LESSONS AND LEGACIES IX

LESSONS AND LEGACIES IX

Memory, History, and Responsibility:
Reassessments of the Holocaust,
Implications for the Future

*Edited and with an introduction by Jonathan Petropoulos,
Lynn Rapaport, and John K. Roth*

NORTHWESTERN UNIVERSITY PRESS   EVANSTON, ILLINOIS

Northwestern University Press
www.nupress.northwestern.edu

Copyright © 2010 by Northwestern University Press. Published 2010. All rights reserved.

Printed in the United States of America

10 9 8 7 6 5 4 3 2 1

ISBN 978-0-8101-2638-1 (cloth)
ISBN 978-0-8101-2639-8 (paper)

Library of Congress Cataloging-in-Publication Data are available from the Library of Congress.

∞ The paper used in this publication meets the minimum requirements of the American National Standard for Information Sciences—Permanence of Paper for Printed Library Materials, ANSI Z39.48-1992.

*Dedicated in loving memory of
Jennie Staub Roland
November 24, 1901–September 7, 2005*

A very special lady who truly inspired people, and brought light and love to all those who knew her. A sweet and gentle soul with a lifelong thirst for learning.

My mother-in-law had to drop out of school at a young age to go to work and help support her immigrant family. She spent her life giving of herself to her family and to her community—certified to transcribe Braille in both English and Hebrew, regional officer of the Women's Division of United Synagogues of America, a Hadassah president, tutored inner-city schoolchildren (at the age of one hundred)—to mention only a very few of her many contributions.

In her late seventies, Jennie finally began the pursuit of her ever-present dream of acquiring a formal education. She first took the GED exam and then entered the Ohio State University and majored in history. She graduated at the age of eighty-three, the oldest student ever to receive a degree at OSU.

She will long be remembered and loved by all who knew her.

*Theodore Zev Weiss
Holocaust Educational Foundation*

*In memory of
Raul Hilberg
(1926–2007)*

*Whose life and scholarship continue to provide
lessons and legacies that deepen our understanding of memory,
history, and responsibility regarding the Holocaust
and its implications for the future.*

*"The unremitting effort continues for the small incremental gains,
no matter what their cost, lest all be relinquished and forgotten."*
—*Raul Hilberg,* Sources of Holocaust Research

Contents

Theodore Zev Weiss
Foreword — xiii

Jonathan Petropoulos, Lynn Rapaport, and John K. Roth
Introduction — xv

Saul Friedländer
Prologue — 3

I. Memory

John K. Roth
Only in the Dark: Seeing Through the Gloom — 19

Christian Goeschel
Suicides of German Jews During the Holocaust — 30

Simone Gigliotti
Deportation Transit and Captive Bodies:
Rethinking Holocaust Witnessing — 47

Michael Allen
The Atomization of Auschwitz: Is History
Really That Contingent? — 63

II. History

Martin Dean
Typology of Ghettos: Five Types of Ghettos
Under German Administration — 85

David Silberklang
Defining the Ghettos: Jewish and German
Perspectives in the Lublin District 106

Alexander V. Prusin
Jewish Ghettos in the Generalbezirk Kiew,
1941–1943 124

Rachel Iskov
Jewish Refugees from the Surrounding
Communities in the Warsaw and Łódź Ghettos 139

Tim Cole
Contesting and Compromising Ghettoization,
Hungary 1944 152

III. Responsibility

Jonathan Petropoulos
Prince zu Waldeck und Pyrmont: A Career in
the SS and Its Murderous Consequences 169

Susanna Schrafstetter
When Perpetrators Compensate Victims:
Karl Hettlage and the Politics of Indemnification
in West Germany 185

Suzanne Brown-Fleming
The Vatican and the Nazi Movement,
1922–1939: New Sources and Unexpected
Findings on the Vatican's Response
to Reichskristallnacht 203

Lissa Skitolsky
Suspending Judgment for the Sake of Knowledge:
Agamben's Approach to Auschwitz 215

IV. Post-Holocaust Issues

Michael Meng
Did Poles Oppose or Collaborate with the Nazis?
Problems with Narrating the Holocaust
in Poland 233

Paul B. Miller
Just Like the Jews: Contending Victimization
in the Former Yugoslavia ... 251

Jerry Fowler
Equivocal Talismans: The UN Genocide
Convention and the Responsibility to Protect ... 269

V. Epilogue
Compiled and introduced by John K. Roth

John K. Roth
Ethics During and After the Holocaust ... 291

Christopher R. Browning
Encountering Ethical Dilemmas in Writing the
History of the Holocaust ... 294

Peter Hayes
Ethics and Corporate History in Nazi Germany ... 300

Claudia Koonz
Taking Jean Améry's "Grudge" Seriously ... 304

Rebecca Wittmann
Torture and the Ethical Implications of
the Holocaust ... 311

Berel Lang
Two Ethical Issues ... 316

John K. Roth
Postscript ... 321

List of Abbreviations and Acronyms ... 325

Notes on Contributors ... 329

Theodore Zev Weiss

Foreword

THIS IS THE NINTH VOLUME OF SCHOLARLY ESSAYS THAT ARE BEING published as an outgrowth of the Lessons and Legacies Conferences that the Holocaust Educational Foundation sponsors in partnership with major centers of higher learning. Our partner for Lessons and Legacies IX was Claremont McKenna College in Claremont, California. John Roth, Jonathan Petropoulos, and Lynn Rapaport served as chairs, and we extend our thanks and appreciation for their devotion to ensuring the success of the conference.

These conferences sponsored by the Holocaust Educational Foundation have become very important and integral for the professors who are working throughout the world in Holocaust Studies, as well as for the graduate students in the field who will be joining the ranks of those teaching the Holocaust to future generations. We are particularly grateful to the professors who attended from countries outside the United States—from Poland, Germany, Austria, Denmark, Sweden, Great Britain, and Israel, to mention a few.

The Lessons and Legacies Conference is only one of the areas in which the work of the Holocaust Educational Foundation has made remarkable strides. We have also added a biennial conference in conjunction with Yad Vashem in Israel. Fifty-one professors traveled to Israel in December of 2007 to participate in a conference with Israeli scholars. It was a very gratifying experience for all the participants, and one that we plan to continue.

The Summer Institute for Holocaust and Jewish Civilization has graduated more than five hundred professors and graduate students to teach Holocaust courses all over the world. The institute, meeting at Northwestern University, continues to teach the participants the history and culture of the Jewish people who were targeted for extinction.

We are very grateful for all the wonderful professors throughout the world who dedicate their efforts to teaching present and future generations about the Holocaust.

Jonathan Petropoulos, Lynn Rapaport, and John K. Roth

Introduction

IN EARLY NOVEMBER 2006, MORE THAN TWO HUNDRED SCHOLARS from around the world gathered at Claremont McKenna College in Claremont, California, for Lessons and Legacies, the biennial conference sponsored by the Holocaust Educational Foundation in Skokie, Illinois. The 2006 conference was the ninth in the series but the first to be held on the West Coast. Under the cosponsorship of the Claremont McKenna Center for the Study of the Holocaust, Genocide, and Human Rights, which was founded in 2003, the scholars came to sunny Southern California to reexamine how the darkness of the Holocaust, Nazi Germany's genocidal attempt to destroy the European Jews and other "inferior" people, rightly continues to shadow human existence more than sixty years after World War II left the Third Reich in ruins.

Titled with the conference themes—*Memory, History, and Responsibility: Reassessments of the Holocaust, Implications for the Future*—this book contains revised and peer-reviewed versions of the cutting-edge research that was focused in more than seventy Lessons and Legacies paper presentations, workshops, and roundtable discussions. Diverse fields and approaches—including but not limited to history and literature, philosophy and religion, film, and gender studies—were amply represented, even while the conference remained mindful of Saul Friedländer's significant keynote address, which urged scholars to make their Holocaust research more integrated. Friedländer's lead essay here, as well as his magisterial two-volume history *Nazi Germany and the Jews,* shows this task to be as difficult as it is valuable. By no means, however, did the difficulty end there, for at the time of the conference and indeed as this book appears, the specter of genocide in Darfur and other human rights atrocities elsewhere reveal that whatever the lessons of the Holocaust may be, the legacies of that catastrophe have not been sufficient to prevent or eliminate human-made mass death.

"Uncomfortable truths," wrote Auschwitz survivor Primo Levi, "travel with difficulty."[1] What makes truths uncomfortable is that they are fraught and burdensome. Their load does not travel easily, nor is their arrival gladly greeted or their persistence eagerly accepted. In all of these senses, exploration of reassessments and implications related to the Holocaust and its aftereffects could lead to one of the most uncomfortable truths of all, namely, that in many ways the world would be better off without human beings and our all-too-destructive history.

Alan Weisman thought in that vein when, between Lessons and Legacies IX and the appearance of this volume, he published his 2007 book called *The World Without Us*. Although Weisman did not concentrate on the Holocaust (his book is packed with cargo consisting of twenty-first-century threats concerning climate change and global warming), there are provocative links between these two volumes.

Based on extensive scientific, anthropological, and historical research, Weisman invited his readers to consider what would happen to planet earth if human life disappeared completely. Over time, he asked, how would the natural world change? As centuries and millennia passed, what traces of human existence, if any, would remain?

Humanity, Weisman emphasized, has arrived in the cosmos recently, at least if one considers how long the galaxies and earlier life-forms existed before anything resembling human life evolved. The emergence of that life made history. Consciousness of past, present, and future grew and expanded. Eventually, human memory led to the recording of experience in storytelling, art, and writing. Then through contemporary forms of communication such as radio, film, television, and the Internet, people became linked together ever more closely. In time's eons, however, these developments are but brief episodes. Long after human beings have come and probably gone, the universe will continue.

Anyone who reads *The World Without Us* becomes newly aware that, in the cosmic scheme of things, one's life and the existence of one's people, nation, culture, or religion may turn out to be insignificant. Weisman's purpose, however, was not to argue that humanity's existence lacks importance and meaning. On the contrary, while urging us to gain perspective about our finite place in reality, he wanted

INTRODUCTION • xvii

people to feel deeply that our humanity is distinctive and precious, that what we think and do makes a huge difference. Human activity has tremendous implications not only in history but also for our world's environment and even for the vast universe that is earth's home and ours as well.

Weisman wanted his readers to understand that humanity has done great harm in and to the world. He has even suggested that there may well be ways in which the world would be better off without human beings who consume, even ravage and destroy, its splendor. His predominant points, however, are that nature has immense recuperative power and that too much of irretrievable value would be lost if the world were really to exist without us. What is needed, he urged, is a renewed sense of respect, reverence, and responsibility for the gift of life and the wondrous universe in which it moves and has its being.

The World Without Us does not concentrate on the Holocaust, the subject of *Memory, History, and Responsibility*, but the implications the two volumes have for each other are noteworthy. First, Weisman's thought experiment leads to reflection on the significance of history and on the importance of particular events within it. A part of his analysis indicates that human consciousness may eventually disappear from reality. If that happened, history would be null and void; arguably, it would be as if no particular event had happened, because historical awareness, and in that sense history itself, depends on memory. Historical documents would decay, artifacts would erode, places would eventually disappear virtually without a trace. If anything human did remain—Weisman thinks plastics of various kinds are among the human artifacts that have the best prospect of lasting longest—the chances of detecting their meaning would probably be slim or none. By this cosmic standard, no human event, including the Holocaust, looms very large.

At the same time, if people are to heed Weisman's urgently needed call for a renewed sense of respect, reverence, and responsibility for the gift of life, then the Holocaust and memory of it loom very large indeed. A key reason for this assertion is that Adolf Hitler, his German followers, and their allies engaged in much more than a thought experiment when they launched their genocide against the Jewish people and other so-called inferior groups. From 1933 to 1945, they acted on their antisemitic and racist creed with an arrogant tenacity. That creed entailed that it would be better for their world, indeed for the world as a whole, if entire human groups were consigned to oblivion. What followed was a systematic, bureaucratic, unrelenting, state-sponsored process of destruction that, under the cover of World War II, annihilated two-thirds of Europe's approximately nine million Jews and millions of other defenseless children, women, and men as well.

Nazi Germany's genocidal project was not entirely successful, but as the chapters in this book make clear, its aims came too close for comfort. If there is not to be a world without us, then we ignore the Holocaust at our peril. Disrespect for the particularity and diversity of human existence harbors selfishness, insensitivity, and hubris, which, in turn, can spark devastating violence, none of which makes humanity fit for survival.

An uncomfortable truth for scholars is that the articles they write and the books they produce do little to guarantee that humanity is fit for survival. Nevertheless, good scholarship has contributions to make toward such fitness. This book does so by directing attention to what Friedländer's prologue calls "the magnitude, the complexity, and the interrelatedness of the multiple components" of the Holocaust's history and its reverberations.

Arguably, there is no history if memory is absent. Therefore, perhaps nothing reflects the ingredients that Friedländer identifies more than issues that swirl through Holocaust-related memory and memories, which are appropriately highlighted in part 1 of the book. It takes up the challenges of reassessment and implication-tracking in the following ways. John Roth explores whether it can make sense to say that the Holocaust's dead can speak and, if it does make sense, what the dead can communicate, especially where uncomfortable truths may be concerned. Christian Goeschel plumbs other depths by studying the suicides of German Jews during the Holocaust; he shows that such acts did not originate solely from despair, but were also motivated by efforts to preserve dignity and as acts of self-assertion, among other reasons. Simone Gigliotti takes one into the horror of the deportation transports that consigned so many to death as they traveled to Auschwitz and other destinations of destruction. Using a variety of sources, including unpublished testimonies and memoirs, she offers a kind of "thick description" of victims' experiences on the transports that usually proceeded at "unbearably slow speeds." Michael Allen's reexamination of Auschwitz, the Holocaust's epicenter,

INTRODUCTION • xix

complicates in good ways the previous scholarship that has been done about that infamous place; his exploration of the issue of whether or not Auschwitz was initially conceived as a death camp has important implications for long-standing historiographical debates about the Nazis' decision-making process. Allen sees the camp as central to the origins of the genocide and argues for a "recontextualization of Auschwitz in the 'Final Solution.'"

Historical research comes to the fore in part 2, which reflects new research on the Nazi-established ghetto as a key structure in the Holocaust's devastation. Taken together, if not individually, these five chapters can be read as a positive response to and illustration of Friedländer's call for an integrated approach to the writing of Holocaust history. Martin Dean provides a useful taxonomy of the types of ghettos established by the Germans—and in the process, he combats the tendency to view ghettos (as well as the inhabitants' experiences there) in an undifferentiated and stereotypical manner. David Silberklang focuses on the ghettos in the Lublin district as he explores the interactions between Jews and Germans. In Lublin, the ghettos were often not closed, especially in medium-sized cities and towns, and this situation afforded relatively better living conditions for Jews than in other parts of the Generalgouvernement. Alexander Prusin advances insight about ghettos in Ukraine, a region that only recently has received the study by Holocaust scholars that it deserves. Using both German and Soviet sources, Prusin argues for the "relatively decentralized Nazi approach to the ghettoization process." Rachel Iskov assesses what happened to Jewish refugees who were uprooted from small towns and rural areas and sent to ghettos in major cities such as Łódź and Warsaw. Tim Cole then turns his attention to the ghetto-related struggles in Hungary that ensued in 1944 after the Germans occupied the territory of their faltering allies. Cole argues for the importance of local factors in determining "the nature and shape of ghettoization."

One can scarcely read the chapters on the ghettos without confronting the uncomfortable truth that the Holocaust was a vast human failing in which the web of responsibility reached far and wide. The timely chapters in part 3 of the book take steps to show what is involved in the difficult task of fairly measuring responsibility for the Holocaust's suffering and grief. Focusing on Schutzstaffel (SS) General Prince Josias zu Waldeck und Pyrmont, Jonathan Petropoulos evaluates some of the roles that German aristocracy played in those outcomes. Susanna Schrafstetter focuses on Karl Hettlage, a devout Catholic who was not a National Socialist, as she provides a case study of a bureaucrat whose problematic career stretched "from the persecution of Jews to the indemnification of victims of Nazism." Indeed, despite his religious faith, Hettlage became a perpetrator; and despite his complicity in the crimes of the regime, he emerged as an influential official in the postwar negotiations about compensation for victims. Suzanne Brown-Fleming uses newly available Vatican archives to take stock of the Vatican's responses to Reichskristallnacht, the vicious November 1938 pogrom that was a key prelude to the "Final Solution." This case study permits a reconsideration of the responses of Pope Pius XI and future Pope Pius XII to the increasingly radical anti-Jewish policies of the Nazis. Lissa Skitolsky then draws on the philosopher Giorgio Agamben to suggest that study of the Holocaust entails engagement with uncomfortable truths that reach well beyond Nazi Germany to "the depravity of the sociopolitical world in which we still live."

These questions about responsibility form the bridge to part 4, which considers a variety of lingering post-Holocaust issues. Michael Meng wrestles with the vexed and vexing problem of the relationship between Poles and Germans during the Nazi occupation of Poland. What mixtures of opposition and collaboration were there at the time, and how is that picture—including its implications for contemporary Polish identity—clouded or clarified by findings that have emerged in recent years? Reminding us of the uncomfortable truth that "Never again!" is a slogan now as empty as it is repeated, Paul Miller addresses ethnic cleansing in the former Yugoslavia, and Jerry Fowler explores the limitations of the Genocide Convention adopted by the United Nations (UN) in the shadow of the Holocaust in 1948. Intended to facilitate both "prevention" and "punishment" and also to establish principles about how governments treat their own citizens, the UN Genocide Convention has fallen short of the goals of many of its backers and is best understood, in Fowler's words, as an "equivocal talisman." Pursuing related topics about responsibility, part 5 concludes the book with a discussion on ethics during and after the Holocaust. It features contributions from John Roth, Christopher Browning, Peter Hayes, Claudia Koonz, Rebecca Wittmann, and Berel Lang.

One uncomfortable truth after another awaits the reader of *Memory, History, and Responsibility*. Such truths are among the Holocaust's most telling lessons and legacies. For the readers and writers of this book alike, it remains to be seen how difficult the journeys of those truths will be, for that determination depends largely on what happens after the last page of this book is turned. Beyond our writing and reading, what we do shall reveal whether the world is better with—or without—us.

NOTES

The editors would like to thank Claremont McKenna College student Becky Grossman for her thoughtful and careful work helping to prepare this volume.

1. Primo Levi, *The Drowned and the Saved,* trans. Raymond Rosenthal (New York: Vintage Books, 1989), 159.

LESSONS AND LEGACIES IX

Saul Friedländer

Prologue

THE NEED FOR AN INTEGRATED HISTORY OF THE HOLOCAUST FIRST became clear to me during the debates of the middle and late 1980s, and particularly as a result of the confrontation with Martin Broszat regarding his 1985 "plea for the historicization of National Socialism."[1] One of Broszat's arguments was directed against the traditional representation of the Third Reich as a simplistic, black-and-white rendition that had to give way to various shades of gray. Broszat's barely hidden subtext, which emerged during our exchange of letters in 1988, contended that the Jewish survivors' perception of this past, as well as that of their descendants, albeit "worthy of respect," nonetheless represented a "mythical memory" that "coarsened historical recollection" and hampered the more rational course of German historiography (particularly of a younger generation of historians).[2]

This view perpetuated the intellectual segregation of the history of the Jews during the Nazi epoch and left it, at best, to Jewish historians. My own work, begun in 1990, was meant to show that no distinction was warranted among historians of various backgrounds in their professional approach to the Third Reich, that *all* historians dealing with this theme had to be aware of their unavoidably subjective approach, and that all could muster enough self-critical insight to restrain this subjectivity. What mattered most to me in my own project was the inclusion of the Jewish dimension, along with all others, within an integrated historical narrative.

In this essay, I shall first address the very notion of an integrated history of the Holocaust, then turn to some narrative and interpretive choices demanded by such an approach, and, finally, evoke the kind of concrete issues that this form of history may bring up.

THE CONCEPT OF AN INTEGRATED HISTORY OF
THE HOLOCAUST

David Moffie was awarded his doctorate in medicine at the University of Amsterdam on September 18, 1942. In a photograph taken at the event, Professor Ariens Kappers, Moffie's supervisor, and Professor H. T. Deelman stand on the right of the new M.D. and assistant D. Granaat stands on the left. Another faculty member, seen from the back, possibly the dean of the medical school, stands at a large desk. In the dim background, the faces of some of the people crowded into the rather exiguous hall, family members and friends no doubt, are barely perceptible. The faculty members have donned their academic robes, while Moffie and assistant Granaat wear tuxedos and white ties. On the left side of his tuxedo jacket, Moffie displays a palm-sized Jewish star with the word "Jood" inscribed on it.[3] Moffie was the last Jewish student at the University of Amsterdam under German occupation. Shortly thereafter, Moffie was deported to Auschwitz-Birkenau. He survived, as did 20 percent of the Jews of Holland; according to the same statistics, most of the other Jews present at the ceremony did not.

The picture raises some questions. How, for example, could the ceremony have taken place on September 18, 1942, although Jewish students were excluded from Dutch universities as of that date? The editors of "Photography and the Holocaust" found the answer: The last day of the 1941–42 university year was Friday, September 18; the 1942–43 semester started on Monday, September 21. The three-day break allowed Moffie to receive his doctorate before the ban on Jewish students became mandatory.

In other words, the university authorities agreed to use the administrative calendar against the intention of the German decree. This decision signaled an attitude that had been widespread at Dutch universities since the fall of 1940; the photograph documents an act of defiance, on the rim of the occupier's laws and decrees.

Other issues arise. The deportations from Holland started on July 14, 1942. Almost daily, Germans and local police arrested Jews on the streets of Dutch cities to fill the weekly quotas. Moffie could not have attended this public academic ceremony without having received one of the special (and temporary) 17,000 exemption certificates that the Germans allocated to the Jewish Council. The picture thus indirectly evokes the controversy surrounding the methods used by the heads of the Council to protect, for a while at least, some of the Jews of Amsterdam and abandon the great majority of Dutch and foreign Jews to their fate.

The "Jood" sewn on Moffie's coat, which meant that the new M.D. was to be murdered, does not appear in block letters or in any other commonly used script. The characters had been specially designed for this particular purpose (and similarly drawn in the languages of the other countries of deportation: for example, "Jude," "Juif," and "Jood") in a crooked, repulsive, and vaguely threatening way that was intended to evoke the Hebrew alphabet and yet remain easily decipherable. And it is in this inscription and its peculiar design that the situation represented in the photograph reappears in its quintessence: the Germans were bent on exterminating the Jews as individuals and on erasing what the star and its inscription represented—"the Jew."

Thus, from one single snapshot the viewer gets the intimation of a vast number of interactions—between German ideological delusions and administrative measures; Dutch institutions and individual choices; Jewish institutions and, at the center of it all, the fate of a Jewish individual. Translated into words, narrated within its context, interpreted at various levels of significance, the photo can be seen as a metonymic illustration of what could be defined as an integrated history of the Holocaust.

Why would an integrated history of the Holocaust be necessary? First, the history of these events cannot be limited to German decisions and measures only; it has to include the initiative and reactions of authorities, institutions, and the most diverse social groups throughout the occupied and satellite countries of German-controlled Europe. Second, at each stage Jewish perceptions and reactions, collective or individual, cannot and should not be considered as a separate domain within any general historical rendition, as they affected, in various degrees, all other elements of this history. Finally, a simultaneous representation of the events—at all levels and in all different places—enhances the perception of the magnitude, the complexity, and the interrelatedness of the multiple components of this history. Let me very briefly address each of these points.

We do not need to belabor the fact that the history of the extermination of the Jews of Europe cannot stop at the borders of the Reich, nor can it be limited to German decisions and measures. One aspect of the German and European scene, marginalized at times, demands, however, to be stressed: the awareness among European elites and populations of what these anti-Jewish measures and policies meant. Nowadays, we know that a considerable amount of information about the extermination was available throughout Europe and this from a rather early stage on. The Polish underground was openly referring to the mass murder as soon as it started. In Switzerland in midsummer 1942, the federal authorities, including the police, explicitly evoked the consequences of the hermetic closing of borders for Jews. In Germany itself, the fate of the Jews was quite openly alluded to at various levels of the population.

"In Bereza-Kartuska, where I stopped for lunch," Wehrmacht Private H. K. wrote home on June 18, 1942, "1,300 Jews had just been shot on the previous day. . . . Men, women, children had to undress completely and were then liquidated with a shot in the back of the neck. The clothes were disinfected and used again. I am convinced that if the war goes on much longer, the Jews will be turned into sausage and served to Russian war prisoners and to Jewish specialized workers."[4] A few months later, on December 7, 1942, Private S. M., on his way to the front, wrote home from the town of Auschwitz: "The Jews arrive here, that is to Auschwitz, at a weekly rate of seven to eight thousand; shortly thereafter, they die a 'hero's death.'" And he added: "It is really good to see the world."[5]

In Minden (Westphalia), the inhabitants had been discussing the fate of deportees from their own town as early as December 1941 and had publicly mentioned that Jews who were unable to work were shot. A few weeks later, in February 1942, Bishop Wilhelm Berning of Osnabrück noted that admittedly there was a plan to exterminate all the Jews.[6] Whereas, here and there, small groups or individuals risked their lives in trying to help the hounded victims, no social segment or global institution (the churches, peasantry, the business world) intervened.

Let us turn to the Jewish dimension of this history. Within the essentially non-Jewish-centered historiography, when Jewish behavior is even referred to at all, it remains almost entirely centered on institutional-collective Jewish behavior—that is, on the decisions of Jewish leadership groups or on some of the best-known attempts at resistance (the uprising of the Warsaw ghetto, for example). But, in fact, the main mode of interaction among the Jews of occupied and satellite Europe, the Germans, and the surrounding populations took place at a far more elementary level. From the very outset, any steps taken by individual Jews or by Jewish groups to hamper the Nazi effort (bribing officials, policemen, or denunciators; paying families to hide children or adults; fleeing to woods or mountains, going to small villages, or disappearing into large cities; converting to Christianity; joining resistance movements; stealing food—anything that came to mind and led to survival) all represented obstacles, be they minimal, on the Nazi path. It is at this micro level that Jewish interaction with the forces acting to implement the "Final Solution" needs to be studied and integrated into the wider domains of this history.

The history of the destruction of European Jewry at the level of individuals can be reconstructed from the perspective of the victims on the basis of postwar depositions, interviews, and memoirs, but mainly from diaries and letters owing to the unusually large number written during the events and recovered over the following decades. These diaries and letters were written by Jews of all countries, all walks of life, all age groups, either living under direct German domination or within the wider sphere of persecution. Of course, the diaries have to be used with the same critical attention as any other document. Yet, as a source for the history of Jewish life during the years of persecution and extermination, they remain crucial and irreplaceable.

Hundreds, probably thousands of witnesses confided their observations to the secrecy of their private writings. Major events and the entire gamut of daily incidents, the attitudes and reactions of the Jews themselves and those of the surrounding world—which the diarists recorded—have merged into an increasingly comprehensive, albeit at times contradictory, picture. These witnesses described in great detail the initiatives and daily brutality of the perpetrators, the reactions of populations, and the life and destruction of their own communities, but they also recorded their own everyday worlds of despair, rumors, illusions, and hope, in constant succession, mostly to the end.

"My dear little Daddy, bad news: After my aunt, it's my turn to leave." Thus began the hasty pencil-written card sent on February 12, 1943, from Drancy, by seventeen-year-old Louise Jacobson to her father, who still lived in Paris. "I am in excellent spirits," she went on, "like everybody else. You should not worry, Daddy. First, I am leaving in very good shape. This last week, I have eaten very, very well. I got two packages by proxy, one from a friend who was just deported, the other from my aunt. Now, your package arrived, exactly at the right moment. . . . We leave tomorrow morning. I am with my friends, as many are leaving. I entrusted my watch and all my other belongings to decent people from my room. My daddy, I kiss you a hundred thousand times with all my strength. Courage et à bientôt, your daughter Louise."[7]

On February 13, 1943, Louise left for Auschwitz in transport number 48 with one thousand other French Jews. A surviving female friend, a chemical engineer, went through the selection with her. "Tell them that you are a chemist," Irma had whispered. When her turn arrived and she was asked about her profession, Louise declared: "student." She was sent to the left, to the gas chamber.[8]

Such personal chronicles, such individual Jewish voices, are also the most immediate testimonies about dimensions of ongoing events usually unperceived in other sources. Like flashes that illuminate parts of a landscape, they confirm intuitions, they warn us against easy generalizations, they tear through the smugness of scholarly detachment. Mostly, they just repeat the known, but they express it with unmatched forcefulness. Thus, reminiscing about the murder of some twelve thousand Jews in Stanislawow on October 12, 1941, a young female diarist, Elsa Binder, brought up the fate of her two friends, Tamarczyk and Esterka: "I hope," Elsa wrote, "that death was kind to Tamarczyk and took her right away. And that she didn't have to suffer like her companion, Esterka, who was seen being strangled."[9]

Finally, simultaneous representation adds an essential dimension to the historical perception of the Holocaust; it need not be solely transnational. It can apply to several categories of events usually not linked to one another, occurring at the same time in the same country. Thus, in late December 1941, the decision to exterminate all the Jews of Europe had been taken. At the same time, the main representative institution of the German Evangelical Church, the Church Chancellery, responding to a violently antisemitic stance taken by several local churches adhering to the German-Christian line, issued a statement of its own denying any solidarity with converted Jews. This was made brutally clear in a circular letter published on December 23 by the Chancellery's deputy director, Günther Fürle:

> The breakthrough of racial consciousness in our people, intensified by the experience of the war and the corresponding measures taken by the political leadership, has brought about the elimination of Jews from the community of us Germans. This is an incontestable fact, which the German Evangelical Churches, which serve the one eternal Gospel within the German people and live within the legal domain of this people as corporations under public law, cannot heedlessly ignore. Therefore, in agreement with the Spiritual Council of the German Evangelical Church, we request the highest authorities to take suitable measures so that baptized non-Aryans remain separate from the ecclesiastical life of the German congregations. The baptized non-Aryans will have to find the ways and means to create their own facilities to serve their particular worship and pastoral needs. We will make every effort to help obtain permission for such facilities from the responsible authorities.[10]

Nobody was fooled by the last sentence of the Chancellery's statement. The Confessing Church protested, but its protest was that of a minority and did not call for any countermeasures. A few weeks earlier, several Catholic bishops, led by Bishop Johann Konrad von Preysing of Berlin, circulated a text meant to express support for converted German Jews sent to the East. The majority of the Bishops' Conference, led by Cardinal Bertram, rejected any such motion, even in its most timid phrasing. Of course, neither Protestants nor Catholics addressed the fate of the nonconverted Jews. In other words, as the deportation from Germany started and, mainly, as the first extermination sites were activated or built, Adolf Hitler and his acolytes could rely on the passivity of the only counterforce that once had challenged the regime about its criminal policies, about the murder of the mentally ill.

The simultaneity of the decision to murder all the Jews of Europe and the declared nonintervention of the Christian churches regarding converted Jews sets the early phase of the "Final Solution" in its wider German context. The same context takes on an additional tragically ironic dimension as, at the very same time, in the last days of 1941, in the Reich and all over occupied Europe, Jews were celebrating their oncoming liberation in view of the Soviet successes in front of Moscow. Only in Vilna and somewhat later in Warsaw did a tiny group become aware that the overall extermination was just starting.

NARRATION AND INTERPRETATION

It may be unusual to devote space to problems of narration in discussing a project in history in which, by definition, all the attention should be focused on conceptualization and interpretation. In fact, problems of narration almost defeated my own project and are liable to remain a major obstacle for similar endeavors. We are dealing with events that occurred in Germany, in every single country of occupied and satellite Europe, and well beyond. We are dealing with institutions and individual voices, with ideologies, religious traditions, and so on. No general history of the Holocaust can do justice to the interaction of this diversity of elements by presenting them as independently juxtaposed; they have to be presented in their simultaneity and their interrelatedness. Moreover, in following the fate of individual Jews, a chronological unfolding of the entire process becomes unavoidable.

It is impossible, in our context, to discuss narrative issues at any length. Sudden cuts in the narration and abrupt changes of perspective are methods common in film but hardly so in history. Yet, this could well be the only possible solution to an otherwise insoluble quandary. Thus—and this represents the core issue—such a project imposes a return to chronicle but, as historian Dan Diner pointed out, not to a form of chronicle that predated conceptualization. In this case, chronicle remains the only recourse after major interpretive concepts have been tried and found lacking.

Nonetheless, such a form of chronicling does not exclude partial interpretations, nor does it exclude assumptions about the general historical context of the Holocaust (the crisis of liberalism in continental Europe, for example). More pointedly, it does not exclude general assumptions about the historical place of the extermination of the Jews within the vast array of Nazi goals and policies. This last issue brings us back to a point that was implicitly questioned in Broszat's argument: the centrality of the Holocaust within the general history of National Socialism.

The promoters of the historicization agenda stressed quite correctly that Nazi crimes had been set at center stage in the history of the Third Reich for the needs of the postwar trials. Later, the centrality of the criminal dimension and the black-and-white representation supposedly became imperative for a historiography aimed at educating the German nation (eine volkspädagogische Geschichtsschreibung).

Thus, according to the same view, the time had come to perceive the criminal policies of the regime within a much wider and differentiated context and, in any case, a context not necessarily centered on the Jewish issue. The persecution and extermination of the Jews of Europe became but a secondary aspect of policies pursued toward entirely different goals. These goals included, for example, creation of a new economic and demographic equilibrium in occupied Europe by way of murdering "surplus" populations and facilitation of German colonization by way of ethnic reshuffling and decimation of Eastern populations. Most recently, the context has broadened to include the systematic plunder of Europe's Jews to allow the waging of the war without putting too heavy a material burden on German society or, more precisely, on the economic and social aims of Hitler's Volksstaat. Several of these interpretations, and particularly the last one, found a major echo in Germany after the war.

Such an approach, cannot, however, answer some fundamental questions. Why did Hitler decide to exterminate the Jews after robbing them of all of their assets? Why did the Nazi leader personally decide, in the fall of 1943, to forge ahead with deportation of the Jews of Denmark and those of Rome, notwithstanding the serious risks involved (the possibility of unrest in Denmark, of the Pope's public protest) and the nonexistent "benefits" of both operations? Why did Heinrich Himmler reject the Wehrmacht's repeated requests to keep specialized Jewish workers from extermination?

The secondary function attributed to the anti-Jewish policies cannot address apparently marginal yet telling occurrences such as these: the personal demand by the Reichsführer-Schutzstaffel (SS) to Finland's prime minister that his country deliver its thirty to forty foreign Jews into Germans hands; the deportation of the small and impoverished Sephardic Jewish communities from the Aegean Islands in July 1944; or, finally, the roundup and deportation of hundreds of Jewish children from France to Auschwitz a few days before the liberation of Paris.

The only approach that seems possible in the writing of an integrated history of the Holocaust has to set the Jewish issue at the very center of the Nazi regime's worldview and policies. "All in all," Joseph Goebbels noted after a long conversation with Hitler at the end of April 1944, "a long-term policy in this war is only possible if one considers it from the standpoint of the Jewish question."[11] This crazed obsession was enthusiastically supported and implemented by Hitler's closest acolytes, by party and state agencies, by officials and technocrats at all levels of the system, and by important segments of the population. The "logic" behind this anti-Jewish passion was constantly spewed by the regime's propaganda. In fact, propaganda molded an increasingly ominous image of "the Jew" as the lethal and relentlessly active enemy of the Reich, intent on its destruction. Thus, within the same hallucinatory logic, once the Reich had to fight on both fronts, East and West, without the hope of a rapid victory and with some early intimations of defeat, Hitler opted for immediate extermination. Otherwise, as he saw it, the Jews would destroy Germany and the new Europe from within as he believed they had done in 1917–18. And, after the military situation became ominous, the extermination was accelerated to its utter limits.

QUESTIONS, ANSWERABLE AND UNANSWERABLE

An integrated history leads in and of itself to comparative queries and, more generally, to connections otherwise but dimly perceived. A prime example could be the lack of an overall Jewish solidarity in the face of catastrophe. In late 1939 and early 1940, the German Jewish leadership attempted to bar endangered Polish Jews from emigrating from the Reich to Palestine, to keep all emigration openings for German Jews only. Native French Jewish leadership (the Consistoire) repeatedly demanded that the Vichy government make a distinction between the status and treatment of native Jews and of foreign ones. The Jewish Councils in Poland, particularly the Council in Warsaw, were granting a whole array of privileges to members of the local Jewish middle class who could afford paying bribes, while poor Jews, the refugees from the provinces, and the mass of those devoid of any influence were increasingly pushed into slave labor or abandoned to starvation and death. Cooperation and neutral help were hardly possible between the local Jews of the Łódź ghetto and the deportees from the Reich and the Protectorate of Bohemia and Moravia. In Westerbork, German Jews, the elite of the camp, closely working with the German commandants, protected their own and put Dutch Jews on the departure lists, while, previously, the Dutch Jewish elite had felt secure, convinced that only refugees (mainly German Jews) would be sent to the local camps and then deported. The Christian

Jews' hatred of their Jewish brethren, and vice versa, particularly in the Warsaw ghetto, is notorious.

Notwithstanding all tensions, however, it should be mentioned that widespread welfare efforts and educational and cultural activities were open to all in many Jewish communities. Moreover, a strengthening of bonds appeared within small groups sharing a specific political or religious background. Such was typically the case in political youth groups in the ghettos, among members of the same political party in the camps, and, of course, among this or that group of Orthodox Jews. In looking at the big picture, we may reach the conclusion that in a majority of cases, specific ethnic-cultural, political, or religious bonds shared by members of any number of subgroups took precedence over any feeling of shared "Jewishness."

The comparisons that belong to the very essence of an integrated history may also raise questions that do not allow for any clear answer. Thus, on June 27, 1945, the world-renowned Jewish-Austrian chemist Lise Meitner, who in 1939 had emigrated from Germany to Sweden, wrote to her former colleague and friend Otto Hahn, who had continued to work in the Reich. After mentioning that he and the scientific community in Germany had known much about the worsening persecution of the Jews, Meitner went on: "All of you have worked for Nazi Germany and never tried even some passive resistance. Certainly, to assuage your conscience, here and there you helped some person in need of assistance but you allowed the murder of millions of innocent people, and no protest was ever heard."[12] Meitner's cri de coeur addressed through Hahn to Germany's most prominent scientists, none of them active Nazi Party members, none of them involved in criminal activities, could have applied as well to the entire intellectual and spiritual elite of the Reich (with some exceptions, of course) and to wide segments of the elites in occupied or satellite Europe.

An even more unsettling aspect of the same question arises in regard to the attitude of the Christian churches. In Germany—again with the exception of a few individuals, none of whom belonged to the higher reaches of the Evangelical or Catholic Churches—no Protestant bishop or Catholic prelate protested publicly against the extermination of the Jews. When men of goodwill such as Bishop von Preysing of Berlin or the Württemberg Bishop Theophil Wurm, the voice of the Confessing Church, were ordered to stop their attempts at confidential protests, they submitted.

If we take into account that, generally speaking, the German situation was replicated in most occupied European countries, except for limited protests in Holland and among a few French bishops (some of whom then recanted), the question assumes its full significance. That an important number of personalities belonging to Europe's intellectual or spiritual elites did not take a public stand against the murder of the Jews is easily understood. That even a few prominent voices were not publicly heard on the overall European scene is puzzling; that not a single person of major stature was ready to speak out remains, as some other aspects of this history, a continuous source of disbelief.

NOTES

This chapter is based on Saul Friedländer's keynote address to the Lessons and Legacies conference at Claremont McKenna College. Delivered on November 2, 2006, Friedländer's address drew on his work *The Years of Extermination: Nazi Germany and the Jews, 1939–1945,* which was forthcoming at the time and published subsequently in 2007.

1. See Martin Broszat, "A Plea for the Historicization of National Socialism," in *Reworking the Past: Hitler, the Holocaust, and the Historians' Debate,* ed. Peter Baldwin (Boston: Beacon Press, 1990).

2. See also Saul Friedländer, "Some Thoughts on the Historicization of National Socialism" and Martin Broszat and Saul Friedländer, "A Controversy About the Historicization of National Socialism," in *Reworking the Past.*

3. This photograph is reproduced on the cover of Sybil Milton and Genya Markon, eds., "Photography and the Holocaust," special issue, *History of Photography* 23, no. 4 (Winter 1999). All details about the individuals depicted are from the caption of the photograph.

4. Walter Manoschek, ed., *"Es gibt nur eines für das Judentum—Vernichtung": Das Judenbild in deutschen Soldatenbriefen 1939–1944* (Hamburg: Hamburger Edition, 1996), 58.

5. Ibid., 63.

6. Ludwig Volk, ed., *Akten deutscher Bischöfe über die Lage der Kirche, 1933–1945,* vol. 5 (Mainz: Matthias-Grünewald-Verlag, 1983), 675n.

7. Louise Jacobson and Nadia Kaluski-Jacobson. *Les Lettres de Louise Jacobson et de ses proches: Fresnes, Drancy, 1942–1943* (Paris: Laffont, 1997), 141.

8. Ibid., 41–42.

9. Elsa Binder's diary, quoted in Alexandra Zapruder, ed., *Salvaged Pages:*

Young Writers' Diaries of the Holocaust (New Haven, Conn.: Yale University Press, 2002), 301ff., particularly 315.

10. Quoted and translated in Wolfgang Gerlach, *And the Witnesses Were Silent: The Confessing Church and the Persecution of the Jews,* ed. Victoria Barnett (Lincoln: University of Nebraska Press), 194.

11. Joseph Goebbels, *Die Tagebücher von Joseph Goebbels,* ed. Elke Fröhlich (Munich: K. G. Saur, 1995), part 2, vol. 12, 202.

12. Quoted in Ute Deichmann, *Biologen unter Hitler: Porträt einer Wissenschaft im NS-Staat* (Frankfurt: Fischer Taschenbuch, 1995), 372.

I. MEMORY

John K. Roth

Only in the Dark: Seeing Through the Gloom

Some truths are glimpsed only in the dark.
—Robert Pogue Harrison, The Dominion of the Dead

SOME OF THE INTERVIEWS CONDUCTED IN 1946 BY AMERICAN PSYchologist David P. Boder are among the earliest with persons who survived the Holocaust. Using the wire recording technology that was state of the art at the time, Boder interviewed "about seventy people, representing nearly all creeds and nationalities in the DP [displaced person] installations in the American Zone." He recorded 120 hours of testimony, which was translated, he said, "to keep the material as near to the text of the original narratives as the most elementary rules of grammar would permit." Eight of these interviews were published by the University of Illinois Press in 1949.[1] The last one contains the testimony given in Munich by a man named Jack Matzner on September 26, 1946.

Born in Wiesbaden, Germany, Matzner, who was forty-two when the interview took place, was a Jew of Polish descent. Deported from Germany to Poland in 1938, he illegally returned to Germany for a time, and then he and his family were reunited in Antwerp, Belgium. On May 14, 1940, soon after the Germans occupied Belgium, Matzner went to France. Eventually arrested, he was deported to the East. The account he gave to Boder after surviving "fifty-five months of concentration camps" included two episodes that were deeply embedded in his memory.[2]

First, Matzner recalled a work assignment in the Polish winter of 1941 to 1942. Several of the men assigned to dig holes for telegraph poles froze to death. Matzner had to carry some of them from the work site back to Lager Fürstengrube, near Katowice. "I shall never forget," he told Boder, "the impression that is made by the face of a man frozen to death. I got the impression that these people were laughing. You notice on the faces a kind of transition, as if at the beginning of the agony the people distort their faces, and for the onlooker it creates the impression that they are laughing. These dead men, dead from freezing—and this expression remains on their faces as if they were laughing."[3]

Second, in 1945, Matzner was inside Germany as a slave laborer for Heinkel Aviation Industries. On one occasion, he was beaten and then imprisoned in a flooded cellar with "about ninety or ninety-five people," many of whom were already in water that was "chest high." Matzner's account to Boder continued as follows: "Those who were lying there were already dead. And those who were standing had arranged the bodies of the dead in such a manner that they could stand or sit on them. Otherwise the ones who were still living would also have drowned. I did the same thing. I found myself a place at the wall. I dragged two bodies which were under the water and arranged them against the wall, and I sat on them. And so I remained in the water, counting from that morning, exactly two days and two nights."[4]

Boder interviewed Matzner, but perhaps with those frozen and drowned Jews from Matzner's account in mind—to say nothing of the millions who had been starved and beaten to death, shot, or gassed—he ended the introduction to his book with these words: "The verbatim records presented in this book make uneasy reading. And yet," he added, "they are not the grimmest stories that could be told—I did not interview the dead."[5] That last thought-provoking phrase—I did not interview the dead—became his book's title.

The frozen corpses that Matzner carried back to the lager did not laugh. The corpses on which he sat may have saved him from drowning, but they said nothing about their fate or his. Boder could not interview the dead because the dead do not speak. Nor, it might be added, should one even imagine interrogating the dead, for to do so would create a temptation that ought to be resisted. It is not the prerogative of the living to speak for the dead. With the Holocaust's murdered Jews foremost on his mind, the Auschwitz survivor Elie Wiesel underscored this point emphatically in his Nobel Peace Prize acceptance speech in Oslo, Norway, on December 10, 1986. "No one may speak for the dead," said Wiesel; "no one may interpret their mutilated dreams and visions."[6]

The living have no right to put words into mouths that death has silenced. The Holocaust, at least sensitive reflection upon it, seems to enjoin warnings and imperatives of that kind. Failure to heed them runs too many risks. To use Lawrence Langer's phrase, those risks include preempting the Holocaust by thinking that there is some meaning to find that transcends the mute abjection of corpses such as those that move grotesquely in the early postwar film footage from "liberated" concentration camps, which shows lifeless, rotting bodies being bulldozed into mass graves, hundreds at a time.

Cautionary principles of the kind mentioned above are well worth remembering. Nevertheless, it may be no less important to think twice about them, for there are countervailing currents that deserve attention if philosophical and particularly ethical reflections about the Holocaust are to be at their best. Consider, then, at least two significant issues that warrant attention. First, to what extent is it true that the dead, including people murdered in the Holocaust, do not and cannot speak? Second, to what extent is it sound to say that no one should or even can speak for the dead, including those drowned or frozen, starved or beaten to death, shot or gassed during the Holocaust?

My response to the first of those questions—to what extent is it true that the dead, including people murdered in the Holocaust, do not and cannot speak?—is informed by a study that scarcely alludes to the Holocaust, let alone focuses on that event, and yet has insights that are pertinent for Holocaust studies and Holocaust-related philosophy in particular. I refer to Robert Pogue Harrison's 2003 book called *The Dominion of the Dead*.

The point of departure for Harrison's eloquent and interdisciplinary book involves deep reflection on a fundamental and distinctive fact about human life: namely, that in one way or another we human beings bury our dead. This action takes place because human beings have memories; it also takes place for memory's sake. Absent memories, the dead would not even be forgotten, they would just be left to decay and disappear. Present memories, however, mean that we do not forget the dead, at least not entirely. In some ways, the dead even have dominion over us and rightly so, for we consciously dispose of their remains in ways that keep them—the dead and usually their remains—with us. That presence of an absence can affect people and policies profoundly.

Already, of course, the Holocaust may make one quarrel with Harrison's account. The German burning of Jewish bodies was the antithesis of an act of remembrance; it was intended to be part of the process that would obliterate Jewish life—and memory of it—root and branch. The remains of the Jewish dead were to be scattered in smoke and ash so as never to be retrieved. Even the vast number of mass graves from killing-squadron actions in the East had to be exhumed and their remains burned, not only to cover the killers' tracks but also to ensure that erasure of Jewish presence was complete. Nevertheless, not even the Nazi mind could free itself entirely from remembering the Jewish dead.

Trauma related to the murder of Jews and to the grisly work of corpse disposal often left its marks on the perpetrators, silent though they usually chose to be about it. Arguably even more important, if the Jewish dead were forgotten, the Nazis' frantic efforts to destroy Jewish bodies without a trace would have lacked the "sense" that it made in the Third Reich's genocidal ideology. Nazism's many contradictions included a key fact: its antisemitism entailed that Nazism had to remain preoccupied with the Jewish dead, or its identity would have been lost. It can even be said that the Jewish dead, owing to the Nazis' obsession to make the world judenrein (empty or "clean" of Jews), had a kind of dominion over Nazi life. Dead Jews haunted the Nazi "mindscape" as they do the psychological and geographical terrain of postwar Germany to this day.

As for those who resisted the Third Reich and the Holocaust— take Matzner and Boder as examples—remembering those who were utterly bereft of the rites of burial is central to what it means to speak of the Holocaust as an unprecedented catastrophe.[7] Thus, even taking into account the overwhelming disrespect for the dead, to say nothing of the living, that characterized the Holocaust, the integrity of Harrison's governing claims still stands: the Holocaust's dead remain definitely with us, and to some extent that presence can and, I would say, should exercise a kind of dominion.

To be human, Harrison argued, "is a way of being mortal and relating to the dead. To be human means above all to bury."[8] Those propositions, which have their applicability in the Holocaust and its aftereffects, made Harrison especially interested in how "we follow in the footsteps of the dead" and what it can mean to speak about what he called the "indwelling of the dead in the worlds of the living."[9] Much of that indwelling pertains to ways, literal and figurative, in which the dead can be said to speak. During his Nobel Peace Prize acceptance speech, Elie Wiesel may have had something akin to this insight in mind, for in addition to contending that no one may speak for the dead, he underscored how much he sensed their presence.

The dead do speak, including, and in some ways especially, the Holocaust-related dead. For instance, the voices of perpetrators such as Adolf Hitler and Joseph Goebbels can still be heard in multiple ways through their writings or even through recordings of their voices. Much could be said about what the Nazi dead may have to say, but in this reflection I am concentrating on the Jews who were annihilated by Hitler and his followers. In their writings and in some cases through recordings of their voices, Anne Frank, Primo Levi, and non-Jews such as Charlotte Delbo can still be heard in multiple ways as they testify about what happened during the event that is now called the Holocaust. Today, their voices are among those of the dead. Increasingly, the tens of thousands of survivor testimonies that have been collected in recent years also include the voices of the dead. Relatively soon all of those testimonies will have to be heard in that way, for the time is rapidly approaching when the term "survivor of the Holocaust" will apply only to the dead. Meanwhile, among the living are people who can still hear quite directly the voices of family members, friends, or acquaintances who experienced the Holocaust, some of them surviving and others not. While even the survivors may no longer be alive, their presence can be very real. Their remembered voices, their speaking, can be immensely moving and powerful.

Harrison did not miss the mark when he contended that "the dead are not content to reside in our genes alone, for genes are not *worlds*, and the dead seek above all to share our worlds."[10] Here it might be objected that Harrison enlivened the dead, that he gave them an existence that they do not and cannot have. But this objection does not hold, because human existence cannot be what it is apart from our dying, from our awareness that our lives, at least on this earth, do not last forever, and that our being here unavoidably, if not from desire, leaves its mark behind, faint and tracelike though that mark may be. What we leave behind when we die and after we are dead reveals—a corpse alone can do so—that the dead do seek to share the worlds of the living. To a considerable extent, moreover, that sharing works. No human identity is possible without the dead; they inform us profoundly. "As human beings," Harrison wrote, "we are born of the dead."[11] In that sense, the dead have an afterlife. Although it does not depend on immortality or resurrection, the afterlife of the dead is nonetheless one that can and does speak.

But can that really be the case if the Holocaust is the benchmark? Is Harrison's analysis credible when one considers the corpses that Matzner lugged or sat upon, the remains bulldozed into pits at Bergen-Belsen, the thousands of Jewish bodies converted into ash and smoke as the Sonderkommando units did their gruesome work, day after day, at the Nazis' behest in Birkenau's gas chambers and crematoria? Contrary to the direction in which such questions seem to go, Harrison's points are arguably even more deeply applicable, at least in some of their dimensions, in these cases that may involve persons who are nameless strangers to us.

Apart from the presence of the Holocaust's dead, there is no Holocaust, no sense of unfathomable and irremediable loss, no horror, no despair of the kind that an honest encounter with the Holocaust makes inescapable. Both in their individual particularity and in their collective enormity, the Holocaust's dead speak in the sense that their reality, their presence, is what grounds our awareness of what the Holocaust was and is. It goes without saying that there is no justification of the Holocaust in this insight. The Holocaust's dead signify unredeemable disaster. What, in particular, the Holocaust's dead communicate, if anything, beyond that recognition is another matter, one to be taken up more fully later in this chapter. But that the Holocaust's dead, anonymous to us or intimately known, inform and communicate with the living can scarcely be denied without denying the Holocaust itself.

If the Holocaust's dead can and do speak, what do they say? To what extent, moreover, is even the raising of that question a temptation to speak for the dead—including those drowned or frozen to death, starved or beaten to death, shot or gassed during the Holocaust—and is it a temptation that ought to be resisted? Already it has been noted that there are writings and recordings to which one can turn to obtain some responses to these questions. The thoughts and voices of the once-living-but-now-dead live on, often with great authority. But Harrison's *The Dominion of the Dead* proposed something intriguingly and profoundly paradoxical that goes beyond remains of that kind. The book did so because Harrison has suggested, I believe, that the dead-in-their-muteness still speak. Indeed, as this essay's title and governing epigraph suggest—Harrison's book is the source of both—Harrison contended that "some truths are glimpsed only in the dark." To discern them as fully as possible means turning to "those who can see through the gloom." These are the dead, including the dead-in-their-muteness, who "possess a nocturnal vision" that involves such seeing.[12]

Again, objections come to the fore, especially when the Holocaust's dead are at the center of attention. Their eyes do not see; every flicker of life is long gone from them. Far from seeing through the gloom, the dead of the Holocaust constitute that darkness of oblivion. Apart from legal fictions, it is even problematic to say that the dead possess anything, least of all vision. Harrison's view, it seems, is not insightful because it is not true.

As with other aspects of Harrison's account, a second glance is important here, too. In a sense of *owning* that is distinctively theirs, the dead, including the dead-in-their-muteness, do *possess* something of the utmost significance. They do so because they *embody* a facticity that is *nocturnal*, if by such words one alludes to the darkness that death itself signifies. Without sharing the nocturnal vision that only the dead can give us (and, in that sense, they possess it), the living are blind—blind, at least, to what befalls us and may await us with regard to death's particularities, which are always real and often hideously so. Like no others, the Holocaust's dead and their brothers and sisters who are the victims of other genocides make us see these realities.

Even granting Harrison this much, however, is it still not misleading or mystifying to suggest as he did that the dead are "those who can see through the gloom" and that "in moments of extreme need" one ought to turn to them because "some truths are glimpsed only in the dark"? Such analysis might be credible if one thinks of those writings and recordings that the once-living have left behind. With the Holocaust in mind, turning to Primo Levi or Charlotte Delbo could make sense of Harrison's claims. I take Harrison, however, to have been holding a more radical position, one that pointed to something more fundamental about the reality, the afterlife, of the dead as dead.

The dead, including the dead of the Holocaust, we may say, are simply dead. But to say even that is far from being as simple as it may seem. A person's death is not his or hers exclusively or alone. It belongs to others as well, which becomes evident in the fact that there is a corpse to dispose of—or at least there is awareness that every human death involves a body, even if no one disposes of it. When one dies, and the Holocaust's dead are no exception to this fact, one unavoidably gives his or her death to others, who do with it what they will. In Harrison's view, this means that the dead can "speak from beyond the grave as long as we lend them the means of locution; they take up their abode in books, dreams, houses, portraits, legends, monuments, and graves as long as we keep open the places of their indwelling."[13]

To follow where Harrison's thought may lead, consider one of the minimalist dialogues that Elie Wiesel has written from time to time, specifically an imagined exchange called "A Father and His Son."[14] In this dialogue, Wiesel does two things, which occur repeatedly in his collection of Holocaust-related dialogues. First, in Harrison's words, he lends the dead the means of locution; he keeps open the places of their indwelling. Wiesel allows them to speak, and in "A Father and His Son," the father, who is one of the Holocaust's dead, asks his living son, who is a Holocaust survivor, "Who will speak for me?" Wiesel's dialogue answers. In doing so the second thing emerges. It consists of a twofold putting of words in the mouth of the dead—first, by having the dead speak in the dialogue and then by emphasizing that the son is trying to speak for the dead father, trying to say what the dead one would say if he could but cannot. "Who will speak for me?" asks the dead father in Wiesel's Holocaust dialogue. "We try," the son replies. "You must believe me. We try." Such trying, the dialogue goes on to suggest, can make one weary, a testimony revealing that honest, credible speaking of and for the dead must concentrate both on the darkness that only the dead can make one see and on the reluctance to see that darkness insightfully, which blinds the living.

Do Wiesel's dialogue and his Nobel injunction against speaking for the dead contradict each other? Here it may be well to note that Wiesel has said that the words "and yet . . . and yet" are among his favorites.[15] In the dialectic of "and yet . . . and yet," the injunction should not be ignored; it must always be kept in play. Nevertheless, fidelity to the dead, bearing witness for them and for the living as well, may sometimes require breaking the injunction by speaking for the dead while always remembering that no one could fully recall or interpret for them what Wiesel rightly called their mutilated dreams and visions. Meanwhile, the dead, even in their muteness, can speak through us. Indeed, if we do not allow them to speak through us, we betray one of the most penetrating ways in which the dead of the Holocaust deeply wanted to indwell in our worlds. Again and again, the dying asked, as the father did in Wiesel's dialogue, to be remembered, to be spoken for—not just spoken of—as those whose lives were laid waste by atrocity.

Does being faithful to that last will and testament of theirs require putting words in their mouths so that they can speak? That is a good question, a right one, which should make us think long and hard. Yes, it does involve putting words into their mouths, but perhaps those words, if carefully considered and thoughtfully uttered, can be at least versions of what the dead would say if they could but cannot. If we keep open the Holocaust places of their indwelling, the dead of Auschwitz and Treblinka, the frozen and drowned bodies that Jack Matzner saw, have much to say to us. To some extent, that saying may involve our imagination as well as our eloquence, but that saying also depends on the stark facticity of their deaths and of the acts that caused them.

In our seeing them, in our discerning what their presence-as-absence in our lives may mean, the sight of the dead may penetrate through the gloom of death and help us to see, in the dark, truths that are always ignored at our peril, not least because such ignorance tends to expand the abysmal count of those whose lives have been wasted by violence, brutality, and genocide. It should go without saying that there is nothing triumphal or necessarily redemptive in these angles of vision. The sight/site of the dead, including the dead of the Holocaust, withholds, in Harrison's words, "a presence at the same time as it renders present an absence. The disquieting character of its presence-at-hand comes precisely from the presence of a void where there was once a person."[16] Yet the truths that can be glimpsed and most profoundly heard only in the dark of that presence of a void may have much to teach.

To note but one possibility of that kind, Harrison stressed that a debt, an "essentially insoluble" one, is owed to the dead.[17] This claim makes sense because no one is "self-authored," and we all "follow in the footsteps of the dead."[18] If that insight encompasses the Holocaust's dead, especially its victims, what is the debt that perhaps can be glimpsed fully only in the dark of the presence of a void? How could one start to respond to that debt and its obligations, keeping in mind that it is impossible to pay and meet them completely because the dead are dead?

Here, I believe, a combination of cautious restraint and bold statement must remain in respectful tension with one another. Restraint is needed because the bold responses that are right and good are also likely to sound like clichés if they are articulated. Silence followed by action that resists death's waste may be the wisest course. But silence, even when accompanied by action that resists death's waste, may be insufficient and irresponsible.

Perhaps one way to begin stating the truths that are glimpsed only in the dark, at least where the Holocaust is concerned, is not so simply to say, "Yes, we all are dying and will soon be dead, but no one's death should come *that way*." What *that way* was and means is unutterable, partly because one cannot interview the dead. But also just because that realization persists—revealing as it does that, in David Boder's words, "the grimmest stories" are not the ones that are told—responses in word and deed that can "see through the gloom" may be found. Such seeing would not dispel the Holocaust's gloom. Nothing can do so. But *seeing through* might suggest another combination: namely, a linking of *seeing through* as enduring to the end, however bitter it may be, with a *seeing through* that entails doing as much as one/we can to find the ways that keep the gloom from overwhelming us.

The Dominion of the Dead had such Holocaust-related perspectives in mind when Harrison drew his book, and I draw my reflection to a close by observing that the dead can be "our guardians. We give them a future so that they may give us a past. We help them live on so that they may help us go forward."[19]

NOTES

1. David P. Boder, *I Did Not Interview the Dead* (Urbana: University of Illinois Press, 1949), xiii.

2. Ibid., 200.

3. Ibid., 209.

4. Ibid., 217.

5. Ibid., xix.

6. See the speech as it is reprinted in Elie Wiesel, *Night,* trans. Marion Wiesel (New York: Hill and Wang, 2006), 117–20, especially 118.

7. This point is augmented by contrast with the Nazi pomp and circumstance that could be found at Third Reich funerals such as the one that honored Reinhard Heydrich, one of the key masterminds of the Holocaust, after his death on June 4, 1942, following wounds inflicted by Czech resistance fighters who ambushed him near Prague on May 27 of that year. For helpful details on such matters, see Jay W. Baird, *To Die for Germany: Heroes in the Nazi Pantheon* (Bloomington: Indiana University Press, 1992), especially 213–18.

8. Robert Pogue Harrison, *The Dominion of the Dead* (Chicago: University of Chicago Press, 2003), xi.

9. Ibid., ix, x.

10. Ibid., 84.

11. Ibid., xi.

12. Ibid., 158–59.

13. Ibid., 153.

14. See Elie Wiesel, *A Jew Today,* trans. Marion Wiesel (New York: Random House, 1978), 139–42 and especially 143.

15. See, for example, Wiesel's 1978 interview with John S. Friedman in Robert Franciosi, ed., *Elie Wiesel: Conversations* (Jackson: University Press of Mississippi, 2002), 96.

16. Harrison, *The Dominion of the Dead,* 92–93.

17. Ibid., 154.

18. Ibid., ix.

19. Ibid., 158.

Christian Goeschel

Suicides of German Jews During the Holocaust

DURING THE HOLOCAUST, SUICIDE BECAME A ROUTINE PHENOMEnon among German Jews. This chapter sheds new light on German-Jewish responses toward Nazi racism and the Holocaust.[1] There is, to be sure, some literature on suicides of German Jews in Nazi Germany. In 1984, historians Konrad Kwiet and Helmut Eschwege argued that suicides of German Jews were not necessarily acts of resistance but nevertheless disturbed the bureaucratic process of the deportations and therefore were acts of deviation, if not of opposition.[2] Kwiet and Eschwege studied suicide largely as a statistical incidence in the wider context of other Jewish responses to Nazi racism, such as open resistance, going into exile, or hiding. And they were mainly interested in the aggregate political effects of suicide. This chapter goes beyond a discussion of suicide as a statistical incidence. It instead focuses on what motivated Jews to commit suicide. Statistics, however elaborate, disregard individual fates and circumstances. Can German-Jewish suicides really be considered a form of resistance against Nazism?

The Nazis claimed to be the arbiters of the lives of Jews once the deportations started in 1941. In this bleak context, the overwhelming majority of German-Jewish suicides derived from personal despair and the desire to preserve individual dignity. Nazi racial policies coalesced in a condition of anomie, a transmutation of normal life and its norms and values, prompted by the collapse of hope, that increases the likelihood of suicide. Emile Durkheim originally developed the concept of anomic suicide as a way to explain suicide as a social phenomenon, but this concept helps us understand the suicides of German Jews in the Third Reich in their wider political and private implications as well.[3] This essay is divided into three sections: a survey of Jewish suicides in

Nazi Germany until the outbreak of the war; Jewish suicides during the deportations, including discussion of suicide notes and police investigations; and suicides in the concentration and death camps.

SUICIDES BEFORE THE WAR

In the months after the Nazis came to power on January 30, 1933, they frequently and arbitrarily attacked Jews. Many Jews committed suicide.[4] The severe Nazi anti-Jewish measures and laws such as the boycott of Jewish businesses on April 1, 1933, the Law for the Renewal of the Professional Civil Service of April 7, 1933, and the creeping "Aryanization" of Jewish business not only caused severe financial problems but also humiliated many Jews who had perceived themselves as Germans. On April 13, 1933, Dr. Hans Bettmann, a Jewish lawyer, shot himself in a Heidelberg cemetery after being dismissed from court.[5] Many other Jewish professionals committed suicide when the Nazis gradually forced them out of their jobs. Most of these professionals thought of themselves as Germans and not as Jews, especially if they were registered members of a Christian church.[6] A journalist noted in his diary on April 24, 1933, that he had recently been to a Jewish cemetery in Berlin. There he saw many new double graves. A friend told him that these were the graves of couples who had committed suicide together.[7]

The Nazis initially welcomed Jewish suicides. Fritz Rosenfelder, a Jewish businessman from Stuttgart and a passionate member of a local sports association, shot himself in the summer of 1933. His club, like most sports associations at that time, was about to expel him, alongside its other Jewish members. His suicide note conveys his feeling of stigmatization:

> My dear friends!
>
> Herewith my final farewell! A German Jew could not stand living with the feeling that the movement with which the German nation wants to be saved regarded him as a traitor. I depart without hatred and resentment. An inner desire inspires me—may reason return in due course! . . . What a Jew feels—you may understand from my action. How much I would have preferred to sacrifice my life for my fatherland! Don't mourn—but try to enlighten and to help the truth become victorious.[8]

The aggressively antisemitic Nazi paper *Der Stürmer*, edited by Julius Streicher, Gauleiter of Franconia, quoted from Rosenfelder's suicide note and commended his suicide as a positive contribution to the solution of the Jewish question in Germany:

> If the Jew Fritz Rosenfelder wanted to contribute to a change of the attitude of Germans towards the Jews, he died in vain. We think of him, now that he is dead, without any feelings of "hatred and resentment." On the contrary, we feel happy for him and would not mind if his racial comrades sent their regards in the same way. Then, "reason will have returned to Germany," with the Jewish question solved in a simple and peaceful manner.

To stress the point, Streicher's paper printed the story on its front page. It blamed Jews for the alleged 220,000 German suicides between 1918 and 1933. If Jews committed suicide, *Der Stürmer* declared, this would only be just.[9]

Some historians claim that the Jewish suicide rate dropped after the boycott of 1933 and after the promulgation of the Nuremberg Laws in 1935. It is impossible to verify this claim statistically because national suicide statistics did not specifically refer to Jewish suicides. Allegedly, Jews felt less threatened and thought that their legal position had been clarified.[10] However, what is clear is that the Nuremberg Laws of 1935 and the increasing legal discrimination suffered by German Jews prompted many to commit suicide. The criminalization of sexual relationships between those branded as racial Jews and non-Jews in the Nuremberg Laws did lead to some suicides of Jews accused of race defilement that might not have happened otherwise.[11]

Mostly, it was Jewish partners in such relationships who committed suicide. Courts treated Jewish suspects much more harshly than their non-Jewish partners.[12] In addition to the Nuremberg Laws, Jews had to cope with a string of local anti-Jewish measures and violence throughout this period, with only a brief and partial letup in the first half of 1936 when the Berlin Olympic Games loomed and the regime, as a consequence, did not want to offend international opinion.[13]

The Berlin Jewish community was worried so much about the growing number of suicides that in 1937 its leaders commissioned an academic study on the subject. The results were reported in a Dutch press circular in November 1937. The study revealed that Jewish suicide levels had sharply increased after 1933. This increase was partly due to the changing age structure of the German-Jewish population. Generally, young Jews left Nazi Germany, whereas older people remained. Elderly people are more prone to kill themselves than young people.[14] In addition, some of the increase in the suicide rate probably resulted from the Great Depression.[15] The Gestapo banned publication of this study, since it clearly linked Nazi racial policies and suicides among German Jewry.[16]

The direct effects of the Nazi regime on Jewish suicides became clearer after the Anschluss of Austria in March 1938. Here, antisemitic violence surpassed anything seen in Germany up to that point. Hundreds of Austrian Jews committed suicide. Immediately after the Anschluss, Anna Freud asked her father, psychoanalyst Sigmund Freud, whether it would not be a good idea to commit suicide. Freud, who shortly thereafter immigrated to England, is said to have told her: "Why? Because they would like us to?"[17]

In the ten days from March 12 to March 22, 1938, at least ninety-six Viennese Jews committed suicide. But the Nazis claimed that only fifty suicides had to do with what they euphemistically called the "change in the political situation in Austria." Concerned with Nazi Germany's image abroad, Joseph Goebbels downplayed the very high number of Jewish suicides on March 30, 1938, in a newspaper article: "In Vienna, there are at present fewer suicides than before, with the main difference being: Some time ago only Germans shot themselves and now there are also Jews [who commit suicide]."[18] Again, the Nazis welcomed Jewish suicides. According to a contemporary British account of Nazi racial policies, Nazi officials forced Viennese Jews to sign a declaration committing themselves to their imminent emigration. Then the Nazis told the Jews that the "way to the Danube [was] always open," thereby encouraging them to kill themselves. After a Jewish shopkeeper had committed suicide together with his family in Vienna, storm troopers plastered his shop windows with posters saying "Please imitate."[19] The Anschluss, with its accompanying antisemitic excesses, gave a tremendous boost to antisemitism across the whole of Germany. It was a significant step toward the long-term Nazi aim: to purge Germany of the Jews.

On November 9, 1938, the Nazis set synagogues and Jewish businesses on fire across Germany. Not only were at least ninety-one Jews killed, according to official Nazi accounts, but also there were several hundred suicides in the wake of Kristallnacht.[20] The pogrom and the violence meted out against Jews clearly indicated that Jewish life would scarcely be possible in Nazi Germany.

Two cases allow us to consider individual German-Jewish reactions to Kristallnacht. The first case is that of Dr. Emil H., a seventy-three-year-old Jewish doctor. On November 11, 1938, a Hamburg local police office investigated his suicide attempt. He had overdosed on morphine. His sister told the police that he "had been depressed over the last few days." He had been forced, like all Jewish doctors across Germany, to close down his surgery for non-Jewish patients by the end of September 1938.[21] On November 18, Dr. H., having survived his suicide attempt, appeared at the police station and declared: "As a result of my tragic and personal circumstances, I have recently been so desperate that I did not want to live any longer and attempted to take my life." He did not mention the pogrom explicitly, probably because he was afraid that the Nazis might retaliate against his family. The shock of the violence and the Nazi invasion of people's homes meant a palpable loss of any security for Jews. Those who survived the pogrom were never the same again. Dr. H. was determined to die, and finally killed himself on November 28, 1938. His wife went to the police station and handed in a death certificate and two suicide notes, which the police typed up and put into Dr. H.'s file.[22] His first suicide note of November 11, 1938, reads:

> My dear Else!
> It will be incredibly difficult to depart from you. I have loved you so much. Be thanked for all your love and faithfulness! Keep on loving the children and grandchildren! Please apologize and think with love of me. Your unhappy H.
> Say hello to Henny and thank her for all her love. I do not want to be given a post mortem, only if my insurance demands it. If that's all right for you, give my fur to E. and my watch to my little godchild.

Jewish suicides in the Third Reich were generally not expressions of hatred toward those left behind or against their own unloved self. Relatives usually did not condemn suicides for violating religious taboos. In the profoundly upsetting environment of the Third Reich, suicide became an acceptable way out of despair.[23] In his second, more desperate suicide note, which Dr. H. wrote before his second and finally successful suicide attempt, he underlined his wish to die: "My dear

Else! I cannot live any longer and I do not want to live anymore. Let me sleep quietly, do not call a doctor and don't let them take me to hospital! Thanks for all your love. Your H."[24] Between the lines, he suggested that Nazi antisemitism was the cause of his suicide.

The second case is that of Hedwig Jastrow, a seventy-six-year-old former teacher. She killed herself on November 29, 1938. In her farewell missive she declared:

> Nobody must undertake any attempts to save the life of someone who does not want to live! It is not an accident, nor an attack of depression. Someone leaves her life whose family has had German citizenship for 100 years, following an oath and has always kept this oath. For 43 years, I have taught German children and have helped them in all misery and for much longer, I have done welfare work for the German Volk during war and peace. I don't want to live without a fatherland, without a Heimat, without a flat, without citizenship, being outlawed and defamed. And I want to be buried with the name my parents once gave me and bequeathed to me, which is impeccable. I do not want to wait until it gets defamed. Every convict, every murderer, keeps his name. It cries to heaven.[25]

Jews would be forced to carry the name "Sara" or "Israel" from January 1, 1939.[26] Jastrow emphasized her Germanness and her service to the German nation during World War I. She refused to accept her removal from German society by the Nazis. The notion of honor also played an important role in Jastrow's suicide note as she saw herself "outlawed" and "defamed." She thought it better to die than break the Nuremberg Laws, which she found dishonorable. The Nuremberg Laws had reduced German Jews from full citizenship to the status of subjects, but only the pogrom of 1938 and, proximately, eviction from her flat destroyed Jastrow's hopes for the future. Her suicide does indeed seem to have been an act of self-assertion of her right to keep control over her life and body.[27] Rather than cope with more discrimination and humiliation, she preferred to decide for herself when it was time to die.

Again, the Nazis explicitly welcomed Jewish suicides. In Hofgeismar, a small town in Hesse, the local representative of the Schutzstaffel (SS) intelligence service, the Sicherheitsdienst (SD), reported on November 17, 1938: "Unfortunately, there have been no suicides or cases of death at this time."[28] The string of local and national Nazi racial policies directed at the removal of the Jews from the public, such as the "Aryanization" of Jewish business, the ban on visiting the most important public places in Berlin (December 1938), the curfew enforced after the outbreak of war, and the introduction of the yellow star in September 1941, meant their "social death."[29] This social death was certainly an important factor creating an environment in which suicides could more easily occur.

SUICIDES DURING THE DEPORTATIONS

After some earlier precedents, the first systematic deportations of German Jews began in October 1941. Only about 160,000 Jews were still in Germany, many of them elderly.[30] The more advanced the age, the more likely someone will commit suicide.[31]

Once the deportations began, Nazi attitudes toward Jewish suicides underwent a fundamental transformation. No longer did the Nazis encourage Jews to commit suicide.[32] The Nazis increasingly regarded themselves as the final arbiters over the lives of Jews. At the beginning of the deportations in 1941, the Berlin Gestapo issued transport orders a week before the actual deportation. But later, they changed this policy and generally did not tell Jews in advance of their deportation, because many Jews had used the interim period to kill themselves.[33] In Würzburg, if a Jew who had been on one of the deportation lists committed suicide, the local Gestapo rounded up another Jew to fill the place that had become vacant.[34] The authorities were determined not to be "cheated" and to round up all Jews. Once the deportations began, policemen routinely inspected the pharmacy of the Berlin Jewish hospital to ensure that no poison had been issued to Jews.[35] An eyewitness later remembered what had happened to those who had attempted suicide, but who survived: "If not successful, suicide was a criminal offense!" Typical of the Third Reich, this practice did not have a legal basis. The Gestapo denied survivors any food and put them onto the next available transport to the East.[36]

Suicide levels dramatically increased after 1941. The Jewish cemetery in Berlin-Weissensee recorded 811 funerals in 1942, compared with 254 in 1941. On March 23, 1943, Martha Liebermann, widow of the famous painter Max Liebermann, aged eighty-five, was also interred in this cemetery. She committed suicide after receiving her deportation order.[37] By then, there was a special ward in the Berlin

Jewish hospital dedicated to failed suicides. This fact, more clearly than any quantitative data, suggests that suicide had become an everyday phenomenon within the Jewish community. Doctors at the Berlin Jewish hospital were debating whether or not to treat people who had attempted to take their lives, since they knew that once recovered they would be deported and killed anyway.[38]

Suicide statistics show a clear chronological correlation between the deportations and the Jewish suicide curve.[39] In Berlin, where most German Jews lived at that time, the suicide rate was at 450 per 100,000 in 1942, more than ten times higher than the corresponding rate for non-Jews. Most people who committed suicide were female and elderly. This pattern reflected the Berlin Jewish community's demographic structure. Elderly German Jews were not really able to assert themselves, other than by committing suicide—unlike younger people who could, at least until late 1941, hope to leave Germany or go into hiding.

But statistics leave out individual fates and circumstances, and it is to them that we now turn. Suicide notes and police investigations sometimes provided a voice to those who ended their lives during the Holocaust. Furthermore, these files allow us to go beyond Marion Kaplan's useful survey of survivors' memoirs written after the Holocaust that documents suicides in the context of a far more terrible death in the camps.[40]

Many German Jews overdosed on sleeping pills. These drugs ensured a relatively easy and private death. As the war went on, sleeping pills became very expensive. Carrying potassium cyanide and barbiturates was a matter of everyday routine for many Jews by that time. In many cases, carrying poison gave Jews a strong sense of control over their fate and made them feel prepared for any eventuality. This culture of being prepared to die by one's own hand was an important stage—well before making the actual decision to die.

The pensioner Dora G. from Prenzlauer Berg, a Berlin working-class district, gassed herself in her kitchen on March 4, 1943. She was due for deportation and announced her suicide to her neighbors. She left a suicide note, written under great stress and therefore almost illegible, on the kitchen table. In it, she declared:

> For forty long years I have been married to Aryans, in my first marriage in America. . . . For 34 years married to an Aryan, had

no contact to Jews, brought up the children in an Aryan way and took them to holy Communion, exercised no Jewish influence on them . . . did not marry according to Jewish faith, 1905 in America, married according to Protestant rituals . . . never did any harm to anyone, always worked (as a girl and as a woman) . . . I am only sorry for my dear ill husband. I like to die, there I am safe.[41]

Dora G.'s suicide note reads like a complaint against the Nazis. She emphasizes her "Aryan" and Protestant identity. She did not feel Jewish and refused to accept being deported like the other Berlin Jews.

Margarete L., a fifty-eight-year-old widow from the middle-class Wilmersdorf district of Berlin, took cyanide on March 4, 1943. She had been married to a Lieutenant Colonel and had received her deportation order for that day. According to the police, she told her friends that she would under no circumstances accept deportation. In her very brief suicide note, she, too, underscored her German identity as an officer's widow: "I depart from life voluntarily! Margarete Sara L., nee Levy, *widow of a Lieutenant Colonel.*"[42] Most Jews who committed suicide in the Third Reich were highly acculturated, like Margarete L. and Dora G. Both referred to their "Germanness." Such language was common in German-Jewish suicide notes. Some men even wore their medals from World War I when they killed themselves.[43] Following the widespread bombings of German towns, the Nazis became more determined to fulfill their plan to expel the Jews from Germany and to murder them.[44] The deportations in early 1943 were accomplished in a particularly cruel and humiliating way in Berlin. The Nazis rounded up Jews on the streets who were not expecting their deportation and immediately took them to the transit camps. On March 6, 1943, Helene M., Ella H., and Bruno H., all in their early sixties, were found dead in a transit camp. They had managed to smuggle in sleeping pills and, in a last attempt to retain their dignity, took them together and died. The criminal police laconically wrote: "Reason of the deed is fear of evacuation."[45]

People facing their immediate deportation sometimes chose very violent means of suicide, reflecting their sheer despair. On August 23, 1943, two Gestapo officers rang the doorbell of forty-eight-year-old Sophie Z. to arrest her for deportation. She did not answer. The first officer remained downstairs, while the other one ran upstairs to Frau Z.'s flat to break down her door. Suddenly, she opened the toilet window and leapt into the backyard. She died on the way to the Jewish hospital.[46]

Having non-Jewish spouses initially protected some Jews from deportation, following Adolf Hitler and Hermann Göring's decree defining "privileged" and "nonprivileged" mixed marriages in the winter of 1938. Once their non-Jewish partner had died, they also fell prey to the Nazis.[47] The Nazis enforced this policy until 1945. Sixty-nine-year-old widow Natalie G., who was Jewish according to the Nuremberg Laws, overdosed on sleeping pills on March 11, 1945. Her non-Jewish husband had died a few days earlier. She was facing deportation. In her suicide note, she wrote:

> My last will and testament. I . . . have decided that because my beloved husband is gone, I, too, will leave this life voluntarily. It is my wish that we be buried together . . . and that this wish be granted. I am so weary of life and have been through so much that I cannot dissuade myself from this course. I am now the third victim in my family. Kind regards to all of my neighbors.[48]

Natalie G. explicitly mentioned the known deaths of her relatives. Some Jews, like Natalie G., knew from summer 1942 onward that deportation meant death.[49]

Most German Jews committed suicide in private, but many Jews wrote suicide notes to publicize their desperate situations. They rightly assumed that the police would read their suicide notes. Contrary to their intentions, Jewish suicides did not shock Nazi authorities, so Jewish suicides were not effective political weapons. In the context of the deportations, suicide was above all an action to keep control of the self and to evade the deportations and what came after.

SUICIDES IN THE CAMPS

Most of the Jews deported to concentration or death camps either died on the way or were murdered in the camps themselves. But, contrary to conventional wisdom, there were some suicides within the concentration camps.[50] Some have claimed that there were relatively few suicide attempts in the camps. Under extreme life-threatening conditions, "there is a tremendous increase in the self-preservation instinct," one scholar noted.[51] Allegedly, the inmates' depersonalization did not allow them to reflect on suicide. This depersonalization was particularly common among the so-called Muselmänner, inmates who had lost their individuality and desire for self-preservation but were so apathetic that they lacked even the will to kill themselves.[52] The SS severely punished suicide attempts, since suicide was an expression of self-determination and thus ran counter to the Nazis' absolute claims over the lives and bodies of the inmates.[53]

Yet suicides did occur in the concentration camps. On September 8, 1942, the Hamburg lawyer Otto B., a Jew, committed suicide by running into the electrical fence in the Mauthausen camp. The SS wrote to his wife that her husband had been cremated and that she could apply for a death certificate by sending in seventy-two pfennigs.[54] In a Ph.D. thesis written in 1943 at Columbia University, the Austrian Jew Paul Neurath, an inmate of Dachau and Buchenwald after the Anschluss until he escaped in May 1939, drew an intriguing picture of SS attitudes toward suicide. At least at this stage, these responses appeared almost entirely arbitrary: "If a guard wants to drive someone into suicide, he subjects him to chicanery until he [the inmate] cannot stand it any longer; if he wants to kill him immediately, he does; but if he wants to prevent the suicide, the man who has undertaken the failed attempt receives twenty-five lashes."[55]

Jean Améry, an Auschwitz survivor, later remembered that "only relatively few had decided to run into the barbed wire," since many inmates feared being severely punished by the SS for failed suicide attempts.[56] According to Hermann Langbein, an Austrian survivor of Auschwitz, suicide was always a widely discussed idea there. However, due to the constant and unbearable torture and humiliation, there were relatively few suicides, because, Langbein claimed, the individuality of the inmates had already been totally destroyed.[57] Auschwitz was both an extermination camp and a labor camp: for those who were not taken to the gas chambers immediately on arrival, there was always some hope of survival. In camps dedicated primarily to extermination, such as Treblinka, the situation was different, and suicide out of sheer despair was so widespread that the SS forced Jewish inmates to go on night watch to prevent other inmates from killing themselves. Nevertheless, many Jews in Treblinka committed suicide, either by taking poison they found in the luggage of those who had already been gassed or by hanging themselves.[58] German Jews usually had the means to commit suicide with sleeping pills and therefore avoided suffering much pain. Poorer Eastern European Jews (less likely to kill themselves because they were generally less acculturated and more religious than German Jews) often resorted to more violent methods such as jumping out of windows or exposing themselves to shootings by camp guards.[59]

Nevertheless, it often remained difficult to differentiate between murder and suicide in Nazi camps. The SS frequently falsified death statistics and claimed that someone had committed suicide to deny responsibility for murdering an inmate or torturing an inmate to death.

DESPAIR AND DIGNITY

Nazi racial policies, the removal of Jews from civic society, and the deportations coalesced in a condition of anomie. This reversal of normal life and its norms and values increased the likelihood of suicide, prompted by the collapse of hope in the possibility of a future.[60] Jewish institutions—synagogues, community centers, schools, clubs, and societies—had been severely weakened in the wake of events in 1938, and Jewish society in Germany had been atomized as well as ostracized. Durkheim's concept of anomie, originally developed to explain suicide as a social phenomenon, clearly applies to the suicides of many German Jews in the Third Reich. But those German Jews who committed suicide in the Third Reich were not simply alienated from existing society as in Durkheim's study of anomie. Rather, they were convinced that the society in which they existed had been destroyed. Until the pogrom of 1938, many German Jews—if they did not emigrate—tried to adapt to life in the racial state. Suicide levels mounted each time the Nazis launched direct actions (the April 1933 boycott of Jewish shops, the Anschluss, and the pogrom of 1938), but levels also subsided temporarily afterward.

Jewish suicides in the Third Reich were not simply acts of despair. Suicides very often tended to be carefully planned to coincide with the start of the deportations. Maintaining some form of dignity was probably a more important motive than despair. Most German-Jewish suicide victims were highly acculturated. They did not accept that the Nazis branded them as "racial" Jews and therefore did not have much contact with the Jewish community. Many did not feel bound by Jewish religious taboos against suicide.

Although Durkheim's concept of anomic suicide helps explain

the suicides of German Jews outside the concentration camps, the comparatively rare incidence of suicides within the concentration and death camps does not fit Durkheim's theory, regardless of whether this relative scarcity resulted from the lack of opportunities for inmates to kill themselves. For all the arbitrary decisions that governed life and death in the camps, the highly regimented rule-bound environment provided inmates with a structure to their lives. The common means to commit suicide with dignity, such as poison, were not readily available. Killing oneself by running into the wire was not a dignified or honorable end but a kind of surrender to the superior forces of the camp's brutal environment. The terrible punishments meted out to failed suicides were a powerful deterrent. In a single-purpose extermination camp like Treblinka, suicides were most probably acts of despair.

During the Holocaust, suicide could no longer be an expression of hatred and anger toward those left behind. Despite Jewish religious proscriptions against suicide, it became a routine phenomenon as the last resort to preserve one's dignity and agency vis-à-vis Nazi racial policies that eventually left no freedom for Jews—other than suicide.[61] Jewish suicides in the Third Reich, especially during the deportations, were, therefore, acts of self-assertion rather than acts of resistance against the Nazis' murderous policies.[62] The history of the suicides of German Jews reminds us that the vast majority of Jews who were left in Germany after November 1938 were fairly elderly. They could not be expected to go into hiding, and their will to live may have been less—as was, undoubtedly, the ability or desire to start a new life elsewhere. The way in which German Jews reacted to the Holocaust, therefore, depended not least on their age. Suicide, a highly individual act that sheds light on wider trends and circumstances, highlights Jewish reactions to Nazi racism on a broader as well as on an individual level.

NOTES

1. This chapter uses some material previously published as "Suicides of German Jews in the Third Reich," in *German History* 25 (2007), 22–45. It is republished here with permission of the German History Society. For an extended discussion, see my *Suicide in Nazi Germany* (Oxford: Oxford University Press, 2009).

2. Konrad Kwiet and Helmut Eschwege, *Selbstbehauptung und Wider-*

stand: Deutsche Juden im Kampf um Existenz und Menschenwürde 1933–1945 (Hamburg: Christians, 1984), 194–215, here 196.

3. Emile Durkheim, *Suicide: A Study in Sociology* (London: Routledge, 1952), 201–39.

4. Kwiet and Eschwege, *Selbstbehauptung und Widerstand*, 200.

5. Comité des Délégations Juives, ed., *Das Schwarzbuch: Tatsachen und Dokumente. Die Lage der Juden in Deutschland 1933* (1934; repr. Frankfurt: Ullstein, 1983), 521.

6. For case studies, see Michael Kater, *Doctors Under Hitler* (Chapel Hill: University of North Carolina Press, 1989), 177–221; Günter Plum, "Deutsche Juden oder Juden in Deutschland?" in *Die Juden in Deutschland, 1933–1945: Leben unter nationalsozialistischer Herrschaft*, ed. Wolfgang Benz (Munich: C. H. Beck, 1988), 36–74.

7. Monika Richarz, *Jüdisches Leben in Deutschland: Selbstzeugnisse zur Sozialgeschichte, 1918–1945* (Stuttgart: Deutsche Verlags Anstalt [DVA], 1982).

8. *Jüdische Rundschau,* April 25, 1933, quoted in Comité des Délégations Juives, *Schwarzbuch,* 522. Note the awkward style of this suicide note.

9. *Der Stürmer,* no. 30 (July 1933).

10. Kwiet and Eschwege, *Selbstbehauptung und Widerstand,* 200.

11. For background, see Alexandra Przyrembel, *"Rassenschande": Reinheitsmythos und Vernichtungslegitimation im Nationalsozialismus* (Göttingen: Vandenhoeck and Ruprecht GM, 2003), 185–488.

12. Hans Robinsohn, *Justiz als politische Verfolgung: Die Rechtsprechung in "Rassenschandefällen" beim Landgericht Hamburg 1936–1943* (Stuttgart: DVA, 1977), 142.

13. Richard J. Evans, *The Third Reich in Power* (New York: Penguin, 2005), 570–73.

14. Paul A. Nisbet, Ronald W. Maris, Alan L. Berman, and Morton M. Silverman, "Age and the Lifespan," in *Comprehensive Textbook of Suicidology,* ed. Maris, Berman, and Silverman (New York: Guilford, 2000), 127–44.

15. "Jüdische Bevölkerungsstatistik," in Benz, *Die Juden in Deutschland, 1933–1945,* 733; see also "Die Juden und jüdischen Mischlinge in den Reichsteilen und nach Gemeindegrößenklassen 1939," *Statistisches Jahrbuch für das Deutsche Reich* 59 (1941/42), 27.

16. Wiener Library London, Press Clippings Collection 3, reel 33, Joodsche Perscommissie voor byzondere Berichtgeving, November 3, 1937; compare with Kwiet and Eschwege, *Selbstbehauptung und Widerstand,* 201.

17. Quoted in Peter Gay, *Freud: A Life for Our Time* (London: Dent, 1988), 622.

18. Quoted in Eckart Früh, "Terror und Selbstmord in Wien nach der Annexion Österreichs," in *Fünfzig Jahre danach: Der 'Anschluß' von innen*

und außen gesehen, ed. Felix Kreissler (Vienna: Europaverlag, 1989), 216–26, here 220.

19. Gustav Otto Warburg, *Six Years of Hitler: The Jews Under the Nazi Regime* (London: Allen and Unwin, 1939), 247.

20. Richarz, *Jüdisches Leben,* 57. Kwiet and Eschwege, *Selbstbehauptung und Widerstand,* 202.

21. Kater, *Doctors Under Hitler,* 200–201.

22. On suicide notes, see Nils Retterstøl, *Suicide: A European Perspective* (Cambridge: Cambridge University Press, 1993), 101–2.

23. Marion Kaplan, *Between Dignity and Despair* (New York: Oxford University Press, 1998), 181.

24. Staatsarchiv Hamburg, 331-5 Polizeibehörde—Unnatürliche Sterbefälle, no. 57/39 (note the awkward style of his suicide notes). On Jews in Hamburg in the Third Reich, see Ina Lorenz, "Das Leben der Hamburger Juden im Zeichen der 'Endlösung'" (1942–1945), in *Verdrängung und Vernichtung der Juden unter dem Nationalsozialismus,* ed. Arno Herzig and Ina Lorenz (Hamburg: Christians, 1992), 207–47.

25. Landesarchiv Berlin (hereafter LAB), A. Pr. Br. Rep. 030, Tit. 198B, No. 1943; for a different interpretation, see Ursula Baumann, *Vom Recht auf den eigenen Tod: Die Geschichte des Suizids vom 18. bis zum 20. Jahrhundert* (Weimar: Hermann Böhlaus Nachfolger, 2001), 373–76.

26. Evans, *The Third Reich in Power,* 575.

27. Richarz, *Jüdisches Leben,* 65.

28. SD-Außenstelle Hofgeismar. Judenaktion, November 17, 1938, printed in *Die Juden in den geheimen NS-Stimmungsberichten 1933–1945,* ed. Otto Dov Kulka and Eberhard Jäckel (Düsseldorf: Droste, 2004), 320.

29. Kaplan, *Between Dignity and Despair,* 184.

30. Kwiet and Eschwege, *Selbstbehauptung und Widerstand,* 54.

31. Nisbet, Maris, Berman, and Silverman, "Age and the Lifespan," 127–44.

32. Suicide was not a criminal offense in Nazi Germany, despite Nazi attempts to criminalize it in the mid-1930s.

33. Wiener Library London, Eye Witness Accounts, P.III.a. no. 1095.

34. Herbert Schott, "Die ersten drei Deportationen mainfränkischer Juden 1941/42," in *Wege in die Vernichtung: Die Deportation der Juden aus Mainfranken 1941–1943,* ed. Albrecht Liess (Munich: Generaldirektion der Staatlichen Archive Bayerns, 2003), 73–166, here 139.

35. Kwiet and Eschwege, *Selbstbehauptung und Widerstand,* 206–7.

36. Quoted in Richarz, *Jüdisches Leben,* 431.

37. Martin Riesenburger, *Das Licht erlöschte nicht: Dokumente aus der Nacht des Nazismus* (East Berlin: Union-Verlag, 1960), 39–40.

38. Hildegard Henschel, "Aus der Arbeit der Jüdischen Gemeinde Berlin während der Jahre 1941–1943: Gemeindearbeit und Evakuierung von Berlin, 16 Oktober 1941–16 Juni 1943," *Zeitschrift für die Geschichte der Juden*, 9 (1972), 33–52. See also the more reliable account by Rivka Elkin, *Das Jüdische Krankenhaus in Berlin zwischen 1938 und 1945* (Berlin: Edition Hentrich, 1993), 42–43.

39. LAB, A. Pr. Br. Rep. 030, Tit. 198B, No. 1623–1626.

40. Kaplan, *Between Dignity and Despair*, 180–81.

41. LAB, A. Rep. 358-02, No. 142671.

42. LAB, A. Rep. 358-02, No. 142676 (original emphasis).

43. Kaplan, *Between Dignity and Despair*, 181.

44. Marion Kaplan, "Jewish Daily Life in Wartime Germany," in *Probing the Depths of German Antisemitism: German Society and the Persecution of the Jews, 1933–1941*, ed. David Bankier (New York: Berghahn, 2000), 406.

45. LAB, A. Rep. 358-02, No. 142565, Kriminal-Inspektion Mitte, March 9, 1943.

46. LAB, A. Rep. 358-02, No. 137482, Selbstmord durch Sprung aus dem Fenster, August 26, 1943.

47. On mixed marriages, see Beate Meyer, "The Mixed Marriage: A Guarantee of Survival or a Reflection of German Society During the Nazi Regime?" in Bankier, *Probing the Depths of German Antisemitism*, 54–77.

48. LAB, A. Rep. 358-02, No. 144354, suicide note of Natalie G., March 11, 1945.

49. Eric A. Johnson and Karl-Heinz Reuband, *What We Knew: Terror, Mass Murder, and Everyday Life in Nazi Germany* (Cambridge, Mass.: Harvard University Press, 2005), 51.

50. Kwiet and Eschwege, *Selbstbehauptung und Widerstand*, 209. On the concentration camps, see generally Ulrich Herbert, Karin Orth, and Christoph Dieckmann, eds., *Die nationalsozialistischen Konzentrationslager—Entwicklung und Struktur* (Göttingen: Wallstein, 1998).

51. Thomas Bronisch, "Suicidality in German Concentration Camps," *Archives of Suicide Research* 2 (1996), 129–44, here 142.

52. Ibid., "Suicidality," 139–40.

53. Wolfgang Sofsky, *Die Ordnung des Terrors: Das Konzentrationslager* (Frankfurt: S. Fischer, 1993), 73.

54. Forschungsstelle für Zeitgeschichte Hamburg 6262, Konzentrationslager Mauthausen, Kommandatur to Frau Gertrud B., September 14, 1942.

55. Paul Martin Neurath, *Die Gesellschaft des Terrors: Innenansichten der Konzentrationslager Dachau und Buchenwald* (Frankfurt: Suhrkamp, 2004), 134.

56. Jean Améry, *Jenseits von Schuld und Sühne* (Stuttgart: Klett-Cotta, 1977), 41. See also Irene Heidelberger-Leonard, *Jean Améry. Revolte in der Resignation: Biographie* (Stuttgart: Klett-Cotta, 2004).

57. Hermann Langbein, *Menschen in Auschwitz* (Vienna: Europaverlag, 1972), 144–49, here 144.

58. Yitzhak Arad, *Belzec, Sobibor, Treblinka: The Operation Reinhard Death Camps* (Bloomington: Indiana University Press, 1987), 223–25.

59. Kaplan, *Between Dignity and Despair*, 183.

60. Durkheim, *Suicide*, 208–39.

61. See by way of comparison Kaplan, *Between Dignity and Despair*, 180–84.

62. Kwiet and Eschwege, *Selbstbehauptung und Widerstand*, 196.

Simone Gigliotti

Deportation Transit and Captive Bodies: Rethinking Holocaust Witnessing

WITH THE FOLLOWING LETTER, ZALMEN GRADOWSKI, A MEMBER OF A Sonderkommando at Auschwitz-Birkenau, issued an invitation:

> Let us walk through those rushing cages. Look, here is the sad and desperate human throng sitting and standing, plunged into a deep, nightmarish meditation. The monotonous sound of bumping wheels is heard . . . it lies on the heart like a heavy burden and harmonizes perfectly with the atmosphere of weirdness. It seems as if the trip had lasted a whole eternity already. We boarded the eternally traveling Jewish train, directed by strangers.[1]

Gradowski's "eternally traveling Jewish train" provides entry into victims' memories of deportation journeys. What can be gleaned from this space of suffering in the Holocaust? Historians have interpreted the administration of deportation as a model of Nazi bureaucratic efficiency at the high point of World War II. This high point was the commission of the "Final Solution of the Jewish Question," the Nazi-coined euphemism for the mass murder of European Jewry. The "Final Solution" involved the deportation of an estimated three million Jews from ghettos across Europe to concentration and extermination camps in occupied Poland between 1941 and 1944. This transportation occurred in no more than 2,000 trains, a statistically insignificant number when compared to the German Railways' overall volume of traffic, which ran on average 30,000 trains per day in 1941 and 1942, declining to about 23,000 trains daily in 1944.[2] The relativization of this figure should not, however, detract from the afflictions of deportees. The sometimes unbearably slow speeds of transports on account of their low priority behind war freight, the antiquated conditions of the engines carrying thousands of deportees, and improvised planning by Schutzstaffel (SS) leaders and bureaucrats that affected the trains' inconsistent departures all contributed to harrowing transit conditions for deportees. An analysis of the deportation transit remains largely neglected in the historiography of the victims' suffering, yet it is crucially revealing about what makes a Holocaust witness. In this essay, I argue that testimonies of transit stimulate a rethinking of the perceptual and visual bases of Holocaust witnessing, of which this captivity was one example.

Nazi policy promoted the social death of the Jews before mid-December 1941, when Adolf Hitler announced to his inner circle the decision to commit to a coordinated plan for their explicit physical murder on a continental scale. Between 1933 and 1941, Jews' ambitions of belonging within German society had been increasingly undermined through a series of measures that ranged from assaults on the person, the group, and symbols of Jewish cultural identity and livelihood to practices of segregation, expulsion, and relocation. This destruction process, as the political scientist Raul Hilberg has labeled it, occurred in four phases that mark transitions from social to physical death: identification as Jews through laws, decrees, race hygiene beliefs; material expropriations of Jewish property and business; concentration of Jews in larger towns and ghettos; and annihilation by disease, starvation, killing squads, and gassings in camps.

Imprisonment marked the spatial and social world of Jews as primary victims of Nazi policy in Europe, and this imprisonment was intensely and painfully felt in suffocating captivity in deportation. The practice of deportations from ghettos to extermination and concentration camps did not occur on a widespread scale until the middle of 1942, and it represented a bridge between concentration and annihilation. For the deportees, however, the experience of these train journeys felt like an endless captivity. The intentional deprivation of basic provisions of food, water, and disposal of human waste during transit was, as Primo Levi wrote, a "systematic negligence" and a "useless cruelty," "a deliberate creation of pain which was an end in itself."[3]

While an examination of deportation train journeys places the reader into this space, the interpretation of victims' experiences of transit, like other traumatic Holocaust experiences, is conflicted and fraught. Where does the experience of bodily pain begin and end, and how does embodied memory negotiate experience? For the deportees, the corporeal degradation of their journeys cannot be so easily spoken or written about. Consequently, the inability to express in words the physicality of bodily pain is perhaps the most striking feature of testimonies. While many of the conditions of transit anticipated the camp regime of depersonalization and defilement, the conditions of deportation transit were arguably more intensely endured and remembered for their impact because of the temporal brevity of transit when compared with longer-term confinement in ghettos and camps. Excruciating compression, the erosion of personal space and possibility for intimacy, severe hunger, deteriorating health and hygiene threats, the destabilization of sight, and the overpowering and choking stench of excrement, urine, and vomit all characterized this space. And despite the varying points of origin, dates, and climates of deportation, testimonies corroborate each other in their accounts of affliction. This feature of corroboration does not ignore moments of exceptionality in deportation, where deportees traveled in passenger trains, had room to move, traveled with few others, and carried plentiful food provisions. In my analysis of unpublished testimonies and depositions, published memoirs, oral histories, and video testimonies, a narrative sequence of transit clearly emerges: the boarding and loading of the carriages and adjustment to the space; the conditions of, and responses to, transit; and the emergence of journey fatigue and inability to perceive time. In its telling, the journey is relived as a mobile chamber of restless and fluid meaning.

The violent entry of deportees into the carriages is commonly represented as entrapment, affecting spatial boundaries and social intimacy, sharing, thoughts on other deportees' coping mechanisms, and rumors about the location of a shared, yet mostly unconfirmed, fate. Distress is imprinted in the testimony of Marek S., who was deported to Majdanek in April 1943. He wrote:

> Finally, one by one, we reach the train platform. I cannot describe the bestial scenes that are taking place as we enter the wagons. Finally, we are inside the wagon. There are 75 of us. That is not many. Supposedly, 120 to a wagon went to Treblinka. On the walls, one can see the various inscriptions left behind by people who were bidding farewell to the world in this way. In the evening, it becomes suffocating. The window is nailed shut. Movements become heavy and sluggish. There is no air to breathe. We throw everything off,

sprawling passively on the floor. Old women and some children fall to the ground. They are dying. Dr. Grozienski pulls out a vial of poison. He stares blankly at his wife with a crazed look and at Dr. Hayman and his wife as well. However, he does not have the courage to make use of it.[4]

Erika A., deported from Greece, recalled that "packed together, dragging their children and luggage, people disappeared into the railway cars. On each car a sign specified: 'Capacity 40 soldiers or eight horses.' The cars were painted in a rusty red color, they had no windows at all apart from a skylight, very high up, left and right, protected by wire. As the doors shut you could not see anything inside; you could hardly hear anything. You saw only an occasional hand through a skylight."[5] Gisela S. was deported from Theresienstadt to Auschwitz in late 1944. The shock of her adjustment is evident as she tried to find a seating place for her mother:

> We were shoved into cattle cars. I was able to secure a seat for her on the only bench available. I sat nearby on the floor, squeezed among many people. I looked around and saw written on the wall of the car 'Arrived in Auschwitz' on such a date. . . . I now knew for sure where we were headed, yet I did not tell anyone. If others saw the writing, they didn't tell either. We traveled two nights and a day under the most horrid conditions. We had not enough air, no water, no toilet facilities and were practically sitting on one another. People were fighting with each other making matters even worse.[6]

Adjustment to confinement was also a dilemma for Ya'akov G., who was deported in January 1943 from the Sanok ghetto in Galicia to Bełżec and who escaped during transit: "When they put us in all together into the wagons, there was no place to stand or sit. Some of the people sat on the floor, some stood and then every hour we exchanged positions."[7] The plea for understanding overcrowding is evident in Leon Cohen's account, although the discomfort was somewhat relieved through uncommonly plentiful food provisions. Cohen used the word "packed" in reference to the sensory feeling: "Seventy of us were packed into each cattle car. Their sole contents were two dustbins for relieving ourselves (under scrutiny of our guards) which could only be emptied at the next station. For seventy people, our only ventilation was a small opening, about 40 cm by 70 cm, which was crisscrossed by barbed wire. But we were also amazed to find masses of fresh food—bread and fruit as well as two water containers."[8]

Other recollections reconfirmed the urgent need to impose a code of spatial exchange. Primo Levi offered that "one must take turns standing or squatting," for "lying down was out of the question, and we were only able to sit by deciding to take turns."[9] In Charlotte Delbo's carriage, "the aged were silent and dazed. All of them formed groups, sharing their blankets, rolling up clothing to use as pillows,"[10] while Eva Quittner reported that "some of the people stood up to stretch their numbed bodies and give the ones sitting down a little more room. This was to become the routine for the duration of the journey."[11]

Zofia P.'s deportation to Bełżec was immersed in decline. She wrote:

> The doors of the cars are shut, it is dark and tense, impossible to stretch out your arms, absolutely no air to breathe. Everybody strangles and chokes and you feel as if a rope were tied around your neck, such a terrible heat as if the fire had been set under the car. About ten people from our group are placed near the door, whoever has hairpins, nails, fasteners, starts to bore between the boards to get a little bit of air. People behind us are in much worse plight, they take off their clothes and as if obsessed by bestiality and madness, they are hawking, choking, and driven into utmost despair. After a long waiting, the train is in motion, a sigh of relief emanates from the mouths of those who are still alive, they hope that now more air will find its way into the car, or maybe it will start raining and a few drops will penetrate through, but none of those miracles happen. I notice that there is more and more free space, people die and we are seated on their dead bodies. The remaining are raving and wild, mad from suffering. They quarrel between themselves about water that doesn't exist. Mothers hand their children urine to still their thirst. We have in our car no more than 20 people still alive.[12]

It is clear that entrapment produced unparalleled and unrelenting misery. But how could language do justice to these primal scenes? Language was often declared futile to describe acts of excretion and urination and their uncontainable and fermenting effects. In his 1976 book *The Survivor: An Anatomy of Life in the Death Camps,* Terrence Des Pres coined the phrase "excremental assault" principally to describe the impact of "mineral movement" in the camps. Although he acknowledged the defilement in the "locked boxcars," his focus on the camp world neglected the sustained transport invasions of excrement, urine, and vomit as a combined preparation for the defilement of individuals in the camps.

The stench of human waste carried both actual and symbolic invasions during transit. Contamination, threats to hygiene, and insultingly inadequate provisions for sanitation persist as themes in deportees' testimonies. To defecate and urinate publicly was shameful, a break with the bounds of civility. People lay down on floorboards of freight cars to find the smallest crack, desperate to inhale air unpolluted by excrement, urine, vomit, and dead bodies. The excruciating need for water "got so bad that people began drinking their own urine," which would sometimes "burn the throat."[13] Others, like Rena Gelissen, unsuccessfully tried to avoid the degradation of public excretion: "I'm sorry . . . but I could not hold myself any longer. Some people are shocked, hiding their eyes in shame but sooner or later one must follow suit or mess themselves."[14]

Where was the train headed, when would it stop, and what would be done with those who died in transit? Although such questions concerned the deportees, they were overtaken by the excrement bucket's unavoidably putrid smell and spillage, worsened by the jerking movement of the train. The latrine bucket defined the sensory memory of transport shame. Rena Gelissen wrote that "the sound of the improvised lavatory soon became unbearable. At every jolt, there was a worrying ploshing noise," and "the stinking air was unbreathable, the ventilation nil."[15] Abraham K. wrote that "it is impossible to describe the tragic situation in our airless, closed freight car. It was one big toilet, the stink in the car was unbearable,"[16] and "nobody thought about food, only about air and water."[17]

Gizel Berman anguished not only over excreting in public but also about the internal anxiety of reaching the bucket: "Each time the train stopped, the bucket for waste and the bucket for water would be emptied and filled respectively. This meant that we all had to perform our most private needs in public, men and women alike. I remember thinking, 'I will wait until dark—but in the dark accidents can happen more easily. What if I'm thrown off balance? What if several people need to go at the same time?' I couldn't stop thinking about this one subject, and about how lucky we were to have claimed a spot well away from the corner where the toilet had been placed."[18]

Eva Gross compared her journey to the toilet bucket as running an emotional marathon course:

> I stole myself into another world. My sleep was too short. I awoke in a sweat and had an urge to go to the pail. I stood up, but immediately, I was down again. There was no foot path on what seemed to be a kilometer-long obstacle course. I reached out with both hands and poked in the dark. There was no place to take a step. When I thought I had secured a spot for one foot, I discovered something like an arm beneath it. Then I stepped on someone's chest. In desperation, I decided to grope ahead with my hands before putting down my feet again. Bending low, the strong body odors nauseated me.[19]

The shameful association victims attached to stench continues the conversations of cultural historians and their assessments of the value of the senses in interpreting past experiences and what kind of knowledge they impart. In "Charting the Cultural History of the Senses," Alain Corbin investigated the hygienic disorder of smell, considering the boundaries of its perceived and unperceived symbolism. Corbin contended that the tension of interpreting the senses' meaning was social: sight and hearing were rational senses, touch was a fundamental sense, and taste and smell were senses of survival, which revealed the ostensibly true nature of things.[20] The senses have also been interpreted as predominantly Western and binary in construct, symbolizing nature and culture, savagery and innocence. Corbin argued that "it is only when our faculty of smell is impaired for some reason that we begin to realize the essential role olfaction plays in our sense of well-being."[21] As I have suggested, deportee testimonies associated stench with putrification, moral corruption, and a regression to primality. In describing the effects of transports, deportees referred to primality by comparing their transport method and violent entry into the carriage to the transport methods for sheep or cattle, presumably to their deaths in an abattoir.

While freight cars, goods wagons, and (occasionally) passenger cars were used in deportations across Europe, many deportees felt they were treated and were forced to behave "like animals," an indication of feeling victimized, beyond the human, and beyond care. Words such as "marched," "herded," "shoved," "packed," and "squeezed" were commonly used to describe the packlike movement to the carriage and subsequent entrapment. Quite often, the dehumanization was complete when deportees described themselves as "animals" instead of "like animals." The reduction to what survivors described as an "animal-like" condition from sitting in excrement, inhaling its toxic stench, and excreting before others confirmed an ultimate objective of the Nazis, which was to create a "death world" for the Jews. As suggested by the philosopher Edith Wyschogrod, "By reducing victims to animal status, the death-world strips them of the symbolic truths of their existence and consigns them to death forever."[22] While actual cattle cars were very infrequently, if at all, used in deportations, it is clear that the unsettling yet frequent use of the term "cattle car" in testimonies has become a victims' phrase of empowerment and a semantic vindication of inhumane treatment. As shown, testimonies of transit's depersonalization and degradation painfully evoke the force and perpetrators' intentional sadism and disregard for deportees' welfare and seriously undermine the credibility of the perpetrators' statements that the journeys were intended to resettle the deportees for labor purposes.

Given these atrocious conditions, how did deportees manage to survive this space and resist the onslaught of bodily decline, a metamorphosis that is indelibly associated with the death of the human? The violated body of deportees was asked to survive misery as a normative state of deportation transit, as recalled by Vera Laska:

> The stench of excrement is overpowering. The woman on the floor emits a putrid smell. There are over a dozen corpses by now in the wagon. They are taken off, thrown on the platform. A bucketful of water is hurled in, cooling those at the middle. Perhaps they were able to swallow a mouthful. Most of the precious liquid drips down through the floorboards. It only intensifies the stench of human waste and vomit. Women cry, shriek, tear their hair. One is hysterically laughing. I will myself to think of ice and snow melting in my mouth, but my palate is dry, my tongue glued to the roof of my mouth. I repeat to myself: cogito ergo sum; as long as I think, I still exist. But thoughts are becoming hazy. Perhaps I am not even here. But I am hanging on to the large hook over the window, not high enough to hang myself. No, I have no intention to oblige the unleashed demons of bestiality and do away with myself.[23]

The possibility of sustaining a visual truth of transit was consistently compromised by other sensory intrusions such as those described by Vera Laska. Menacing were the tunes of the locomotive: the sound of wheels turning, whistles blowing, and brakes screeching. Viktor Frankl recalled hearing the train's whistle before the utterance of the word "Auschwitz" made its impact on the group psyche:

> Fifteen hundred persons had been traveling by train for several days and nights: there were eighty people in each coach. All had to lie on top of their luggage, the few remnants of their personal possessions. The carriages were so full that only the top parts of the windows were free to let in the gray of dawn. Everyone expected the train to head for some munitions factory, in which we would be employed as forced labor. We did not know whether we were still in Silesia or already in Poland. The engine's whistle had an uncanny sound, like a cry for help sent out in commiseration for the unhappy load which it was destined to lead to perdition. Then the train shunted, obviously nearing a main station. Suddenly a cry broke from the ranks of anxious passengers, 'There is a sign, Auschwitz!' Everyone's heart missed a beat at that moment. Auschwitz—the very name stood for all that was horrible: gas chambers, crematoriums, massacres. Slowly, almost hesitatingly, the train moved on as if it wanted to spare its passengers the dreadful realisation as long as possible: Auschwitz![24]

Parallel to the incapacitating conditions of transit, deportees revealed that reduced space also produced negotiations: spatial stress was observed in the need to form alliances and friendships with fellow passengers, to indulge in and eavesdrop on conversations about other people, to block out annoying and hysteric screams, to express indifference to the shared plight of the carriage, and to practice a form of transport etiquette by showing care in the sharing of food, water, and space. Singing among deportees, such as Zionist youth songs, was common, yet people also fought, entertained each other with macabre death stories, and told jokes.

While journeys provoked some deportees to behave with occasionally compassionate and life-affirming actions, others withdrew from this space, as they perceived emotional distance and detachment to be essential to survival. A consistent theme in testimonies is the preoccupation with decline, in terms of managing its presence and potential in claiming psychologically vulnerable deportees. An extreme but all too unfortunately tempting example of decline was suicide. Its temptation and occurrence during transit implicated deportees in a community of ethics and reluctant responsibility. Josef B. reported that "in my wagon was over hundred people together" who "couldn't breathe, and they locked the doors, there was barbed wire and small windows, and the train started to move, and one man he hanged himself in the train with a belt, and they tried to cut him off."[25] Clara L., deported from Hungary to Auschwitz, saw that the doctor of the ghetto had smuggled "an entire hospital supply of morphine" onto the train, and he used it to take his own life. As the train journeyed closer to Auschwitz, Clara asked her mother "if she would want to have this way out, and she said no. She was a very religious woman and apparently decided this is what is going to be."[26]

Suffocation caused additional deaths. Helen K., deported to Majdanek, recalled in her video testimony her family's futile fight for life. She made a frustrated plea to her interviewer to understand her trauma in terms corroborated by other deportees, that is, as a discrete death space; she mourned, "My brother died in my arms. My younger brother and my husband's two sisters. There was not enough oxygen for all those people. They kept us in those wagons for days. They wanted us to die in the wagons. You know the cattle cars with very little windows?"[27]

While the conditions of Holocaust transit induced symbolic and actual deaths and inhibited life, making more "efficient" (from the Nazi perspective) the intended destruction before arrival at the camps, the survivors' struggles to make this trauma explicable to an audience without a comparable experience of captivity remains deeply agonizing. It is clear that survivor testimonies of deportation provide a narrative order to the experience of forced movement from the ghetto, transit trauma, and arrival at the camps. Yet it is also clear that the corporeal significance of the journeys—that is, the tellability of bodily pain endured during transit—persists as a disordered and frustrating sensory memory that remains unsatisfyingly expressed in written or spoken forms.

The tellability of transit's bodily pain relates to a wider issue of what makes a witness in different spaces and locations of incarceration and requires rethinking of the links between perceptual opportunities to witness in different locations of Nazi persecution and the consequent impact on what can be testified to. Making sense of transit suffering is crucially dependent on what is told about it, who does the telling, and the forums available for it.

The authors of transit witnessing, namely the deportees, were very ordinary people without pretension to literary acclaim or evocative insight about human behavior in extremity. They were by far the majority of Holocaust survivors, but their testimony remains unclaimed and displaced by a scholarly preference for "classic" texts about Holocaust victimization. Yet it was the ordinary witnesses who were forced by the violence of history to become messengers but with despairingly few listeners or readers. There are thousands of these testimonies, but who has heard of their authors—Leo Bretholz from Vienna; Warsaw ghetto fighter Benjamin Piskorz, who told his story to David Boder in an Italian displaced persons' camp in 1946; and Rosa Ferera from Rhodes? Could it be that a lack of critical interest in their journeys is reflective of the scholarly marginalization of abundant unpublished testimonies that evince minimal literary distinction or revelations about the human condition or behavior in extremity? This reading implies that what constitutes a meaningful Holocaust experience is arguably less the content of the story than the drama and sophistication of its telling, the revelation of a previously mystifying experience in language that rewrites the Holocaust as a continuing cultural moment of disruption, mourning, and return.

Indeed, in what ways can the ordinariness and ostensible anonymity of deportation testimony challenge the existing scholarly reliance on long-published literary classics and visual witness as a speaking position for Holocaust suffering? The primacy given to the sight basis of witness truths, particularly from the Holocaust, and their inheritance to scientific visualization are grounded in the relatively unchanging hierarchy of the senses—that sight, hearing, and smell were human senses, while taste and touch were characteristic of animal traits.[28] Several historians of the senses see their value in cultural and social terms, a mediated process of the civilized world, where perception is the product of a multisensory experience. David Howes has advanced the paradigm of emplacement to suggest the "sensuous interrelationship of body-mind-environment."[29] But this emplacement is what Holocaust transit provides only in part, an embodied witness of indeterminate locations and feared destinations, where the cattle car's freight of passengers becomes the defining architecture of confinement.

One way of ethically responding to these testimonies is to isolate the integrity of bodily experience and claim a position of silence for it. Abjection is intimate and personal and cannot be shared. This reading suggests that experiences of transit are without words and without image. As Roberta Culbertson noted about trauma narratives in general, they "obey none of the standard rules of discourse: they are the self's discourse with itself, a channel between the conscious and unconscious that speaks a body language."[30] The New Zealand anthropologist Michael Jackson would concur with Culbertson on the work of silence; he has argued that the ethnographic impulse of "coexistence" with suffering is perhaps the most that can be achieved through an ethical engagement with the other.[31] Yet the quest for explanation remains paramount: "Can the intellectual succeed in accomplishing what the sufferer cannot? Or are our attempts to communicate or publicize the pain of others little more than stratagems for helping us deal with the effects this pain has had on us?"[32] Silence, Jackson claimed, might be a more effective ethical response than talk, a deliberate muting that has long prevailed in intellectual responses to how victims' experiences of the Holocaust should be interpreted.[33] How does one compensate, Jackson inquired, for the "sheer banality of suffering—the fact that though it is so devastating to the sufferer, there is little that he or she can say about it, except recount the kind of matter-of-fact summaries of events?"[34] Indeed, while there might be no "final vocabulary" for doing justice to experience, there is an argument for rethinking approaches to embodied experiences that testify to overwhelming pain in this summary-like manner.

In that spirit, it is useful to revisit Gradowski's request to enter the "rushing cages" and remain in their scenes of relentless distress, emotional trauma, and decline. How do these conditions compel a rethinking of what conditions make and break a witness during transit? How does the lack of location, of deportation transit being unanchored to a site-specific location such as a ghetto or a camp, influence embodied perception and corporeal memory? How do the survivors themselves go beyond chronicle and interpret transit's relentless misery?

This last question merits being the concluding question. By their very survival, camp inmates testify to an experience of death in chambers that were not in the camps but in the cattle car. It is the mobile chamber of the cattle car that for many survivors remains inadmissible in social discourse, as suggested in Ruth Klüger's description of her transport from Theresienstadt to Auschwitz in her acclaimed memoir, *Still Alive*. She wrote:

If I look at a map today, I see that the distance from Theresienstadt to Auschwitz is not very great. Yet it was the longest trip I have ever taken. The train stood around, it was summer, the temperature rose. The still air smelled of sweat, urine, excrement. A whiff of panic trembled in the air. It's from this experience that I think I have an idea of what it must have been like in the gas chambers. The feeling of having been abandoned, which is not the same as having been forgotten. We knew we hadn't been forgotten, because the railroad car stood on rails, had a direction, would arrive. But abandoned in the sense of discarded, separated, trashed and tossed in an old crate, like last birthday's worn-out toy.[35]

Klüger's comparison is not as disturbing as it may sound given that many testimonies of transit are a post hoc interpretation. Rather the comparison is a telling comment about why survivors have made that appeal in the first place. The comparison, I would argue, is a critique of the marginalization of the cattle car "death" in interpretive writing about victims' experiences during the Holocaust. The collaborative testimony of transit struggled to find validation for the journey's corporeal aura once the horrible reality of the gas chambers in the camps was exposed. This reality was the essential basis to representations of the camps' horror and mass death as the epicenter of what Sidra Ezrahi has called the "symbolic geography" of the Holocaust, and all other experiences outside of it as peripheral. Ezrahi argued that representations of the Holocaust, ranging across historical writing, literature, and survivor testimony, mark it as a universe consisting of "concentric circles," of which the gas chamber was the center or black hole, and that to have spent the war years avoiding that fate was to have inhabited the "outer circles" of that universe.[36] By this logic, she wrote, "Multiple points of reference or departure are not equally valid but rather mark degrees of separation from the 'Event' itself."[37] While deportees traveled to the center of the concentric circles to reach that epicenter of witness authenticity, testimonies of transit destabilize the persistent trauma of the concentration camp universe from fixed locations or geographies.

The witness's appeal to the gas chamber experience as an experiential stand-in for the symbolic and actual death of deportation transit delivers, I believe, not an ending. Rather, the feeling of death in the cattle cars permits a critical rethinking about whether or not the overburdened senses and embodied witnessing of Holocaust deportees are, as the historian of the body Anthony Synnott has asked, "valid or invalid ways to knowledge."[38]

NOTES

1. Zalmen Gradowski, "Letter to a Friend," in *Amidst a Nightmare of Crime: Manuscripts of Members of Sonderkommando,* ed. Jadwiga Bezwinska, trans. K. Michalik (Oświęcim, Poland: State Museum at Oświęcim, 1973), 78. See also Gideon Greif, *We Wept Without Tears: Testimonies of the Jewish Sonderkommando from Auschwitz* (New Haven, Conn., and London: Yale University Press, 2005), 20–32.

2. In contrast, the Deutsche Reichsbahn ran an average of just under two Jewish transports (or Sonderzüge) per day. See Alfred C. Mierzejewski, "A Public Enterprise in the Service of Mass Murder: The Deutsche Reichsbahn and the Holocaust," *Holocaust and Genocide Studies* 15, no. 1 (Spring 2001), 36.

3. Primo Levi, *The Drowned and the Saved,* trans. Raymond Rosenthal (New York: Summit Books, 1988), 109.

4. Testimony of Marek Sznajderman, in *The Last Eyewitnesses: Children of the Holocaust Speak,* ed. Wiktoria Śliwowska, trans. Julian Bussgang and Fay Bussgang (Evanston, Ill.: Northwestern University Press, 1998), 240.

5. Erika Amariglio, *From Thessaloniki to Auschwitz and Back: Memories of a Survivor from Thessaloniki* (London: Vallentine Mitchell, 2000), 51.

6. United States Holocaust Memorial Museum (hereafter USHMM), Record Group (hereafter RG) 02, "Survivor Testimonies," American Gathering Conference Collection, Gisela Adamski Sachs, "Unpublished Testimony," RG-02.002*08, frame 00384.

7. Testimony of Ya'akov Gurfein, in *The Trial of Adolf Eichmann: Record of Proceedings in the District Court of Jerusalem,* Session 21, vol. 1 (Jerusalem: State of Israel, Ministry of Justice, Trust for the Publication of the Proceedings of the Eichmann Trial in Cooperation with the Israel State Archives and Yad Vashem—the Holocaust Martyrs' and Heroes; Remembrance Authority, 1998), 332.

8. Leon Cohen, *From Greece to Birkenau: The Crematoria Workers' Uprising,* trans. J. Gormezano (Tel Aviv: Salonika Jewry Research Center, 1996), 13. See also Leon Cohen's interview, "We Were Dehumanized, We Were Robots," in Greif, *We Wept Without Tears,* 286–309.

9. Levi, *The Drowned and the Saved,* 86.

10. Charlotte Delbo, *Auschwitz and After,* trans. R. Lamont (New Haven, Conn.: Yale University Press, 1995), 290.

11. Eva Quittner, *Pebbles of Remembrance* (Sydney: Kerr Publishing, 1993), 227.

12. USHMM, RG-02, "Survivor Testimonies," American Gathering Conference Collection, Zofia Pollack, RG-02.002*22.

13. Harry Gordon, *The Shadow of Death: The Holocaust in Lithuania* (Lexington: University Press of Kentucky, 1992), 141.

14. Rena Kornreich Gelissen, *Rena's Promise: A Story of Sisters in Auschwitz* (Boston: Beacon Press, 1995), 51.

15. Ibid., 16.

16. Abraham Kszepicki, quoted in Yitzhak Arad, *Belzec, Sobibor, Treblinka: The Operation Reinhard Death Camps* (Bloomington: Indiana University Press, 1987), 63.

17. Ibid.

18. USHMM, RG-02, "Survivor Testimonies," Gizel Berman, "The Three Lives of Gizel Berman," RG-02.157; Acc. 1994.A.0235, 111.

19. USHMM, RG-02, "Survivor Testimonies," Eva Gross, "Prisoner 409," RG-02.111; Acc. 1994.A.202, 187.

20. Alain Corbin, "Charting the Cultural History of the Senses," in *Empire of the Senses: The Sensual Culture Reader,* ed. David Howes (Oxford: Berg, 2005), 136.

21. Constance Classen, David Howes, and Anthony Synnott, *Aroma: The Cultural History of Smell* (New York: Routledge, 1994), 1.

22. Edith Wyschogrod, *Spirit in Ashes: Hegel, Heidegger and Man-Made Mass Death* (New Haven, Conn.: Yale University Press, 1985), 114.

23. Ibid.

24. Viktor Frankl, *Man's Search for Meaning: An Introduction to Logotherapy,* trans. I. Lasch (London: Hodder and Staughton, 1964), 6–7.

25. USHMM, RG-50, "Oral History," interview with Josef B., RG-50.030*0047.

26. See "Clara L.," testimony in *Witness: Voices from the Holocaust,* eds. Joshua Greene and Shiva Kumar (New York: Simon and Schuster, 2001), 106.

27. See "Helen K.," testimony cited in ibid.,108.

28. Anthony Synnott, *Body Social: Symbolism, Self and Society* (London: Routledge, 1993), 132.

29. David Howes, "Introduction," in *Empire of the Senses,* 7.

30. Roberta Culbertson, "Embodied Memory, Transcendence, and Telling: Recounting Trauma, Re-establishing the Self," in *New Literary History* 26, no. 1 (1995), 178.

31. Michael Jackson, "The Prose of Suffering and the Practice of Silence," *Spiritus* 4 (2004), 54.

32. Ibid.

33. Ibid., 55.
34. Ibid.
35. Ruth Klüger, *Still Alive: A Holocaust Girlhood Remembered* (New York: Feminist Press at the City University, 2001), 92.
36. Sidra DeKoven Ezrahi, "Questions of Authenticity," in *Teaching the Representation of the Holocaust,* eds. Marianne Hirsch and Irene Kacandes (New York: Modern Language Association of America, 2004), 54.
37. Ibid.
38. Synnott, *Body Social,* 128.

Michael Allen

The Atomization of Auschwitz: Is History Really That Contingent?

CHRISTOPHER BROWNING CONCLUDED THAT ACTIVITY AT AUSCHWITZ in the fall of 1941 "does not yet suggest the camp's future role in the Final Solution."[1] In another passage he, like most contemporary historians as well as the recent popular documentary *Auschwitz*, took pains to emphasize that Auschwitz was decidedly *not* founded as a death camp.

True enough. Heinrich Himmler's orders to build the concentration camp in February of 1940 included no instructions to murder the European Jews. Yet to stress so emphatically the *non*origins of genocide at Auschwitz seems misplaced. The Schutzstaffel (SS) *did found* Auschwitz, like Stutthof or Lublin/Majdanek, as an institution for ethnic cleansing. The Nazi state established these camps shortly after the conquest of Poland, both to suppress the Polish population and to enforce the regime's racial supremacy—including grand "Aryan" settlement designs. Even though gas chambers did not appear at Auschwitz until 1941, its original mandate was clearly murder. It would have satisfied quite plainly some of Raphael Lemkin's lesser definitions of genocide.

Moreover, insistence that Auschwitz *was not*, at first, a death camp should not serve to conceal the fact that gas chambers really did not take long in coming. The overwhelming stress placed on the contingency of the "Final Solution," Germany's "cumulative radicalization," and, more recently, the importance of isolated regional initiative as key elements of the Holocaust should not obscure how swiftly things progressed—or how closely events throughout German-occupied Europe all converged.

Only fifteen months passed between the arrival of Auschwitz's first inmates and the first experimentation with Zyklon B to kill them. Auschwitz began ad hoc gassings at roughly the same time that Einsatzgruppe B Commander Arthur Nebe and chemists from the Reich Criminal Technical Institute began their own tentative experiments with explosives and exhaust gas near Minsk. Some have objected that the first homicidal use of Zyklon B in Block 11 of Auschwitz in September 1941 claimed only the lives of Soviet prisoners of war (POWs). Thus it is widely assumed that this constitutes no evidence that the SS was preparing for the extermination of the Jews.[2] Yet Nebe also experimented with POWs. Contemporary historians seem to insist on the decontextualization of Auschwitz in a way that members of the SS themselves would certainly never have entertained. To believe that such events occurred in isolation, one must assume that officers in the SS conducted operations in hermetic ignorance of each other or that, unique to Auschwitz, experimentation with the methods of mechanized killing that targeted one group were not conceived with other groups of victims in mind.

Are not the obvious continuities also worthy of emphasis? In the fall of 1941, Auschwitz turned to Topf & Söhne, the same firm that had simultaneously secured contracts to supply another known death camp, Mogilew, with gas chambers and crematoria. Arthur Nebe conducted his macabre experiments under the jurisdiction of Higher SS and Police Leader (HSSPF) Erich von dem Bach-Zelewski, who had earlier helped to site Auschwitz in Upper Silesia. The Mogilew plan seems to have been Bach-Zelewski's brainchild, but the contingencies of war quickly rendered it impractical. The camp was never built. In consequence, in August 1942, Auschwitz installed Bach-Zelewski's Mogilew gas chamber–crematoria units in Birkenau. The same firm, Topf & Söhne, worked on both projects throughout. Gerhard Peters, the chief executive officer of the gas chamber and Zyklon B manufacturer Degussa, admitted after the war to discussing the use of his company's products for the murder of human beings and clearly consulted with concentration camp personnel.[3] The SS Business Administration Main Office erected a coordinating office to oversee the special design of the Mogilew and Auschwitz projects.[4]

If the dense context of events and personnel surrounding Auschwitz-Birkenau "does not yet suggest" the camp's future role in the "Final Solution," what could possibly suffice to do so? Those who are wont to emphasize contingency note that Auschwitz's new gas chambers lagged behind the completion of an entire archipelago of other death camps. But did they really?

True enough, the new crematoria of Birkenau were not finished until the spring of 1943. Not until May 1942 did excavation for the foundations begin. Even then, the SS did not complete these buildings until almost a year later. Ironically, in 1943, the Central Construction Directorate turned the buildings over to the camp for operations at precisely the time that a great lull in transports actually set in. The gigantic banks of fifteen crematoria furnaces, probably one of the most widely recognized images of the Auschwitz-Birkenau complex, actually played little role in the Holocaust until the Hungarian Action of 1944. If Auschwitz was to be a "Capital of the Holocaust," why would the SS have waited so long?[5]

Yet delays in construction of this complex are less mysterious than many contemporary narratives imply. There was, first of all, nothing unusual about postponing new construction in the harsh Polish winter. The site for Bełżec, like that for Birkenau, was planned in October of 1941, and like Birkenau its construction was also delayed until the following spring. Unlike Birkenau, however, Bełżec was a simple ad hoc affair. The very complexity of Birkenau repeatedly got in the way. Bełżec was built of scavenged lumber and a discarded tank engine. The new gas chamber of Birkenau required reinforced concrete and below-grade excavation. Pouring and properly setting concrete below freezing is not just difficult, it is simply impossible.

Over and above normal delays, prisoners and perpetrators alike testified that shortages repeatedly held up Birkenau's construction. Herta Soswinski, forced to work in the Building Materials Supply Office, made clear that the SS had to accord special priority to the crematoria in order to get any materials at all: "One thing is certain. Everyone active in the Construction Directorate, its works, and its land-use, especially regarding the gas chambers and crematoria, had to be informed, because otherwise the planning and building supply materials could not have been had at all."[6] The lack of seemingly trivial building supplies like bituminous paper (needed to create moisture barriers for the basement) could postpone construction for weeks. The Central Construction Directorate could not secure the electric blowers for Birkenau's ventilation system—a system designed from the first rudimentary drawings in the fall of 1941, never altered, and repeatedly singled out as evidence of gas chambers by numerous expert witnesses—until as late as February of 1943.[7] As Rudolf Höss stated after the war, "Almost no building materials were ever at hand."[8]

Moreover, the crematoria should not be treated in isolation from what was going on only three kilometers away in Auschwitz's main camp or in the woods just beyond Birkenau's perimeter. When we consider the context of Auschwitz in its entirety, the assertion that the camp somehow "lagged behind" seems curious at best. The Central Construction Directorate hastened to complete ad hoc gas chambers when its "high-tech" killing complex lagged behind. Crews of prisoner-masons converted two confiscated farmhouses—the so-called "red" and "white" houses, also called Bunker 1 and Bunker 2—in a matter of days. The first bunker was completed as early as March 1942 and maybe earlier.[9] Meanwhile, experimentation with gassing continued in the "old crematoria" of the Auschwitz main camp, where Topf & Söhne engineer Kurt Prüfer witnessed it early in 1942.[10] To suggest that delays in the completion of Birkenau's crematoria imply that Auschwitz remained at the margins during the origins of the "Final Solution" not only fails to account for the context of genocide elsewhere; it also divorces Birkenau from the context of the very concentration camp complex in which it was located.

This essay makes a small plea for the recontextualization of Auschwitz in the "Final Solution." Current accounts, for all their virtues, increasingly present the camp as marginal during the origins of genocide. Key evidence suggests the contrary. This essay focuses on the expert testimony of prisoners forced to serve in the many offices of Auschwitz-Birkenau.[11] They had to help design, build, and maintain the equipment used to destroy the European Jews.

I will call such prisoners "gray-collar workers." They were no less bureaucrats than the perpetrators who worked as "white-collar workers." Bureaucrats occupy a prominent place in popular impressions of the Holocaust, as lurid terms like "technocrats of extermination" or "desk-job murderers" suggest. But perhaps because prisoner-bureaucrats so poorly fit the stereotypes of bureaucracy generated by academic scholarship and the popular imagination alike, the role of the gray-collar worker has been almost completely overlooked.[12]

It is striking that prisoner-draftsmen worked alongside SS architects and had to prepare diagrams for their approval. Prisoners formed the bulk of skilled technicians in the camp, and Auschwitz's many offices would have quickly collapsed without them. It is simply baffling that this rich source has been almost completely neglected.[13] These prisoners were both insiders and outsiders. On the one hand, they witnessed Auschwitz from the inside. On the other hand, precisely for this reason, they were acutely aware that the systems they helped build and maintain could easily sweep them up among the vast number of the dead.

THE "DATING" GAME AND THE HOLOCAUST AS A PARADIGM OF MODERN CATASTROPHE

In particular, testimony by gray-collar workers suggests that we should bring Auschwitz back to the center of accounts of the origins of the "Final Solution." This testimony can shed new light on what some have begun to ridicule as the "dating" game, that is, the ongoing and nearly Casaubonian attempt in Holocaust studies to nail down a precise date for the origins of the "Final Solution."

Unlike older scholarship that depicted events at Auschwitz in the fall and winter of 1941–42 as conclusive evidence that Adolf Hitler's state decided to murder the European Jews, more recent accounts of the origins of the "Final Solution" have assigned little importance to Auschwitz.[14] For the most part, this assessment rests on the work of Robert Jan van Pelt and Jean-Claude Pressac.[15] Their microchronology of the design and construction of the gas chambers presented what I will call a "transformation narrative." They argued that the new giant crematorium of Birkenau, first planned in October 1941, initially contained only "ordinary" morgues and furnaces but no gas chambers. If Auschwitz-Birkenau was to evolve into a death camp, the SS had to transform these designs incrementally. Thus Auschwitz appears paradoxically divorced from the nearly frenetic experimentation with mechanized genocide almost everywhere else in the occupied East.

There is more to this question than minor issues of microchronology and the "dating" game. Auschwitz is the key to whether and how we consider the Holocaust to be a manifestation of modern organized society. To understand how this is so, consider that the transformation narrative reinforces an important trend in regional studies. Walter Manoschek, Dieter Pohl, and Thomas Sandkühler have provided some of the best and earliest work in this tradition.[16] Historians increasingly have argued that the most important decisions seem to occur at the periphery, albeit monitored and confirmed at the center. Regional uncoordinated initiative provided a key and perhaps *the key* impetus in the "Final Solution." "In the end," wrote Sandkühler, "the endeavor to build gassing installations must be sought in local initiative."[17] In such accounts, the Holocaust evolved out of the overwhelming disorganization of German institutions at the fringes of German society.

This actually reverses the entire premise of authors of the first generation of Holocaust studies. Both Hannah Arendt and Raul Hilberg insisted that genocide was, above all, a crime of modern organized society.[18] The new regionalism implies the opposite. Some, like Dieter Pohl, have declared, "The instruments used to carry out the Final Solution in Eastern Europe bear the character of a complete *debureaucratization*" (emphasis in the original).[19] In particular, regional studies stress discontinuity at every stage and cast doubt on any coherent, overarching decision for the "Final Solution," at least until long after the fact of actual mass murder in the East.[20]

Pressac and van Pelt's transformation narrative plays an important role in this argument in a curious way. It is exceedingly hard to argue that Auschwitz's gas chambers came into being as anything other than the coordinated outcome of Berlin's interaction with technical professionals within both the SS and modern corporations. If this happened—as the transformation narrative implies—during a belated, evolutionary process, then local initiative would still seem paramount. Thus if we can date with precision when and how centralized institutions acting in concert initiated designs for gas chambers, this date can tell us whether Auschwitz resulted from a distinctive synthesis of modern technology, industry, and the state or whether it was merely an accident of "mission creep."[21] The latter implies inertia and unintended consequences; the former dynamic ongoing innovation. And if the latter proves true, Auschwitz stands as a warning that modern institutions can run amok without anyone really knowing it.[22] But if Auschwitz embarked on the Holocaust from the beginning, historians need a more realistic assessment of why and how modern organizations can become barbarous.

THE SURVIVOR AS EXPERT WITNESS

In postwar trials, gray-collar prisoners gave testimony as technically trained experts. Among them were engineering professors and architects as well as skilled technicians, electricians, plumbers, masons, and construction foremen. Numerous juries dismissed their testimony in the most perfunctory manner, and it is only a slight exaggeration to say that professional historians have done much the same thing. Gray-collar prisoners were nearly unanimous that gas chambers were easily discerned from the first drawings that came into their hands. For instance, not a single surviving professional of the Central Construction Directorate of Auschwitz testified that the crematoria of Birkenau had to be transformed or adapted.

Wladyslaw Plaskura, a professor of engineering, stands as one of several examples. His impossible predicament also shows just how dark the "gray zone" could become. Plaskura's family home lay little more than ten miles from the camp. He and his brother Josef entered Auschwitz in June 1940 among the camp's first political prisoners. By September, Wladyslaw was working in the construction offices, first as a Kapo. Later he had to install "blind" showerheads in the old crematoria of Auschwitz's main camp. He also served as a draftsman. In May 1943 he was released from custody, but only on condition that he continue as a civilian employee of the Central Construction Directorate. This employment was compulsory. The chief of the Political Office, Maximillian Grabner, threatened him and intimated what might happen to his brother Josef if anyone found Wladyslaw troublesome.

Plaskura saw the camp with a professional eye and discussed it with other professionals.[23] Thus it is hardly surprising that his testimony makes reference to salient details: "One could clearly recognize in the plans of Crematoria II and III that here a gas chamber would be erected. I cannot remember if 'gas chamber' was written on the plans. On the basis of the installations, however, one could see what it was all about." As with many other witnesses, perpetrators as well as survivors, Plaskura singled out systems that caught his eye: "There were these ventilation ducts and openings where the Zyklon B was to be thrown in." When the judge pressed him for further details, Plaskura elaborated: "There are different kinds of ventilation. In this case, however, the ducts out of which the Zyklon B gas was to be sucked out of the room were built in."[24]

The close collaboration between the private firm that built these facilities, Topf & Söhne, and the SS is now well known. Less well known is that SS architects and engineers also relied on gray-collar workers in the design and construction of the system. The wire-mesh columns for introducing Zyklon B gas or the "gas-tight doors" are absent in the major architectural plans and seem to have been made "in-house."[25] Gray-collar workers are likely the only source of evidence we will ever have on some of this work.

Consider Bronislaw Galuszka, who worked in Auschwitz's metals shop. In "early 1942" he recalled being handed "drawings of the most primitive kind," likely just crude sketches:[26]

> [The SS officers] left the plans they brought with them in the office in order that we might prepare the materials. The officers . . . did not tell us what the plans represented, but on the basis of the descriptions and the drawings themselves we could orient ourselves. These had to do with . . . certain equipment for the gassing of prisoners in the gas chambers. One drawing represented the installation for introducing the crystals of gas . . . I remember it exactly.[27]

Given the nature of this work and their expertise, it is hardly surprising that prisoner-technicians speedily gained insight into the intent of the designers of the new crematoria and gas chambers. We can also assume that plans delivered into the hands of skilled prisoners for fabrication do not represent the *origins* of genocide but rather a much later stage in the preparation for it. It is highly unlikely that Bronislaw Galuszka's SS overseer came up with the idea to manufacture the wire-mesh columns on his own, and if he did, Galuszka gave no indication of this. Rather, Galuszka was of the opinion (almost universally confirmed in testimony from both gray-collar workers and former SS architects) that the planning originated in Berlin.

Some might suggest that survivors had a vested interest in making the SS appear much more deliberate than was really the case. Might they not have read the obvious nature of the killing compound backward into its contingent origins? In *The Case for Auschwitz,* Robert Jan van Pelt cautioned, for instance, that a paradox "underlies every historical narrative . . . even in Auschwitz—each moment unfolds with no certainty of outcome."[28] This echoes brown-collar defendants like Walter Dejaco, the head of the Auschwitz engineering design bureau, who complained about one witness: "In hindsight, it is easy for [former prisoner-engineer Rudolf] Kauer to say that a technical person can easily recognize what the plans are about."[29]

But the testimony of civil engineer and political prisoner Rudolf Kauer is by far the most unusual, for in most respects Kauer overtly sided with his former oppressors. Kauer entered Auschwitz in May of 1941.[30] In postwar trials, prosecutors exposed the fact that Kauer took bribes to retract incriminating testimony against the notorious sadist Wilhelm Boger, among others. When asked in a 1972 Vienna Auschwitz trial why he did this, Kauer simply admitted, "I didn't want to leave . . . condemned men in the lurch."[31]

Yet despite his strange behavior and his proclivity to identify with his former jailers, Kauer's testimony is remarkably consistent regarding the "transformation" narrative. That is, it offers no support for it. From testimony in 1963: "The gas chambers were built according to [SS architect Walter] Dejaco's plans . . . from the beginning in the planning"; or in 1972: "I could recognize in the plans that men would be gassed"; or in one angry letter to the District Court of Vienna, which degenerated into a diatribe against Hermann Langbein for being anti-German, Kauer remained steadfast on this point:

> One can perceive a feverish work in the correspondence from this time period concerning the technical solution of the ways and means to carry out mass murder through the application of poison gas . . . with such methods that resembled mass production.[32]

Kauer merely went on to insist that "the defendant Dejaco was too young at the time and had not progressed far enough professionally so that he could design a facility of such complexity."[33] Had the crematoria required retrofitting, it is strange, to say the least, that Kauer's exculpatory statements did not highlight this.

It is also important to note that survivors did not hesitate to point out transformations when they actually did occur. Survivors recalled, for instance, ad hoc renovations of the small farmhouses west of Birkenau, the so-called Bunker 1 and Bunker 2. Squads of prisoner-masons were forced to brick up the windows. Doors were made gas tight with no more than paper tape.[34] The "old crematoria" of the Auschwitz main camp likewise involved extensive reengineering, and several prisoners recalled this.[35] Simply put, when the original purposes of buildings were altered in significant details to serve radically new purposes, gray-collar prisoners did recognize this immediately and spoke plainly about it after the war.

BEYOND THE "DATING" GAME?

The testimony of prisoner-engineers, prisoner-technicians, and prisoner-architects offers little confirmation of the transformation narrative currently accepted as consensus. Instead, it suggests a different narrative, one more in accord with recent scholarship that once again stresses continuity.[36] Most witnesses stated plainly that gas chambers were clear to them from the first diagrams that they encountered. Primary documents leave no doubt that these diagrams originated in October and November of 1941. Auschwitz was not marginal during the origins of the "Final Solution." The SS embarked upon the invention of gas chambers in Auschwitz at the same time they did so everywhere else.

Perhaps most significant, the engineers of Topf & Söhne corroborate prisoner testimony. Both production engineer Gustav Braun and Topf's ventilation expert Karl Schultze testified in Soviet captivity that plans for gas chambers dated to 1941. Kurt Prüfer, who repeatedly sought to imply that planning and design work began much later, eventually revised his testimony when interrogators contradicted him with documentary evidence. He then admitted to learning of gas chambers in "early 1942."[37]

And even during interrogations in which Topf managers denied knowledge of the gas chambers, neither Prüfer nor any other Topf engineer ever alleged that plans for "normal" morgues or "ordinary" furnaces had to be transformed, adapted, or altered to fit an evolving, dimly discernible intention to make over Auschwitz into a death camp. Rather, it was their clear impression that Auschwitz participated fully in concerted efforts to perfect methods of extermination—"the latest technology [that] had become in every real way a death factory according to the needs of the camp," as Prüfer put it.[38] In Soviet interrogations, Topf engineers merely tried to avoid their own personal association with the initiation of such plans. Prüfer even recalled one SS man plainly bragging outside Crematorium I in January 1942 that "he knew something of the construction of gas chambers in which the SS had gassed people with motor exhaust ... and that they [the SS at Auschwitz] had improved on that."[39]

As this statement shows, Auschwitz proceeded with full knowledge of the Holocaust in Eastern Europe. Just as an SS man frankly told Prüfer that Auschwitz had "improved" on gassings elsewhere, so too did genocidaires from other killing camps know about Auschwitz. Josef Oberhauser, who worked in the T4 "euthanasia" program and helped build Bełżec, testified after the war that Viktor Brack, head of Main Office II of the Führer's Chancellery, came to Lublin and discussed Auschwitz: "One had decided to eradicate the Jews with gassing. In concentration camp Auschwitz one had already gathered a certain amount of experience."[40] People at Bełżec knew of Auschwitz and were also discussing it with central authorities from Berlin. Moreover, the camp counted as a precedent for the "Final Solution"—not a latecomer in need of "transformation."

What does this evidence all imply, finally, beyond the "dating" game? Clearly the new regional studies are right to open our eyes to local initiative.[41] Testimony yields plentiful evidence that SS men on location did everything they could to facilitate genocide. Even the exculpatory Rudolf Kauer spoke of "feverish" effort. Other survivors confirmed this: "The whole Construction Directorate oriented itself to this one thing, to finish these plans with special energy."[42] When design engineer Walter Dejaco's work was done, Zbigniew Gosczynski recalled, he got promoted and the office threw him a party.[43] Work shaded into pleasure. This is only one indication that some, at least in the SS, found excitement at Auschwitz.

But if plentiful local initiative fueled Auschwitz's development, there was also *far more* than this. Little was exclusively "local" about it: "Dejaco had made the plans ahead of time," recalled Kauer. "They were not in agreement, because Mr. Prüfer of the firm Topf & Söhne said, 'it won't work that way.'"[44] Auschwitz was, in short, coengineered. Auschwitz reached across the breadth of Europe, and other institutions reached into it. It operated as most contemporary scholars of industry and organization would expect: it not only mobilized the conscious initiative of its employees but also called on the expertise of modern institutions elsewhere. Private contractors worked closely alongside the SS. The gas chambers constituted a minor research and development project. Witnesses, whether white, gray, or brown collar, also acknowledged nearly unanimously that the SS's central Office Group C–Construction coordinated the effort from start to finish. Primary documents confirm this as well.

In early November 1941, Topf engineer Kurt Prüfer announced that the Office Group C–Construction of the SS Business Administration Main Office was organizing a special bureau "to work only on crematoria . . . in view of the importance and difficulty of the new design [of Birkenau's crematoria] that is to be created for you [i.e., Auschwitz-Birkenau]."[45] This was not the outcome of competition among local bureaucrats striving to gain a prominent place among the genocidaires of Nazi Germany by "working toward the Führer." The witness testimony of expert survivors is also nearly unanimous that the new crematoria of Birkenau were purpose-built for extermination. The collective engineering of genocide did not happen in a vague, evolutionary process. However much designs were subject to alterations—as any moderately complex artifact always is—the crematoria of Birkenau were meant from the beginning as a machine for genocide. Only one former SS architect alleged a version of events that even remotely conformed to the transformation narrative that historians now accept as consensus, but his testimony was transparently mendacious.[46] Birkenau's *novel* (hardly "normal") design was part of an overarching initiative.

CONCLUSION

The great Hessian attorney Fritz Bauer once warned against "atomizing the holistic event" of the Holocaust, particularly at Auschwitz.[47] Microchronology, he cautioned, parses everything into discrete episodes. Even the most unitary event can then seem infinitely contingent rather than a crime of organized society.[48] He feared that petty details could swamp the Auschwitz case by dividing criminal activities into the minutiae of decontextualized fragments. Bauer was concerned that such an analysis would befuddle jurors. The defense might make out even the most coherent events as unpredictable unintended consequences. Historians purportedly prefer complexity to simple explanations, but Bauer well knew that microchronologies could dress up great simplicities and masquerade them as complexity.

At least concerning Auschwitz, we have begun to place exaggerated importance on one building's minor alterations of staircases, doorways, or other marginal details. Overarching continuities are consigned to lesser status than such trivia.

Bauer was also acutely aware of one other thing, which bears receiving far more attention than it currently does. Microchronological treatments of evidence, the decontextualization toward which they tend, and, indeed, the entire "transformation narrative" originated in the defense strategies of patently mendacious and culpable perpetrators.[49] This does not mean that a host of hardworking, honest, contemporary historians are somehow on the side of the "bad guys"—that microchronologies are somehow all inevitably tainted or even that they are necessarily flawed. But it does suggest that historians should approach microchronology with more conscious reflection than is currently the case.

Should we not, at the very least, be asking if history is really all *that* contingent?

NOTES

I would like to express my sincere thanks to Charlie Syndor, Nicholas Terry, and Peter Hayes for reading and commenting on earlier drafts of this essay. I thank Christian Hufen for helping me translate Soviet interrogation files from the handwritten Cyrillic. The research for this essay was supported by National Science Foundation Scholars Award SES-0408827.

1. Christopher Browning and Jürgen Matthäus, *The Origins of the Final Solution: The Evolution of Nazi Jewish Policy, September 1939–March 1942* (Lincoln, Neb.: Bison Books, 2004), 358. Hans Mommsen, *Auschwitz, 17. Juli 1942. Der Weg zur europäischen 'Endlösung der Judenfrage'* (Munich: Deutscher Taschenbuch Verlag, 2002), 167. Laurence Rees, *Auschwitz: A New History* (New York: Public Affairs, 2005), 63, 73, 80, 168. Because Auschwitz is excepted from the more general context of the fall and winter of 1941, many accounts touch only briefly on early gassings there, for example, Peter Longerich, *Politik der Vernichtung. Eine Gesamtdarstellung der nationalsozialistischen Judenverfolgung* (Munich: Piper, 1998), 457, 515–16, and Götz Aly, *'Endlösung' Vokerverschiebung und der Mord an den europäischen Juden* (Frankfurt: Fischer, 1995), 361. This pattern holds for historians at pains to stress discontinuity as well as those who wish to reassert continuity, as, for example, Philippe Burrin, *Hitler and the Jews: The Genesis of the Holocaust*, trans. Patsy Southgate (New York: Hodder Arnold, 1994), 115–32, especially footnote 15. Or, more recently, Wolf Gruner, "Von der Kollektivausweisung zur Deportation der Juden aus Deutschland (1938–1945)," in *Die Deportation der Juden aus Deutschland. Pläne—Praxis—Reaktionen 1938–1945,* eds. Birthe Kundrus and Beate Meyer (Göttingen: Wallstein, 2005), 51–56.

2. Karin Orth, "Rudolf Höß und die 'Endlösung der Judenfrage': Drei Argumente gegen deren Datierung auf den Sommer 1941," *Werkstattgeschichte* 18 (1997), 45–57.

3. Peters's role and the networks in which he moved are discussed at

length by Paul Weindling, *Epidemics and Genocide in Eastern Europe 1890–1945* (Oxford: Oxford University Press, 2000), 254–55, 262, 305.

4. Kurt Prüfer to Karl Bischoff, November 21, 1941, United States Holocaust Memorial Museum (hereafter USHMM) Record Group (hereafter RG) 11.001M: 41 (512:1:314).

5. Peter Hayes, "Auschwitz, Capital of the Holocaust," *Holocaust and Genocide Studies* 17 (2003).

6. Herta Soswinski, April 6, 1966, Zeugenvernehmung, Signature V526/1-155, Dokumentationsarchiv des österreichischen Widerstandes (DöW) microfilm roll 1106. This statement is confirmed by perpetrator testimony, for example, Karl Möckel, July 7, 1947, Übernahme von Baulichkeiten (Krematorien) durch die Standortverwaltung, USHMM 1998.A.0247, roll 5.

7. Central Construction Director—Auschwitz Karl Bischoff to Topf & Söhne, February 11, 1943, reprinted in "Krematorium III"; Jean-Claude Pressac, *Auschwitz: Technique and Operation of the Gas Chambers* (New York: Beate Klarsfeld Foundation, 1989), 360.

8. Rudolf Höss, April 15, 1946, testimony, Signature V526/1-155, DöW microfilm roll 1107.

9. See for instance the testimony of one of the masons, Otto Locke, February 25, 1972, Zeugenvernehmung, Signature V526/1-155, DöW microfilm roll 1107. Locke dates the conversion of Bunker 1 to February 1942.

10. Kurt Prüfer, March 4, 1948, interrogation by 3. Department of MGB (MGB translates as Ministry of State Security), USHMM RG-06.025*08 (Central Archives of the Federal Security Services of the Russian Federation, N-19262).

11. Anonymous, November 26, 1944, excavated 1952, buried notebook of the Sonderkommando, in *Amidst a Nightmare of Crime: Manuscripts of Prisoners in Cremation Squads Found at Auschwitz,* ed. Jadwiga Bezwinska and Danuta Czech (New York: Howard Fertig, 1992), 111–22; Eric Friedler, Barbara Siebert, and Andreas Kilian, *Zeugen aus der Todeszone. Das jüdische Sonderkommando in Auschwitz* (Lüneburg: Zu Klampen, 2002); Gideon Greif, "Die 'Sonderkommandos' von Auschwitz-Birkenau. Ein historischer Überblick," in *Wir weinten Tränenlos . . . Augenzeugenberichte der jüdischen 'Sonderkommandos' in Auschwitz* (Cologne: Böhlau, 1995); Filip Müller, *Eyewitness Auschwitz: Three Years in the Gas Chambers* (Chicago: Ivan R. Dee, 1999); Miklos Nyiszli, *Auschwitz: A Doctor's Eyewitness Account* (New York: Arcade, 1993). The horrible predicament of those in the Sonderkommandos, the prisoner detail that operated the gas chambers, is reasonably well known and has even been the subject of a film, *Grey Zone* (2001), directed by Tim Nelson.

12. This is not to say that survivor testimony has been neglected, only

that historians rarely turn to it as evidence of the "Final Solution." The huge outpouring of literature on survivor experience usually highlights survivor trauma, postwar identity, the limits of representation, or the nature of memory. See, for example, Giorgio Agamben, *Remnants of Auschwitz: The Witness and the Archive,* trans. Daniel Heller-Roazen (New York: Zone Books, 2002). See also Lawrence Langer, "Interpreting Survivor Testimony," in *Writing and the Holocaust,* ed. Berel Lang (New York: Holmes and Meier, 1988). Saul Friedländer, *The Years of Extermination: Nazi Germany and the Jews, 1939–1945* (New York: HarperCollins, 2007), is an attempt to transcend the divide between event-based history and history of experience.

13. Admirably, some histories seek to integrate prisoner experience into the history of institutions—for instance, Bernd Wagner, *IG Auschwitz: Zwangsarbeit und Vernichtung von Häftlingen des Lagers Monowitz 1941–1945* (Munich: K. G. Saur, 2000), especially 112–25. Most recently, Jonathan Petropoulos and John Roth have tried to redress this neglect with the edited volume *Gray Zones: Ambiguity and Compromise in the Holocaust and Its Aftermath* (New York: Berghahn, 2005).

14. Raul Hilberg, *The Destruction of the European Jews* (New York: Holmes and Meier, 1985), 881. Browning and Matthäus, *The Origins of the Final Solution,* 241, recently repopularized the once conventional dating of the "Final Solution" to the summer of 1941 but did not utilize Kommandant Rudolf Höss's testimony. This testimony is widely considered to be inaccurate (Karin Orth, "Rudolf Höß und die 'Endlösung der Judenfrage,'" 45–57). For important recent work on Auschwitz, see Sybille Steinbacher, *'Musterstadt' Auschwitz. Germanisierungspolitik und Judenmord in Ostoberschlesien* (Munich: K. G. Saur, 2000); Wagner, *IG Auschwitz;* and the review essay of Peter Hayes, "Auschwitz, Capital of the Holocaust."

15. Pressac, *Auschwitz: Technique;* Robert Jan van Pelt, *The Case for Auschwitz: Evidence from the Irving Trial* (Bloomington: Indiana University Press, 2002).

16. Walter Manoschek, *'Serbien ist Judenfrei' Militärische Besatzungspolitik und Judenvernichtung in Serbien 1941/1942* (Munich: Oldenbourg, 1993). Dieter Pohl, *Nationalsozialistische Judenverfolgung in Ostgalizien 1941–1944. Organisation und Durchführung eines staatlichen Massenverbrechens* (Munich: Oldenbourg, 1996). Thomas Sandkühler, *'Endlösung' in Galizien: der Judenmord in Ostpolen und die Rettungsinitiativen von Berthold Beitz 1941–1944* (Bonn: Dietz, 1996).

17. Sandkühler argued that this took place while Heinrich Himmler and Reinhard Heydrich were still contemplating options and had no plans for a systematic "Final Solution" (Sandkühler, *'Endlösung' in Galizien,* 165). Walter Manoschek (*'Serbien ist Judenfrei,'* 190) emphasized that, in Serbia, General Franz Böhme (placed in charge of counterpartisan operations)

needed no order from Berlin but rather "spontaneously made the decision to murder the Jews."

18. Donald Bloxham, *Genocide on Trial: War Crimes Trials and the Formation of Holocaust History and Memory* (Oxford: Oxford University Press, 2001), 149–52, 185–220.

19. Pohl, *Nationalsozialistische Judenverfolgung in Ostgalizien 1941–1944,* 405.

20. This is also true of studies of much later phases of the Holocaust. See Götz Aly and Christian Gerlach, *Das letzte Kapitel. Realpolitik, Ideologie und der Mord an den ungarischen Juden 1944/1945* (Stuttgart: Deutsche Verlags Anstalt, 2002), 256.

21. Hans Mommsen *(Auschwitz, 17. Juli 1942)* still insisted on a "lite" version of this interpretation. For the classic statement of this thesis, see Hilberg, *The Destruction of the European Jews,* 18. This approach essentially dates back to Martin Broszat, "Hitler und die Genesis der Enlösung," *Vierteljarhshefte für Zeitgeschichte* 25 (1977), 739–75. "Cumulative radicalization" also comes from Hans Mommsen.

22. This monitory lesson has clearly influenced Robert Jan van Pelt, who at one point implied that technology itself drove the process. He suggested that "the presence of the powerful ventilation system charged the [normal] design [of Crematorium II] with a genocidal potential which would require small modifications to actualize." Robert Jan van Pelt and Debórah Dwork, *Auschwitz 1270 to the Present* (New York: W. W. Norton, 1996), 271, see also 268, 324. This argument implies that technology gave the nudge to genocidal intentions rather than the reverse. Van Pelt is clearly more rigorous than Pressac. Nevertheless, he suggested that a corpse slide was eliminated from Crematorium II and a stairwell added at a completely different location. Although it is true that a new stairwell was added, the corpse chute can still be seen in the ruins of Birkenau (ibid., 324; and van Pelt, *The Case for Auschwitz,* 443, 474), despite the fact that this contradicts eyewitness claims, which van Pelt also cited (*The Case for Auschwitz,* 205). Likewise, van Pelt mistook the forced draft of the furnace for the forced-air ventilation of the gas chamber (*The Case for Auschwitz,* 330). These are not grave mistakes, and the most careful historians make them. Nevertheless, the tendency to see every alteration as evidence that the intentions of the SS were in flux seems to underlie these mistakes. The core of the system remained stable throughout the history of design and construction: the gas chambers' ventilation system, the massive bank of crematoria, and the smooth planning of workflow through the building.

23. Zbigniew Gosczynski, March 3, 1972, Zeugenvernehmung, Signature V526/1-155, DöW microfilm roll 1107; Dr. Stanislaus Klodzinski, February 8, 1972, testimony, Signature V526/1-155, DöW microfilm roll 1107.

24. Wladyslaw Plaskura, Prof. schlesischen Polytechnik in Gleiwitz, February 17, 1972, testimony, Signature V526/1-155, DöW microfilm roll 1107.

25. Samuel Itzkowitz, 1996, survivor video, Holocaust Video Archives—Shoah Visual History Foundation (hereafter HVA-SVHF), interview by Miriam Davidow. Robert Jan van Pelt (*The Case for Auschwitz,* 206–7) pointed out that this work was carried out in the camp's in-house workshops. These were partly under the Zentralbauleitung (ZBL) and partly under the German Equipment Works, an SS corporation to which the ZBL transferred some of its workshops in late 1942 and early 1943. In practice, the Kommandantur also maintained work crews of specialists. See Stbaf. Chef VuWHA Amt III C to Oswald Pohl, September 24, 1940, Monatsbericht, USHMM 1998.A.0247, roll 1; Z. A. Finkmann to Deutsche Ausrüstungswerke (Deutsche Ausrüstungswerke; German Equipment Works), January 13, 1943, Ausführung von Tischlerarbeiten für hiesige Bauvorhaben, Pánstwowe Muzeum Oświęcim (hereafter PMO, or Polish State Museum of Auschwitz) AuII BW 30/34; Höss's orders, August 20, 1942, Kommandantur-Befehl, USHMM RG-11.001M.03:20 (502:1:32).

26. Bronislaw Galuszka, November 4, 1965, Zeugenvernehmung, Signature V526/1-155, DöW microfilm roll 1106.

27. Ibid. The most cited account is Michael Kula, June 11, 1945, Zeugenvernehmung by Jan Sehn, Signature V526/1-155, DöW microfilm roll 1107. Compare to Rees, *Auschwitz: A New History,* 67, 73, 80, 168.

28. Van Pelt, *The Case for Auschwitz,* 217. It is important to remember that we are talking not about a "Luther-to-Hitler" argument but rather about whether seasoned, trained professionals in modern organizations have some idea about what they do from month to month. Is history really *that* paradoxical?

29. Walter Dejaco trial testimony, February 15, 1972, Signature V526/1-155, DöW microfilm roll 1107.

30. Danuta Czech, *Auschwitz Chronicle, 1939–1945* (New York: Henry Holt, 1990), 64.

31. Testimony of Rudolf Kauer, February 2, 1972, Signature V526/1-155, DöW microfilm roll 1107.

32. Rudolf Kauer, Zeugenvernehmung, September 18, 1963, Signature V526/1-155, DöW microfilm roll 1106; Rudolf Kauer, February 2, 1972, trial testimony, Signature V526/1-155, DöW microfilm roll 1107; Rudolf Kauer to Geschworrenengericht beim Oberlandsgericht, Vienna, February 21, 1972, Signature V526/1-155, DöW microfilm roll 1108.

33. Rudolf Kauer to Geschworrenengericht beim Oberlandsgericht, Vienna, February 21, 1972, Signature V526/1-155, DöW microfilm roll 1108.

34. Jiri Beranovzky, February 23, 1972, trial testimony, Signature V526/1-155, DöW microfilm roll 1107; Ludwik Lawin, September 7, 1966, Zeugenvernehmung, Signature V526/1-155, DöW microfilm roll 1106; Otto Locke, February 25, 1972, Zeugenvernehmung, Signature V526/1-155, DöW microfilm roll 1107; Leopold Moszynski, September 7, 1966, Zeugenvernehmung, Signature V526/1-155, DöW microfilm roll 1106; Wladyslaw Plaskura, Prof. schlesischen Polytechnik in Gleiwitz, February 17, 1972, testimony, Signature V526/1-155, DöW microfilm roll 1107.

35. Tadäus Joachimowski, February 29, 1972, Zeugenvernehmung, Signature V526/1-155, DöW microfilm roll 1107; Otto Locke, February 25, 1972, Zeugenvernehmung, Signature V526/1-155, DöW microfilm roll 1107; Eugenius Nosal, February 8, 1972, testimony, Signature V526/1-155, DöW microfilm roll 1107.

36. Wolf Gruner, "Von der Kollektivausweisung zur Deportation der Juden aus Deutschland (1938–1945)," in *Die Deportation der Juden aus Deutschland. Pläne—Praxis—Reaktionen 1938–1945;* Martin Cüppers, *Wegbereiter der Shoah: Die Waffen-SS, der Kommandostab Reichsführer-SS und die Judenvernichtung 1939–1945* (Darmstadt: Wissenschaftliche Buchgesellschaft, 2005), especially 142–238. Wendy Lower's research on the Ukrainian headquarters of Himmler (Hegewald) and Hitler (Werwolf) and their direct association with ethnic cleansing in this territory far to the east not only emphasized continuity between "center" and "periphery" but also called into question whether this is a meaningful distinction whatsoever. Wendy Lower, *Nazi Empire-Building and the Holocaust in Ukraine* (Chapel Hill: University of North Carolina Press, 2005), 151–55, 162–79. See also Tobias Jersak, "A Matter of Foreign Policy: 'Final Solution' and 'Final Victory' in Nazi Germany," *German History* 21 (2003). Jersak sought to put the Holocaust in the global perspective of World War II (much in the tradition of Gerhard Weinberg) rather than atomizing the Holocaust in a microchronological perspective.

37. Gustav Braun, February 12, 1948, interrogation by 3. Department of MGB, USHMM RG-06.025*08 (Central Archives of the Federal Security Services of the Russian Federation, N-19262); Karl Schultze, March 11, 1948, interrogation by 3. Department of MGB, USHMM RG-06.025*08 (Central Archives of the Federal Security Services of the Russian Federation, N-19262). See Kurt Prüfer, March 4, 1948, interrogation by 3. Department of MGB, USHMM RG-06.025*08 (Central Archives of the Federal Security Services of the Russian Federation, N-19262); and Kurt Prüfer to Bischoff, November 21, 1941, USHMM RG-11.001M: 41 (512:1:314).

38. Kurt Prüfer, March 4, 1948, interrogation by 3. Department of MGB, USHMM RG-06.025*08 (Central Archives of the Federal Security Services of the Russian Federation, N-19262).

39. Quote: ibid. See also Gustav Braun, February 12, 1948, interrogation by 3. Department of MGB, USHMM RG-06.025*08 (Central Archives of the Federal Security Services of the Russian Federation, N-19262). See also Karl Schultze, March 11, 1948, interrogation by 3. Department of MGB, USHMM RG-06.025*08 (Central Archives of the Federal Security Services of the Russian Federation, N-19262).

40. Josef Oberhauser dated this to the early spring of 1942. Sandkühler, *'Endlösung' in Galizien*, 175.

41. Steinbacher, *'Musterstadt' Auschwitz*, especially 278.

42. Zbigniew Gosczynski, March 3, 1972, Zeugenvernehmung, Signature V526/1-155, DöW microfilm roll 1107.

43. Ibid.

44. Rudolf Kauer, February 2, 1972, trial testimony, Signature V526/1-155, DöW microfilm roll 1107.

45. Kurt Prüfer to Bischoff, November 21, 1941, USHMM RG-11.001M: 41 (512:1:314).

46. Walter Dejaco, Zeugenvernehmung, June 7, 1971, Signature V526/1-155, DöW microfilm roll 1106. See Michael Thad Allen, "Realms of Oblivion: The Vienna Auschwitz Trial," *Central European History* 40 (2007), 1–32.

47. Werner Renz, "Der erste Frankfurter Auschwitz-Prozeß. Völkermord als Strafsache," *Zeitschrift für Sozialgeschichte des 20. und 21. Jahrhunderts* 15 (2000), 20.

48. This is particularly true because we know most instructions for the "Final Solution" were passed on orally. And we lack conclusive evidence of all that was not recorded in verbal conversation or messages passed by telephone and radio. When historians have turned up evidence of such communications, as Richard Breitman and Martin Cüppers have done, there is little doubt that local initiative was coordinated and informed by the intentions of a centralized state. Richard Breitman, *Official Secrets: What the Nazis Planned, What the British and Americans Knew* (New York: Allen Lane, 1998). Cüppers, *Wegbereiter der Shoah*, especially 142–238.

49. Allen, "Realms of Oblivion," 1–32.

II. H·I·S·T·O·R·Y

Martin Dean

Typology of Ghettos: Five Types of Ghettos Under German Administration

IN A RECENT PRESENTATION, YEHUDA BAUER OBSERVED WITH RESPECT to the shtetlekh of eastern Poland that since no official definition of a shtetl existed, he felt obliged to make up his own. This observation reflects my own experience in defining and describing the types of ghettos established for Jews by the Germans in Eastern Europe during the Holocaust. Not only has nobody seriously attempted a comprehensive listing of ghettos before, but also there is not an agreed definition of what comprised a ghetto, nor is there any detailed typology.[1] The Germans themselves adopted widely differing definitions of ghettos across time and space.

This essay will present a sampling of the initial results from *German-Run Ghettos*, the second volume of the multivolume *Encyclopedia of Camps and Ghettos* being prepared by the United States Holocaust Memorial Museum (USHMM), for which more than 850 entries have been completed. Five main types of ghettos will be examined using specific examples: open ghettos, enclosed ghettos, destruction ghettos, transit ghettos, and remnant ghettos. In about 1,150 cities, towns, and shtetlekh of German-occupied Eastern Europe, roughly two million Jews were confined to ghettos, where they suffered persecution and exploitation prior to their destruction.

OPEN GHETTOS

Was a fence or wall the defining characteristic of the ghetto, or were there also open ghettos, known as Jewish residential districts (Jüdische

Wohnbezirke), where Jews were not contained by a physical barrier but were still forced into overcrowded dwellings, with severe punishments for leaving the demarcated area without permission?[2]

Evidence has been found so far of open ghettos in more than one hundred locations in the German-occupied regions of Poland and the Soviet Union. In Distrikt Lublin of the Generalgouvernement,[3] which David Silberklang discusses in his essay in this volume, there were possibly as many as thirty open ghettos (depending on definition), without the German authorities necessarily declaring them as such. To resolve these questions, some definition of an open ghetto is required, and close attention has to be paid to the descriptions in the various sources from perpetrators, victims, and bystanders.

Open ghettos will be included in *Encyclopedia of Camps and Ghettos* insofar as there was some form of forced resettlement in which all Jews were collected together and separated from the non-Jewish population. In most cases, there were also strict regulations controlling those entering and leaving the open ghetto. For example, in Uman, in Generalkommissariat Kiew (Kyyiv) within Reichskommissariat Ukraine (RKU), the "Jewish district" was not physically isolated and only lightly guarded, but Jews were forbidden to leave. Those who did were severely punished.[4]

In what was to become the Generalkommissariat Shitomir (Zhytomyr), also in RKU, several open ghettos were established by the military administration in July 1941, for example, in the towns of Chudnov, Liubar, Dzerzhinsk, and Rogachov. The Jews were resettled into a few streets in each town and were prevented from leaving without permission and were prohibited from trading with the non-Jewish population. These ghettos were first decimated and finally liquidated in a series of Aktions conducted by the German and Ukrainian police over the following months.

Several open ghettos have been identified in Distrikt Krakau (Kraków) of the Generalgouvernement. In Neumarkt (the name the Germans gave to Nowy Targ) a Jewish residential district (open ghetto) was created in May 1941. It was located between Kraśińskiego, Waksmundzka, Nadwodna, Jana Kazimierza, and Doroty streets, comprising roughly one thousand square meters. Initially about two thousand Jews from Nowy Targ and the surrounding region were concentrated there. According to a report by the Kreishauptmann in

Nowy Targ from June 1941: "The Jews in Neumarkt are currently being concentrated in a ghetto, which later on is to absorb the Jews from the other locations [in the Kreis]."[5] The open ghetto was very small and run-down. From October 15, 1941, leaving the Jewish residential area without a special permission was punishable by death.[6] Other examples of open ghettos in German-occupied Poland include Bełchatów in Reichsgau Wartheland, where the Germans established a Jewish residential area (with clearly marked boundaries but not physically enclosed) on March 1, 1941, and Zmigród Nowy in Distrikt Krakau.[7]

DESTRUCTION GHETTOS

Another significant category is that of destruction ghettos, used by the German forces primarily as a collecting point or holding pen in direct connection with the destruction of the Jewish population.[8] In some destruction ghettos, there was no long-term planning for the support of Jewish life, such as the provision of sufficient food or the employment of Jews as forced laborers. In some places, however, the Germans deliberately exploited designation of a ghetto to delude Jews into believing that more permanent plans were being made for them, to ease the process of destruction. Some of the short-lived and improvised ghettos established in Lithuania fit this category.

Evidence from the small town of Jurbarkas in Lithuania indicates that the term "ghetto" was used to mean a few buildings where Jews were held under guard. In mid-August 1941, the district commissar in Siauliai ordered the establishment of Jewish ghettos in the larger towns of the district, but in Jurbarkas, such ghettos had been created even before this order was given.[9]

In postwar testimony, the former Lithuanian police chief in Jurbarkas stated that "after the first shootings in June, mass arrests were carried out by a group of police and auxiliary police. The arrested Jewish men were transferred into the ghetto. . . . I think that there were two ghettos, both in Dariaus and Gireno Streets, guarded by police and auxiliary police."[10] Further perpetrator testimony states that "the Jews with their children and the elderly were placed in the ghetto, which was a building surrounded by barbed wire. . . . There the Jews lived under prison conditions. Nutrition was bad, consisting of cabbage soup and a little bread. They were driven to work under guard and had to clean rubbish from the houses and the streets and do other most disgusting and difficult work, with food being scarce."[11]

On August 21, 1941, there were still 684 Jews in the Jurbarkas ghettos, 64 of whom were engaged in forced labor.[12] On September 4–6, those Jews deemed unfit for work—about 400 women and children—were driven into the yard of the "Talmud-Torah," which served as the women's ghetto. They were then escorted to pits near Kalnenai and murdered by Lithuanian police under German direction. On September 12, only 272 Jews were still alive, including 73 who were working.[13] Those Jews were murdered shortly afterward by a small killing squad from Kaunas (Kovno), again assisted by the local police. The destruction ghettos in Jurbarkas existed for only a few weeks and were used primarily as staging areas for the killings, although some food was supplied and forced labor imposed during the ghettos' short existence.

Another example of a destruction ghetto was that in Khar'kov. When the German 6th Army captured the city in late October 1941, the policy of eliminating entire Jewish communities had been in operation behind the advancing Eastern Front for some two months. Both the army and the police prepared the ground for the implementation of the "Final Solution" in the city. At a military conference, Field Command Post (Feldkommandantur) 787 stated on November 4: "Since most of the Jews are still hiding, an Aktion against the Jews is anticipated only after some time."[14] Initially, various reprisal Aktions were taken against Jews and suspected Communists. In mid-November Sonderkommando 4a of Einsatzgruppe C, commanded by Standartenführer Paul Blobel, arrived in Khar'kov.

First the Jews were registered separately as part of a citywide census. Then they were concentrated into a makeshift ghetto. Einsatzgruppe C reported:

> An area was chosen, where the Jews could be housed in the barracks of a factory district. Then, on 14 December 1941, the city commandant ordered the Jews to move into the area by 16 December. The evacuation of the Jews went off without a hitch, except for some robberies as the Jews were marched into their new quarters. . . . So far, no report is available on the number of Jews arrested during the evacuation. At the same time, preparation for

the shooting of the Jews is under way. 305 Jews who spread rumors against the German army were shot immediately.[15]

The ghetto consisted of twenty-six residential "barracks" attached to a machine-tool factory.[16] Only 861 residents were evicted to make space for more than ten thousand Jews, resulting in severe overcrowding in the ghetto.[17] "Living conditions" reflected the German intention only to contain the Jews until they had been murdered. A Soviet report based on local testimony described conditions in Khar'kov's "Jewish district" or "ghetto" as follows:

> The doors and windows in the barracks into which the Jewish population was herded were broken, and the plumbing and heating were ruined. Hundreds of people were settled in barracks intended for sixty or seventy people. In the ghetto . . . the Germans starved people and prevented them from going out to get water and food. At night people were prevented from going outside even for the needs of nature. Anyone spotted violating the established regime was immediately shot. Many people became sick and died. The corpses of the dead remained in the barracks. Taking them outside was not permitted. . . . Every day the Germans made new demands to deliver warm clothing, watches, and other valuable objects. If these demands were not met because nothing was available, "soldiers" [probably German police, ed.] would take several dozen people from the barracks and shoot them.[18]

A contemporary report by Police Battalion 314 confirms that "from 17 December 1941, to 7 January 1942, the companies took it in turn to guard the ghetto. During the guard duty of the First Company, Jews trying to leave the ghetto who did not stop when called, were shot by the ghetto guards."[19]

In this way as many as fifty people were shot each day until the end of December.[20] The total liquidation of the Jews began on January 2, 1942. It lasted several days because Soviet air raids interrupted the shootings in the Drobitskii Yar Ravine outside the city. In all, more than nine thousand people were shot.[21]

In the Generalgouvernement there were also several ghettos that existed only very briefly, like the ghetto in Baranów Sandomierski, established to facilitate the extermination of the Jews of the town and its environs in summer 1942. The Baranów ghetto was set up on June 30,

1942, and liquidated only three weeks later on July 20, 1942.[22] The ghetto encompassed part of the marketplace and sections of adjoining streets. Anticipating disaster, some Jews (including two policemen) managed to escape from the ghetto, but most of the escapees were recaptured and perished later.[23]

ENCLOSURE OF GHETTOS

The process of enclosing or sealing off ghettos, which sometimes took place several months after the initial establishment of an open ghetto or Jewish residential district, demonstrates the essential links between open ghettos and enclosed ghettos. Three examples illustrate how this looked in practice.

In Łokacze, in Volhynia, the enclosure of the ghetto represented the completion of a gradual process. First, at the beginning of November 1941 the Jews of Łokacze were forced into a ghetto, centered on one of the synagogues. About half of the Jewish houses were confiscated. The ghetto initially remained open. Jews from other small towns and villages nearby were forced into the ghetto. These Jews had to leave most of their property behind. In addition to the 1,400 Jews residing in Łokacze, another 800 were brought in. This resulted in terrible overcrowding: some people moved into rooms without windows or lived in stables.

On January 5, 1942, the town authorities requested that the Judenrat construct a fence around the ghetto. The ghetto enjoyed a brief respite in January as the local German gendarmerie chief went on leave for fifteen days and his more lenient replacement allowed the construction of the fence to languish. By February, however, the ghetto fence had been completed. It was two meters high, wrapped in barbed wire. The enclosure of the ghetto made trading with the local peasants more difficult, and punishments for leaving the ghetto also became more severe. Now the Ukrainian police began to shoot on sight Jews caught outside the ghetto. For example, one man was shot on March 16, instantly causing black market prices to rise by 50 percent.

In Łokacze, deaths from disease due to overcrowding in the ghetto started before its enclosure. However, the construction of the fence and especially the stricter guard regime that followed marked a considerable intensification of persecution.[24]

For the town of Kozienice in Distrikt Radom of the Generalgouvernement, the establishment of a Jewish residential district (open ghetto) and its subsequent conversion into an enclosed ghetto is clearly documented in the monthly reports of the Jewish Council to the Gestapo. At the end of December 1941, the Jewish Council reported: "In connection with the Order on the Restriction of Movement for the Jews (Aufenthaltsbeschränkung), the Council has—on the orders of the authorities—at the end of this month prepared the . . . creation of a Jewish Residential District in Kozienice and . . . the resettlement of Jews living outside the Residential District."[25]

The ghetto was not enclosed until five months later, as a subsequent Jewish Council report described: "In accordance with the Order of the Kreishauptmann of Radom Land, the Council has completed fencing in the Jewish Residential District, whereby a separate and enclosed quarter of the town has been established."[26]

The ghetto in Dereczyn (Derechin), in Generalkommisariat Weissruthenien (now Belarus), was set up in several stages, such that it is not possible to specify a precise date for its establishment. Soon after their arrival, the Germans evicted Jews from some of the best houses, taking them for themselves. Then, during the winter of 1941–42, the German administration issued certificates to those Jews deemed "essential" on account of their skills as craftsmen, although some Jews were also able to buy such certificates using bribes. These "essential" Jews, consisting of about five hundred people, were permitted to live in their own collective area composed of workshops, to which non-Jews also had access in order to request their services. Probably in March 1942, the remaining few hundred Jews from the nearby villages of Holynka, Jeziornica, and Kolonia Sinaiska were brought to Dereczyn and confined within the same small area as the two thousand or so "nonessential" Jews living in Dereczyn.

By May or June of 1942 at the latest, the ghetto for the non-craftsmen had become enclosed, and according to one account some 2,880 Jews were living together crammed into only thirty-four small cottages.[27] Its area comprised the entire Schulhof and the premises of the tailor's Bet HaMedrash, called the Hayatim Schul, up to the Kamienitzya. The entry to the ghetto was through the yard between the wall to Slutzky's house and the wall to Bebbeh Rabinovich's house. The ghetto was surrounded with barbed wire and guarded by the local police. Due to poor sanitary conditions, there were epidemics in the ghetto and many Jews died of disease and starvation.[28] German police and their collaborators liquidated the ghetto in Dereczyn on July 24, 1942, murdering some 2,500 Jews.

Other ghettos, such as that in Nowogródek, were enclosed from the moment of their creation, but the various stages involved in setting up certain ghettos helps to account for the sometimes contradictory information in the various sources regarding the date of their establishment.

TRANSIT GHETTOS

An important and largely neglected category is that of the transit ghetto. The Polish historian Robert Kuwałek highlighted this category in connection with his extensive research on the Bełżec extermination camp. The case of Izbica, as summarized by Kuwałek, illustrates some of the unique conditions that developed in a transit ghetto that was also an open ghetto.[29]

From the end of 1939, the town of Izbica in Distrikt Lublin (Generalgouvernement) became a collecting point for many Polish Jews resettled by the Germans from Polish towns farther to the west that had been incorporated into the Third Reich, including Głowno, Koło, Kalisz, and Łódź. In 1940 and 1941, Jews were also resettled into Izbica from the cities of Krasnystaw and Lublin. By August 1941, about seven thousand Jews were living in Izbica, including nearly two thousand resettled from other places.[30] In March and April 1941, the Germans transported about one thousand persons to Izbica from Lublin. An enclosed ghetto did not exist in Izbica at the time. The entire town was one large open ghetto bordered on three sides by hills and on the fourth (Tarnogór) side by the Wieprz River. Izbica became a Jewish enclave. From the start of 1941, Jews were not allowed to leave the designated borders of the town on pain of death or even to move freely within the town. Economic activity nevertheless continued.[31]

After the Wannsee Conference, Izbica became a transit ghetto for Jews deported from the Protectorate of Bohemia and Moravia (Theresienstadt), Germany, Austria, and Slovakia. The choice of Izbica as a transit ghetto reflected its location on the main rail line between Lublin and Bełżec, where the Nazis established an extermination camp in November 1941. Izbica was the largest of the Nazi transit ghettos in Distrikt Lublin; other transit ghettos included Piaski,

Rejowiec, Zamość, Opole-Lubelski, Dęblin-Irena, Siedliszcze, Chełm, Włodawa, and Międzyrzec Podlaski.

The first transport to Izbica arrived on March 11, 1942, carrying some one thousand Czech Jews deported from Theresienstadt. In total, seventeen transports arrived in Izbica, bringing more than fifteen thousand Jews to the town by early June 1942.[32] Since the foreign Jews arrived in Izbica while Polish Jews were still in the town, there was severe overcrowding and no space for the deportees. The German authorities crammed them into houses occupied by the Polish Jews. Up to thirty people were forced to share a small room with broken windows, such that they had to stand up all day and all night.[33]

After a few days, the Germans carried out the first mass deportation Aktion, taking some of the Polish Jews to an unknown location. The function of the transit ghetto in Izbica became one in which the inmates had to wait for an available place to stay, and all the buildings were overcrowded. Living conditions and hygiene were terrible for the Jews who arrived from abroad. The deportees also suffered from hunger. Not until the summer of 1942, when Jews were being sent to the extermination camps, did the occupation officials provide rations for the Jews. Deaths from starvation and exhaustion occurred daily.[34]

Cultural conflicts were common between the Polish Jews and the Jews who arrived in Izbica from abroad. The majority of the non-Polish Jews were assimilated, had liberal attitudes toward religion, and did not speak Yiddish. The conflict was exploited and deepened by the Germans, who deliberately set the groups against each other. In 1942, they set up one Judenrat for the Polish Jews and one for the Jews transported to Izbica from abroad.[35] Two branches of the Jewish Self-Help Association also functioned in Izbica, one for each group. During the course of the various Aktions, the non-Polish Jewish policemen arrested Polish Jews, and Polish Jewish police arrested non-Polish Jews.[36]

On March 24, 1942, about 2,200 Polish Jews were sent to the extermination camp at Bełżec. During the Aktion, several dozen Jews were shot on the spot by the local Schutzstaffel (SS) officers Kurt Engels and Ludwik Klemm, and the bodies were buried in the Jewish cemetery.[37] The deportations were supervised by officers from the SS training camp in Trawniki and by the German gendarmerie from Krasnystaw, assisted by the local Polish police.

The next Aktion took place May 12–15, 1942. The Germans organized a mass deportation throughout the entire Krasnystaw district. First, several hundred Jewish men—both Polish and non-Polish—were sent from Izbica to the Majdanek concentration camp. A second group consisting of about four hundred persons was deported to the extermination camp in Sobibor.[38]

After a short time, the Polish Jews began to comprehend the fate of the deportees to Bełżec. During subsequent cleansing Aktions, many people tried to escape and hide in Izbica or in the nearby forests. Most of the non-Polish Jews at this time obediently assembled in the Izbica marketplace, from where they were led away in columns to the Izbica railway station. The Jews from abroad recognized more slowly the fate of those deported.[39] In June and July 1942, the Germans conducted further deportations to the extermination camps in Bełżec and Sobibor. Then, until the fall of 1942, no further deportations were carried out, although the Germans conducted several executions of Jews in the town.[40]

In October 1942, Izbica became the central ghetto for Polish Jews in the Krasnystaw district. Several thousand Jews were brought to Izbica from Krasnystaw, Żółkiewka, Turobin, and also from places within the Zamość district. The last Jews from Zamość and Krasnobrod were driven to Izbica on foot. It is not known exactly how many Jews were in Izbica at that time, but one may estimate that about six thousand Jews came to the town from the liquidated ghettos.[41] In mid-October 1942, more than five thousand Jews were deported from Izbica in the largest of the "resettlement" Aktions. The operation was directed by SS forces from Izbica, Zamość, and Lublin. This Aktion was particularly bloody. At least five hundred persons were shot on the platform of the railway station in Izbica. The Jews who remained alive were transported to Bełżec and Sobibor.[42]

Shortly after these mass deportations, the Higher SS and Police Leader (HSSPF) in the Generalgouvernement ordered the creation of a small ghetto in Izbica. All of those Jews who survived the last deportation were collected in this ghetto, namely those found hiding in Izbica or the nearby wooded areas, and also the Jews who had escaped from other ghettos. The ghetto consisted of several buildings near the Altmanów Tannery on Stokowa and Cicha streets, near the former brick factory at Kulik (today, Fabryczna Street). The small ghetto remained an open ghetto. Jews worked there in the tannery

TYPOLOGY OF GHETTOS • 95

and the brick factory. Its main purpose was to attract Jews who were hiding elsewhere in the region.[43]

RESTGHETTOS (REMNANT GHETTOS)

This final phase of the Izbica transit ghetto introduces another important type of German-run ghetto, the remnant ghetto. In several places, ghettos were established only for a much-reduced Jewish population just following a large-scale killing or deportation Aktion. In such cases, often a selection preceded the Aktion and the remnant ghetto held only those deemed necessary for specific types of work, together perhaps with their families or others who had gone into hiding and emerged thereafter to join the inmates of the ghetto. In the occupied territories of the Soviet Union, the wave of mass killings in the fall of 1941 led to the establishment of a number of such remnant ghettos after only a few months of German occupation.

For example, in the town of Nieśwież, Generalkommissariat Weissruthenien (now Nesvizh in Belarus), the German military commandant (Ortskommandant) ordered the entire Jewish population to gather in the marketplace on October 30, 1941. When people turned up in their best clothes, the Germans selected the skilled workers together with their families on the basis of a list. During the selection German troops, Lithuanian auxiliaries, and local Belorussian police suddenly appeared and surrounded the marketplace.

Belorussian police escorted the selected group (about 585 people) to the high school. German soldiers and Lithuanian auxiliaries took the remaining Jews in the marketplace (approximately four thousand) and shot them at two separate sites. The surviving 585 Jews were then moved into the ghetto, an area 250 meters long and 150 meters wide surrounded by barbed wire, where they lived in very overcrowded conditions. This pattern was common for several ghettos in Generalkommissariat Weissruthenien and Reichskommissariat Ukraine, which were set up only for workers and their families in the wake of large-scale Aktions.[44]

A similar mass-killing Aktion preceded the establishment of what became a remnant ghetto in the Ukrainian town of Litin, Generalkommissariat Shitomir (Zhytomyr). Early on the morning of December 19, 1941, a squad of German Security Police from Vinnytsia arrived. Reinforced by the local German gendarmerie and Ukrainian police, they surrounded the streets on which the Jews lived. These police forces drove the Jews from their homes, killing some in the process. Then they escorted them to a nearby Red Army base, together with other Jews brought in from the surrounding villages. At the Red Army base, the German authorities selected about two hundred craftsmen and their families. German SD men and Ukrainian police escorted the remaining two thousand or so people to ditches that had been dug two kilometers away and shot them.[45]

The selected Jews were moved into a ghetto over the next two hours. The ghetto comprised a few houses on two narrow streets. The Germans also brought into the ghetto those Jews who had hidden during the mass shooting and emerged thereafter. About three hundred Jews were concentrated in the ghetto surrounded by a fence. The Jews were prohibited from leaving on pain of death. Although food was scarce and hunger severe, nobody was allowed to go to the market to obtain food.[46]

One of the most important functions of such remnant ghettos, apart from the exploitation of remaining Jewish labor, was to attract Jews back out of hiding following the large Aktions. This was the case with regard to the large ghetto in Głębokie (Glubokoye), Generalkommissariat Weissruthenien, which served as a main collecting point for Jews after a series of liquidation Aktions in the region in the early summer of 1942.[47] In August 1942, the office of the Gebietskommissar in Głębokie spread news of an amnesty for Jews in hiding, if they gave themselves up and came to the Głębokie ghetto.[48] On account of the difficulties in finding a safe place to hide, many Jews accepted this offer, despite their natural doubts as to its sincerity. For instance, as many as five hundred Jewish escapees from the Szarkowszczyna ghetto went into the Głębokie ghetto, which was subsequently liquidated in August 1943.

Some historians have interpreted the infamous announcement of Higher SS and Police Leader Krüger on "The Establishment of Jewish Residential Districts" (Errichtung jüdischer Wohnbezirke) in a few towns in the Radom, Kraków, and Galicia regions (Distrikte Radom, Krakau, and Galizien) as serving primarily this function of attracting Jews out of hiding.[49] Certainly many of the listed ghettos attracted large numbers of desperate Jews unable to find shelter once the Germans also imposed the death penalty on persons caught hiding Jews and their families.

The complex history of the successive ghettos in Sandomierz illustrates how some of these remnant ghettos in the Generalgouvernement functioned in practice. In the weeks following Krüger's announcement that Sandomierz would be one of the four remaining Jewish residential districts in the Radom region,[50] many Jews came to Sandomierz out of hiding from the surrounding areas, raising the Jewish population to more than six thousand. Most remained suspicious of German intentions but could not find any other way to survive. One reason for their desperation was the hostile attitude of many Polish partisan groups who turned away or betrayed Jews fleeing to the forests. Only relatively few escapees, such as ten-year-old Sara Glass, whose parents found her a safe refuge with Janina Szymanska in the village of Mokrzyszow near Tarnobrzeg, were able to remain in hiding for more than a few weeks.[51]

This "second ghetto" in Sandomierz, established after the deportation of some three thousand Jews on October 28 and 29, 1942, was located in about twenty single-story houses around Jewish Street (Yiddisher Gas) and on part of Zamkower Street. It was surrounded by a fence two meters high and guarded by German police.[52] One survivor described conditions there as "terrible. It was so dirty. People were lying in the streets, hungry.... I've never seen such filth."[53] About twelve Jews had to share a room, and some lived in attics or on the street. Jews were able to barter remaining valuables for food with local peasants across the fence, but the meager rations issued by the Judenrat consisted only of bread and a little soup once per day. Jews had to go out of the ghetto under close guard to reach the bathhouse and queue for water. A communal toilet was established on an elevation toward the Christian quarter, but sanitary conditions were appalling and disease was rife. Those who fell sick and reported to the hospital were generally murdered after just a few days. Many Jews tried to flee from this hell.[54]

On January 7, 1943, units of the SS, the German gendarmerie, Polish police, and Latvian and Ukrainian auxiliaries surrounded the ghetto. During the night these forces threw in bombs, setting a few houses on fire, and shot at anyone who approached the ghetto fence. Then on the following morning they rounded up and deported most of the roughly seven thousand Jews in the ghetto. During the roundup the Germans selected about three hundred men who were fit for work and sent them to the labor camp at Skarżysko-Kamienna. The other deportees were placed into freight cars holding more than 120 people each destined for the Treblinka extermination camp, where they were murdered.[55]

Following the Aktion on January 7, the Germans again announced that those who came out of hiding and returned to the ghetto would not be harmed and established a "third ghetto." About 180 people emerged and returned to Jewish Street to join 120 people who had been excluded from the deportation. These Jews were employed in clearing out the ghetto. On April 15, 1943, the Germans selected young and healthy Jews and sent them to the labor camp at Pionki. Those remaining, including fifteen children, were shot. This Aktion finally liquidated the ghetto, and most of the buildings were demolished. Local Poles searched through the rubble for any hidden valuables.[56]

NUMBERS OF GHETTOS BY REGION

Even as research on the United States Holocaust Memorial Museum's volume *German-Run Ghettos* approaches its conclusion, it is still not possible to say exactly how many German-run ghettos there were in total or how many of each type existed. As this small sampling illustrates, German-run ghettos can be divided into several different types with a variety of functions. Indeed, many ghettos fall into several of these categories, either at once or successively. Some types of ghettos have not been included here, such as the rural ghettos of Grozdiec and Rzgów, established to hold the Jews of the Konin region, as the research still has to be done. However, there is no doubt that the final results of this project will considerably advance our knowledge of the number of ghettos there were, conditions in them, and the role they played in the Holocaust.

Until recently, the most common estimate for the total number of ghettos was something in excess of 400. This figure reflected the number of ghettos documented in the Generalgouvernement (including Distrikt Galizien), together with those territories incorporated into the Reich (Warthegau, Oberschlesien, and Ostpreussen), and Distrikt Białystok. However, there were more than 230 additional ghettos in Reichskommissariat Ukraine (including more than 130 in Generalkommissariat Wolhynien-Podolien alone), and also another 250 or so in Russia and Belarus combined (not counting more than

120 mostly short-lived destruction ghettos—existing for less than two months—in the Baltic states), bringing the overall total to more than 1,150.

The central aim of *German-Run Ghettos* and the area in which it will break new ground is primarily with regard to the many smaller, previously undocumented ghettos. In addition, it will serve as an important reference source for the larger ghettos, such as those in Warsaw, Kraków, and Minsk, also providing an archival and bibliographical survey. The work will present a much clearer picture of how many ghettos there were, what typologies each ghetto falls into, how long the ghettos existed, and roughly how many Jews were held in each place. Many smaller and in most cases relatively unknown ghettos, such as those in Snów, Stołowicze, Shpola, Yalta, Jeremicze, and Iarun will be carefully documented and finally put on the map.

NOTES

1. The author of the present essay is the editor of *German-Run Ghettos, Mostly in Poland and the USSR* (hereafter *German-Run Ghettos*), which is volume 2 of the multivolume *Encyclopedia of Camps and Ghettos, 1933–1945*, begun in 1999 by the United States Holocaust Memorial Museum (hereafter USHMM). Since 1999 Yad Vashem has also begun preparing its own lexicon of ghettos; it will be interesting to compare the results of the two projects in terms of numbers of ghettos, definition, and typology.

2. Dieter Pohl noted that in Ukraine many ghettos more closely resembled the open-ghetto model. Pohl, "Schauplatz Ukraine: Der Massenmord an den Juden im Militärverwaltungsgebiet und im Reichskommissariat 1941–1943," in *Ausbeutung, Vernichtung, Öffentlichkeit: Neue Studien zur nationalsozialistischen Lagerpolitik,* ed. Norbert Frei, Sybille Steinbacher, and Bernd C. Wagner (Munich: K. G. Saur, 2000), 158.

3. Locations in the Generalgouvernement will be identified according to their wartime German designations, with current spellings given in parentheses if they differ.

4. Alexander Kruglov, draft entry for "Uman" received for USHMM's *German-Run Ghettos*.

5. Czesław Pilichowski, ed., *Obozy hitlerowskie na ziemiach polskich 1939–1945: informator encyklopedyczny* (Warsaw: Państwowe Wydawnictwo Naukowe, 1979), 342; report of the Kreishauptmann in Nowy Targ for the period from September 17, 1939, to May 31, 1941, in *Faschismus—Getto—Massenmord; Dokumentation über Ausrottung und Widerstand der Juden in*

Polen während des zweiten Weltkrieges, eds. Tatiana Berenstein and Artur Eisenbach (Berlin: Rütten and Loening und Jüdischen Historischen Institut, Warsaw, 1961), 64; USHMM Record Group (hereafter RG) 15.019.M, reel 14 (Ankieta Sadów Grodzkich [hereafter ASG] sygn. 48 b), 189.

6. *Justiz und N-S Verbrechen* (hereafter *JNSV*), vol. 21, Laufende Nummer (hereafter Lfd. Nr. or "running number") 593 (Amsterdam: Amsterdam University Press, 1979), 182; *Biuletyn Żydowskiego Instytutu Historycznego* (1959) no. 30, 96; *Remembrance Book of Nowy Targ and Vicinity* (Translation from *Sefer Nowy Targve ha seviva*), ed. Michael Walzer-Fass (Tel Aviv: Townspeople Association of Nowy Targ and Vicinity, 1979), 57–58; USHMM RG 15.019.M (Court Inquiries About Executions, Mass Graves, Camps, and Ghettos), reel 14 (ASG sygn. 48 b), 189.

7. Pilichowski, *Obozy hitlerowskie na ziemiach polskich 1939–1945,* 93; Michael Albertini, *Die Verfolgung und Vernichtung der Juden im Reichsgau Wartheland 1939–1945* (Wiesbaden: Harrassowitz, 2006), 200.

8. Roman Mogilansky (*The Ghetto Anthology* [Los Angeles: American Congress of Jews from Poland and Survivors of Concentration Camps, 1985], 345) used the term "Nazi Death-Traps for Jews" with regard to ghettos in the occupied territory of the Soviet Union. But many of the ghettos he described existed for six months or longer. Wendy Lower, "Facilitating Genocide: Nazi Ghettoization Practices in Occupied Ukraine, 1941–1942," in *Life in the Ghettos During the Holocaust,* ed. Eric J. Sterling (Syracuse, N.Y.: Syracuse University Press, 2005), 120–21, has described how in Berdichev and Zhytomyr "the ghetto served mainly as a temporary staging area while Nazi killing units were mustered for the killing *Aktion*."

9. Sources for Jurbarkas include Christoph Dieckmann and Saulius Sužiedėlis, *Lietuvos žydų persekiojimas ir masinės žukynės 1941 m. vasarą ir rudenį: šaltiniai ir analizė* [The persecution and mass murder of Lithuanian Jews during summer and fall of 1941: Sources and analysis] (Vilnius: Margi raštai, 2006). Also Lithuanian Central State Archive, Vilnius (hereafter LCVA), 1753-3-4, 36–37, order of the district commissar in Siauliai, August 14, 1941, which only reached Jurbarkas on August 27, 1941.

10. Protocol of the interrogation of Mykolas Levickas, November 24, 1948, Lithuanian Special Archive (hereafter LYA), B.14142/3, 47–48.

11. Protocol of the confrontation of P. Kairaitis with the witness J. Keturauskas, June 21, 1948, LYA, B.16816, 69–70.

12. Reply of Mayor Gepneris on August 21, 1941, to the letter from the head of the district in Raseiniai of August 16, 1941, LCVA, 1753-3-13, 22.

13. Zevulun Poran, ed., *Sefer HaZikaron LeKehilath Yurburg-Lita* (Tel Aviv: Organization of Former Residents of Yurburg, 1991), 392 and 406–7. In the report of Einsatzkommando 3 on shootings carried out up to Sep-

tember 10, 1941, 412 victims were recorded for Jurbarkas; see Bundesarchiv Berlin (hereafter BAB), R 70 Sowjetunion 15, 80, and 84. See also LCVA, 1753-3-13, 58, letter of Mayor Gepneris to Kreischef in Raseiniai, September 12, 1941, which indicates that not all Jews had been shot by this date.

14. Besprechung bei der Feldkommandantur Charkow am 4.11.1941: Kreigstagebuch (hereafter KTB, or War Diary) 57 ID/Ib, quoted in Hamburger Institut für Sozialforschung, ed., *Vernichtungskrieg: Verbrechen der Wehrmacht 1941 bis 1944. Ausstellungskatalog* (Hamburg: Hamburger Edition, 1996), 96.

15. BAB, R 58/215-20, Ereignismeldung UdSSR (Union der Sozialistischen Sowjet-Rupubliken) Nr. 164, February 4, 1942.

16. A poor-quality photograph of several of the barracks taken in 1943 can be found in Iurii M. Liakhovitskii, *Poprannaia mezuza: Kniga Drobitskogo iara. Svidetel'stva, fakty, dokumenty o natsistskom genotside evreiskogo naseleniia Khar'kova v period nemetskoi okkupatsii 1941–1942*, no. 1 (Khar'kov: Osnova, 1991), 64.

17. Alexander Kruglov, draft entry for "Khar'kov" received for *German-Run Ghettos*.

18. *Dokumenty obviniaiut: Sbornik dokumentov o chudovishchnykh prestupleniiakh nemetsko-fashistskikh zakhvatchikov na sovetskoi territorii*, no. 2 (Moscow: Ogiz-Gospolitizdat, 1945), 307–9.

19. BAB, R 2104/25 (Reichshauptkasse Beutestelle), Police Battalion 314 report on 83 dollars and 850 Swedish crowns handed in, dated January 24, 1942, signed Christ, Obltn. d. Schupo. u. Kp. Führer. The role of Police Battalion 314 in guarding the ghetto was confirmed by Karl G., a former unit member, who also described the mass shooting of the Jews of Khar'kov; see *Hessiches Hauptstaatsarchiv*, Wiesbaden, 631 a, 1868, 2551-5, statement of Karl G., November 9, 1964.

20. Account of Maria Markovna Sokol, "What I Survived in Kharkov," Khar'kov, November 1943, in Ilya Ehrenburg and Vasily Grossman, *The Complete Black Book of Russian Jewry*, ed. and trans. David Patterson (New Brunswick and London: Transaction, 2002), 37–41. Maria Sokol managed to survive subsequently with the aid of Russian papers from a woman who had died. Lidia Gluzmanova also complained of insufficient heat and water and that she was hungry all the time; see USHMM, RG-50.226*0010.

21. According to a document issued by the Soviet Extraordinary State Commission on September 5, 1943, more than fifteen thousand Jews were executed. They were buried in two trenches. One contained eight to ten thousand corpses, the other, about 350 meters away from the first, contained five to six thousand. However, the second trench was hardly investigated. The number of corpses in it was estimated by eye. It is entirely possible that it contained the remains either of prisoners of war (military ammunition

was found in the trench) or of non-Jewish civilians. In addition, the figure of fifteen thousand exceeds (by five thousand) the number of registered Jews. It is unlikely that so many Jews could have evaded registration. It should also be kept in mind that some of the registered Jews were killed before January 1942, and that for various reasons still other Jews were not resettled into the factory barracks. *Dokumenty obviniaiut,* issue 2 (Moscow: Ogiz-Gospolitizdat, 1945), 307–12. A German translation of the Soviet Extraordinary State Commission Report of September 5, 1943, can be found in Bundesarchiv-Ludwigsburg (hereafter BAL), AR-Z 269/60, Dokumentenband, 164–69.

22. *Pinkas Hakehilot: Encyclopedia of Jewish Communities. Poland. Vol. 3. Western Galicia and Silesia* (Jerusalem: Yad Vashem, 1990), 62; N. Blumenthal, *Sefer Yizkor Barnov* (Jerusalem: Yad Vashem, 1964), 205. I am grateful to Samuel Schalkowsky for summarizing these sources in Yiddish for the "Baranów Sandomierski" entry for the USHMM's *German-Run Ghettos.*

23. At first they were hidden by Gentiles, who, for payment, later either turned them over to the Nazi authorities or killed them personally; see Blumenthal, *Sefer Yizkor Barnov,* 208–10.

24. Michael Diment, *The Lone Survivor: A Diary of the Lukacze Ghetto and Svyniukhy, Ukaine* (New York: Holocaust Library, 1992), 38–72.

25. USHMM Archives Acc. 2003.406.1, A-077, Aeltesten-Rat der jüd. Bevölkerung Kozienice, report of December 31, 1941 (two pages):

In Zusammenhang mit Anordnung über die Aufenthaltsbeschränkung der Juden, hat der Rat,—auf Befehl der Behörden,—am Ende dieses Monats ihrer, mit Errichtung des jüdischen Wohnbezirks in Kozienice und mit Umsiedlung ausserhalb des Wohnviertels ansässiger Juden, verbundenen und bereits noch im Gang werdenden, Arbeiten vorgenommen.—Der Obmann des Rates.

26. Ibid., A-140, Ältesten-Rat der jüd. Bevölkerung Kozienice, report of May 15, 1942 (two pages):

Der Anordnung des Herrn Kreishauptmanns Radom-Land gemäss, hat der Rat die Abzäunung des jüdischen Wohnviertels durchgeführt, wodurch ist ein abgesondertes und geschlossenes Stadtviertel entstanden.—Der Obmann des Rates.

27. Jewish Historical Institute, Warsaw (hereafter AŻIH), 301/2140 and 301/4695, testimony of the accountant Reich. An English translation is available: Y. Reich, "We Were Slaves . . . ," in *The Dereczin Memorial Book: A Book of Remembrance Honoring the Communities of Dereczin, Halinka, Kolonia-Sinaiska,* ed. Yekhezkiel Raban, trans. Jacob Solomon Berger (Mahwah, N.J.: J. S. Berger, 2000), 211–12. It is not clear whether this number of 2,880 also included the 500 "essential" workers living outside the ghetto.

28. BAL, II 202 AR-Z 180/67, Dokumenten Band (hereafter Dok. Bd.), 7–8, statement of Vladimir Varfolomeyevich Ogorodnikov on February 19, 1968; Katya Bialosotsky-Khlebnik, "During the Days of Slaughter," in *The Dereczin Memorial Book,* 242.

29. See especially Robert Kuwałek, "Die Durchgangsghettos im Distrikt Lublin (u.a. Izbica, Piaski, Rejowiec und Trawniki)," in *"Aktion Reinhardt": Der Völkermord an den Juden im Generalgouvernement 1941–1944,* ed. Bogdan Musial (Osnabrück: Fibre, 2004): 197–232. This section on transit ghettos is based on Kuwałek's draft entry for "Izbica" received for volume 2 of the *Encyclopedia of Camps and Ghettos.*

30. AŻIH, 211/138, report on the situation in Izbica, August 16, 1941, 24–25.

31. AŻIH, 301/5953, testimony of Stefan Sendłak: "Ostatni etap przed śmiercią," 3–4; testimonies of Janina Kić and Helena Błaszczyk in the private collection of Robert Kuwałek.

32. Robert Kuwałek, "Getta tranzytowe w dystrykcie lubelskim," in *Akcja Reinhardt. Zagłada Żydów w Generalnym Gubernatorstwie,* ed. Dariusz Libionka (Warsaw: Instytut Pamięci Narodowej, 2004), 143–44; and Robert Kuwałek, "Das Durchgangsghetto in Izbica," in Jaroslava Milotova, Ulf Rathgeber, and Michael Wögerbauer, *Theresienstädter Studien und Dokumente* (Prague: Sefer, 2003), 326–27.

33. Archive of Jewish Museum in Prague, Collection of Memoirs, Tape No. 162, interview with Hela Danielova née Troller.

34. For further details about conditions in Izbica, see Kuwałek, "Das Durchgangsghetto," 328–32. On living conditions in the transit ghetto of Piaski, see Else Behrenfeld-Rosenfeld and Gertrud Luckner, eds., *Lebenszeichen aus Piaski: Briefe Deportierter aus dem Distrikt Lublin, 1940–1943* (Munich: Deutsche Taschenbuch Verlag, 1970).

35. AŻIH, 301/29, testimony of Chaskiel Menche; Arndt Müller, *Geschichte der Juden in Nürnberg 1146–1945* (Nuremberg: Stadtbibliothek Nürnberg, 1968), 288.

36. Interview given by Thomas-Toivi Blatt in 2000, in the private collection of Robert Kuwałek.

37. Tatiana Berenstein, "Martyrologia, opór i zagłada ludności żydowskiej w dystrykcie lubelskim," *Biuletyn Żydowskiego Instytutu Historycznego,* no. 21 (1957), 70. Instytut Pamięci Narodewej (hereafter IPN) in Lublin, OKL/Ds. 3/67, statement of Irena Pańko. Pańko's statement came from IPN, the Polish Institute of National Remembrance, Warsaw (previously the Main Commission for the Investigation of Nazi Crimes in Poland).

38. Zofia Leszczyńska, *Kronika obozu koncentracyjnego na Majdanku* (Lublin: Wydawnictwo Lubelskie, 1983), 76; Yitzak Arad, *Belzec, Sobibor,*

Treblinka. The Operation Reinhard Death Camps (Bloomington: Indiana University Press, 1999), 390.

39. Interviews with Thomas-Toivi Blatt, 2000, and Janina Kić and Halina Błaszczyk, 2003, in the private collection of Robert Kuwałek.

40. Kuwałek, "Das Durchgangsghetto," 334.

41. AŻIH, 301/72, testimony of Leon Feldhendler. From Zamość alone, some three to four thousand Jews were forcibly transferred to Izbica.

42. Ibid.; *JNSV,* vol. 20, Lfd. Nr. 316, Landgericht Kassel (hereafter LG) 3a Ks 1/51, verdict in the case of R., former official of the German Kreishauptmannschaft in Krasnystaw (Andere Massenvernichtungsverbrechen Izbica bei Lublin), 603–29.

43. R. Adamski, *Izbica nad Wieprzem* (memoir); manuscript in the collection of the Bełżec Memorial Museum, 64; interview with Thomas-Toivi Blatt, 2000, in the private collection of Robert Kuwałek.

44. Moshe Lachowicky, *Churban Nesvizh* [Yiddish] [The destruction of Nesvizh] (Tel Aviv: Committee of Emigrants from Nesvizh, 1948), 6–18; Shalom Cholawski, *Soldiers from the Ghetto* (San Diego and New York: Barnes and Co., 1980), 53–55; David Farfel, *In Nesvizh Ghetto and Naliboki Woods* [Hebrew] (Ramat Gan, Israel: 1995), 49–51; Yad Vashem Archive (hereafter YVA), O-3/2746; Fortunoff Video Archive, testimony of E. Farfel; and David Farfel's draft entry on "Nieśwież" received for *German-Run Ghettos.*

45. YVA, M-33/196, pp. 6–16; BAL, II 204a AR-Z 135/67, 556–57 (Abschlussbericht). This report indicates that 300 men, 500 women, and 1,186 children were murdered.

46. YVA, O-3/7372, O-3/6401; interview with David Irilevich on April 5, 2005, in the possession of Albert Kaganovitch; Albert Kaganovitch's draft entry for "Litin" received for *German-Run Ghettos.*

47. On the wave of killings in the region in May and June, see National Archive of the Republic of Belarus, 370-1-483, 15, report of the district commissar in Głębokie on the Jewish Aktion, July 1, 1942.

48. USHMM, Art and Artifacts, Acc. 1998.89, "Survival in German-Occupied Poland," 46; Szmerke Kaczerginski, *Hurbn Vilne: umkum fun di Yidn in Vilne un Vilner gegnt . . . : zamlung fun eydus: bavayzn oder dokumentn* [Yiddish] (New York: Aroysgegebn fun dem fareyniktn Vilner hilfs-komitet in Nyu-York durkh Tsiko bikher-farlag, 1947), 155.

49. Police decree issued by HSSPF Krüger of the Generalgouvernement, November 10, 1942, in Berenstein and Eisenbach, *Faschismus,* 344–45.

50. Ibid.

51. Israel Gutman, ed., *The Encyclopedia of the Righteous Among the Nations: Rescuers of Jews During the Holocaust—Poland* (Jerusalem: Yad Vashem, 2004), 802–3.

52. Amnon Ajzensztadt, *And the Earth Did Not Cover the Blood* [Yiddish]

(Toronto: Farlag Tsentrale fun di Tzosmerer Organizatsies, 1962), 72; Evah Feldenkraiz-Grinbal, ed., *Et ezkerah: sefer kehilat Tsoizmir (Sandomiyez)* (Tel Aviv: Irgun yots'e Tsoizmir be-Yisra'el: Moreshet, bet'edut, a. Sh. Mordekhai Anilevits', 1993), 555; Archives of the Center for Contemporary Jewish Documentation (CDJC), testimony of B. C. regarding Sandomierz.

53. USHMM, RG-50.155*0007, oral history interview with Ruth Muschkies Webber, February 2, 1987.

54. Feldenkraiz-Grinbal, *Et ezkerah: sefer kehilat Tsoizmir,* 554; CDJC, testimony of B. C. regarding Sandomierz.

55. Feldenkraiz-Grinbal, *Et ezkerah: sefer kehilat Tsoizmir,* 553–52.

56. Ibid., 552–51; see also AŻIH, 302/94.

David Silberklang

Defining the Ghettos: Jewish and German Perspectives in the Lublin District

"ALL NIGHT THERE WAS VERY HEAVY MILITARY TRAFFIC.... I HAVEN'T seen such heavy traffic for a long time.... People involved in studying political events are sure that something big will happen soon."[1] What Dr. Zygmunt Klukowski observed on January 15, 1941, was part of the Wehrmacht's preparations for Operation Barbarossa. During the first months of 1941, large concentrations of German troops began to gather in the Generalgouvernement and especially in the Lublin District. Klukowski recorded their intensive activity in his diary—laying and expanding roads, building bridges and airfields, and so on. Parallel to this, on January 28 he noted German preparations for "new initiatives" regarding the Jews.[2]

Earlier that month, on or before January 11, Dr. Walter Bausenhardt, head of the district's Housing Department, met Lublin Judenrat leaders to discuss a "voluntary" transfer of Jews out of Lublin as a preparatory step to creating a ghetto in Lublin. The space to be allotted for the ghetto was not large enough to house all 43,000 Jews.[3] On January 17, Lublin District Governor Ernst Zörner "recommended" that his county chiefs and mayors concentrate Jews into fewer communities to eliminate them from trade and to better control smuggling.[4]

It was also at this time that Reich Security Main Office (RSHA) head Reinhard Heydrich spelled out his plans for the coming months of massive population movement. He envisioned moving 831,000 Poles and Jews from the German-annexed territories of western Poland to the Generalgouvernement. They would be replaced by 200,000 Volksdeutsche. In addition, 10,000 Jews would be brought to the Generalgouvernement from Vienna. General Governor Hans Frank and his senior aides approved these plans on January 15.[5]

DEFINING THE GHETTOS • 107

When German authorities discussed forcibly resettling large numbers of Poles and Jews in early 1941, they were continuing a discussion of grandiose demographic engineering plans that had been ongoing since the beginning of the war. By the end of 1940, tens of thousands of Jews had been deported into the Lublin District from western Poland, the Third Reich, Kraków, and various prisoner of war (POW) camps, and many thousands of local Jews had been uprooted from their homes.

Bausenhardt's discussion with the Lublin Judenrat on relocating Lublin Jews and creating a ghetto came against the background of fifteen months of forced population movements of Jews and the establishment of ghettos in various other places in Poland. But the Germans found that the general demographic planning, the military planning, and anti-Jewish planning all conflicted with each other. Moreover, between fall 1940 and summer 1941, officials in the Generalgouvernement and in Lublin were implementing conflicting anti-Jewish policies: concentration for security and control reasons and in preparation for future measures; and dispersal from existing or planned German areas for security or "aesthetic" reasons. These contradictory policies of concentration and dispersal led to ad hoc decisions designed to resolve specific problems as they arose.[6]

DEPORTATIONS TO LUBLIN

This round of deportations from western Poland had actually begun earlier. From October 1940 through January 1941, nearly five thousand Jewish POWs were sent to camps in the Lublin District. In December 1940 and in March 1941, respectively, more than three thousand Jewish civilians each from Mława and Konin in the German-annexed areas were deported to the district.[7] The Konin deportations came on the heels of the arrival of more than three thousand Jews from Vienna in February and March 1941. Dozens of people died in transit and others after arrival.[8] These were primarily older people not capable of working, and they arrived ragged, frozen, and starved and had to be housed in community buildings in the already overcrowded Jewish quarters.[9]

Within the Generalgouvernement, deportations to the Lublin District during this period came primarily from Kraków, at Frank's initiative. Between November 29, 1940, and April 2, 1941, more than nine thousand Jews were expelled to the Lublin District in order to "cleanse" Frank's capital.[10] These Jews arrived on more than forty transports and were dispersed among more than thirty localities. In addition, many thousands of Jews were deported within the Lublin District, partly in connection with the creation of the Lublin ghetto.

In all, more than 23,500 Jews were "resettled" into the Lublin District from October 1940 to April 1941.[11] At the same time, some 15,000 Jews were relocated out of municipal Lublin and dispersed among many small communities, while the remaining Jews were ordered into a ghetto. These numbers do not take into account those Jews who moved "illegally" from place to place of their own accord. A conservative estimate of the number of newly uprooted Jews in the Lublin District during this half-year period would be 84,000, or more than one-fourth of the district's Jewish residents. If the constant movement of people into and within the district of their own accord could be quantified, it would add many thousands to the previous estimate and raise the proportion of newly uprooted Jews in the district to more than one-third.

WEHRMACHT NEEDS AND GHETTOIZATION

These deportations clogged the roads and hampered Wehrmacht preparations for Operation Barbarossa. At the same time, Wehrmacht security needs hampered the civilian government's ability to deal with the massive influx of deportees. On March 12, 1941, the Lublin District's Interior Department complained to the Generalgouvernement's Interior Department that the plethora of closed military areas had made it impossible to deal with housing more deportees in addition to housing those within the district who needed to be resettled.[12]

On March 25, 1941, Schutzstaffel (SS)-Obergruppenführer Georg Wilhelm Friedrich Krüger, the Generalgouvernement's Höhere SS- und Polizeiführer, ordered a temporary halt to all resettlements on the grounds that troop movements and Wehrmacht needs took precedence.[13] At a Generalgouvernement meeting the same day, Lublin District Governor Ernst Zörner related the interconnection between the expulsion of ten thousand Jews from Lublin earlier that month, ghettoization of the remaining Jews, and making room for the Wehrmacht.[14] The plan was to remove the Jews from sensitive security areas by scattering them in nonmilitary areas or confining them to ghettos.

DEFINING THE GHETTOS • 109

March and April 1941 brought a flurry of ghettoization in the Generalgouvernement's district capitals and several other large towns that was also connected with the Wehrmacht's security and space considerations. Frank issued a ghettoization decree for Kraków on March 3; Zörner decreed a ghetto for Lublin on March 24; and ghettos were set up in Radom (March 29), Kielce (early April), Częstochowa (April 9), and Zamość (early April) shortly afterward. The close timing and similarities of these actions reflect central planning, in contrast to prior practice.[15]

The "voluntary relocation" from Lublin, in which more than 15,000 Jews left the city for other localities in the district, began in the midst of the arrival of the deportees from Konin, which aggravated the chaos and suffering. The Lublin expulsions came in two stages: the brutal deportation that took place March 10 through 13, when more than 10,000 Jews were relocated into more than one hundred localities, and the less brutal stage that began during the latter part of March and continued over several months. The German civilian administration wanted to have only 20,000 Jews in the ghetto; 23,000 needed to leave. However, only a few more than 15,000 Jews "voluntarily" relocated out of Lublin in 1941.[16] The Lublin Judenrat did not always know where the Jews had been taken, and their arrival at their new destinations was not always coordinated.[17] On the receiving end, the communities were often ill equipped to deal with such large numbers of refugees.[18]

The Lublin Judenrat appointed a committee of seven of its members to coordinate the relocations. The Lublin JSS (Jüdische Soziale Selbsthilfe, or Jewish Social Self-Help organization) under Marek Alten tried to follow the routes of the deportees and arrange aid for them at their destinations as needed. However, it was difficult to trace all the expulsion routes. They found that 1,250 mostly well-off Jews had gone to Rejowiec; 2,300 mostly poor Jews had gone to Siedliszcze, where a public kitchen had been set up; and 3,200 had gone to Sosnowice. This was in addition to the large numbers who had gone to very small towns and villages. Sosnowice had had only 412 Jews prior to this refugee influx, and the situation in Sosnowice highlights the turmoil into which the deportations had thrust the Jews.[19]

Ongoing forced population movements within the district further complicated these attempts to trace and help expelled Jews. For example, on April 17, 1941, 250 Jews were expelled from Izbica to

Siennica Różana, where there was no JSS representative. Alten asked the JSS representative in Krasnystaw to visit these refugees and report on their needs.[20] Less than three weeks later, 1,400 Jews from Krasnystaw were themselves expelled from their town and sent to fifteen different localities in the county.[21]

The Lublin ghetto was situated in the old Jewish quarter, where many of the Jews of the city were already living. The area was quite small, and 20,000 people would have been very crowded there. This was why District Governor Zörner pressured the Judenrat to find an additional 15,000 Jews to "volunteer" to leave the city, and the Judenrat feared that many of the expelled Jews might return.[22] The Germans consented to increase the number of ghetto residents to 25,000 and tried to entice more Jews to move out of Lublin by opening additional areas in the district and extending the deadline to leave Lublin.[23] But this measure met with only limited success.

Once the move into the ghetto was completed on April 24, Lublin Mayor Fritz Sauermann ordered a census to be taken that night. The Judenrat counted 34,149 Jews in the ghetto, and there were 504 families (approximately 2,220 people) still living outside the ghetto.[24] Thus, there were 16,000 more Jews in Lublin than the Germans had originally intended. This meant more severe overcrowding, more starvation, and more suffering. More people entered the ghetto all the time. "Voluntary" emigrants from Lublin were secretly returning, and Jews from other districts continued to sneak into Lublin in search of better living conditions.[25] Thus, the severe overcrowding was, in a sense, aggravated by the Jews' choice.

Preparations for some sort of ghettoization in other parts of the Lublin District began in January 1941. Following the January meetings between Bausenhardt and the Lublin Judenrat's five-man presidium and Zörner's January 17 "recommendation" that his county chiefs and mayors concentrate Jews into fewer communities, Zörner issued a new Aufenthaltsbeschränkung (residence restriction) for the district's Jews on February 15—as of July 1, no Jew could leave the Jewish quarter without special permission. Violators would be punished with three months in prison and a fine of 1,000 zloty. On June 27, Zörner extended the deadline to October 1.[26]

The Lublin governor's action is a bit puzzling. On the one hand, it can be understood as being part of the larger picture of ghettoization and limitation of the Jews in concert with security interests and Wehrmacht needs. Yet, on the other hand, the delay in the implementation of the limit on the Jews' freedom of movement—from February 15 to October 1—seems to run counter to such interests. If the order were implemented as decreed, then Jews would not have been limited to the Jewish quarters until after the invasion of the USSR was under way. Moreover, the threatened punishment for violating the decree was very mild by Nazi standards. Ghettoization, apparently, was not yet urgent. Yet the flurry of ghettoization in the Generalgouvernement's district capitals and several other larger cities and towns mentioned previously would seem to indicate the opposite.

There were at least three other ghettos in the Lublin District in spring 1941—Zamość, Opole-Lubelski, and Piaski. Ghettoization in Zamość followed a similar pattern to that in Lublin in many ways. Karl Voss, in the Kreishauptmann's office, informed the Judenrat in March of the plans for a ghetto, and the Jews were ordered into the ghetto in early April, with a May 1 deadline. The Nowa Osada neighborhood set aside for the ghetto was heavily Jewish before the war, which meant that many Jews did not leave their homes as part of the ghettoization, although those who lived in the old city and others in the new city did. As in Lublin, the number of Jews in the ghetto (7,000) was smaller than the prewar Jewish population (12,000), with a small number of Jews receiving permission to remain in their homes outside the ghetto. As in Lublin, this was an open ghetto—no fence—and Jews could leave the area, which meant that they could find ways to trade with the local non-Jews. However, the crowding in the Zamość ghetto was somewhat less severe than in Lublin or in the towns that had received large numbers of refugees but had no official ghetto. On May 1, German and Polish police and other forces searched for Jews who had not yet moved to the ghetto. Approximately 250 people were discovered and expelled to Komorów, and several days later, several hundred more Jews were seized and sent to nearby Krasnobrod.[27]

The ghettoization in Opole-Lubelski and Piaski differed from that in Zamość and Lublin in that these ghettos housed more Jews than had lived in these communities before the war. The Opole ghetto was established in March by Kreishauptmann Alfred Brandt, with at least 7,500 Jews, a majority of them refugees. The Piaski ghetto was established by Lublin-Land Kreishauptmann Emil Ziegenmeyer in two stages—a Jewish neighborhood in early 1940 and a fenced-in ghetto in June 1941. Here, too, most of the ghetto population were refugees, and the crowding was very severe.[28] The variations in conditions and ghettoization patterns in the Lublin District reflect decentralized decision-making regarding details of anti-Jewish policy, even where the general trend had some central planning.

The gradually tighter restrictions imposed on the Jews in 1941, further limiting where they could live and move, hindered their contacts with the local non-Jewish population and their access to food. These restrictions affected especially the Jews who had been concentrated in Jewish quarters or ghettos. Four types of Jewish communities developed in this period: rural, urban nonrefugee, small refugee centers, and ghettos.

In rural areas, such as Stężyce, the Jews' dispersal among small towns and villages and their employment in officially sanctioned agricultural work helped them avoid contact with Germans and keep themselves and their families fed.[29] Urban nonrefugee areas, such as Hrubieszów and Dęblin-Irena, had received relatively small numbers of refugees, and the Jews continued to live without a formal ghetto and to have limited access to local farmers and therefore to food and information.[30] Small refugee centers included small localities that had received many refugees but had not been put under a ghetto regime, such as Siedliszcze. Here, the increased numbers of Jews looking for contacts and food made contact with the local farmers somewhat more difficult. The fact that many of the refugees were not local people, including many who did not speak Polish or Ukrainian, further hindered contacts and food acquisition.

In the ghetto, such as Lublin, food access was now much more restricted. Strict food rations were imposed by the German civilian authorities in 1941. These restrictions varied according to supplies, crop yields, and the whim of the mayor, which led to widespread hunger but not starvation. Yet even under such a ghetto regime, all but one of the ghettos were open, and this situation enabled some contact to continue. Compared with Warsaw, Lublin was still a better place to be, so refugees continued to sneak into the Lublin District.[31]

IDENTIFYING THE GHETTOS

As summer 1941 progressed, with the German invasion of the Soviet Union well under way and Nazi plans for European Jewry taking shape, Generalgouvernement policy toward Jews began to change.

DEFINING THE GHETTOS • 113

On July 17, 1941, Frank told a Generalgouvernement meeting that ghetto building should be suspended because the Jews of the Generalgouvernement would soon be removed and the Generalgouvernement would serve only as a transit camp for Jews.[32] Still, as part of the developing plans for the Jews of the Reich, the Interior Department of the Generalgouvernement asked the Lublin civilian government to report on ghettos and Judensammelorte (gathering places for Jews) in the district and the availability of space for incoming Jews. This request was passed to Richard Türk, head of the BuF (Bevölkerungswesen und Fürsorge, or Population and Welfare) office in Lublin, who in turn passed the request on to the ten county chiefs and the Lublin Stadthauptmann on September 9. The county chiefs were asked to report by September 27 on three matters: all ghettos that they had established or were planning, all other Sammelorte established or planned, and estimates of Jewish population and the number of additional Jews each county could receive.[33] All but two county heads responded by the deadline, but none was interested in receiving any significant number of additional Jews.[34] The responses indicated that there were few ghettos and few planned, and that there was room for no more than approximately 2,550 additional Jews in the entire Lublin District. Kreishauptmann Hans Lenk in Janów-Lubelski was considering ghettos in seven towns, Hans Augustin was planning a ghetto in Chełm, and Otto Busse was planning ghettos or camps for Hrubieszów and Grabowiec. According to the reports from the county chiefs, there were ghettos only in Lublin and Piaski. There was a Jewish Stadtteil in Opole-Lubelski, a Judenbezirk in Biała-Podlaska, and Jewish quarters in Dęblin-Irena, Zamość, and the cities of Radzyn county. Bełżyce, Chodel, and Bychawa had Judensammelorte. In Biłgoraj county, there was no ghetto, quarter, or Sammelort, but Jews in the town of Biłgoraj were restricted to certain streets.

The Nazi nomenclature in this correspondence can be confusing. Many terms were used to refer to the way in which the Jews' housing and movement were being restricted, while the term "ghetto" was used only in reference to Lublin and Piaski. Did each term refer to a specific type of space or policy for Jews? Türk himself clearly distinguished ghettos from other types of concentrations of Jews in his September 9 letter, but it is not clear if all the county chiefs made the same distinction. Helmuth Weihenmaier, in Zamość, seems to have used the terms "quarter" and "ghetto" interchangeably in his report.

Similarly, the *Krakauer Zeitung* carried a report on May 16, 1941, on the "Judenghetto" in Opole.[35] Does this mean that all the various terms can be subsumed under the concept of a ghetto for purposes of understanding the policy? Yet Alfred Brandt clearly distinguished among terms—there were no ghettos in Puławy county, a Jewish quarter in Dęblin-Irena, and a Stadtteil, not a ghetto, in Opole.[36]

Other terms and ideas raised in some of these reports seem to deepen the confusion. Hans Augustin said he had considered turning the places in Chełm county that had many Jews into a "Judenreservat" [*sic!*], but since there was no room for more Jews, the ghetto in Chełm was postponed and the reservation dropped.[37] Emil Ziegenmeyer argued that the Piaski ghetto and the three Sammelorte in Lublin-Land county were all severely overcrowded. Remarkably, he suggested evacuating Poles from their homes as a way of clearing out space for Jews.[38] Like Ziegenmeyer, most of the county chiefs and the Lublin Stadthauptmann argued that lack of space forced them to allow significant numbers of Jews to live outside the areas set aside for Jews. In fact, in Lublin, 5,000 Jews out of 39,000 (13 percent) were reported to be living outside the ghetto in September.[39] To complicate matters further, the Germans themselves often used the term "ghetto" from early in the war to mean simply the prewar Jewish neighborhood.

Whether for lack of space (e.g., Lublin-Land) or because of the outbreak of a typhus epidemic (e.g., Zamość), the fear of an epidemic (e.g., Puławy), or simple lack of interest in ghettos (e.g., Biłgoraj), two things are clear. From the point of view of the middle echelons in the civilian government in the Lublin District, there was little use for ghettos, and there was no room for additional Jews.

One conclusion from all of the foregoing is again to reiterate the decentralization of the details of anti-Jewish policy until mid-1941. The mere need for such a survey points to the absence of central planning for ghettos, while the general disinterest in ghettos and in taking in additional Jews underscores the authority of the local officials over day-to-day Jewish affairs. Not even pressure from the Wehrmacht or pressure from Frank's office in spring 1941 to create ghettos or in late summer 1941 to desist from creating ghettos changed local authority significantly. And the confusing inconsistency in the officials' terminology suggests that certain basic concepts regarding anti-Jewish policy had not yet reached a stage of common discourse among the Germans. The word "ghetto" meant different things to different officials. The result of the lack of clarity, lack of central ghetto planning, and lack of interest in ghettos in Lublin was that the large majority of Jews in the Lublin District did not live in closed ghettos in 1941.

The Jewish testimonies from the Lublin District also have varying interpretations of ghettoization and other restrictive German policies. Jewish testimony refers to more ghettos (fourteen) than the number reflected in the German documents. Many of these ghettos are called open ghettos in the testimonies, while Biała-Podlaska is referred to alternately as an open ghetto or a Jewish neighborhood. In Tomaszów-Lubelski, the Jews were restricted to two streets in early 1940, while in Janów-Lubelski their residence was restricted to one part of town, and in Radzyn to three streets. In all three cases, Jewish testimony relates relative freedom of movement until well into 1941. In Radzyn, many of the testimonies use the term "ghetto" for the restricted residential area, whereas in Janów-Lubelski they generally do not. Testimonies on Łuków and Biłgoraj differ regarding whether there was a ghetto, while on Opole they differ on the date and whether there was a fence. By comparison, Jews from many other places clearly recalled that there was no ghetto at least as late as near the end of 1941 (e.g., Bełżyce, Hrubieszów, Międzyrzec-Podlaski).

The criteria for defining a ghetto are also not clear from the testimonies. Some relate to residence restrictions as ghettos, while others use the term to describe curfews and restrictions on freedom of movement. In places where German records refer to some form of residence restriction other than a ghetto, Jews often recalled a ghetto, such as Dęblin-Irena. Similarly, in a number of places where the German records do not refer to any kind of ghetto or concentration of the Jewish population, Jewish records refer to a ghetto, as in Włodawa and Kraśnik.

None of this is surprising, since the harsh conditions and brutality that Nazis might have considered "normal" for Jews could easily match Jewish memory of a ghetto existence. What is more surprising is the two cases—Bychawa and Chodel—in which a German Judensammelort was not recalled by the Jews as a ghetto. Large numbers of refugees had been brought to both these little towns in 1939–41, severely worsening living conditions. Yet, whereas the survivor testimonies discuss this, they do not refer to a ghetto.

In the final analysis, how many ghettos were there in the Lublin District in 1940–41, and how many of the district's Jews were living in ghettos? Bogdan Musial and this author have identified four ghettos with approximately 53,500 Jews (about 18 percent of the district's Jews). Yet was this so? This ghetto question is not one of semantics but is rather part of our effort to understand how the Jews lived during this period, what policies the German authorities pursued, and how all this can compare with other places under German rule. By what criteria do we determine if a locality had a ghetto? Which documents provide the answer: German contemporary documents—there was a ghetto only where they believed they had set up a ghetto; or Jewish memory—there was a ghetto wherever Jews felt they had been restricted in a ghetto? A cogent argument can be made for Jewish memory taking preference, since Jewish memory recalled the complexion and texture of the conditions imposed on them. Still, this may be insufficient. The Jewish and German records are not consistent with each other, nor do they have internal consistency.

Scholars, too, have not been consistent in their definitions of a ghetto. Raul Hilberg, for example, cited six characteristics of a ghetto, five of which, such as "the severance of social contacts" between Jews and the non-Jewish population, were instituted in Germany, while the sixth, the creation of separate "Jewish districts, complete with walls," he said was added in Poland and the USSR. For him, the essence of ghettoization was the Jews' isolation from the surrounding population. In Germany, a ghetto was a social-political status and state of mind, whereas in Poland, according to Hilberg's definition, a ghetto was a tightly packed run-down physical space where the Judenrat's nature had changed from forced labor provider to municipality.[40] Hilberg did not distinguish among the variety of conditions in ghettos, or between ghettos established at different times—in 1940, for temporary concentration; in spring 1941, for military security; after Operation Barbarossa, for genocide. And his criterion for the functions of the Judenrat can also be interpreted in more than one way. It could be argued that regardless of the Judenrat's functions, if Jews were not confined to a specific physical space and continued to have contact with Polish neighbors or continued to have limited access to post and telephones, their living conditions differed from those described in Hilberg's definition of a ghetto. As demonstrated, most Jews in the Lublin District continued to live outside of a ghetto at least until the end of 1941.

Yisrael Gutman said ghettos "were, in fact, camps where the Jews were held under duress, with their internal life and organization imposed on them and enforced" by the Nazi regime through violence. He differentiated between the closed ghettos in some of the large cities and those in medium-sized cities and towns, where Jews had more access to food and more freedom of movement.[41] Thus, for Gutman, a ghetto was a physical place for which duress is the basic criterion. Yet, where Jews were permitted to have contact with their neighbors and where Jewish and German sources are unclear regarding the existence of a ghetto, how shall we define it?

Residence under duress and the extent of the restrictions imposed on the Jews are certainly basic criteria for defining a ghetto, regardless of Nazi nomenclature. Regardless of what terms German officials may have used, it is the complexion of the living conditions that determined the ghetto. And our access to that complexion is largely through Jewish records and memory. A ghetto without a fence may have been an "open ghetto," in that it was a residential area imposed on the Jews. However, a community with food, contacts, and travel permits was not living in a ghetto. This does not mean that Jews who were not in a ghetto were living normal lives. The German occupation regime was vicious toward Jews. But at least until the summer of 1941, most of the Jews in the Lublin District were not living in a ghetto.

CONCLUSION

Two enduring aspects of the ghettos in the Lublin District in 1940–41 are particularly striking: the absence of closed ghettos and the concomitant relatively better living conditions for Jews in this district in comparison to other parts of the Generalgouvernement. Moreover, the German considerations regarding creating ghettos were varied. The absence of ghettos and the existence of better conditions should not be mistaken for an absence of antisemitism or lack of agreement with Nazism by the local German authorities. As the German civilians' subsequent enthusiastic and diligent cooperation with the SS in carrying out the deportations to death camps in 1942 indicates, the German civilian authorities in the Lublin District were generally very antisemitic and in full agreement with the regime's anti-Jewish policies.

Why, then, were there so few ghettos in the Lublin District? Until the run-up to the deportations in 1942, ghettos were within the jurisdiction of the civilian authorities in practice, but SS control of much of Jewish affairs meant that the SS could be the ultimate arbiter of ghetto affairs. By not establishing ghettos in the Lublin District, the civilian authorities in effect made the job of the SS more difficult and increased their own involvement in Jewish affairs. Without a ghetto, the SS would have needed increasingly to turn to the civilian authorities for data on the Jews to be able to requisition certain numbers of Jews for various SS forced labor jobs. By not keeping the Jews penned behind a ghetto wall where they could be easy prey for the SS, the civilian authorities made the SS dependent on them for the data available in the population and labor offices and for the exploitation of Jewish manpower that could be derived therefrom. The Jews, then, were more useful to the civilian authorities if there was no ghetto than if there was a ghetto. All of this was conscious local decision-making.

When restrictions on the Jews were tightened and some ghettos were created in the Lublin District in 1941, this was done in connection with German preparations for Operation Barbarossa. Local German civilian authorities' considerations determined the type of ghetto that would be created, if at all, as well as the conditions therein. The civilians employed a variety of restrictions to control the Jews, but they did not see creating ghettos as a necessary feature to achieve this control. Hence, even when ghettos were created, they could be created through dispersal of the Jews rather than concentration. That Jews were dispersed in order to create ghettos is remarkable and seems to contradict our understanding of ghettoization. Yet, when all is said and done, the absence of ghettos in the Lublin District, the dispersal of Jews to create the Lublin ghetto, and the less debilitating living conditions in this district in comparison to other parts of the Generalgouvernement did not reflect serious differences in principle among Nazi officials regarding anti-Jewish policy. The Jews' fate and chances for survival were the same regardless of the conditions—very slim indeed.

NOTES

1. Zygmunt Klukowski, *Diary from the Years of Occupation, 1939–44*, trans. from the Polish by George Klukowski (Urbana: University of Illinois Press, 1993), 132.

2. Ibid., 132–60 (quotation from 134).

3. Nachman Blumental, ed., *Documents from the Lublin Ghetto: Judenrat Without Direction* [Hebrew] (Jerusalem: Yad Vashem, 1967), Protocol 1(62), January 11, 1941, 211.

4. Bogdan Musial, *Deutsche Zivilverwaltung und Judenverfolgung im Generalgouvernement; Eine Fallstudie zum Distrikt Lublin 1939–1943* (Wiesbaden: Harrassowitz Verlag, 1999), 134.

5. Excerpts from a January 15, 1941, meeting of Georg Wilhelm Friedrich Krüger, Josef Bühler, and Hans Frank regarding deportations of Poles and Jews into the Generalgouvernement; Krüger reported on the January 8 meeting at the RSHA with Reinhard Heydrich. Excerpt from Hans Frank, *Diensttagebuch* (1941, I, 1–3), cited in Tatiana Berenstein and Artur Eisenbach, eds., *Faschismus—Getto—Massenmord; Dokumentation über Ausrottung und Widerstand der Juden in Polen während des zweiten Weltkrieges* (Berlin: Rütten und Loening und Jüdischen Historischen Institut, Warsaw, 1961), 60–61; Götz Aly, *"Final Solution": Nazi Population Policy and the Murder of the European Jews,* trans. Belinda Cooper and Allison Brown (London: Hodder Arnold, 1999), 137–39.

6. See, for example, Dieter Pohl, *Von der "Judenpolitik" zum Judenmord; Der Distrikt Lublin des Generalgouvernements 1939–1944* (Frankfurt: Peter Lang, 1993), 87. See also Simon Segal, *The New Order in Poland* (New York: Alfred A. Knopf, 1942), 61–63; Jon Evans, *The Nazi New Order in Poland* (London: Victor Gollancz, 1941), 150–51.

7. On Mława, see Friedrich Heinecke, BuF Lublin to Labor Department Lublin, December 10, 1940, Województwo Archiwum Państwowe w Lublinie (WAPL), Gouverneur des Distrikts Lublin (GDL) 891 (copy in Yad Vashem Archive [YVA], JM/2700, 10,458); unsigned testimony on Mława and Konin in "Oneg Shabbat" archive, YVA, M.10.AR.1/674; Abraham Wein, ed., *Pinkas Hakehillot: Encyclopedia of Jewish Communities, Poland, Vol. IV, Warsaw and Its Region* [Hebrew] (Jerusalem: Yad Vashem, 1989), 284. Transport lists indicate either 3,000 or 3,140 arrivals in the Lublin District from Mława. See WAPL, Rada Żydowska w Lublinie (RZ) 169 and GDL 897, 898. Embarkation lists at the train station in Łódź indicate that 3,259 were deported. Since the deportation conditions were very difficult, it is possible that 3,259 left, yet only 3,140 arrived. See Aly, *"Final Solution,"* 117, 130, n. 40–42.

On Konin, see: List of 1,001 Jews deported from Konin to Izbica, March 10, 1941, WAPL, RZ 169 and GDL 897, 898, and YVA, JM/10454; "Judenaussiedlung Transport Nr. 15/41 10-3-1941, Konin," the deportee list signed by the commandant of Lager Flottwellstrasse 4, the transit camp from whence they departed, WAPL, GDL 897, 898, and YVA, JM/1477; list of 1,000 Jews sent from Konin to Izbica, March 12, 1941, WAPL, RZ 169 and GDL 897, 898, and YVA, JM/10454. Records compiled by the Jüdische

Soziale Selbsthilfe (JSS) in the Lublin District based on Judenrat reports from each locality list 3,141 Jews from Konin, WAPL, RZ 169, and GDL 897. See also Avraham Obarzonek testimony, YVA, M.1.E/1407; Gorzków Judenrat to Marek Alten, March 28, 1941, requesting aid for refugees and local poor families, YVA, JM/1574; undated and unsigned report on Konin and Mława Jews deported to Ostrowiec and Józefów, YVA, M.10.AR.1/674.

8. The records of the Jewish deportees from Vienna show that more than 3,000 Jews were deported. See: "1. Transport von 1000 Juden am 15.2.1941," WAPL, RZ 168, and YVA, JM/1476; "Alle evakuiert aus Wien am 15-II-41 alle Wohnhaft in Opole," compiled by the Opole Judenrat, WAPL, GDL 892; "3. Transport mit 1000 Juden am 26.2.1941," WAPL, GDL 892; "Alle evakuiert aus Wien am 26-II-41 alle Wohnhaft in Opole," WAPL, GDL 892; report by the deportee leader of the second train, Transportleiters Wien to Marek Alten, February 26, 1941, WAPL, RZ 168 and GDL 892 (copy in *Faschismus,* 62–63); "4. Transport mit 1000 Juden am 5-III-41," WAPL, GDL 892, and a second embarkation list in the Lublin Judenrat's possession, WAPL, RZ 168. See also Janina Kiełboń, *Migracje Ludności w Dystrykcie Lubelskim w Latach 1939–1944* (Lublin: Towarzystwo Opieki nad Majdankiem Państwowe Muzeum na Majdanku, 1995), 139, whose estimate of 2,990 deportees is slightly low. See also Abteilung V Kreishauptmann Puławy to BuF Lublin, July 7, 1941, reporting the resettlement of 10,330 Poles in twenty-four localities in the county in June and 2,004 Jews in Opole, WAPL, GDL 153. These Jews were likely only those who had found housing in Opole in this period. A fourth, small group of 43 Jews arrived in the village of Pysznica on April 1.

9. Transportleiters Wien to Marek Alten, February 26, 1941, WAPL, RZ 168 and GDL 892 (copy in Berenstein and Eisenbach, *Faschismus,* 62–63); Marek Alten to JSS Presidium, February 28, 1941, YVA, JM/1574–1575; Zentralstelle für jüdische Auswanderung, Vienna, to Governor, Lublin District, September 18, 1941, WAPL, GDL 892, and YVA, O.53/84.

10. WAPL, GDL 891 contains name lists of Kraków Jews deported to the Lublin District, November 29–December 9, 1940; WAPL, GDL 892, and YVA, JM/10,455 contains name lists of Kraków Jews deported to the Lublin District, January 24–April 2, 1941. See also Kiełboń, *Migracje,* 139, whose estimate of 5,436 for the number of Kraków Jews deported to the Lublin District was considerably and inexplicably lower. See also Friedrich Heinecke, BuF Lublin to Labor Department, Lublin, December 10, 1940, listing the Kraków deportations to the Lublin District for November 29–December 9, 1940, and the seven central destinations, WAPL, GDL 891, and YVA, JM/2700.

11. Musial, *Zivilverwaltung,* 157–59, estimated 23,000 in all of 1940–

DEFINING THE GHETTOS • 121

41, in addition to some 10,000 unregistered refugees. See also Pohl, *Von der "Judenpolitik,"* 53.

12. Secret memo, Alfred Kipke to Eberhard Westerkamp, March 12, 1941, WAPL, GDL 153.

13. Excerpts from a meeting between Georg Wilhelm Friedrich Krüger and Hans Frank, March 25, 1941, in Werner Präg and Wolfgang Jacobmeyer, eds., *Das Diensttagebuch das deutschen Generalgouverneurs in Polen, 1939–1945* (Stuttgart: Deutsche Verlags-Anstalt, 1975), 336–38: Aly, *"Final Solution,"* 144.

14. Aly, *"Final Solution."* See also Berenstein and Eisenbach, *Faschismus,* 64; Pohl, *Von der "Judenpolitik,"* 86–87.

15. Pohl, *Von der "Judenpolitik,"* 86–87, said Frank ordered the creation of ghettos in several large towns and cities in the Generalgouvernement during a February 25–26, 1941, Generalgouvernement meeting, based on Helge Grabitz and Wolfgang Scheffler, eds., *Letzte Spuren: Ghetto Warschau, SS-Arbeitslager Trawniki, Aktion Erntefest, Fotos und Dokumente über Opfer des Endlösungswahns im Spiegel der historischen Ereignisse* (Berlin: Edition Hentrich, 1988), 283, which actually did not mention this meeting.

16. The signed and stamped travel permits can be found in WAPL, GDL 894, 895, and YVA, JM/1478, 1479, 10456, 10457. Name lists of Jews who voluntarily relocated in March, together with their destinations, can also be found in WAPL, RZ 153, and YVA, O.6/403. See also Blumental, *Documents,* Protocols 7, 8, 9 (68, 69, 70), March 16, 20, 21, 1941, 221–25; memo by Dr. Albert Ziegenhirt, March 31, 1941, on a meeting that day of Ernst Zörner, Walter Bausenhardt, Friedrich Schmidt, and himself on the "Judenaussiedlung. Sonderaktion Lublin," WAPL, GDL 892, and YVA, O.51/10, O.53/84; Judenrat announcement, YVA, JM/213/4.

17. Marek Alten, "Vermerk des Vorstandes der JSS in Krakow," March 12, 1941, in Berenstein and Eisenbach, *Faschismus,* 120–21.

18. See, for example, the letter from Erich and Clare Silbermann, deportees from Stettin who were now in Bełzyce, to Margarethe Lachmund in Berlin, on March 16, 1941, reporting the sudden arrival of hundreds of refugees from Lublin in the town and the difficulties in caring for them, in Else Rosenfeld and Gertrud Luckner, eds., *Lebenszeichen aus Piaski; Briefe Deportierter aus dem Distrikt Lublin 1940–1943* (Munich: Biederstein, 1968), 146.

19. Blumental, *Documents,* Protocol 9 (70), March 21, 1941, 224–25; Marek Alten to BuF Lublin, requesting a travel permit for Goldfarb in the district, YVA, JM/1574–1575; WAPL, GDL 894, 895, RZ 153; YVA, JM/1479, 10,457, O.6/403.

20. Marek Alten to JSS Krasnystaw, April 20, 1941, YVA, JM/1574–1575.

21. Musial, *Zivilverwaltung,* 136.

22. Ernst Zörner's ghetto order, WAPL, GDL 892; memo by Emil Ziegenhirt on his meeting that day with Walter Bausenhardt, Friedrich Schmidt, and Ernst Zörner, WAPL, GDL 892, and YVA, O.51/10, O.53/84 (copy in Berenstein and Eisenbach, *Faschismus,* 123–24).

23. Blumental, *Documents,* Protocols 16–20 (77-18), April 1, 2, 5, 10, 13, 1941, 229–34; Ernst Zörner's curfew order in YVA, JM/213/4.

24. The initial count was 33,411, but a careful recount showed a total of 34,149, and this was the final number reported on May 18. See the Judenrat's Jewish Population Office's report of May 18 as well as subsequent reports for the balance of 1941, WAPL, RZ 150, and YVA, O.6/402. The file in WAPL contains all the census records, including street-by-street breakdowns. See also the Judenrat announcement of April 22, 1941, in YVA, JM/213/4.

25. Blumental, *Documents,* Protocol 33 (94), June 14, 1941, 247–48.

26. Ernst Zörner, "Anordnung," June 27, 1941, WAPL, GDL 58, and YVA, O.6/23d and O.6/11b (old YVA file numbers); Musial, *Zivilverwaltung,* 134.

27. Mieczysław Garwin (Garfinkel) testimony in Mordechai Bernstein, ed., *Pinkas Zamość: Yizkor Book* [Yiddish] (Buenos Aires: Central Committee for Pinkas Zamość, 1957), 1126–28; Moshe Frank, *To Survive and Testify* [Hebrew] (Tel Aviv: Ghetto Fighters House and Hakibbutz Hameuhad, 1993), 34; Grzygorz Pawlowski testimony, YVA, O.3/4816; Mieczysław Garwin (Garfinkel) testimony in Wiesbaden in June and July 1962, YVA, TR.10/1146Z, XVII:3724–74.

28. Emil Ziegenmeyer to Abteilung Wirtschaft, June 11, 1941, WAPL, Kreishauptmann Lublin-Land 8 (copy in Berenstein and Eisenbach, *Faschismus,* 126–27); Aleksander Verba, "One Righteous Person in Sodom," and Yosl Goldreich and Hayaleh Goldreich, "In Ghettos and Camps," in *Opole-Lubelski Yzkor Book,* ed. David Shtokfisch [Yiddish] (Tel Aviv: Association of Opole Immigrants in Israel and the Diaspora, 1977), 68, 277. German records indicate 7,500 Jews in the ghetto, whereas other sources refer to as many as 9,000. Perhaps the additional refugees sent there in April 1941 were the basis for the latter number.

29. See, for example, Moshe Zylberszpan testimony, YVA, M.49.E/4137; Harold Werner, *Fighting Back: A Memoir of Jewish Resistance in World War II,* ed. Mark Werner (New York: Columbia University Press, 1992), 23, 28–31, 59–67.

30. See the entries on these towns and others in Abraham Wein, ed., *Pinkas Hakehillot: Encyclopedia of Jewish Communities. Poland. Vol. 7, Districts Lublin. Kielce* [Hebrew] (Jerusalem: Yad Vashem, 1999), 141, 241, and more.

DEFINING THE GHETTOS • 123

31. Musial, *Zivilverwaltung*, 160–61; testimony of Klajnman-Fradkof (YVA, O.33/1134), who recalls receiving 50 grams of bread daily (half the official ration) and 300 grams dark flour per month (less than one-tenth the official ration).

32. Frank, *Diensttagebuch*, 386; Musial, *Zivilverwaltung*, 138–39.

33. Richard Türk to county chief, "Verfügung—Judensammelorte," September 9, 1941, WAPL, GDL 270.

34. The responses came in from September 12, 1941 (Alfred Brandt, Puławy), to October 6, 1941 (Hubert Kühl, Biała-Podlaska), WAPL, GDL 270, and YVA, O.6/47-3 (old YVA file numbers), and JM/10,458. The details of the reports are taken from these sources. Both Dieter Pohl and Bogdan Musial referred to some aspect of this survey, but neither one addressed the entire correspondence and therefore could not fully assess ghettoization in 1941. See Pohl, *Von der "Judenpolitik,"* 93; Musial, *Zivilverwaltung*, 137, 222–23.

35. *Krakauer Zeitung*, May 16, 1941, 5 (Yad Vashem Library, Pfi 48).

36. Alfred Brandt, Puławy, Chef des Amtes, Lublin, September 12, 1941, WAPL, GDL 270.

37. Hans Augustin to Chef des Amtes, Lublin, September 25, 1941, WAPL, GDL 270.

38. Emil Ziegenmeyer to Chef des Amtes, Lublin, September 19, 1941, WAPL, GDL 270.

39. Ibid. Note the increase in the Jewish population since the first ghetto census on April 25, 1941. The expelled Jews were returning.

40. Raul Hilberg, *The Destruction of the European Jews*, rev. ed. (New York: Holmes and Meier, 1985), 158, 227–30.

41. Yisrael Gutman, ed., *Encyclopedia of the Holocaust* (New York: Macmillan, 1990), 579–82.

Alexander V. Prusin

Jewish Ghettos in the Generalbezirk Kiew, 1941–1943

THE FOLLOWING ESSAY AIMS TO RE-CREATE ONE OF THE LEAST KNOWN episodes of the Holocaust in the Soviet Union: the story of the Jewish ghettos in central and eastern Ukraine. In contrast to western Ukraine, where several ghettos existed until late 1943, almost all ghettos in the eastern regions were destroyed in the fall of 1941 and in the spring and summer of 1942. Consequently, their short existence combined with the dearth of primary sources—during the Soviet summer offensive of 1943, the Germans burned much of the regional documentation—make research on the topic quite difficult.

This essay focuses on the ghettoization process in the so-called Generalbezirk Kiew (GBK)—a German administrative unit carved out of the prewar Soviet Kiev and Poltava provinces (oblast').[1] Judging by available sources, such as Soviet and German wartime situation reports, war crimes trial records, and survivors' testimonies and recollections, it appears that the longevity of the ghettos in GBK depended on the will and whim of local German military and civil administration. In accordance with general Nazi guidelines, German officials in charge aimed at the total annihilation of Soviet Jews as the most dangerous racial and political foe of the Third Reich. However, the officials retained a substantial degree of independence governing ghettos, contingent on the needs of the army and the civil administration. In localities with large Jewish populations, the Germans had created the so-called labor ghettos, whose inmates were temporarily deployed to perform a variety of agricultural and construction projects. Small Jewish ghettos became death traps, serving as collection points for Jews before their final liquidation: as soon as the killing units arrived or the local administration had the necessary manpower, they carried out the murders.[2]

THE FORMATION OF THE GHETTOS IN THE SUMMER AND FALL OF 1941

Before the Soviet invasion of Poland in September 1939, Kiev oblast' was home to the largest Jewish community of the USSR—297,409 people including 224,236 in the city of Kiev. In Poltava oblast' the majority of Jews—32,740 out of 46,928—also lived in the largest urban centers of Poltava and Kremenchuh.[3] Such concentrations of Jews in towns and cities emanated from the expansion of the Soviet education system and medical facilities and the drive to industrialization in the interwar period. A high level of literacy among Jews, combined with state support for education among ethnic minorities, contributed to the fact that by the mid-1930s, Jews constituted the highest percentage of high school and college graduates, attaining positions in the Communist Party, the civil service, and the army. Accordingly, since Soviet contingency plans prioritized the evacuation of industries, state institutions, specialists, and state and party functionaries to the east, large numbers of Jews who had belonged to the aforementioned categories and their families were evacuated in the summer and early fall of 1941. In Kiev alone, about two-thirds of the Jewish population—approximately 140,000 people (of the total 335,000 evacuees)—left between July and September of 1941. Similarly, between 50 and 70 percent of the Jews in Poltava oblast' were also evacuated.[4]

In late September 1941, in the area west of the Dnieper River, the German military was replaced by a civil administration. Kiev oblast' on the west bank was named the Generalkommissariat (or Generalbezirk) Kiew and became a part of the Reichskommissariat Ukraine (RKU) headed by Erich Koch. The left bank of Kiev oblast' and the entire Poltava oblast' remained under the jurisdiction of the Rear Army Group Area South until September 1942, when it was also transferred to the RKU. In each Generalbezirk, supreme power rested in the hands of the Generalkommissar, who supervised the district chiefs—Gebietskommissars. Military commandants performed similar functions in the left-bank area. On both sides of the Dnieper River, low-level administrative posts were filled with reliable Ukrainians and Russians.[5]

The blueprint for ghettoization in the Soviet Union was the so-called Brown Folder, which defined ghettos as the means to separate Jews from the rest of the population and exclude them from social, cultural, and economic life. In early May 1941, Alfred Rosenberg, who would head the Reich Ministry of the Occupied Territories, issued the guidelines regarding the ghettoization process. Jews in the occupied territories were to be removed from all spheres of public life, concentrated in ghettos, and forced to work at road and building construction and agriculture. All Jewish property was to be registered and confiscated. After the launch of Operation Barbarossa, several additional decrees stipulated the deployment of Jewish men and women between the ages of fourteen and sixty into labor details and the supervision of the ghettos by the Jewish Councils and the Jewish police.[6] The RKU government issued similar instructions to create "Jewish living districts" in localities with more than two hundred Jews. The ghettos were to be tightly sealed off, and the inmates were prohibited from leaving the premises without a special authorization. Although on paper Jewish laborers were to be paid for their services, special taxes were levied on Jews so that all payments went back to the RKU treasury.[7]

The German military matched the initiative of its civilian counterparts. In mid-July 1941, the commander of the Rear Army Group Area South, Karl von Roques, had ordered the creation of Jewish ghettos and formation of labor details to be deployed to clean out the rubble and repair streets. Jewish communities were to pay for transportation and equipment. Jewish religious services were prohibited and religious artifacts confiscated. Further directives of the German High Command specified the racial definition of "Jew" according to the Nazi regulations, authorized the registration and labeling of the Jews, and ordered the formation of Jewish Councils.[8]

The ghettoization process began with the registration and labeling of Jews by the Ukrainian town and village councils. The councils also assisted the military in selecting ghetto sites such as stables, abandoned factories, schools or school yards, and military barracks. The size of the ghettos varied according to the Jewish population. Thus, in a large prewar Jewish enclave in Bila Tserkva (Kiev oblast'), up to 4,000 Jews from the town and vicinity were ghettoized in the former military barracks and a brick factory. In Zvenyhorodka (Kiev oblast'), the ghetto was confined to several houses in the northern part of the town, where at least 2,000 Jews from the district and Jewish refugees from western Ukraine and Belarus shared a very limited space. In the left-bank area, one of the largest ghettos was in Kremenchuh (Poltava oblast'), where about 3,000 Jews were confined to the military barracks in the suburb of Novo-Ivanivka. In contrast to the bulk of the ghettos in the GBK, the military commandant in Kremenchuh ordered the ghetto fenced, apparently as a preemptive measure against "Jewish sabotage." In Pyriatyn (Poltava oblast'), the ghetto grew by the spring of 1942 from several hundred to 1,500 Jews, while in Kobeliaky (Poltava oblast') no more than 100 older Jews were confined to the ghetto on the outskirts of the town. Since the Kobeliaky military commandant expected that the ghetto would soon be liquidated, the food rations for the ghetto inmates were drastically reduced.

That the Germans counted on the existence of the ghettos to be short-lived was attested to by the ghettos' makeshift character. Most were not fenced, and in several places, such as Myrhorod and Lokhvytsia (Poltava oblast'), Jews were allowed to live in their own houses and apartments. Some small Jewish communities of several dozen individuals were not ghettoized at all. As long as the German army needed Jewish skills, a number of blacksmiths, tailors, and shoemakers were allowed to operate outside the confined areas. Altogether, by October 1941 approximately 35,000 to 40,000 Jews were confined to twenty-eight ghettos in GBK and in the military-controlled area.[9]

Life in the ghettos was strictly regulated by numerous restrictions and prohibitions. Entering and leaving the premises without a special permit was forbidden. The Ukrainian police set up checkpoints, and those who avoided ghettoization or were apprehended outside the ghetto were shot as an example to deter others. Maintaining contact with non-Jews was also prohibited, although in the Zvenyhorodka ghetto inmates were occasionally allowed to go to the local market to buy food. The Germans appointed Jewish elders selected from the Jewish intelligentsia or religious Jews. For example, in Uman' one of the councilmen was a well-respected Dr. Rabinovich (later hanged by the Germans). In Bila Tserkva, two individuals—Samburskii and Tabachnik, appointed respectively as councilman and deputy—apparently were of far more modest social origins. These elders were to oversee the collection of valuables and furniture (in the countryside of cattle and poultry) from the ghetto inmates. In several large ghettos, the administration also ordered the formation of the Jewish police to enforce order among the inmates. Survivors from Uman' recall the policewoman Ida Teplitskaia-Shkodnik who, in an attempt to curry favor with the Germans, was especially brutal to her fellow Jews.[10]

A day in the ghetto began with the formation of labor details. Under the supervision of the Jewish Councils, all inmates, with the exception of small children, were dispatched to various work sites, depending on the needs of the German administration. In the summer and early fall of 1941, Jews in Piatyhory, Bohuslav, and Skvira (Kiev oblast') collected harvest. The need for Jewish agricultural laborers was attested to by the fact that initially they were remunerated with grain. In Chernobyl', the inmates collected metal scrap; in Ol'shany, they cleaned fuel containers and repaired roads; in Bila Tserkva, they felled trees and collected harvest; in Cherkasy and Korsun', they picked up garbage and cleaned the streets; and in Tarashcha, Makariv, and Bohuslav, they repaired roads. Some Jewish women cleaned German officers' quarters and worked as maids in German hospitals. With the beginning of winter, the ghetto inmates were deployed to clear snow from roads. In some localities, Jewish laborers received rations of flour or millet, usually between 200 and 400 grams of bread a day; nonworking family members received no more than 200 grams. Because of the German food-reduction policies and corruption among Ukrainian councilmen, most of the ghettos faced starvation by late September and early October of 1941.[11]

The threat of death was an ever-present psychological burden as the Germans used reprisals for any alleged "transgressions," such as an undelivered quota of work or the violation of curfew. For example, in Uman', where fire broke out in a German office, several Jews were publicly hanged. The conditions became especially precarious as the first cold set in. Since the ghettos had no heat or electricity and water had to be brought in from neighboring wells, those in the ghettos soon were afflicted by a wave of epidemics. Fearing the spread of diseases, the Germans allowed the Jewish medical personnel to attend the inmates in several ghettos. In Ol'shany (Kiev oblast'), a small cadre of doctors and nurses treated ghetto inmates, and in Kremenchuh, two Jewish doctors also provided services to the Ukrainian population. In the Zvenyhorodka ghetto, Dr. Starosel'skaia maintained a clinic, where she performed complicated surgeries without necessary medications and equipment. Two Jewish dentists also treated Jews and German officials.[12]

In comparison to the German military officials, who viewed the ghettos as a temporary labor source for the needs of the army, the civil administration was poised to implement Adolf Hitler's worldview to turn Ukraine into a huge German colony. In this regard, the social profile of German officials in the RKU is informative. Known as the "Ostnieten" (eastern nobodies), they were largely unemployed party hacks and low-ranking officials for whom appointments in the East were the only way for promotion and economic gratification. Since they had no special skills or qualifications outside of their party credentials, they were eager to substitute the lack of education and expertise with ideological zeal and brutality, especially with regard to the people who were marked for annihilation. Hence, they became true satraps in their domains and ruled as they pleased. Extortion was a daily routine as German officials, as well as passing military units, robbed Jews of remaining valuables, clothing, dishes, and shoes. Periodically, the administration imposed "contributions" on the ghettos, which the Jewish Councils had to deliver in a limited time. For example, in the early winter of 1941, the Bila Tserkva ghetto was "fined" 300,000 rubles.[13]

Robbery, economic exploitation, and deliberate starvation of Jews served as the tools for the ethnic "remapping" of Ukraine, and once the front line had stabilized in the late fall of 1941, the killing units returned to the localities they had "combed" during the previous summer. In Uman' in early August, the Sonderkommando 4b murdered the Jewish intelligentsia. Then, on September 21, 1941, the town newspaper, *Uman'skyi holos,* alleged that the mutilated corpses of the victims in a local prison were the "handy-work of Jewish Communists." A pogrom ensued as German soldiers and the Ukrainian police, accompanied by a local mob, entered the ghetto on a killing spree. Jewish women and children were locked up in the basement of the Pioneers' House, where many suffocated or were trampled to death. Adult Jews were rounded up and murdered in the prison. The Einsatzkommando 5, which arrived in the town shortly thereafter, complained that the pogrom disrupted the "planning" for mass executions. Miron Demb, who survived the massacre, believed that the ghetto was doomed to extinction because Jews had no more gold to pay off the German administration. On September 22 and 23, after some semblance of order was restored, the Einsatzkommando 5 and the Order Police murdered about 1,400 Uman' Jews. A group of young

Jewish women was spared and deployed to road construction, using gravestones from the Jewish cemetery.[14]

The attitudes of the Ukrainian population toward the ghettos varied from direct participation in German anti-Jewish policies to providing assistance and shelter for the Jews. All survivors and eyewitnesses stressed the deadly role of the Ukrainian police, which in many localities supervised the ghettos and imposed its own "contributions"— robbing the Jews at will. It hunted Jews who escaped or avoided ghettoization, and it participated in mass executions with or without German supervision. While the Ukrainian police were forbidden to enter the ghettos during the day, they preyed on the ghetto inhabitants at night, assaulting them and plundering their quarters. Ukrainian guards also constantly harassed and brutalized Jewish labor details. Some Ukrainians and Russians entered ghettos to sell or barter food for Jewish valuables, enriching themselves at the expense of their former neighbors. In other instances, Ukrainians moved into empty Jewish apartments knowing full well what had happened to the residents.[15] However, Jewish survivors have admitted that they managed to escape death because of the bravery and kindness of individual Ukrainians and Russians. Galina Klotsman, who posed as a Ukrainian in Pyatyhory, recalled that local Ukrainians were helpful to her, while one policeman warned the ghetto inmates of impending actions. The mayor of Kremenchuh, Synytsia Verkhovs'kyi, provided Jews with false baptism certificates and was later executed by the Germans (while he might have acted out of goodwill, German reports insinuate that Verkhovs'kyi took bribes from Jews for his services).[16]

The expedited destruction in the eastern regions of the USSR impeded the creation of any organized resistance. In contrast to Lithuania, Belarus, and East Galicia, where the traditional structure of Jewish communities contributed to the resistance, the Soviet Ukraine largely saw acts of individual defiance. Thus, in GBK, some Jews escaped from the ghettos and joined the partisans, while others avoided the registration, wandered in the countryside, concealed their ethnicity, and posed as Ukrainians or Russians.[17]

THE LIQUIDATION OF THE GHETTOS

In comparison to the Ostland (the Baltic regions and Belarus), where economic considerations forced the German civil administration to slow down the killing, there was no letup in the annihilation of Jewish populations in eastern Ukraine. Since the problems with food supplies—largely due to Soviet scorched-earth policies and German requisitions of foodstuffs—effectively put Ukrainian urban areas on the brink of starvation, the Germans reasoned that further reductions of food rations for the population would remedy the situation. As Berlin imposed high delivery quotas on the occupied territories in the fall of 1941, the German administration began rapidly reducing food rations for non-Germans, especially Jews. All incapable of work were deemed "superfluous mouths" and therefore marked for annihilation. As most of the ghettos in the GBK were deprived of any financial means, they had outlived their usefulness. Hence, both racial and economic considerations were the driving forces behind the resumption of mass murder.[18]

With the energetic assistance of the German military and civil administration, the Einsatzgruppe C and the forces of the Higher SS and Police Leader (HSSPF) Friedrich Jeckeln (Hans Prützmann since late October) continued their murderous work. Public announcements indicated that the ghetto dwellers would be "resettled" and had to have warm clothing and provisions for several days (a ruse used to pacify the fears of the victims). On September 28, 1941, after the 17th Army Command requested that anti-Jewish reprisals be carried out for the damage of cables in town, 1,600 Jews of the Kremenchuh ghetto were murdered. Between late October and the end of November, Jeckeln organized several additional killing actions, which resulted in the deaths of 8,000 Jews from the town and its environs. On November 22 and 24, the Field Commandant Office of Kremenchuh reported that the town was "almost cleansed" of Jews; two Jewish doctors were spared to service the local population. At the same time, the Sonderkommando 4b liquidated the ghetto in Poltava and turned Jewish belongings and furniture over to the Ukrainian city council for further distribution among the population. By December, the majority of Jewish males on both sides of the Dnieper River had been killed. In certain small localities, the Ukrainian police did the killing or escorted victims to the collection points for mass executions.[19]

The so-called "second sweep" in central and eastern regions of Ukraine began in the winter rather than—as generally contended by most scholars—in the spring of 1942. It can be reasoned that there was no specific instruction from Berlin to resume the annihilation, but local German officials took the initiative as soon as they had the means to do so. Again, the "Jewish question" was viewed as the core of economic and security issues. Thus, the administration anticipated that the murder of Jews would solve the food-supply problem. In addition, since Jews were allegedly fomenting resistance, their murder would nip the growing partisan movement in the bud. Indeed, in January 1942 the Einsatzgruppe C and the HSSPF reported the appearance of partisans in the left-bank area near Lubny, Poltava, Hadiach, and Zen'kiv. Hence, a large antipartisan sweep was deemed suitable, and the ghettos were liquidated because they were regarded as the hotbeds of resistance. The arrival of Hitler's personal security detail (Reichssicherheitsdienst) to the military-controlled area spurred the Germans into action. Authorized to secure the ground for Hitler's headquarters in Poltava, the unit apparently coordinated the efforts of the police and security formations to "cleanse" the region of Communists, partisans, and Jews. In January, the Order Police began a large antipartisan operation in the western part of Poltava oblast', killing Jews in the ghettos of Zen'kiv, Hadiach, Dykan'ka, and Opishnia. Military commandants often stimulated the killing, requesting that the "Jewish problem" within their jurisdiction be solved as soon as possible. Simultaneously, the killing accelerated in the RKU area. In January and February, the gendarmes and the Ukrainian police shot about five hundred Jews in Bila Tserkva, and in March, the Security Police oversaw the murder of several groups of Jewish men, women, and children.[20]

As soon as the roads cleared in the early spring, the total destruction of the ghettos began. The initiative originated with the RKU headquarters, which was determined to "remove" Jews not employed in German enterprises and constructions. On March 1, 1942, Erich Koch authorized Prützmann to take over "Jewish affairs" in the RKU. In turn, Prützmann passed the order to the chief of the Security Police and Security Service (Sipo/SD) in the RKU, Max Thomas. In April, Reinhard Heydrich visited Ukraine and, according to the testimony of the chief of Kiev Gestapo Hans Schumacher, gave Thomas final instructions to liquidate the Ukrainian Jewish population. Thomas ordered all the Sipo/SD commanders to report how many Jews were still in the areas of their jurisdiction and to begin killing.[21]

On the left bank, the final liquidation of the ghettos began on March 20, when von Roques ordered his subordinates to assist an

SD commando headed by SS-Hauptsturmführer Karl Plath in the "cleansing" of the area. Aided by the Order Police and the Ukrainian police, the commando swept through Poltava region, killing all remaining Jews except a few hundred employed by the army. Between May and August, the military repeatedly reported that the "terrain within the jurisdiction of the [Rear Army Group Area South] can be considered free of Jews."[22] On the right bank, the destruction of the ghettos corresponded to large-scale antipartisan operations in Chernihiv, Kiev, and Zhytomyr regions. Concurrently, in March and April, the gendarmerie and the Ukrainian police killed Jews in smaller ghettos. On March 17, the liquidation of the Shpola ghetto began: 800 Jews were murdered, and 500 of the younger inmates were sent to the construction camps near the town, where most perished by December 1942. The German administration also spared 13 Jewish tailors and blacksmiths who survived until 1943. The destruction of the Uman' ghetto proceeded along similar lines. On April 22, 1942, the Germans selected able-bodied inmates, who were sent to construction sites along the so-called Durchgangstrasse IV, a strategic route connecting East Galicia via Uman' to Dnipropetrivs'k. The remaining Jews were shot.[23] In Zvenyhorodka ghetto, the Germans concentrated approximately 1,500 Jews from the town and the district. In June they separated able-bodied individuals, who were sent to the Durchgangstrasse IV. Jewish craftsmen and their families were also temporarily spared until August 1943. The remaining 1,375 people were shot in the nearby meadow.[24]

Thus, by the summer of 1942, the majority of the ghettos were destroyed. Nevertheless, the German civil administration retained small Jewish enclaves and disregarded Heinrich Himmler's insistence on the total liquidation of Jews. Even his own "watchdogs"—the Security Police—employed Jewish laborers at the agricultural estate of Myshelovka near Kiev as well as in Uman', where Gebietskommissar Rudiger also maintained a small ghetto until November 1942 (some sources indicate until January 1943).[25]

Most surviving Jews were employed at the Durchgangstrasse IV. Initiated in October 1941, the Durchgangstrasse required large labor details, and for this purpose the SS deployed Soviet prisoners of war and Jews. Consequently, in the GBK, the SS transferred the survivors of the ghetto massacres to several construction camps at Buky, Smil'chentsi, Budyshchi, Dariyev, and Nemorozh. Conditions in the camps were similar to conditions in the ghettos, except that the number of inmates was much smaller and those no longer capable of working were immediately liquidated (whereas in the ghettos, the inmates were targeted for destruction as a whole). The inmates, who lived in barracks, pigsties, and stables, wore armbands with the Star of David and were prohibited from leaving the quarters. They received meager portions of millet and 200 grams of bread daily. For this, they labored fourteen hours a day uprooting tree trunks or working in sand and stone quarries. In the summer of 1943, Jews from the Nemorozh camp also helped Ukrainian agricultural workers collect and dry tobacco leaves and, in Zvenyhorodka, they harvested peas. Constantly brutalized by Ukrainian and Lithuanian guards, the camp inmates were subjected to frequent "selections," and those no longer able to work were shot. The last Jewish labor camps were liquidated in the summer of 1943.[26]

The history of the Jewish ghettos in the Generalbezirk Kiew (as well as in central and eastern Ukraine) reveals the relatively decentralized Nazi approach to the ghettoization process. The fact that the bulk of the ghettos were unfenced and lightly guarded suggests that the Germans did not plan to keep them operational for long. In fact, although the ghetto inmates served German economic interests by performing a wide variety of work, the availability of Ukrainian laborers rendered them only temporarily useful and, hence, easily eliminated. In addition, the smaller numbers of the Jewish communities in the East—in comparison to Belarus and East Galicia—made them an easy target for the killing units. Because of this, the longevity of the ghettos depended entirely on the will of the local civil or military administration, which often acted contrary to the orders from Berlin: the use of Jewish laborers at the Durchgangstrasse IV was a case in point. Nevertheless, German military and civil officials in the GBK concurred that the eventual destruction of the ghettos was absolutely necessary for the ethnic remapping of Ukraine—in accordance with Hitler's racial visions—as well as for the security of the occupied territories, where Jews were allegedly the main driving force behind the resistance. Therefore, the ghettoization process was but a short transitional stage in the "Final Solution" in eastern and central Ukraine.

NOTES

1. In 1941, most of the present-day Cherkasy oblast' was a part of Kiev oblast'. All Ukrainian localities appear in their modern spelling, except those integrated into the English language (for example, "Kiev" instead of "Kyiv").

2. For the classification of the ghettos in the USSR, see Martin Dean, "Ghettos in the Occupied Soviet Union: The Nazi 'System,'" in *The Holocaust in the Soviet Union: Symposium Presentations* (Washington, D.C.: United States Holocaust Memorial Museum [hereafter USHMM]—Center for Advanced Holocaust Studies, 2005), 40–44.

3. Iu. A. Poliakov et al., *Vsesoiuznaia perepis' naselenia 1939 goda: osnovnye itogi* (Moscow: Nauka, 1992), 69; Wila Orbach, "The Destruction of the Jews in the Nazi-Occupied Territories of the USSR," *Soviet Jewish Affairs* 6, no. 2 (1976), 41–43.

4. USHMM, Record Group (hereafter RG)-11.001M, Accession 1993.A.0085 (Osobyi Archive [Moscow] records, 1932–45 [cited as Osobyi Archive]), reel 92, l. 15; phone interview with Alexandra Erkis, August 10, 2002; phone interview with Dora Mordushenko, August 23, 2002.

5. National Archives and Records Administration (hereafter NARA), RG 238, Series M898, "Prosecution Exhibit 43 (Nuremberg Oberkommando der Wehrmacht [hereafter NOKW, or Nuremberg Armed Forces High Command] 1471)," r. 12, frame 0294; *Nimets'ko-fashys'ts'kyi okupatsiinyi rezhym na Ukraini: zbirnyk dokumentiv i materialiv* (Kiev: Derzhavne vydavnytstvo politychnoi literatury, 1963), 131–41.

6. Yitzhak Arad, "Alfred Rosenberg and the 'Final Solution' in the Occupied Soviet Territories," *Yad Vashem Studies* 13 (1979), 267, 273, 275; *Trial of the Major War Criminals Before the International Military Tribunal (IMT)* (Nuremberg: 1947), 25: 302–3.

7. Tsentral'nyi derzhavnyi arkhiv vyshchykh orhaniv vlady i upravlinnia Ukrainy (hereafter TsDAVO), fond 3206, opys 2, sprava 30, lists 13zv, 23-23 opp. site; Dieter Pohl, "Schauplatz Ukraine: Der Massenmord an den Juden im Militärverwaltungsgebiet und im Reichskommissariat 1941–1943," in *Ausbeutung, Vernichtung, Öffentlichkeit: Neue Studien zur nationalsozialistischen Lagerpolitik,* ed. Norbert Frei, Sybille Steinbacher, and Bernd C. Wagner (Munich: K. G. Saur, 2000), 158.

8. NARA, RG 242, T315, r. 2217, frame 000111; Norbert Müller, "Massenverbrechen von Wehrmachtorganen an der sowjetischen Zivilbevölkerung im Sommer/Herbst 1941," *Zeitschrift für Militärgeschichte* 8, no. 5 (1969), 548; Pohl, "Schauplatz Ukraine," 141–42.

9. Derzhavnyi arkhiv Kyivs'koi oblasti (hereafter DAKO), r-4758/2/26, ll. 5–6; r-4758/2/50, l. 35; F. D. Sverdlov, ed., *Dokumenty obviniaiut.*

Kholokost: svidetel'stva Krasnoi Armii (Moscow: Nauchno-prosvetitel'nyi tsentr "Kholokost," 1996), 51–52; Ilya Ehrenburg and Vasily Grossman, *The Complete Black Book of Russian Jewry* (New Brunswick, N.J.: Transaction Publishers, 2002), 20; Pinchas Agmon and Iosif Maliar, eds., *V ogne katastrofy (Shoa) na Ukraine: svidetel'stva yevreev-uznikov kontslagerei i getto, uchastnikov partizanskogo dvizheniia* (Kirzat-Heim, Israel: Izdatel'stvo "Beit lokhamei kha-gettaot," 1998), 151, 205.

10. USHMM, RG-31.018 "Post-War Crimes Trials Related to the Holocaust, 1937–1943" (cited as USHMM-SBU [archive of Sluzhba Bezpeky Ukrainy, or the Security Service of Ukraine]), r. 4, spr. 1747fpd, ll. 24, 32, 33–35; "V Umani. Vospominaniia Mani Faingold. 1944," in *Neizvestnaia chernaia kniga* (Jerusalem: Yad Vashem and GARF, 1993), 190–92 ; "Chto ia perezhil v fashistkom plenu," 193.

11. USHMM, RG 50.226 # 0015, interview with Galina Klotsman; RG 50.226 #0024, interview with Dmitrii Mironenko; RG-50.226 #0022, interview with Bronya Medvinskaia; USHMM-SBU, r. 3, spr. 19896, tom 3, l. 14; r. 4, spr. 1747fpd, ll. 24, 32, 33–35; Tsentral'nyi derzhavnyi arkhiv hromads'kykh orhanizatsii Ukrainy (hereafter TsDAHOU), 62/9/4, ll. 157–58; 166/3/351, ll. 1–3; 166/3/256, l. 1; 166/3/242, ll. 38–39; Derzhavnyi arkhiv Cherkas'koi oblasti (hereafter DaChO), r-51/1/20, l. 10; Grigorii Basovskii, "V etot den't nemtsy reshili unichtozhit' ves' lager'," in *Zhivymi ostalis' tol'ko my: svidetel'stva i dokumenty*, ed. Boris Zabarko (Kiev: Zadruga, 2000), 46. "V Umani," 190–92; "V mestechke Piatigory Kievskoi oblasti. Vospominaniia Raisy Zelenkovoi," in *Neizvestnaia chernaia kniga*, 167–68; "V gorode Shpola i iego okrestnostiakh. Rasskazy mestnykh zhitelei. Zapisal uchitel' Krugliak [1944 g.]," in *Neizvestnaia chernaia kniga*, 183.

12. TsDAVO, Kolektsiia materialiv i fotodocumentiv (hereafter KMF) 8/2/157, t. 1, l. 244; Agmon and Maliar, *V ogne katastrofy*, 151–53, 196–97; USHMM, RG 50.226 #0016, interview with Lubov Krasilovskaya; RG 50.226 #0032, interview of Tatyana Pit'kina (Shnaider); DAKO, 4758/2/20, l. 30; USHMM-SBU, r. 7, spr. 7250, l. 97; "V Umani," 190–92; "Chto ia perezhil v fashistkom plenu," 193.

13. TsDAVO, 3206/4/6, l. 1a; 3206/2/22, l. 34; NARA, RG 242, T-454, r. 91, frame 244–45, 947; r. 16, frame 1116; T-501, r. 5, frame 838, 846; r. 6, frame 192–95, 244, 557–58, 561–63; DAKO, r-4758/2/26, ll. 5–6; TsDAHOU, 166/3/242, l. 36; USHMM-SBU, r. 3, spr. 19896, t. 3, l. 41; Miron Demb, "Zhyvimi ostalis' tol'ko my," in *Zhyvymi ostalis' tol'ko my*, 130; "V Umani," 185, 190–92; "Chto ia perezhil v fashistkom plenu," 193.

14. NARA, RG 242, T175 (Ereignissmeldung, n. 119, October 20, 1941), r. 234, frame 976; USHMM, Osobyi Archive, r. 92, l. 16; USHMM-SBU, r. 4, spr. 1747fpd, ll. 19–20, 163; Samuil Gil', *Krov' ikh i segodnia govorit: o katastrofe i geroizme yevreev v gorodakh i mestechkakh Ukrainy* (New

JEWISH GHETTOS IN THE GENERALBEZIRK KIEW • 137

York: 1995), 131–32, 161–62; "V Umani," 185; Demb, "Zhivymi ostalis' tol'ko my," 131–37.

15. USHMM-SBU, r. 4, spr. 1747fpd, ll. 33–35; r. 5, spr. 4452, tom 2, ll. 7–24; TsDAHOU, 166/3/242, ll. 38–39; "V Umani," 190–92 ; "Chto ia perezhil v fashistkom plenu," 193.

16. NARA, RG 242, T501, r. 7, frame 000499, 000504; TsDAVO, KMF 8/2/157, t. 2, ll. 75, 238; 4620/3/236, l. 144; TsDAHOU, 62/9/4, ll. 157–58; 166/3/242, ll. 37–39; DaChO, r-51/1/20, l. 10; USHMM, RG 50.226 #0015, interview with Galina Klotsman; "V mestechke Piatigory," 179–81.

17. NARA, T175 (Ereignissmeldung UdSSR, n. 94, September 25, 1941), r. 233, frame 2722586; T501, r. 33, frame 000391; r. 349, frame 000483, 000486, 000569–000570, 000611.

18. Yitzhak Arad, "The Holocaust of Soviet Jewry in the Occupied Territories of the Soviet Union," *Yad Vashem Studies* 21 (1991), 26–27; Rolf-Dieter Müller, "The Failure of the Economic 'Blitzkrieg Strategy,'" in Horst Boog, Jurgen Forster, Joachim Hoffman, Ernst Klink, Rolf-Dieter Müller, Gerd R. Ueberschar, and Edwald Osers, *Germany and the Second World War: Volume IV: The Attack on the Soviet Union* (Oxford: Clarendon Press, 1998), 1163–64; Martin Dean, *Collaboration in the Holocaust: Crimes of the Local Police in Belorussia and Ukraine, 1941–1944* (New York: St. Martin's Press, 2000), 53; Pohl, "Schauplatz Ukraine," 160.

19. NARA, RG 242, T501, r. 33, frame 000398, 000400, 000486; DAKO, 4758/2/45, l. 8; DAPO, r-3388/1/688, ll. 6–7; TsDAVO, KMF 8/2/157, t. 1, l. 244; TsDAHOU, 166/3/242, ll. 38–39; 166/2/34, l. 1; USHMM-SBU, r. 3, spr. 19896, tom 3, ll. 107–10, 115; r. 4, spr. 56141, l. 17–18, 37–38, 52zv.; r. 5, spr. 63088, tom 2, ll. 7–9; tom 6, ll. 13–15.

20. NARA, RG 242, T-175 (Ereignissmeldung UdSSR, n. 156, January 16, 1942), r. 235, frame 2722675; T501, r. 7, frame 415, 424; USHMM, RG 48.004M (Military-Historical Institute [Prague] records, 1941–44), "Kommandostab (KdoS) des Reichsführer-Schutzstaffel (RFSS)," card 2, r. 1, frame 100899; card 3, r. 1, frame 100950, 100955; Bundesarchiv-Ludwigsburg (hereafter BAL), B162 AR(Z) 6501251, "Ermittlungsverfahren gegen die Angehörige des Polizeiregiment 'Süd,'" Bd. II, Bl. 376–77.

21. TsDAVO, 3206/2/3, ll. 12–14; 3206/2/14, ll. 5–6; KMF 8/2/175, ll. 99, 148; NARA, RG 242, r. 39, frame 000259–000261, 000267–000268; BAL, AR(Z) 6000015, "Ermittlungsverfahren gegen Robert Mohr," Bd. 1, Bl. 56; Pohl, "Schauplatz Ukraine," 162.

22. NARA, RG 238, M898, Prosecution Exhibit 1320 (NOKW 2909), r. 23, frame 1009; RG 242, T175 (Meldung, n. 191, April 10, 1942), r. 235, frame 2724193; RG 242, T501, r. 33, frame 617; r. 349, frame 000107, 000179; r. 7, frame 000429, 000643, 000650, 000880; r. 33, frame

000643; BAL, AR 6502359, "Ermittlungsverfahren gegen die Angehörige der Sk. Plath," Bd. V, Bl. 4274; DAPO, r-1876/8/104, l. 5; r-1876/8/98, l. 1; r-3388/1/1086, l. 1; TsDAHOU, 166/3/242, ll. 1–2, 4–5; TsDAVO, KMF-8/2/157a, l. 392; KMF-8/2/175, t. 1, l. 100, t. 2, l. 212; KMF-8/2/157, t. 2, l. 222; KMF-8/2/195, l. 69.

23. USHMM-SBU, r. 4, spr. 1747fpd, ll. 15–17, 21; TsDAHOU, 1/22/269, tom 1, l. 118; 166/3/351, l. 3; 7021/65/241, ll. 46, 87–88; TsDAVO, 3676/4/317, l. 7; Ehrenburg and Grossman, *The Complete Black Book*, 25–26; "V gorode Shpola," 183; Gil', *Krov' ikh i segodnia govorit*, 163–64.

24. Interview with Fania Shubinskaia (Sapozhnikova), in *Zhyvymi ostalis' tol'ko my*, 522–23; Agmon and Maliar, *V ogne katastrofy*, 209; testimony of T. E. Shnaider (Pipkina), in Iu. M. Liakhovitskii, *Perezhivshie katastrofu: spasshiesia, spasiteli, kollaboranty, martirolog, svidetel'stva, fakty, dokumenty* (Khar'kov-Jerusalem: Biblioteka gazety "Bensiakh," 1996), 139; testimony of Grigorii Basovskii, in *Zhivymi ostalis' tol'ko my*, 46–47.

25. BAL, AR(Z) 6000015, "Ermittlungsverfahren gegen Robert Mohr," Bd. 1, Bl. 131; Dokumentensammlung Verschiedenes, Bd. 70, 152–54; AR(Z) 5800021, Ermittlungsverfahren gegen Erich Ehrlinger u.a., Bd. 3, Bl. 1849–1857; Bd. 3a, Bl. 1871–73, 1887, 1895, 1899; Bd. 5, Bl. 3175; Bd. 12, Bl. 384, 388–89; Handakte III, Bl. 1–3; AR(Z) 6300020, "Ermittlungsverfahren gegen die Angehörige des Einsatzstabes 'Durchgangstrasse IV,'" Bd. 5, Bl. 118; Bd. 6, Bl. 464.

26. TsDAVO, 3206/2/164, l. 49; DAKO, 4758/2/20, l. 30; BAL, AR(Z) 6300020, "Ermittlungsverfahren gegen die Angehörige des Einsatzstabes 'Durchgangstrasse IV,'" Bd. 4, Bl. 73; Bd. 5, Bl. 118; Bd. 7, Bl. 138; Bd. 9, Bl. 1709; Bd. 12, Bl. 1969; Bd. 16, Bl. 2816–2817; Bd. 18, Bl. 3259–3275; USHMM, RG-50.226 # 0015, interview with Galina Klotsman; RG-50.226.0032, interview with Tatyana Pit'kina (Shnaider); RG-50.226 # 0016, interview with Ljubov' Krasilovskaia; Agmon and Maliar, *V ogne katastrofy*, 15–21, 156–60; "Fania Shubinskaia (Sapozhnikova) (1926 g.)," in *Zhyvymi ostalis' tol'ko my*, 522–23; Basovskii, "V etot den't nemtsy reshili unichtozhit' ves' lager'," 46–47; "V mestechke Piatigory," 170–71; "V gorode Shpola," 183–84; Agmon and Maliar, *V ogne katastrofy*, 15–21, 156–60, 198–99, 206–11.

Rachel Iskov

Jewish Refugees from the Surrounding Communities in the Warsaw and Łódź Ghettos

THE JEWISH INHABITANTS OF TOWNS AND VILLAGES IN THE VICINITY of Łódź and Warsaw suffered a rupture in their lives when they received deportation orders to the central ghettos in those cities. Along with their former lives in the provincial ghettos, they left behind most, if not all, of their possessions. Deportation selections also tore families apart. These Jews arrived to the central ghettos as impoverished remnants of families. The ghettos were unable to meet the needs of the new arrivals: the extra mouths to feed and bodies to shelter exacerbated the already devastating hunger and overcrowding that Jews suffered in both ghettos. The refugees found it difficult to establish themselves, and they struggled to adapt to life in the new ghettos. The experiences of the refugees and their relations with local Jews in the Łódź and Warsaw ghettos also provide insights into historiographical questions about ghetto life and Holocaust studies: "who knew what, when, and how?" and "gray zones."

In this essay, I examine the provincial Jews; I will not be discussing the "western" Jews deported into the Łódź and Warsaw ghettos from greater Nazi Germany. Those Jews faced a different set of challenges than the refugees from provincial ghettos. They were culturally and linguistically different from the "eastern" Jews of Poland. They had greater difficulty adapting to ghetto life. Describing western Jews deported into the Łódź ghetto, Holocaust scholar Hanno Loewy has explained that "without the possibility of becoming gradually accustomed to the privations and the heavy physical work, and forced into the role of pariahs among pariahs in the ghetto, the Jews from the West succumbed with frightening speed to hunger and disease."[1]

A couple of differences were notable between the circumstances for refugees in the Łódź and Warsaw ghettos. First, the size of the refugee population in Warsaw was considerably larger. By April 1941, one out of every three Jews in that ghetto was a refugee.[2] This number included evacuees that fled to Warsaw at the beginning of the war. The Jewish community in Warsaw established refugee shelters much earlier than was necessary in Łódź.

Conditions in the refugee shelters were terrible in both ghettos, but in Warsaw, they were more desperate. Pervasive hunger and epidemics caused mortality rates in the shelters to soar. According to eminent Holocaust historian Isaiah Trunk, a growth in the typhus epidemic in the Łódź ghetto in June 1942 was attributable to Jews deported from nearby towns, among whom some were infected with typhus. The epidemic did not spread into the ghetto, he has explained, because of preventive measures taken by the Health Department.[3] The spread of typhus was more extensive in Warsaw than in Łódź. Trunk has accounted for this disparity by noting that the refugee shelters in the Warsaw ghetto "became nests for the spread of typhus."[4] This was despite the "superhuman efforts" of the doctors, who, as an anonymous Warsaw ghetto diarist noted, made daily rounds of assigned buildings, worked long hours in hospitals, struggled to obtain soap rations and disinfectants, and lectured on hygiene.[5]

Beginning in the winter of 1941, soon after the Warsaw ghetto was sealed, tens of thousands of refugees were deported into the ghetto from towns and villages in the vicinity. Deportations continued in waves until July 1942, that is, just before the great deportation action in the Warsaw ghetto. Deportations into Łódź from the provincial ghettos began in September 1941 and continued until August 1942. In sum, close to twenty thousand Jews were "resettled" to the Łódź ghetto. Some of these refugees were selected again for deportation soon after their arrival and were shipped to work or death camps.

Refugees in the Łódź and Warsaw ghettos experienced similar hardships from the moment they received their deportation orders, despite differences in the circumstances and conditions. Whether or not the refugees arrived with their family and possessions, from their selection and transportation to the new ghetto to the conditions of the shelter to which they were assigned, including hunger, disease, and overcrowding, and their ability to adapt to the new ghetto, the refugees suffered under their new and tragic circumstances.

In the course of my research, I interviewed a Holocaust survivor who was deported with his mother from the Brzeziny ghetto to the Łódź ghetto in May 1942. His testimony provides important insights about the "resettlement" experience, and I will quote excerpts from his testimony throughout this essay. I interviewed George Fox in the summer of 2006 in Toronto, Canada. He was born in Brzeziny on February 13, 1916, to Isaac and Rebecca, and had two older brothers, Max and Samuel, and a twin sister, Chana. He grew up in Brzeziny and Chemnitz, Germany, and completed Gymnasium in Brzeziny. Before the war, Fox worked as an office clerk, and he was called to the Polish army in 1939. He was wounded during the war and sent to a military hospital in Lublin, from which he escaped. He returned to Brzeziny and he and his family lived in the Brzeziny ghetto until May 17, 1942, when it was liquidated.

RESETTLEMENT

The Jews experienced terrifying and tragic events during the deportation actions to the Warsaw and Łódź ghettos. Deportations to Łódź included a selection, where families were torn apart, as "productive" Jews were divided from family members who could not work due to their age or physical condition. These selections forcibly separated children from their parents, husbands from wives, and sisters from brothers. Families were divided for transport to work camps, to the central ghetto, and to their deaths. In his postwar testimony, Moniek Kaufman notes a poignant moment for him during the liquidation action in the Bełchatów ghetto: the German authorities had gathered all the Jews into the courtyard of the synagogue and, as a worker with an identity card, Moniek had been selected for life in the Łódź ghetto. He was looking around for his family, when suddenly, his mother's gaze caught his, and she "picked up a little child, my six-year-old little brother, who from far away, said good-bye to me, waving his little hand. Unfortunately," he remarked, "it was a farewell forever."[6]

George Fox described the murderous events of the liquidation action that tore families apart in the Brzeziny ghetto:

> Two days before the ghetto was liquidated, on the fifteenth of May [1942], they called all mothers who had children from one minute to ten years old, that they have to come to this-and-this Marysin

place. They took us young people, maybe forty young people, to help these mothers to the trucks, from the trucks. We came over there. We had to take away the children from the mothers, deliver them to the trains. . . . I witnessed by myself in that same night, they took three little babies. In my opinion, one baby was about six months old, the other maybe nine months old; boys. The third one was maybe a year old. They took them by their little legs, the little babies, and threw them with their heads against the iron doors from the trains so the brains spread out right there. And those mothers who had been screaming and crying loudly were shot right on the spot. And after that, they sent us back to the ghetto. . . . [S]ix hundred children [were] killed at that time, [taken] away from us. Nobody came back.[7]

His graphic depiction could very well describe the liquidation actions in other ghettos. An account of a selection in the Pabianice ghetto on May 16, 1942, for example, records that "shocking scenes were played out there."[8] The entry describes the brutal separation of children from parents and the resulting panic that ensued. During such actions, the elderly and the sick were also selected for deportation to the "unknown," which today we know was the killing center at Chełmno. The remainder of the population—that is, Jews with work cards—was deported to work camps or the central ghetto.

Unlike the case of "resettlement" actions to the Łódź ghetto, Jews deported to the Warsaw ghetto from neighboring towns traveled as complete or near-complete families, especially before 1942. Some of these communities suffered more than one deportation order. Ten-year-old Regina Geszyt and her family, for example, were forcibly resettled first from Stryków to Głowno to Łowicz in February 1940. During that deportation action, they were robbed of their possessions by the German authorities and their rapacious neighbors, who "carried away everything they liked, before our eyes." They were later deported to the Warsaw ghetto when the Łowicz ghetto was liquidated.[9]

LEAVING THEIR GHETTO

With the deportation order and the selection, another horrific ordeal began for the Jews. Though circumstances varied across the provincial ghettos, in most cases Jews were given short notice of their imminent departure. They hastened to pack for their journey. Most refugees were permitted to travel with only a few possessions. George Fox explained, "We had only our belongings, which was nothing and nothing, just a little clothing because we couldn't take a bed, we couldn't take anything into another city."[10] In Kalisz, Gestapo agents informed the Jews in their workplaces that they would have to leave the ghetto within the hour: "Everyone went back to their apartments and, under the eyes of the police, began to pack their belongings in feverish haste."[11] They had to part with these last possessions when leaving Kalisz and received empty promises from the German authorities that their baggage would follow.

Moniek Kaufman described the deportation action in the outskirts of Bełchatów in the early morning hours of August 11, 1942, when the Bełchatów ghetto was liquidated. These Jews were rounded up at night, Moniek explained, because the Germans feared they would escape or hide if the action began in the city center. The Germans "cleared one Jewish apartment after another, and they drove those present half-naked to the courtyard of the synagogue."[12] In the Bełchatów ghetto as well, the Jews were given no warning and no opportunity to put together a few of their belongings.

Many Jews arrived to the ghettos with only the clothing they were wearing, either because they were seized from their homes or places of work or they lost their baggage to pilfering guards along the way. The liquidation of the provincial ghettos completed the pauperization of the Jews from the small communities, as Nazis had ordered they leave their ghetto homes and abandon their few remaining possessions. Moreover, the Jewish communities in the central ghettos appropriated for general distribution the food and coal the refugees had brought. The new arrivals thus became dependent on the generosity of their new ghetto. The Jewish community and self-help organizations in the ghettos provided some assistance to these Jews, including shelter and a modicum of food. Nevertheless, these Jews were among the most disadvantaged and vulnerable in the Łódź and Warsaw ghettos.

THE JOURNEY TO THE CENTRAL GHETTOS

The deported Jews experienced harrowing journeys on foot or by truck or wagon to the Łódź and Warsaw ghettos. They suffered fear and anxiety about their destinations and those of their relatives, and mourned the loss of family members, their ghetto homes, and familiar domestic life. They also endured unhealthy conditions and loss of dignity on overcrowded vehicles or abuse and the threat of death for straggling walkers. George Fox described his journey on foot from the Brzeziny ghetto:

> Going there, what I witnessed with my eyes—three people they killed. Two men and one woman [were] shot. And one man was a little heavy size . . . so he couldn't walk so fast . . . and he was going slower and slower, he was [falling] behind. So I just turned around, [and] they took this man and put him in over there, and he died over there. I didn't see how he died, because we had to go and not look back.[13]

The deported provincial Jews suffered brutal treatment unfamiliar to most during their journey. Szlama Jakubowicz was ten years old when the Germans began rounding up the Jews in Sochaczew for deportation to the Warsaw ghetto in February 1941. The German authorities there gave the Jews two options: go voluntarily or wait for the transport to take them forcibly. His family chose to go voluntarily, and when his mother cried, Szlama told her "if the Germans come, they will beat us."[14]

While families in some communities had previously experienced forced resettlement, and many had experienced the loss of home and property to "Aryanization" as well as the loss of loved ones to deportation and death, most Jews were subjected to new forms of dehumanization during the deportation actions. At the end of their traumatizing and terrorizing transports, they faced yet another tragedy: life in the Łódź and Warsaw ghettos.

ADAPTING TO LIFE IN THE NEW GHETTO

The situation of the deportees continued to deteriorate after their arrival. I asked George Fox about his introduction to life in the Łódź ghetto. He explained that conditions were worse in Łódź than in Brzeziny. Hunger in Brzeziny was bad, he told me, but it did not compare to Łódź.

> The first soup [in the Łódźer ghetto], very truthfully, I'm admitting it: When I received my first soup, it was red beets in hot water. Not even cooked. So I tasted it [*he makes a disgusted face*] and I spilled it out on the street. The people around me—the Jewish people—

they were willing to kill me! And I didn't realize why! They said, "The first of all, you can sell it, we will pay you for it, and the second, this is your nutrition." I woke up. I was thinking of Brzeziny. We had a little potato, we had a little vegetable, and here we got nothing anymore, just this dirt. . . . But on the second day, I ate it; this was very tasty already![15]

Refugees suffered severe hunger and faced mass starvation alongside the local populations. They also shared the common experience of living in overcrowded conditions, because their arrival exacerbated the endemic housing shortage in the ghettos. In both ghettos, the Jewish Councils sought to place the new arrivals in their own rooms soon after their arrival. George Fox said he and his mother were assigned one room on the day they arrived. Not all refugees were so fortunate, especially in the Warsaw ghetto, where deportees languished in refugee shelters.

These refugee shelters were appallingly overcrowded. According to the anonymous woman who kept a diary in the Warsaw ghetto, they "housed masses of people who had been deprived of their homes," some with several dozens of people living in a room.[16] The shelters did not provide adequate housing for the newcomers: many were without beds, running water, and heat. Describing the terrible conditions in the Warsaw ghetto shelter to which his family was assigned, Chil Brajtman complained that there were no windowpanes: "The frost plagued, the soup froze in the bowl."[17] Brajtman wrote his testimony as part of an Oyneg Shabes pedagogical project at a children's institution in the Warsaw ghetto. In brief reports recorded in March and April 1942, they wrote about hunger and the terrible conditions in the shelters. They also described their parents' efforts to find work. Refugee families found it difficult to establish themselves in the already oversaturated job markets. Often, the work they found was undesirable, involving heavy labor or health risks. Dawid Jakubowicz, who was deported from Kowale Pańskie to the Łódź ghetto on July 20, 1941, found work at the Radegast station, loading the trains. "People died like flies from the hard work and the lack of food," he explained. And they were maltreated by their overseer: four people were assigned to carry twenty kilograms of coal within four hours, and if the work wasn't finished the overseer whipped them.[18]

Even after a deportee found a job, the family continued to suffer from hunger and the ghetto conditions. George Fox noted that he had several jobs in various workshops in the Łódź ghetto. Despite his labors, he did not receive enough food to sate his hunger, and he worried, too, about his sick mother, who could not work. Sara Widawska, who was deported with her family to the Warsaw ghetto from Łowicz, wrote in her Oyneg Shabes report that her father could not get a job. Her mother worked as a cleaning lady, but they still struggled. Sara explained:

> In December 1941 . . . my father was swollen with hunger, lay down in bed, and when he got up once, to go to an acquaintance for help, he fell on the street and died. Mommy lost her job, because she had less and less strength. She died of hunger four weeks after my father.[19]

Like Sara's parents, many of the new arrivals died of hunger in the shelters. The German administrations did not allocate additional food for the refugees, so the paltry ration supply for the ghetto populations was divided among more mouths. Hunger was a significant theme running through the Oyneg Shabes testimonies by the orphaned children. They described, as well, various efforts they made to acquire additional food for themselves and their families. Bajla Grinberg wrote that days would go by when she did not eat at all. She began to beg, and she explained, "I was often ashamed, but hunger nagged."[20] Some Jews sold or traded the few possessions they brought with them to the ghetto, for additional food. Still others stole, in an attempt to survive and help their family members.

In his interview, George Fox told me that he went out at night to steal a piece of coal and, if he could, a piece of food. He wanted to help his mother, who was sick and swollen from hunger edema. He related a story of what happened when he stole from a bakery in the Łódź ghetto in September 1942: "I stole a little flour and put it in my pocket. You can realize how much I could have taken, how much this is. But unfortunately, the Jewish police [caught] me and they sentenced me to six months in prison in Łódźer ghetto." I was astounded when he told me he continued to steal in prison. He explained:

> I had to do it. When you're hungry, you have to steal. If they kill me, they kill me. What difference does it make? I'm not ashamed to say it. . . . I was pretty smart, privileged and lucky they didn't catch me. Otherwise they would kill me. I was even able to help my

mother. She came to the fence and I threw over some little pieces of bread, a couple tomatoes every day. . . . I made a little hole in the backyard over there, covered it up at nighttime. Every morning she came and picked it up. I helped my mother how much I could.[21]

I asked him whether he stole in Brzeziny. "No, no," he replied, "only in Łódź." Could he account for this difference? I asked. He explained that in the Łódź ghetto, the circumstances were more dire, the hunger more desperate. And yet, I know hunger was severe in Brzeziny, too. His twin sister and his grandmother both died of starvation in Brzeziny. His mother was healthier in Brzeziny; she was still able to work. In Łódź, she was weak and ill. He shared even the smallest bit of food with her. He told me: "I had nothing to spare for my mother, I still gave her a little tiny piece. She didn't want to take. I said you have to take."[22]

GRAY ZONES

When I asked George Fox about relations between local Jews and refugees, he spoke about ghetto social hierarchy and nepotism: "Well, you have a little privilege, if you know some people, [who] live in some different apartments, they took you in; [who worked in] the food, [in] the kitchen, so you got a break off of them. If not, you worked, like a dirty worker."[23] When I heard this, I thought immediately of Starachowice.

In his analysis of survivor testimonies of that labor camp, Christopher Browning has found that the survivors were very critical of the Jewish camp elite in Starachowice. Most of the camp officials came from four important families of the prewar Jewish community, Browning has noted, and the Jews who were the most disenchanted with them were latecomers to the camp from outside Starachowice. They protested the inequality and theft they witnessed, and suffered worse discrimination in response.[24] Browning referred to Primo Levi's concept of the gray zone to introduce his analysis of Jewish inmate relations within the camp.

I also invoke the term "gray zone" to explain the complexity of relationships within the ghettos. There have been many critiques—and many criticisms—of ghetto Jewish Councils. Yet George Fox's observations about nepotism in the Łódź ghetto remind us of the importance of the gray zone for survival strategies and even daily life in the ghettos. Fox struggled with the fact of ambiguous behavior in the ghetto. On more than one occasion, he began to talk about the Jewish Council and, in particular, its president, Chaim Rumkowski. He stopped himself mid-sentence repeatedly, commenting that he did not want to talk about the "bad things" they did. He was uncomfortable speaking about gray zones of Jewish behavior during the war, he explained, because he worried that including negative stories about Jews might spur antisemitism. His unspoken testimony nevertheless draws attention to questions about use and misuse of authority and to relationships between local Jews and refugees in the ghettos.

Impressions of these refugees among the local community were mixed: some were sympathetic to the new arrivals, observing their tragic circumstances. The anonymous Warsaw ghetto diarist, for example, recorded that these Jews were "shipped from outside the city without any possessions or means of support" and relied on local welfare initiatives. "But what kind of life was it," she asked, "with no food, no hope for tomorrow, no energy to go on living?"[25] Others were less understanding, such as Marek Stok, who wrote his testimony while hiding in Warsaw in early 1944. He noted the overcrowding in the ghetto, which was exacerbated by the arrival of refugees. "These masses of people are put up in puny, communal shelters," he wrote. "The filth in these places is horrendous."[26]

Majer Rokitowicz, who was from Łódź, was highly critical of the Jews deported into the Łódź ghetto. He commented on the few privileged newcomers, who exploited the ghetto's poorest by bribing them to take their deportation slips. He noted one provincial Jew who thus saved himself because he had an acquaintance in the Jewish Council, and concluded, "Many Łódźers went, who fell victim [to] foreign Jews."[27] Most local Jews, however, were apathetic to the suffering of the refugees, as they focused on their own struggle for survival. As for the affluent minority in the ghetto, historian Emmanuel Ringelblum noted in his Warsaw ghetto diary that they refused to support refugees, because, as they said, "That won't help; the paupers will die out, anyway."[28]

WHO KNEW WHAT, WHEN, AND HOW

A significant implication of the arrival of the refugees for the local population was the change of mood in the ghettos. The remnants of the provincial ghettos agonized over the fate of family members torn from them and told ominous stories about selections and deportations to the unknown, evoking fear in the local Jews. After the Jews from Pabianice were deported into the Łódź ghetto, the Łódź ghetto chroniclers reported on May 18, 1942, that it was "terrible to see these desperate, lamenting women and men, wringing their hands, from which those nearest and dearest to them had been rudely torn."[29] Two days later, they observed that the arrival of these Jews had a "depressing effect" on the ghetto: "It is no surprise that anyone with small children or old parents awaits the days to come with trepidation."[30]

The refugees did not know where their children and other family members were sent, and asked "where?" fearing they would not see their loved ones again. This questioning, as well as the question "when?" posed by apprehensive Łódźer Jews about their own children, offers insights into the historiographical question "who knew what, when, and how?"

Isaiah Trunk has argued, "From the accounts of the remnants of the liquidated provincial ghettos that were sent to the Łódź Ghetto in May 1942, people knew clearly where the deportees were ending up."[31] Although this statement is true for the Warsaw ghetto, whose inhabitants had better access to information about deportations and the world beyond the ghetto walls, I cannot agree for the Łódź ghetto. I can confidently state that the deportation of refugees into the Łódź ghetto from the liquidated ghettos in 1942 compounded suspicions about the destination of waves of deportations from the Łódź ghetto. For the Jews of the Łódź ghetto, cut off as they were from the outside world, whose "information" came from such capricious sources as the overactive rumor mill and Nazi propaganda, the refugees entering the ghetto played a significant role in clarifying the meaning of the deportations to the "unknown."

The arrival of the refugees deported from the provincial ghettos sent shock waves though the Łódź and Warsaw ghettos. In addition to the fear of deportation instilled in the hearts of the local Jews, this arrival severely worsened ghetto conditions, including hunger, overcrowding, and the epidemics. With time, however, refugees from neighboring towns and villages who were deported into the Łódź and Warsaw ghettos and who did not perish in the refugee shelters integrated themselves into the larger ghetto population. Like the local Jews who were their neighbors in the ghettos, they worked and lived under inhumane conditions and were susceptible to hunger and disease, deportations, and death. As George Fox told me when he was explaining relations between the new arrivals and the local population in the Łódź ghetto, "They accepted us, and they said, 'Don't worry, you'll die, too.'"[32]

NOTES

1. Oskar Rosenfeld, *In the Beginning Was the Ghetto: Notebooks from Łódź,* ed. Hanno Loewy (Evanston, Ill.: Northwestern University Press, 2002), xxv. I am focusing here only on the Jews deported from the provincial ghettos, a less researched group perhaps because those who were not deported out of the ghetto soon after their arrival were absorbed into the ghetto populations.

2. Yisrael Gutman, *The Jews of Warsaw, 1939–1943: Ghetto, Underground, Revolt* (Bloomington: Indiana University Press, 1982), 63.

3. Isaiah Trunk, *Łódź Ghetto: A History,* trans. and ed. Robert Moses Shapiro (Bloomington: Indiana University Press, 2006), 203.

4. Ibid., 205.

5. Michał Grynberg, ed., *Words to Outlive Us: Eyewitness Accounts from the Warsaw Ghetto* (New York: Metropolitan Books, 2002), 41.

6. Żydowski Institut Historyczny (hereafter ŻIH), *Holocaust Survivor Testimonies,* Record Group (hereafter RG) 301, "Moniek Kaufman," number 1413, 17. My translation from the original Polish.

7. Interview with George Fox, Toronto, Ontario, Canada, July 12, 2006.

8. Lucjan Dobroszycki, ed., *The Chronicle of the Łódź Ghetto, 1941–1944* (New Haven, Conn.: Yale University Press, 1984), 178–79.

9. ŻIH, *Holocaust Survivor Testimonies,* RG 301, "Regina Geszyt," number 3678, 3–4. My translation from the original Polish.

10. Interview with George Fox, Toronto, Ontario, Canada, July 12, 2006.

11. Dobroszycki, *The Chronicle of the Łódź Ghetto,* 221.

12. "Moniek Kaufman," 15. My translation from the original Polish.

13. Interview with George Fox, Toronto, Ontario, Canada, July 12, 2006.

14. ŻIH, *Holocaust Survivor Testimonies,* RG 301, "Szlama Jakubowicz," number 2427, 6. My translation from the original Polish.

15. Interview with George Fox, Toronto, Ontario, Canada, July 12 and September 5, 2006.

16. Grynberg, *Words to Outlive Us,* 41.

17. Ruta Sakowska, ed., *Archiwum Ringelbluma: Konspiracyjna Archiwum Getta Warszawy tom 2: Dzieci—tajni nauczanie w getcie warszawskim* (Warsaw: ŻIH IN-B, 2000), 47. My translation from the original Polish.

18. ŻIH, *Holocaust Survivor Testimonies,* RG 301, "Dawid Jakubowicz," number 2243, 3. My translation from the original Polish.

19. Sakowska, *Archiwum,* 47–48. My translation from the original Polish.

20. Ibid., 49. My translation from the original Polish.

21. Interview with George Fox, Toronto, Ontario, Canada, July 12, 2006.

22. Interview with George Fox, Toronto, Ontario, Canada, September 5, 2006.

23. Ibid.

24. Christopher Browning, *Nazi Policy, Jewish Workers, German Killers* (Cambridge: Cambridge University Press, 2000), 103–5.

25. Grynberg, *Words to Outlive Us,* 41.

26. Ibid., 37.

27. ŻIH, *Holocaust Survivor Testimonies,* RG 301, "Majer Rokitowicz," number 869, 3. My translation from the original Yiddish.

28. Jacob Sloan, ed., *Notes from the Warsaw Ghetto: The Journal of Emmanuel Ringelblum* (New York: Schocken Books, 1974), 156.

29. Dobroszycki, *The Chronicle of the Łódź Ghetto,* 181.

30. Ibid.

31. Trunk, *Łódź Ghetto: A History,* 233.

32. Interview with George Fox, Toronto, Ontario, Canada, September 5, 2006.

Tim Cole

Contesting and Compromising Ghettoization, Hungary 1944

IN A GROUNDBREAKING ARTICLE FIRST PUBLISHED MORE THAN twenty years ago, Christopher Browning pointed to the importance of "local initiative" in Nazi ghettoization policy in occupied Poland. Rejecting the approaches adopted by those engaged in the then dominant "functionalist" versus "intentionalist" debate, Browning argued that "[g]hettoization was in fact carried out at different times in different ways for different reasons on the initiative of local authorities."[1] Because ghettos were planned, implemented, and managed locally, they looked different in different places, as Browning's study of the Łódź and Warsaw ghettos in 1940–41 revealed. Looking through to the final year of the war, it is striking how ghettos in another country, Hungary, continued to be shaped in the locality and therefore to vary from each other in significant ways. That ghettos differed begs the questions how and why.

In this essay, in which I examine the planning and implementation of three rather different ghettos in three Hungarian towns and cities in 1944, I highlight the importance of local debates—involving local officials, the press, and "ordinary Hungarians"—over where ghettos were to be established and the form ghettoization was to take. What to do with local "Jews"[2] was not something that was simply an external decision implemented in the locality but was rather the subject of vigorous local debate. The importance of local factors owed much to the political context within which ghettoization was enacted in Hungary. As is well known, the elements of the Holocaust were rapidly implemented in Hungary in the aftermath of the Nazi German occupation on March 19, 1944.[3] Jews were marked with a yellow

CONTESTING AND COMPROMISING GHETTOIZATION • 153

star, and ghettos were established in the larger towns and cities from April 1944 onward. From May 15, mass deportations of Hungarian Jews commenced and over the following eight weeks, some 437,402 Jews were deported, the vast majority to Auschwitz-Birkenau.[4] All of this took place in a country where decision-making still took place within established political structures of national, regional, and local government. There had been personnel changes in key positions, most significantly perhaps within the cabinet and the Interior Ministry, but there were also significant political continuities, especially within localities.[5]

A caveat is in order here. The three towns and cities that I examine differed from those places where ghettoization and subsequent deportation were carried out particularly swiftly. There was an even greater telescoping of the timescale for implementing ghettoization and deportation in towns and cities in Carpatho-Ruthenia and other parts of northeastern Hungary. In those areas, plans for ghettoization were carried out within a matter of days in late April 1944, before ghettoization legislation was enacted nationally at the end of April. Earlier in the month, a secret ghetto order had been issued by one of the new secretaries of state in the Interior Ministry, László Baky, which formed the basis for the rapid implementation of ghettoization in towns and cities in the military operational zone. It was not only ghettoization that was rapidly carried out in this part of Hungary. On May 15, 1944, deportations from Carpatho-Ruthenia also commenced.[6]

Although ghettoization and deportation took place relatively rapidly elsewhere in Hungary—certainly when compared with other countries—they did not proceed at quite the same degree of speed in southern and western Hungary. There, ghettoization was planned and implemented within the framework of national legislation being enacted at the local level, and both more time and space were available for the contesting of ghetto plans. In the places I examine in this essay, ghettoization was discussed and enacted on the basis of the April 28, 1944, national legislation that empowered local mayors or their equivalents to designate buildings for Jewish residential use.[7] In Szeged, a large university city in the south of the country, the ghetto was announced on May 17; in Kiskunhalas, a small market town also in southern Hungary, on May 27; and in Budapest, the capital, between June 16 and 22. In the days and weeks between when ghettoization was first proposed and when it was finally enacted, there was considerable debate. A key issue was the potential impact that creating a single ghetto would have on "non-Jews" who lived in that part of the town or city. This concern was articulated in all three towns and cities—as it was much further afield[8]—and was joined by more specific, localized considerations. My contention is that in all three places, this mix of general concerns about the impact of ghettoization on non-Jews and local issues not only led to weeks of debates over ghettoization but also ultimately influenced the nature and shape of ghettoization implemented in specific places. The result was that ghettoization, when it was enacted, was a compromise.

KISKUNHALAS

According to national legislation, ghettos were to be created in all towns and cities with a total population of more than 10,000. Given that the population of Kiskunhalas exceeded this figure—the 1941 census recorded a total of 33,758[9]—Kiskunhalas was to have a ghetto. The town's mayor, the man charged with implementing ghettoization under national legislation, found himself in the midst of competing views of what the ghetto should look like and where it should be implemented within the town. Members of the local population, and indeed the mayor himself, saw ghettoization as both possibility and problem. Writing to the county prefect on May 8, 1944, the mayor offered mixed messages. Ghettoization was clearly being seized on as an opportunity to reshape the town. In particular, his concern was with the possibilities for creating "Jewish absences" in the town as a result of creating a ghetto.[10] Ghettoization offered the opportunity to move Jews from properties owned by non-Jews and to clear Jews from the main streets and squares of the town. These included the visible areas around the town's market and the town hall—the mayor's own patch, if you like—as well as "three beautiful, large, newly built villa-style buildings," which, from the description, were clearly the best of Kiskunhalas real estate but which, it would seem, were Jewish-owned.[11] This concern with clearing the town's main streets of Jews was being articulated elsewhere and apparently reflected national concerns.[12]

Although the mayor in Kiskunhalas was clear about from where Jews were to be removed, he was less sure about where they were to be placed. He asserted the principles that the Jews were to be concentrated together—"at least 3–4 persons living in one room"—and that their relocation should not bother the majority of the non-Jewish population of the town. He vaguely offered the area around the synagogue as a possible location for a ghetto, but there was far greater specificity about where the ghetto would not be, rather than where it would be, sited.

Underlying this uncertainty about location was a view that creating ghettos presented more problems in a small market town like Kiskunhalas than in a larger city. In Kiskunhalas, there were no large apartment buildings where Jews could be placed and the ghetto sited. Rather, it was a town dominated by small houses surrounded by gardens, cowsheds, pigsties, and henhouses. What is striking in the mayor's representation of living patterns in the town is his juxtaposition of Jews living in comfortable apartments with non-Jewish smallholders living in "modest" houses with "modest" gardens. It is a representation rooted in notions of the Jew as both urban and wealthy. These different living patterns were seen to create problems for the mayor in selecting where to place the ghetto. It was clear to him that non-Jewish smallholders did not want to leave their semirural properties, even for Jewish apartments offering "greater comfort." Therefore, his solution was to suggest relocating only those non-Jews with lesser property rights—tenants of the few small apartment buildings in the center of the town—rather than non-Jewish home owners.[13]

These concerns, first expressed to the county prefect, were rearticulated a few days later to members of the town council. They were informed that Jews were to be removed from the main streets and best properties in the town and placed in apartments in streets surrounding the synagogue, keeping in mind the interests of non-Jews currently living on those streets. These non-Jews were to be given empty Jewish apartments "of the same or even better quality than their present apartments," reflecting the mayor's stated commitment that "ghettoization must be done in such a way as not to be injurious to the citizens of my town." However, it is clear from the mayor's words that his meeting with the county prefect had added a further concern—ensuring that Jews be concentrated in such a way so as to ensure effectiveness and ease of control.[14]

For members of the town council, the idea of creating a single concentrated ghetto in the town, which would be easy to police, raised problems. Specifically, as one town councilor pointed out, the problem was that there was no single area of the town where houses were solely owned by Jews. The result was that implementing concentrated ghettoization would inevitably bring about protests from non-Jewish house owners, which was already happening in the town.[15] This problem was faced by local authorities across Hungary. The reality was that Jews and non-Jews lived not only on the same streets but also in the same apartment buildings. Thus, attempting to separate their living space inevitably meant moving both Jews and non-Jews. It is clear from examining records from Kiskunhalas, Szeged, and Budapest that this was a central concern both to officials charged with implementing ghettoization and to non-Jews living in towns and cities being reshaped into distinct Jewish and non-Jewish space.

One solution to this problem, suggested by another town councilor in Kiskunhalas, was to eschew residential properties altogether and find an alternative place for Jews to be housed. In the case of Kiskunhalas, two potential buildings were proposed—a factory and steam mill.[16] In Szeged, nonresidential locations for the ghetto were popular options, with the local press throwing its weight behind plans for a purpose-built ghetto, and in other cities, nonresidential properties were widely adopted in Hungary as ghetto sites.[17] However, the county prefect's orders to the mayor of Kiskunhalas stipulated that a ghetto should be created within a part of the town[18] and explicitly not in a "camp."[19] There was insistence that the ghetto was to be an urban phenomenon.

If the ghetto had to be placed in residential properties, an alternative to a single closed ghetto area was to designate only Jewish-owned houses within a more loosely defined and larger area. This idea was proposed in the May 15 town council meeting, being seen both as satisfying "the police authorities from the point of view that Jewish living space will be easier to control" and as ensuring that non-Jewish home owners would not be forced to move.[20] It was noted that this "temporary" or "gradual" solution had been adopted in other towns and had met with the approval of none other than the secretary of state in the Interior Ministry, László Endre, where "obstacles" were present to setting up a closed ghetto.[21] When it was finally implemented in Kiskunhalas, ghettoization was a compromise of sorts. There was a degree of concentration and control, with Jews crammed into a limited number of houses that they could leave only with police permission. However, there was also a degree of dispersion. The ghetto was not a single closed area but rather seventeen addresses spread over twelve streets in the town.[22] It is clear that the decision to adopt a dispersed ghetto was a result of concerns with the property rights of non-Jewish home owners.

SZEGED

In Kiskunhalas, local officials created a ghetto for just over five hundred Jews from the town. Only Jews from Kiskunhalas were to be housed in the town ghetto, rather than Jews from surrounding smaller towns and villages, as was the case elsewhere in the county.[23] In Szeged, however, far larger numbers of Jews needed housing. Deciding the precise number of Jews to be housed in individual ghettos was ultimately being done at a county level. The policy of clearing the southern border area of Hungary at the end of April 1944[24] meant that about three thousand Jews from outside of Szeged needed housing, alongside the almost four thousand Jews from the city itself.[25] The Jews from outside the city were housed in the Jewish school, the synagogue, Jewish community headquarters, and a sheep pen,[26] but these were seen as only temporary measures.[27]

By early May, the local press reported receiving "many complaints" about the rumored location of a ghetto in the center of Szeged that was seen to "jeopardize Hungarian-Christian values."[28] As in Kiskunhalas, there were concerns with the impact of ghettoization on the city's non-Jewish population. The press reckoned that the plans for an urban ghetto would displace 3,600 non-Jews (including 100 families who were home owners and thus in a category of those who had additional property rights).[29] But not only the sheer numbers of relocations were contested; the placing of the ghetto at the heart of the city was also disputed. On May 8, "tumultuous scenes" were taking place in Szeged over "the plans for the ghetto" to be located in "the most finely built district" of the city. A public meeting held by the mayor to discuss the matter was cleared by police when it descended into uproar.[30]

At the forefront of opposition to ghetto plans was the local rightist paper, *Szegedi Uj Nemzedék*. It was not simply reporting developments in the run-up to ghettoization but rather offering its own solutions. In particular it advocated alternative sites on the outskirts of the city, whether five settlements in the suburbs or purpose-built barracks on the edge of the city.[31] It was this latter plan, in essence to build a ghetto from scratch, that the paper ran with in May 1944. The plan, which had the support of the city's rightist "Hungarian and Christian population," was being advocated by the Party of Hungarian Renewal, which was reported to be petitioning the Interior Minister, requesting him to act to stop plans to create a ghetto in the center of the city.[32] The local press went to considerable lengths to detail the precise number of barracks that would need to be built, what materials and labor were required, and where all this would come from. Their plan was for the creation of an out-of-town ghetto of 150 barracks—50 meters long, 4.5 meters wide, and 3 meters high. The majority would house the seven thousand Jews living in or recently gathered to the city, with a further six barracks identified for use as a synagogue, school, health care center, hospital, bathhouse, and community office. That ghettoization was being seen as more than simply a short-term measure can be seen in the timescale advocated for creating this Jewish settlement. The estimate was that it would take six weeks, 1,500 Jewish laborers, and 1.5 million pengő to construct the barracks. Ghettoization would therefore be enacted at the end of July at the very earliest and would be an interim measure for the city's Jews, in the paper's words, "until we could get rid of them within the framework of a general European solution."[33]

Although costly in terms of money, materials, and labor, this plan for a purpose-built ghetto on the outskirts of the city was seen not simply as dealing with the immediate problem of where to place the ghetto but also as solving "overnight" a longer-term housing shortage in the city.[34] In the eyes of the local paper, it was the perfect solution. However, the time involved in building a new ghetto from scratch did not fit with the county prefect's desire to undertake the evacuation of Jews "within the shortest time,"[35] and it went against the Interior Ministry directive of May 11 that Jews were "not to be transported to camps."[36] As in Kiskunhalas, ghettoization was to be an urban phenomenon, but an urban ghetto would only be for the city's Jews ("Christian Jews" were to be housed separately), while those Jews gathered into the city from the surrounding area would remain in more makeshift camps on the periphery. The result of the reduction in the number of Jews requiring housing in the city itself was that the closed ghetto would be smaller in scale—thirty-one houses on six streets—and would mean fewer non-Jews would be forced to move.[37] Those non-Jews who did have to move would receive accommodation equivalent to, or better than, the apartments they left.

A critical concern was the interests of non-Jews forced to relocate as a result of the decision to create a fenced ghetto. They were invited to present their requests for vacated Jewish apartments to officials in the city hall, and the costs of cleaning, decorating, and moving into these apartments were to be paid by the city's Jews.[38] More significantly, perhaps, the interests of non-Jews affected by ghettoization had been at the forefront of debates over the size, shape, and location of the ghetto in Szeged during the previous weeks: debates that resulted, to some extent, in compromise in the implementation of ghettoization. A single closed ghetto was created in the center of Szeged, but it was smaller in scale than was originally envisioned.

BUDAPEST

Concerns over the impact of urban ghettos on the non-Jewish population also played a key role in debates over where to locate the ghetto in Budapest. However, these were joined with another set of concerns, which had been briefly referenced in the press in Szeged: the links between ghettoization and Allied bombing.[39] As Nicholas Nagy-Talavera has noted from a study of the wartime Hungarian press, "Jewish responsibility for the strategic bombing of Hungary by the U.S. Army air forces was an axiom for the Fascist press."[40] In Budapest, the press made frequent connections between Allied bombing of the city and the dangers and possibilities of ghettoization. Initially, they signaled the dangers of segregating the city's Jews within a single concentrated ghetto sited in one part of the city, which would open up the rest of the city to Allied bombing, with the assumption that the Allies were the Jews' friend.[41] Interviewed in the pages of *Magyarság*, László Endre responded to these concerns by noting plans to concentrate the city's Jews in several closed Jewish quarters dispersed throughout the city rather than in a single ghetto.[42] In early May, the ghetto plans reflected these concerns: the city's Jews were to be cleared from the city's major streets and squares and placed into seven loose Jewish quarters—three sited on the Buda side of the Danube River and four on the Pest side.[43] Within these seven broad ghetto areas, Jews were to live in buildings with existing Jewish owners and tenants. These plans dealt neatly with the two major concerns circulating in the city—they neither required non-Jews to move nor left the city's non-Jews open to Allied bombing.[44]

In many ways, these ghetto plans appeared to be a perfect solution;

however, they were shelved during May and replaced with plans for a much more dispersed form of ghettoization. The driving force behind these changes was the Interior Ministry, which communicated new decisions relating to ghettoization in the capital to local officials at the end of May. The Lord Mayor was informed that a door-to-door survey would be carried out in the city, and houses would then be identified for Jewish occupation. The choice of houses was to be determined by whether houses had a majority of Jewish or non-Jewish tenants, whether the owner was Jewish or non-Jewish, and what the level of rents was. No longer were the main streets and squares of the city to be cleared of Jews, nor were Jews to be housed in seven loosely identified ghetto areas. They were to live in the houses where they already predominantly lived.[45]

Although the shape of the intended ghetto was broadly acceptable to local officials, the proposed timetable did not meet with their approval. The very rapid implementation of the door-to-door survey—followed swiftly by the designation of houses for Jewish use and the moving into those houses of all the city's nearly two hundred thousand Jews—was contested by local officials. Whereas Endre wanted all of this completed by June 1, local officials wrote to his boss—Interior Minister Andor Jaross—arguing that it would take until the end of August to complete all of the relocations that ghettoization involved, in particular to ensure that non-Jewish interests were not harmed. Such a radically different timescale reflected very different ways of seeing ghettoization. In Szeged, as I have already noted, the press saw ghettoization as something that could be implemented over a course of weeks rather than days. In Budapest it was not the press advocating a timescale of weeks rather than days, but local officials, who did not see ghettoization as the rapidly implemented prelude to deportations at the end of May 1944. However, their superiors in the Interior Ministry understood ghettoization in different terms and insisted that houses be designated for Jewish use by June 10.[46]

Ultimately, this deadline was stretched a little. After the door-to-door survey of all buildings in the capital was completed in early June, 2,639 houses were designated on June 16, 1944, for housing the city's Jews.[47] The press praised the decision to designate houses throughout the city. *Esti Ujság* wrote approvingly of the decision not to adopt a policy of "complete separation," as had been the case in the provincial towns "where a separate area has been designated for them [the Jews]," going as far as claiming for itself some role in making the decision. However, the press was less happy that even such a dispersed form of ghettoization, based on an analysis of where Jews lived in the city, still meant that an estimated twelve thousand non-Jewish families would have to move. As *Esti Ujság* was quick to point out, ghettoization was "not merely a Jewish affair, but closely affects the Christian population also," and "Christians do not willingly leave yellow-star houses, but are forced to by the regulations."[48] Once the list of ghetto houses was published, the press sniffed a Jewish conspiracy, complaining that the city's Jews had grabbed the best properties for themselves.[49] For the non-Jewish and Jewish populations of the city, the days after the issuing of the list of ghetto houses saw a flurry of activity. While some Jews and non-Jews were making arrangements to swap apartments, hundreds of others were writing to the city mayor contesting ghetto designation. About six hundred of these letters survive in the city archives. The majority came from Jews and non-Jews asking to stay put. For the former, this meant requesting that their apartment building be designated as a ghetto house. For the latter, this meant asking that their apartment building be removed from the list of 2,639 properties.[50]

What is striking are the arguments that petitioners put forward to justify their claims. In many ways, these echoed the criteria for classification of ghetto houses that formed the basis of the door-to-door survey and were reported in the press: majority occupation, ownership, and rental rates. Details of the precise number of Jewish and non-Jewish tenants, whether the owners were Jewish or non-Jewish, and how much the rents were feature large in the hundreds of petitions submitted to the mayor. But so do other factors deemed relevant to the petitioners (even if not always to the mayor and other city officials). Some petitioners made much of the quality of the apartment building (whether particularly good or particularly bad),[51] the status of the tenants,[52] the proximity of the house to likely bomb targets,[53] the house's location on the city's main thoroughfares,[54] or its history.[55] What emerges in some petitions is a strong sense that a particular property was either too good for Jews or too bad for non-Jews. In the latter case, the request from non-Jews was for their apartment building to be designated for Jewish use. In a minority of petitions from non-Jews, ghettoization was not something to be avoided but rather an opportunity to move into better apartments previously occupied by Jews.

Perhaps more significantly, several non-Jews and Jews, and in some cases a coalition of both, called on the mayor for a new category to be created—the "mixed house"—and applied to their apartment building.[56] Like the majority of petitioners, their desire was to stay put, but this desire led them, perhaps unwittingly, to challenge the segregation of Jews and non-Jews at the scale of the individual apartment building. This level of segregation characterized ghettoization as it had been framed in the national legislation at the end of April and as it was implemented in Budapest in mid-June. After a full reinvestigation of designated properties, a new definitive list of 1,948 ghetto houses was issued on June 22, in which mixed houses were now accepted by officials. In the regulations issued on June 25 that governed ghettoization in the city, "Christians" were forbidden from hiding Jews or allowing Jews admission "for no matter how brief a period into either Christian houses or *the Christian-tenanted portions of Jewish houses.*"[57] Here was official tolerance for non-Jews to remain in the 1,948 ghetto houses that were to be the home of the city's Jews. To what extent non-Jews stayed put is hard to state categorically. Randolph Braham agreed with the postwar claim of the journalist Jenő Lévai that "close to 12,000" non-Jews remained in the city's ghetto houses, although it is impossible to tell where Lévai got this figure.[58]

That significant numbers of non-Jews did remain living in their apartments in the ghetto houses is suggested from figures from the city's VII district. At the end of November 1944, 144 of the 162 ghetto houses in the area of this district that shortly would be made into the closed Pest ghetto were partly occupied by just over four thousand non-Jewish tenants.[59] If these figures were replicated across the city, it would seem that the vast majority of ghetto houses in Budapest in reality functioned as mixed houses during the summer and autumn of 1944. In the capital, ghettoization in reality meant the segregation of Jews and non-Jews not at the scale of the individual apartment building, as was planned in May and June and was spelled out in the national guidelines, but at the scale of the individual apartment. This amounted to a significant compromise on the part of the authorities, which had much to do with concerns about the impact of ghettoization on non-Jews.

COMPROMISE SOLUTIONS

As the examples of Kiskunhalas, Szeged, and Budapest suggest, not only was ghettoization debated and contested, but also the debates influenced the nature and shape of the ghettoization plan adopted. Perhaps most significantly, concerns with the impact of ghettoization on non-Jews (especially home owners) led to changes in the scale at which it was implemented. In Szeged, the ghetto was scaled down. In Kiskunhalas, instead of creating a fenced ghetto, officials enacted ghettoization at the scale of individual houses. In Budapest, ghettoization was ultimately tolerated, in the summer of 1944, at the level of individual apartments.

These three places were not the only towns and cities in Hungary where there was opposition to ghetto plans. On May 11, 1944, László Endre informed local authorities that "in every city and town in which the gathering of Jews into ghettos cannot be carried through without obstacle for any reason, it will be necessary to await the arrival of the advisors appointed from the Interior Ministry."[60] In early May 1944, the implementation of ghettoization—in southern and western Hungary, at least—was far from a smooth process.

Endre's order could be—and I think was—read as a potential threat within localities. Just before Endre's second visit to Szeged on June 10 to check on progress being made on ghettoization, Szeged's deputy mayor ordered that the ghetto needed to be fenced in, the external windows whitewashed, and the Jewish police force functioning by the day of the visit.[61] Reading his urgent report sheet, one has the sense of a man who wanted to put on a good show for the visiting national official and convince him of the efficiency of city authorities in creating a smoothly functioning ghetto. Within the locality, my sense is that compromises may well have been reached in part to ensure that ghettoization was something implemented locally to avoid intervention from national authorities. In short, in compromising, local officials were listening not only to local opinion but also to the offer—or threat—of national intervention to solve obstacles to the rapid implementation of ghettoization. As officials in Kiskunhalas, Szeged, and Budapest found out, obstacles there might be, but they could be overcome locally through compromise, and this led to the establishing of three rather different ghettos in these three places.

Ultimately, the Kiskunhalas and Szeged ghettos were to prove short-lived places; the Jews in these towns were deported in June 1944. In Budapest, however, an ever-changing ghetto continued to be the home of the city's Jewish population through to liberation in January 1945. In the winter of 1944, the dispersed form of ghettoization adopted in the early summer of 1944 was replaced with a more concentrated form of ghettoization, in which two ghettos were created on the Pest side of the river: the so-called international ghetto and the closed Pest ghetto. But the creation of two ghettos for two distinct categories of Jews in the last months of the war is another story altogether.[62]

NOTES

1. Christopher Browning, "Nazi Ghettoization Policy in Poland: 1939–41," *Central European History* 19, no. 4 (1986), 345.

2. On my use of quotation marks around the word "Jew" to emphasize the constructed nature of the term, see Tim Cole, "Constructing the 'Jew,' Writing the Holocaust: Hungary 1920–45," *Patterns of Prejudice* 33, no. 3 (1999), 19–27, and Tim Cole, *Holocaust City: The Making of a Jewish Ghetto* (New York: Routledge, 2003), 44–48. Subsequent use of the words "Jew" and "non-Jew" in the text should be read with awareness of the problematic and constructed nature of these terms.

3. Such rapidity, however, should not be assumed to be evidence that there was a direct line between the two; see Tim Cole, "Budapest 1944: Changing the Shape of the Ghetto," in *Remembering for the Future: The Holocaust in an Age of Genocide. Vol. 1, History,* eds. John K. Roth and Elizabeth Maxwell (Houndmills, U.K.: Palgrave, 2001), 198–210.

4. Randolph Braham, *The Politics of Genocide: The Holocaust in Hungary* (New York: Columbia University Press, 1994).

5. Judit Molnár, *Zsidósors 1944-ben az V. (Szegedi) Csendőrkerületben* (Budapest: Cserépfalvi Kiadó, 1995), 39–40, 77.

6. Braham, *The Politics of Genocide,* 600–603.

7. Decree no. 1.610/1944 M.E. (Prime Minister's office) (April 28, 1944), *Budapesti Közlöny* 95 (April 28, 1944).

8. On Szolnok, see László Csősz, "'Keresztény Polgári Érdekek Sérelme Nélkül...' Gettósítás Szolnokon 1944-ben," in *Tanulmányok a Holokausztról II,* ed. Randolph L. Braham (Budapest: Balassi, 2002), 203–55.

9. Henrietta Somodi, *Zsidók Bács-Kiskun Megyében* (Budapest: Makkabi, 2001), 124.

10. For more on ghettoization as the creation of "Jewish absences" as well

CONTESTING AND COMPROMISING GHETTOIZATION • 165

as "Jewish presences," see Tim Cole, "Ghettoization," in *The Historiography of the Holocaust*, ed. Dan Stone (Houndmills, U.K.: Palgrave Macmillan, 2004), 65–87.

11. Letter from Kiskunhalas Mayor to County Prefect (May 8, 1944), in Ágnes Ságvári, ed., *Dokumentumok a Zsidóság Üldöztetésének Történetéhez/ Iratok a Bács-Kiskun Megyei Levéltárból* (Budapest: A Magyar Auschwitz Alapítvány, 1994), 28–30.

12. Cole, *Holocaust City*, 84–93, 96.

13. Letter from Kiskunhalas Mayor to County Prefect (May 8, 1944), in Ságvári, *Dokumentumok,* 28–30.

14. Letter from Kiskunhalas Mayor to Town Council (May 13, 1944), in Ságvári, *Dokumentumok,* 30–31.

15. Minutes of Town Council meeting (May 15, 1944), in Ságvári, *Dokumentumok,* 32.

16. Ibid., 33.

17. Braham, *The Politics of Genocide,* 590–777.

18. Letter from Kiskunhalas Mayor to Town Council (May 13, 1944), in Ságvári, *Dokumentumok,* 31.

19. Országos Levéltár (hereafter OL, or Hungarian National Archives), I 120, Pest-Pilis-Solt-Kiskun County Prefect to Mayors re: Designation of Jewish Living Places, 27409/1944 (May 12, 1944).

20. Minutes of Town Council meeting (May 15, 1944), in Ságvári, *Dokumentumok,* 32.

21. Ibid., 32–33.

22. Kiskunhalas Mayor Announcement re: Designation of Jewish Living Places, 5887/1944 (May 27, 1944), in Ságvári, *Dokumentumok,* 35.

23. OL, I 120, Pest-Pilis-Solt-Kiskun County Prefect to Mayors re: Designation of Jewish Living Places, 27409/1944 (May 12, 1944).

24. Braham, *The Politics of Genocide,* 604–5.

25. Ibid., 716–18, 728.

26. United States Holocaust Memorial Museum (hereafter USHMM), Record Group (hereafter RG) 52.007.01, Memo from Szeged Police Headquarters (May 10, 1944).

27. *Szegedi Uj Nemzedék,* May 3, 1944, 3.

28. Ibid., May 5, 1944, 4.

29. Ibid., May 7, 1944, 6.

30. *Népujság,* May 8, 1944, 3.

31. *Szegedi Uj Nemzedék,* May 7, 1944, 6.

32. Ibid., May 7, 1944, 6; May 10, 1944, 4; May 11, 1944, 5.

33. Ibid., May 10, 1944, 4.

34. Ibid.

35. Ibid., May 12, 1944, 3–4.

36. USHMM, RG 52.007.04, 13734/944, Memo from László Endre to Police and Gendarme Headquarters (May 11, 1944).
37. USHMM, RG 52.007.01, Mayoral Decision (23356/1944) on the Establishment of the Szeged Ghetto (May 17, 1944).
38. Ibid.
39. *Szegedi Uj Nemzedék,* May 10, 1944, 4.
40. Nicholas M. Nagy-Talavera, "The Second World War as Mirrored in the Hungarian Fascist Press," *East European Quarterly* 4, no. 2 (1971), 201. See also Péter Róbert, "A Holokauszt a Magyar Sajtóban," in *Tanulmányok a Holokausztról I,* ed. Randolph L. Braham (Budapest: Balassi Kiadó, 2001), 54.
41. Cole, *Holocaust City,* 115–25.
42. *Magyarság,* April 16, 1944, 4.
43. OL, K 148, 1944, 3410.
44. Cole, *Holocaust City,* 84–93.
45. OL, I 17, 323.1944, Letter from the Lord Mayor to the Interior Minister (May 31, 1944); Letter from the Lord Mayor to the Mayor (June 1, 1944).
46. Cole, *Holocaust City,* 95–100.
47. Ibid., 105–15.
48. *Esti Ujság,* June 20, 1944, 3.
49. Jenő Lévai, *Zsidósors Magyarországon* (Budapest: Magyar Téka, 1948), 166.
50. Cole, *Holocaust City,* 131–56.
51. Budapest Főváros Levéltára (hereafter BFL, or Budapest City Archives), IX.2786.1944/147729 (June 17, 1944).
52. BFL, IX/2789.1944/148414 (June 21, 1944).
53. BFL, IX/2784.1944/148145 (June 20, 1944).
54. BFL, IX/2784.1944/148129 (June 19, 1944).
55. BFL, IX/2784.1944/148128 (June 19, 1944).
56. BFL, IX/2784.1944/148191 (June 19, 1944) .
57. Braham, *The Politics of Genocide,* 737–38 (emphasis mine).
58. Jenő Lévai, *Fekete Könyv a Magyar Zsidóság Szenvédéseiről* (Budapest: Officina, 1946), 156; Braham, *The Politics of Genocide,* 735.
59. Új Magyar Központi Levéltár (hereafter UMKL, or New Hungarian Central Archive), XXXIII-5-c-1, XI.23, Jewish Council writings (November 23, 1944).
60. USHMM, RG52.007.04, Memo from László Endre to Police and Gendarme Headquarters, 2872 (May 11, 1944).
61. USHMM, RG 52.007.06, Report Sheet from Mayor to Szeged Police Headquarters, 29237 (June 4, 1944).
62. Cole, *Holocaust City,* 197–220.

III. R·E·S·P·O·N·S·I·B·I·L·I·T·Y

Jonathan Petropoulos

Prince zu Waldeck und Pyrmont: A Career in the SS and Its Murderous Consequences

THE SS WAS A MAGNET FOR ARISTOCRATS.[1] INDEED, THERE WERE TOO many to list here. But to offer one indication of this phenomenon, a cursory glance at the Schutzstaffel (SS) rolls reveals the membership of more than seventy Barons (Freiherrn), ranging from the influential Friedrich Karl von Eberstein (1894–1979), who served as Heinrich Himmler's chief of staff, to rocket scientist Wernher von Braun (1912–1977), to Günther von Reibnitz (1894–1983)—the father of Marie-Christine von Reibnitz, the current Princess Michael of Kent.[2] The SS also included members of the princely houses of Hohenzollern, Hessen, Mecklenburg, Thurn-und-Taxis, Lippe, Brunswick, and Auersperg.[3] While several members of the aristocracy had appointments that were largely honorific, others were leading figures in the SS. In 1938, 18.7 percent of the Lieutenant Generals (Obergruppenführer), 9.8 percent of the Major Generals (Gruppenführer), and 14.3 percent of the Brigadier Generals (Brigadierführer) were members of the aristocracy.[4] Among the Higher SS and Police Leaders (HSSPF), eight of forty-four were drawn from the nobility (Oberschicht).[5] Although it is an exaggeration to use the phrase that was "popularly bandied about after the war that the SS was 'at times almost a nursing home for princes,'" there were organic ties between the nobility and Himmler's elite—the consequences of which were sometimes murderous.[6] The overrepresentation of aristocrats in the SS helped shape the organization's character, contributing a sense of self-assuredness, reinforcing the notion of a pansocial racial community, and suggesting a historical mission, among other elements. Prince zu Waldeck und Pyrmont,

• 169

perhaps more than any other aristocratic member of the SS, embodied and advertised these ideals.

The fact remains that Himmler, while holding ambivalent views about aristocrats, conceived his order as "a new knighthood" and liked to surround himself with nobles.[7] He told one meeting of the Circle of Friends of the Reichsführer-SS that "to fulfill its mission, the SS required as members the best elements of society, 'genuine military tradition, the bearing and breeding of the German nobility, and the creative efficiency of the industrialist, always on the basis of racial selection.'"[8] The Reichsführer-SS conceived his order as a Blutadel (blood nobility) and drew on the resources and traditions of the aristocracy.[9] Himmler had been raised in proximity to princes. His father had been a tutor for the Wittelsbach family, having been an employee of Prince Arnulf von Bayern and supervisor of his son Prince Heinrich.[10] Putzi Hanfstaengl, who was also a student of the senior Himmler, described him as "a terrible snob, favoring the young titled members of his class and bearing down contemptuously on commoners."[11] Indeed, Prince Heinrich von Bayern later became Heinrich Himmler's godfather.[12]

The son of a Gymnasium professor who was attracted to the glamour of the Bavarian royal family, the future Reichsführer-SS spent his youth in a staunchly pro-Wittelsbach milieu (the family even moved to Landshut in 1913—"the administrative seat of the Wittelsbach dukes" with an "Altstadt" that one historian described with the phrase "mediaeval splendour").[13] In 1917, Himmler received 1,000 reichsmarks (RM) as a gift from the chamberlain of his late godfather—Prince Heinrich having been killed in battle the previous year—which Himmler used to pay his way into the elite officers' training program of the 1st Bavarian Infantry. Indeed, the young man reported for training at Regensburg on January 1, 1918, as a Fahnenjunker (officer trainee—a word with strong aristocratic connotations).[14] While Himmler did not remain a monarchist—especially after Prince Rupprecht refused to support the Nazis in the failed Beer Hall Putsch of 1923—he continued to admire many aspects of aristocratic life, including the connectedness to history, the martial heritage, and the sense of honor and duty. He created a pseudo-knightly order at the castle called the Wewelsburg, made plans for an ideological school in Schloss Grünwald near Munich (the birthplace of, in his words, "Ludwig der Bayern, a great German Kaiser"), and exhibited a fixation with the founder of the Saxon dynasty, King Heinrich I ("the

Fowler"; 875–936)—a conqueror of the Slavs.[15] On the anniversary of the king's death, Himmler would visit his tomb in the Quedlinburg Cathedral "and at the stroke of midnight in the cold crypt of the cathedral, Himmler would commune silently with his namesake.... He became so obsessed by his hero that he gradually came to regard himself as a reincarnation of the King."[16]

Himmler also realized the usefulness of aristocrats: the respect they often commanded in Germany and the resources they could frequently commit to the cause. Even before the Nazis came to power, one of Himmler's closest colleagues, Baron Friedrich Karl von Eberstein, "traveled the country recruiting for the SA [Sturmabteilungen] and SS" and helped land, among others, Reinhard Heydrich.[17] Baron von Eberstein, who had the extraordinarily low SS number of 1,386, became the Police President of Munich in 1936 and remained a force in the Bavarian capital until April 20, 1945, when he was fired from all his posts (including General of the Waffen-SS) on orders of Martin Bormann because of defeatism.[18] Eberstein was sacked at a time when Himmler was meeting with Count Folke Bernadotte (1895–1948). The Swedish prince (who had "left" the royal family after marrying without the king's consent) was the vice president of the Swedish Red Cross and worked toward the end of the war to rescue concentration camp inmates and to negotiate an armistice between Germany and the Allies.[19] Himmler did not remain enamored of the traditional aristocracy as a whole throughout the Third Reich. Indeed, he turned on the princes as a caste during the latter part of the war. Historian Gerald Reitlinger argued that it was the replacement of the relatively more genteel Karl Wolff as Himmler's chief aide by the more radical Hermann Fegelein in April 1943 that "marked an important change in the character of Himmler's court."[20] Reitlinger added, "Wolff was a relic of the days when the SS was considered the respectable section of the Party suitable for the sons of princes."[21] Despite the gradual shift, it is important to recognize the linkages between the SS and the aristocracy. To do this, it is helpful to examine the career of Hereditary Prince Josias zu Waldeck und Pyrmont.

CAREER

Prince Josias zu Waldeck und Pyrmont (1896–1967), who had extraordinary and varied experiences during the Third Reich, enjoyed an especially close relationship with Himmler. The eldest son of the last ruling prince in Waldeck (Prince Friedrich abdicated in November 1918), the nephew of the King of Württemberg, and a close relation of Dutch Queen Wilhelmina, Josias was badly wounded (and gassed) in World War I. He was also highly decorated, receiving the Iron Cross First and Second Class.[22] He later volunteered for the Freikorps, where he fought in Upper Silesia in 1919. Waldeck joined the Nazi Party in 1929 and the SS in 1930. He had married one of the sisters of Grand Duke Nikolaus von Oldenburg (1897–1970)—and the Grand Duke's first wife was Waldeck's sister, Princess Helene (1899–1948). The Grand Duke von Oldenburg's two sisters married SS Lieutenant Colonel (Obersturmbannführer) Prince Stephan zu Schaumburg-Lippe and SA Colonel (Oberführer) Harald von Hedemann, making this a tight-knit circle of aristocratic Nazis.[23] During his first year in the SS, Waldeck became chief of Himmler's personal staff.[24] Later, in 1933, he became the aide-de-camp of SS General Sepp Dietrich (1892–1966), who also headed up Adolf Hitler's personal security. That the same year, Waldeck was promoted to Major General (Gruppenführer)—part of his precipitous rise in rank. He also had a brief appointment as a counselor (Legationsrat) in the Foreign Office in 1933 and held a seat in the Reichstag throughout the Third Reich. As of 1935, he headed the SS division in Fulda, putting him in close proximity to Philipp von Hessen (both were based in Kassel), although the latter was a General in the SA. In Kassel, Waldeck created a "Bureau for the Germanification of Eastern Peoples," which promoted the idea of an SS-directed settlement in Eastern Europe.[25] In 1939, Himmler made Waldeck the HSSPF of Weimar, and in this capacity, Waldeck had supervisory authority over the concentration camp at Buchenwald (and more specifically, its Political Department and the Kommandantur). The prince was also a General of the Order Police (General der Polizei)—appointed by Hitler personally in April 1941. The Order Police, as Christopher Browning and others have shown, played a central role in the Holocaust.[26] Waldeck, although never commanding one of the murderous units, was also a General of the Waffen-SS as of July 1944.

Waldeck was severe, hard-driving, and ambitious. To cite two (among numerous) examples: he oversaw an execution commando at the Stadelheim prison near Munich during the Röhm Purge in June 1934, where he helped murder a number of former comrades; and then, on March 12, 1938, the day of the German invasion of Austria, he wrote to Himmler—addressing the letter to the "Reichsführer-SS persönlich"—requesting to be deployed to Austria.[27] He noted that he had once been the leader of an SS division in Austria and wanted to be back where the action was. In November 1938, Waldeck's SS unit in Arolsen was one of the first to launch attacks on local Jews during Reichskristallnacht. Although Joseph Goebbels, who coined the euphemistic phrase, gave his inflammatory speech in Munich on November 9—the night when the violence peaked—Waldeck's troops destroyed the local synagogue and several Jewish businesses on the night of November 7. (There were also violent acts that night in Kassel, where Waldeck had limited authority.) Waldeck was in Munich at a meeting of party leaders and later claimed to have telephoned back to Arolsen and ordered his men to refrain from violence, but the leading scholar of the pogrom in Hesse, Wolf-Arno Kropat, doubts the veracity of this statement.[28] Indeed, considering the culture of discipline in the SS and Prince zu Waldeck's severe demeanor, it is hard to believe that his troops would act against his orders. In April 1942, Waldeck was sent to France. As noted in the *Washington Post* at the time, "Hitler has ordered the merciless repression of terrorism in occupied France, entrusting it to Prince Josias of Waldeck-Pyrmont, old-line Nazi, it was learned today as the wave of incidents started by Pierre Laval's return to power spread to the unoccupied zone, with two bomb explosions at Montpelier."[29] Waldeck was appointed commander of a well-armed "storm troop force." Housed in "mansions or luxurious apartment houses at the edges of the city, they had at their disposal more than 400 tanks parked at strategic points along a 25-mile circle around Paris."[30]

Considerably more trivial, but nonetheless revealing, was the grievance filed against him in September 1941 when a subordinate accused him of "damaging his honor." Waldeck had reportedly castigated the man for "moaning" about his duties in a Luftwaffe flak unit and said to him, "In my eyes, you are a Schwein!"[31] Waldeck's sharp tongue led to a 1941 trial in an SS court in Munich. Later, in another incident that occurred in May 1942, Prince Waldeck ordered the arrest of First Lieutenant (Oberleutnant) Nikolaus Hornig, a Wehrmacht officer who had been transferred to the Order Police because of his prewar experience in the police forces. In November 1941, Hornig had received an order from his battalion commander to oversee the shooting of 780 Russian prisoners. Hornig not only had refused to participate in the killing but also had informed his troops that there were "military and police codes that permitted them to refuse illegal orders."[32] Waldeck believed that his comportment constituted "Wehrkraftzersetzung" (undermining of the military) and arranged for an SS court to hear the case. Oberleutnant Hornig experienced two trials—one in November 1942 and a second one in March 1945 (that Waldeck would pursue the matter this late in the war is indicative of his character). Hornig spent the entire time incarcerated in Buchenwald, although he was a special kind of prisoner under "investigative arrest"—an arrangement in which he kept his rank and pay.[33]

At about the same time the charges were first filed against Hornig (1942), Prince zu Waldeck recommended that Buchenwald Commandant Karl Otto Koch and his notorious wife, Ilse, be sacked because of their embezzlement of more than RM 700,000 in valuables from the camp. Waldeck was instrumental in arranging for them to be transferred to the death camp at Majdanek.[34] They were subsequently put on trial: Koch was found guilty of corruption and hanged at Buchenwald just days before the camp was liberated by General George S. Patton and the American 3rd Army. There has been a debate among historians about Waldeck's direct responsibility in carrying out the sentence, as well as his knowledge of what transpired there. Although he visited the camp some thirty times, he claimed to have entered the protective custody area only "seven to eight times"; furthermore, he claimed to know nothing of the medical experiments conducted by the camp physicians or the killing of Soviet prisoners, among other atrocities.[35] Postwar judges were mixed in their findings about Waldeck, with certain officials believing that for most of the war, "he had no command powers over Buchenwald, his powers being limited to judicial functions over the SS."[36]

There is considerably less doubt, however, about his role in the evacuation of the camp at war's end, where Waldeck oversaw the Germans' efforts to conceal the horror of the site by shipping off inmates—a measure that resulted in thousands of deaths.[37] Waldeck had assumed control of Buchenwald when Wehrkreis IX had become a combat area in the spring of 1945.[38] He was in charge when thousands of inmates (34,000 by one count) were sent on forced marches.[39] Most of these people perished: an Allied investigation team noted in an April 18, 1945, report, "Transportation was not available to move them fast, and in their woefully weak condition, they could not have marched very far.... They have literally vanished into thin air."[40] Actually, there was limited transportation, but this was hardly better treatment. One train that headed south toward Bavaria (and Flossenbürg) took days to reach its destination instead of the projected eighteen hours; only 300 of the 3,105 on board survived the journey without provisions.

While the Prince was responsible for persecution on a vast scale, he still considered himself principled and disciplined. Scholars now generally reject the charge made by Buchenwald inmate and historian Eugen Kogon that Waldeck himself was brazenly corrupt.[41] But this is not to say that he did not profit handsomely from his position in the Third Reich. The manner in which he did so is in itself significant. It concerned the Waldecks' princely property, which, like that of many other noble families, had been transferred to a foundation in the 1920s. For certain properties, such as the castle (Residenz) in Arolsen, the Princes zu Waldeck had only the right of use: they paid a quarter of the upkeep costs, while the state paid the rest.[42] Prince zu Waldeck wanted to change this; especially as of 1938 when the Nazi government passed legislation that provided for the dissolution of trusts and foundations.[43] He therefore turned to another Nazi legal initiative: hereditary farms (Erbhöfe). Intended as a way to protect peasants and small farmers from the voracious expansion of modern agribusinesses, Erbhof status both protected a property and limited the owner's ability to sell it. The Nazis conceived of the Erbhof as a program for small landowners and imposed limits on the size of the holdings (between 18.5 and 212 hectares) that could receive this designation. There were loopholes in the law: when the property had been owned for 150 years and when the applicant was a "worthy German" (verdienten Deutschen). To simplify a complicated story, Prince zu Waldeck arranged for the property in the Waldeck Foundation—including more than 5,000 hectares of farmland and forests—to be declared an Erbhof.[44] This came about when Himmler intervened on his behalf with Reich Minister for Nutrition and Agriculture (and also chief of the SS Race and Settlement Head Office) Richard Walther Darré.[45] What is so striking is how Waldeck secured his financial status—the estate was valued in 1938 at more than RM 1.7 million, making him an extraordinarily wealthy man—and how he couched it in ideological terms.[46] According to Nazi law, an Erbhof was limited "only to a person of German or related blood," and it permitted the owner to call himself a "peasant" (Bauer).[47] Clearly, it was convenient for princes to cloak themselves in the Nazis' populist "blood and soil" rhetoric.

During the Third Reich, Prince zu Waldeck was publicized as a kind of role model for the SS. He was made head of the SS office for riding (Leiter des Deutschen Reitsports), and he frequently competed in international competitions in his SS uniform. Just after the Anschluss in the spring of 1938, Waldeck inquired whether he could serve on the police unit that would accompany Hitler to Rome: his aide addressed the request to Himmler, noting Waldeck would be in Rome from April 24 to May 5 competing in an international riding competition.[48] Himmler wrote back that he could not assign Waldeck to the police detail because the Italians were taking charge of security, but that it would be no problem to invite the Prince to other functions during the Führer's visit in May.[49] Waldeck was a visible figure in the entourage that was photographed by the press during the state visit. He fit the SS ideal in many other ways, too: not surprisingly, Waldeck and his wife had five children, which would earn the latter the Mother Cross in gold, the highest award for bearing children for the Reich.

Prince Waldeck was one of Himmler's favorites, and the Reichsführer-SS made special efforts to take care of him. They used the familiar form of address (one of Himmler's few "Duzfreunden"), and the Reichsführer-SS sent numerous gifts, not only to Waldeck but also to his family: Himmler was godfather to the prince's only son, Volkwin (also known as Wittekind), to whom he sent a regular stream of presents and notes.[50] In March 1943, Himmler requested to his staff that Waldeck be awarded the Military Service Cross with Swords—the highest award granted to Higher SS and Police Leaders. Then an aide wrote back that Waldeck had already received the award the previous year (for service as part of civil defense).[51] Waldeck in turn venerated Himmler and made every effort to honor his SS chief. This included giving Himmler a new train car—a "Salonwagen"—at the conference of SS leaders in Posen in the autumn of 1943 when Himmler made the infamous speeches where he went on record informing subleaders about the genocide.[52]

Waldeck's experiences during the war took a toll on him. In January 1944, SS General Udo von Woyrsch (1895–1982) wrote Himmler and explained how the Prince was suffering from serious eye problems and that "he must constantly smoke and evidently appears shaken."

Woyrsch asked Himmler to intervene—to prohibit Waldeck from smoking and to take better care of himself.[53] The results of this request are not known, but Waldeck did survive the German defeat. He was captured by General Patton's forces at Buchenwald on April 13, 1945—the day the camp was liberated—and imprisoned in various facilities, including the Coburg fortress and a civilian internment camp at Hammelburg.[54]

Waldeck faced two trials in the postwar period.[55] The first was the so-called Buchenwald trial, which was conducted by the Americans at Dachau between April and August 1947. On August 14, 1947, Waldeck was found guilty, sentenced to life in prison, and incarcerated in War Crimes Prison Number 1 at Landsberg, Bavaria. He was relatively fortunate, as twenty-two of the thirty-one on trial, including the second Camp Commandant Hermann Pister, were sentenced to death.[56] A year later, on June 19, 1948, General Lucius Clay (the Military Governor and European Commander in Chief) commuted that sentence to twenty years.[57] Waldeck subsequently underwent a denazification trial back near his home in Hesse—more specifically, in Fritzlar-Homberg. Because he had already received a long prison sentence, it was more his property that was at stake. There was also the historical record, as the entirety of his career and not just his activities in connection with Buchenwald was considered. Utilizing the five-tier scale of the denazification system, with Category I as a main offender and Category V as exonerated, the court placed Waldeck in Category II as "burdened" (belastet) and seized 70 percent of his property (among other sanctions).[58] This occurred on September 17, 1949; yet by November 29, 1950, Waldeck had been released from prison—one of the first to benefit from American High Commissioner John J. McCloy's amnesty program. In July 1953, he received an amnesty from the Hessian Minister President, and this resulted in a huge reduction of his fine, whereby he paid less than half the original sum and remained a very wealthy man.[59] Although he was investigated on several occasions in the late 1950s and early 1960s in connection with the Buchenwald camp complex, the murder of civilian workers, and the Röhm Purge, he was never again imprisoned. Prince zu Waldeck lived out his life in the Federal Republic until his death in November 1967.[60] He passed away in his castle, Schloss Schaumburg near Diez an der Lahn, at the age of seventy-one. His son, Prince Volkwin zu Waldeck und Pyrmont (b. 1936), mentioned earlier as Himmler's godson, became a Lieutenant Colonel (Oberst) in the German Armed Forces and succeeded him as head of the house.[61] In 1993, Volkwin gave his second child the name Josias—a family name, to be sure, but also that of his very problematic father. Furthermore, the family has kept its archives closed to scholars.

CONSEQUENCES AND CONCLUSIONS

Aristocrats were all over the spectrum in terms of their position toward the Nazi regime: from opponents in exile, such as Rupprecht von Bayern, to SS radicals like Waldeck. Although there was a wide range of responses to National Socialism, there existed a special connection between the SS and aristocrats. Himmler had noted, "We want to create an upper class for Germany, selected constantly over centuries, a new aristocracy, recruited always from the best sons and daughters of our nation, an aristocracy that never becomes old."[62] While Himmler never completely disavowed the idea that the aristocracy was susceptible to degeneracy due to inbreeding and unreliable due to their international connections (and these perceptions became more marked toward the end of the Third Reich), his fundamental conception of the traditional elite was a positive one.[63] Clearly Waldeck had qualities that made him attractive to Himmler: among them, that his social standing was exceptionally high.

A key question concerns the representativeness of Waldeck. Were there many others like him? Among princes, the short answer is no. While there were several dozen princes in the SS, none held comparable positions of authority. Also, because Hitler and the other top Nazi leaders turned against princes as a caste in 1943—passing the "Erlass des Führers über die Fernhaltung international gebundener Männer" in the spring of 1943 (which entailed screening them for reliability and sacking most from their positions in the state, party, and Wehrmacht)—most princes did not keep their positions during the latter part of the war.[64] Waldeck, who retained his authority until his capture, was a rarity in this regard. It was also highly unusual among princes to become involved in the persecution and atrocities to the extent that Waldeck did. There were princes who served as important cogs in the Nazi machine—Prince Christoph von Hessen, for example, who was a Lieutenant Colonel (Standartenführer) in the SS and headed up the Forschungsamt (Research Office) in Hermann Göring's Reich

Air Ministry. The Forschungsamt tapped telephones and intercepted telegrams and was indeed part of the totalitarian apparatus, but it passed on the intelligence to other agencies and therefore played a subsidiary role. Prince Christoph, like certain other princes in the SS, may have been a Schreibtischtäter (bureaucratic perpetrator), but he was not handing down death sentences, supervising Order Police, or overseeing death marches from a concentration camp. If one drops down the social ladder a rung—to the "ordinary" aristocrats who were in the SS—then there are comparable figures: SS-Lieutenant General (Obergruppenführer) Erich von dem Bach-Zelewski (1899–1972), for example, who was responsible for the mass murder of thousands of so-called partisans as well as for the crushing of the Warsaw Uprising.

But there is much about Prince Waldeck's career that was representative: like many others of the traditional elite, he lent his support to Hitler and the other Nazi leaders in a successful effort to make them "salonfähig" (socially acceptable), and he helped contribute to what Peter Reichel has called "der schöne Schein des dritten Reiches" (that is, the glamorous façade). Waldeck strived to exhibit his loyalty to the Nazi leaders and to assuage the lingering doubts he had about their reliability, and he avoided serious penalties for his actions by manipulating the postwar judicial authorities. To this one might add that he strived to subvert historical inquiry.[65] The Waldecks are far from alone among the princely families in keeping the records in the house archives closed to historians (the Princes von Hessen are unique in this regard, and even they would not grant unfettered access). There is still much to learn about princes during the Third Reich: this essay represents a modest contribution toward filling the many lacunae.

NOTES

1. Herbert Ziegler, *Nazi Germany's New Aristocracy: The SS Leadership, 1925–1939* (Princeton, N.J.: Princeton University Press, 1989), xiv. Heinz Höhne, *Order of the Death's Head* (London: Penguin, 2001), 135. More generally, see Jonathan Petropoulos, *Royals and the Reich: The Princes von Hessen in Nazi Germany* (New York and Oxford: Oxford University Press, 2006).

2. The data bank of the former Berlin Document Center as well as Bundesarchiv Berlin (hereafter BAB), Berlin Document Center Series 6400 (SS Officers' Service Records), provide the basis for the previously noted

list of Freiherrn in the SS. See also www.stengerhistorica.com. For more on the father of Princess Michael of Kent, see Alan Palmer, *Crowned Cousins: The Anglo-German Royal Connection* (London: Weidenfeld and Nicolson, 1985), 227.

3. For Prince Alfred Auersperg in the SS, see Marianne Enigl, "Der Adel und die Nazis," in *Profil* 22 (May 24, 2004), 37. For more on aristocrats in the SS, see Tino Jakobs, *Himmlers Mann in Hamburg: Georg Henning Graf von Bassewitz-Behr als höher SS- und Polizeiführer im Wehrkreis X, 1933–1945* (Hamburg: Ergebnisse-Verlag, 2001); and Marie Vassiltchikov, *Berlin Diaries, 1940–1945* (New York: Vintage, 1988), 308.

4. Bernd Wegner, *The Waffen-SS: Organization, Ideology, and Function* (Cambridge, U.K.: Blackwell, 1990), 245.

5. Ruth Bettina Birn, *Die Höheren SS- und Polizeiführer: Himmlers Vertreter im Reich und in den besetzten Geibieten* (Düsseldorf: Droste, 1986), 353. Note that the category Oberschicht is comprised of Rittergutsbesitzer (estate owners) and Hochadel (high aristocracy).

6. Wegner, *The Waffen-SS*, 245.

7. Ziegler, *Nazi Germany's New Aristocracy*, xv.

8. G. S. Graber, *History of the SS* (New York: David McKay, 1978), 66.

9. Wegner, *The Waffen-SS*, 77.

10. See Otto Freiherr von Waldenfels, "Legendenbildung um Himmler: Die königlich-bayerischen Edelknaben und die SS," *Zeitschrift für bayerische Landesgeschichte* 26 (1963), 400–407.

11. Ernst Hanfstaengl, *Unheard Witness* (Philadelphia: Lippincott, 1957), 22.

12. Peter Padfield, *Himmler: The Reichsführer-SS* (London: Cassell, 2001), 21.

13. Ibid., 21, 26.

14. Ibid., 29.

15. Karl Hüser, ed., *Wewelsburg 1933 bis 1945: Kult- und Terrorstätte der SS. Eine Dokumentation* (Paderborn: Verlag Bonifatius, 1982); and BAB, NS 19/3356, Heinrich Himmler to Oswald Pohl, February 26, 1944.

16. Höhne, *Order of the Death's Head*, 154.

17. Padfield, *Himmler*, 96.

18. Birn, *Die Höheren SS- und Polizeiführer*, 10, 332.

19. Count Folke Bernadotte was born Prince Oscar of Sweden and later took the title Count of Wisborg. On his activities at war's end, see Yehuda Bauer, *Jews for Sale? Nazi-Jewish Negotiations, 1933–1945* (New Haven, Conn.: Yale University Press, 1994).

20. Gerald Reitlinger, *The SS: Alibi of a Nation, 1922–1945* (London: Heinemann, 1956), 239.

21. Ibid.

22. "Fürst Josias zu Waldeck gestorben," *Kasseler Allgemeine Zeitung* (December 2, 1967), in Kassel Stadtarchiv, SL 2392. Waldeck had been a First Lieutenant (Oberleutnant) in the 3rd Kurhessische Infantry Regiment, Number 83, seeing action in France and the Balkans. See Anke Schmeling, *Josias Erbprinz zu Waldeck und Pyrmont. Der politische Weg eines hohen SS-Führers* (Kassel: Verlag Gesamthochschul-Bibliothek Kassel, 1993), 19.

23. Nikolaus von Preradovich, "Regierende Fürsten im Dritten Reich: Die Herrschaftsgeschlecter des Deutschen Reiches und der NSDAP," *Deutschland in Geschichte und Gegenwart* 2 (1981), 28–30.

24. Padfield, *Himmler*, 102. Schmeling, *Waldeck*, 60–69, 82. Note that the position as Himmler's adjutant was later held by another aristocrat, Ludolf von Alvensleben.

25. In German, "Büro zur Eindeutschung der Ostvölker." Preradovich, "Regierende Fürsten," 28–30.

26. BAB, SSF-217B, appointment of Waldeck as General der Polizei, signed by Adolf Hitler, April 8, 1941. Christopher Browning, *Ordinary Men: Reserve Police Battalion 101 and the Final Solution in Poland* (New York: HarperPerennial, 1998).

27. Schmeling, *Waldeck*, 48. BAB, SSF-217B, Prince Waldeck to Heinrich Himmler, March 12, 1938.

28. Wolf-Arno Kropat, *"Reichskristallnacht": Der Judenpogrom vom 7. bis 10. November 1938—Urheber, Täter, Hintergründe* (Wiesbaden: Kommission für die Geschichte der Juden in Hessen, 1997), 78, 174.

29. Ralph Heinzen, "Hitler Moves to Forestall French Revolt: Orders Drastic Action to Stem Rising Tide of Resistance," *Washington Post*, April 25, 1942, 1.

30. Ibid.

31. BAB, SSF-217B, SS-Standartenführer Moreth to the judge (Scheidmann des Schiedhofes beim Reichsführer-SS), September 24, 1941.

32. David Kitterman, "Those Who Said 'No!'": Germans Who Refused to Execute Civilians During World War II," *German Studies Review* 11, no. 2 (May 1988), 247.

33. Ibid.

34. Schmeling, *Waldeck*, 93–104.

35. National Archives and Records Administration (hereafter NARA), Record Group (hereafter RG) 153, Stack 270, Row 1, Compartment 19, Shelf 5-7, Box 243: Deputy Judge Advocate's Office, "Review and Recommendations," November 15, 1947, 48–49.

36. NARA, RG 153, Row 1, Compartment 19, Shelf 5-7, Box 246, Judge Advocate, EUCOM, U.S. v. Josias Prince zu Waldeck et al., "Summary of Case," April 9, 1948.

37. Eugen Kogon held Waldeck responsible for Koch's execution. Eugen

Kogon, *The Theory and Practice of Hell: The German Concentration Camps and the System Behind Them* (London: Secker and Warburg, 1950), 265. Anke Schmeling argued that the matter was decided by an SS court in Munich and acquitted him of direct involvement in the execution; however, she detailed his involvement in the deaths that resulted from the evacuation of Buchenwald. Schmeling, *Waldeck,* 111–15, 118.

38. The U.S. Deputy Judge Advocate had noted that "following 1944 there existed an order that in the event of a state of emergency, concentration camps would no longer come under the authority of the headquarters at Oranienburg, but under that of the Higher SS and Police Leaders of the areas in which the camps were located." NARA, RG 153, Stack 270, Row 1, Compartment 19, Shelf 5-7, Box 243: Deputy Judge Advocate's Office, "Review and Recommendations," November 15, 1947.

39. At the Buchenwald trial held at Dachau, the prosecution offered different numbers for the Buchenwald camp (and the approximately 100 subcamps): they maintained that in March 1945, there were 103,000 inmates, of whom 49,000 remained on-site in April 1945. This would entail an evacuation of 54,000. See NARA, RG 153, Row 1, Compartment 19, Shelf 5-7, Box 246, Judge Advocate, EUCOM, "Trial Data," April 9, 1948. The number of 34,000 is given in United States Holocaust Memorial Museum (hereafter USHMM), Buchenwald War Crimes Trial Collection, "Report of Investigation Team," April 18, 1945. Note that Waldeck maintained that the Gauleiter and Reich Defense Minister in Thuringia, Fritz Sauckel, had ordered the dismantling of the Buchenwald camp. Waldeck claimed that he refused and acted only when he received an order from Himmler. He claimed that he then transmitted the order to Pister, the Camp Commandant. Furthermore, he maintained that he "did not supervise or control the evacuation, but he assisted the camp commander in every way possible." This testimony must be viewed in the context of a war crimes trial, where he had strong motivation to offer a self-exculpatory version of events. Note that his appeal of the life sentence was denied by the Deputy Judge Advocate. See NARA, RG 153, Stack 270, Row 1, Compartment 19, Shelf 5-7, Box 243, Deputy Judge Advocate's Office, "Review and Recommendations," November 15, 1947, 50.

40. Ibid.

41. Schmeling, *Waldeck,* 116–20. Kogon, *The Theory and Practice of Hell,* 89.

42. Schmeling, *Waldeck,* 71–72.

43. Reichs-Gesetz-Blatt (1938), Teil I, 825, "Gesetz über das Erlöschen der Fideikommisse und sonstiger gebundener Vermögen," July 6, 1938.

44. Schmeling, *Waldeck,* 71–72.

45. BAB, SSF-217B, Richard Walther Darré to Heinrich Himmler, February 11, 1939.

46. Stephan Malinowski, *Vom König zum Führer: Sozialer Niedergang und politische Radikalisierung im deutschen Adel zwischen Kaiserreich und NS-Staat* (Berlin: Akademie-Verlag, 2003), 566.

47. Christian Zentner and Friedemann Bedürftig, eds., *Encyclopedia of the Third Reich* (New York: Macmillan, 1991), 397.

48. BAB, SSF-217B, Adjutant of Waldeck to Heinrich Himmler, April 7, 1938.

49. Ibid., Heinrich Himmler "Aktennotiz," April 13, 1938.

50. Ibid., Heinrich Himmler to Prince Waldeck, December 22, 1944, and January 13, 1945.

51. Ibid., Dr. Fitsner to Dr. Rudolf Brandt, Personal Staff of the Reichsführer-SS, March 5, 1943.

52. Ibid., SS-Obergruppenführer Udo von Woyrsch to Heinrich Himmler, January 25, 1944.

53. Ibid.

54. NARA, RG 319, Stack 270, Row 84, Compartment 11, Shelf 7, Box 324, Prince Waldeck, "Persönliche Angaben," April 26, 1946.

55. Schmeling, *Waldeck,* 115.

56. See the Buchenwald War Crimes Trial Collection, USMM, which includes William Denson et al., *An Information Booklet on the Buchenwald Concentration Camp Case* (Dachau: 1947). See also the review of the appeal in NARA, RG 153, Stack 270, Row 1, Compartment 19, Shelf 5-7, Box 243, Deputy Judge Advocate's Office, "Review and Recommendations," November 15, 1947. As noted earlier, Waldeck's initial appeal of the life sentence was denied.

57. NARA, RG 153, Stack 270, Row 1, Compartment 19, Shelf 5-7, Box 244, EUCOM Commander in Chief, Judgment and Sentence, June 19, 1948.

58. For the September 17, 1949, judgment of the Spruchkammer concerning Prince zu Waldeck, see Schmeling, *Waldeck,* 129.

59. Ibid., 132, 137.

60. Birn, *Höheren SS- und Polizeiführer,* 347.

61. Stadt-Archiv Kassel, SL 2392, "Eine Prinzenhochzeit," in *Kassel Allgemeine Zeitung* (March 4, 1968).

62. NARA, T-175/90/2612447, Heinrich Himmler to SS-Gruppenführer, August 11, 1937. Also Ziegler, *Nazi Germany's New Aristocracy,* 52.

63. Certain scholars have sensed the contradictions in the SS leader's thinking. Heinz Höhne remarked, "For years the Imperial Guard of National Socialism had preached the law of selection on racial and biological

grounds; now, however, the SS began to lure into its ranks sections of the population possessing qualities which appeared in no dictionary of Nazi racial philosophy—prestige, money, and an aptitude for command born of generations spent in positions of authority." Höhne, *Order of the Death's Head,* 134.

64. For more on the May 19, 1943, "Erlass des Führers über die Fernhaltung international gebundener Männer," see Petropoulos, *Royals and the Reich,* 283.

65. Peter Reichel, *Der schoene Schein des Dritten Reiches. Faszination und Gewalt der Faschismus* (Munich: Hanser, 1991).

Susanna Schrafstetter

When Perpetrators Compensate Victims: Karl Hettlage and the Politics of Indemnification in West Germany

THE STORY OF KARL HETTLAGE IS THE STORY OF A PERPETRATOR WHO was not a National Socialist. It is also the story of a career stretching from the persecution of Jews to the indemnification of victims of Nazism. Hettlage, a devout Catholic and former member of the Catholic Center Party, worked for Albert Speer's Generalbauinspektion (GBI), where he took an active part in the expulsion of Berlin's Jews from their homes and in the "Aryanization" of Jewish-owned real estate.[1] When Speer became minister of armaments in 1942, Hettlage became the head of the new ministry's finance division, where he facilitated the exploitation of slave labor. In 1959, he was appointed to the position of state secretary in the West German Ministry of Finance. At the time, Bonn was negotiating a series of agreements with Western European states regarding compensation to the victims of National Socialism.[2] Karl Hettlage, the onetime "Aryanizer," was intimately involved in these negotiations.

Spanning the biographical arc from persecution to indemnification, this essay examines three major aspects of the career of Karl Hettlage. First, how and why did Hettlage, a devout Catholic, become a perpetrator, despite his religious faith? Second, a career stretching from persecution to compensation for Nazi victims illustrates in a particularly tragic way the shortfalls of postwar denazification and the failure to hold high-level functionaries of the Nazi regime accountable. Hettlage's case demonstrates how elites who had maintained a modicum of ideological distance from the Nazi regime managed to transform that distance into an ostensible track record of resistance after 1945.

• 185

Third, and most important, this essay will address the position taken by Hettlage toward West German plans to provide financial compensation for victims of Nazi persecution. Did Hettlage share the majority of West Germans' indifference—if not outright hostility—toward compensation? Hettlage was not the only West German official with a highly problematic past who was involved with indemnification matters. Thus, his case will be analyzed in comparison to those of two similar figures: Hans Globke and Herbert Blankenhorn. Globke, Konrad Adenauer's state secretary in the federal Chancellery, had served as the coauthor of a legal commentary to the notorious Nuremberg Laws of 1935. Herbert Blankenhorn, Adenauer's foreign policy adviser, had served in the Foreign Ministry from 1929 to 1945 and had been a member of the Nazi Party. Both Blankenhorn and Globke played instrumental roles in negotiating the Luxembourg Agreement with Israel and the Jewish Claims Conference in 1952. This essay will show that Hettlage did not fit the pattern of top-level bureaucrats with tainted pasts, like Globke and Blankenhorn, who, under the eye of public scrutiny, adopted positions favorable to compensation. Operating in an environment that was overwhelmingly hostile toward indemnification—the Ministry of Finance—Hettlage exhibited much less magnanimity to the victims of Nazism, even though his attitude was more moderate than that of many West German politicians. Aside from the question of indemnification, a comparison of the careers of Hettlage, Globke, and Blankenhorn can also shed light on the personal motives and career strategies of a class of men whose expertise proved indispensable to the Nazi regime: young, unenthusiastic, perhaps even reluctant, Schreibtischtäter (bureaucratic perpetrator).

PERSECUTION: KARL HETTLAGE IN THE NAZI BUREAUCRACY, 1933–1945

Born in 1902 in Essen, Karl Hettlage grew up in the town of Eschweiler, near Aachen. He took up the study of law in 1921 and received his Ph.D. from the University of Cologne in 1926. He then secured a position in the municipal administration of Cologne before becoming chief of the financial division of the deutscher Städtetag (Association of German Cities). In April 1932, he was elected a Center Party deputy to the Prussian parliament.[3] Despite his membership in that Catholic-oriented party, he was appointed city treasurer of Berlin in

1934, a position that he kept until the spring of 1939.[4] At that point, he became a member of the board of directors of the Commerzbank.[5] In addition, in 1940 he accepted a job with Albert Speer's GBI, the office in charge of the planned reconstruction of Berlin. Hettlage headed the Hauptamt II, responsible for the financial and legal aspects of the GBI.[6] Joseph Goebbels, the Gauleiter of Berlin, had misgivings about Hettlage's appointment, claiming that he was politically unreliable.[7] Yet he conceded that an investigation of Hettlage had not resulted in incriminating evidence and did not pursue the matter.[8]

The GBI worked closely with the Schutzstaffel (SS) to secure enormous amounts of building materials needed to realize Speer's megalomaniacal architectural plans.[9] Stone and bricks were produced by slave laborers in numerous concentration camps under SS supervision. In conjunction with the German Earth and Stone Works (Deutsche Erd- und Steinwerke GmbH) founded by the SS in 1938, the GBI planned for the building of a stone masonry workshop at Oranienburg (Oranienburg II).[10] The labor would be performed by inmates from the nearby concentration camp. Planning for the Oranienburg brickworks (Oranienburg I) had already been under way for some time. Hettlage was in charge of the relevant financial calculations, drafted the contract, and signed it on behalf of the GBI.[11] Once the project was under way, Hettlage supervised its progress for the GBI and transferred the funds to the SS.

To facilitate his grand designs for the reconstruction of the capital city, Speer organized the demolition of entire residential neighborhoods. This created a housing shortage, which, in turn, led Speer and his advisers to arrange for Jews to be evicted from their apartments. Jewish tenants were gradually forced out to make room for "Aryans" whose buildings had been earmarked for demolition. More and more Jews were forced to live in squalor in the shrinking sector of the housing market in which they were still allowed to live.[12] By January 1941, the GBI had moved to a policy of forced eviction, leading to the deportation of the Berlin Jews to the ghettos of Eastern Europe. Hettlage's Hauptamt II was in charge of coordinating these evictions.[13] At the same time, the GBI participated actively in the "Aryanization" of Jewish-owned real estate.[14]

When Albert Speer was appointed Minister of Armaments in February 1942, Hettlage took over the finance division in Speer's new ministry. As Speer's expert for finance, planning, and supply,

Hettlage played an important role in the running of the German war machine. As a founding member of the Mittelwerk GmbH, Hettlage was instrumental in moving the construction of the production of V-2 rockets from Peenemünde to the underground shafts of Thuringia, where slave laborers from the Mittelbau-Dora camp were expected to build the Führer's "miracle weapons" in the final stages of the war.[15] The horrific living and working conditions and the brutal treatment of the inmates killed many thousands. Walter Dornberger, commander at the Peenemünde rocket facility, called Hettlage "probably the most powerful man in the ministry."[16]

RESTORATION: DENAZIFICATION AND RISE IN THE WEST GERMAN BUREAUCRACY, 1945–1949

After the end of the war, Hettlage was detained in camp "Dustbin" at Kransberg castle with other members of the Speer ministry, including Speer himself. Hettlage tried to present himself as a victim rather than as a perpetrator of the Nazi system. He explained that he had never been a member of the Nazi Party, that he had been an opponent of National Socialism, and that he had been in touch with prominent people who had taken part in the assassination attempt against Hitler in July of 1944.[17] In his interrogations and subsequent denazification process, he remained silent about his position at the Generalbauinspektion. His detailed curriculum vitae (CV) mentioned no word of it.[18] Hettlage explained his departure from the position as city treasurer of Berlin by referring to his appointment to the board of directors at the Commerzbank.[19] His position at the Commerzbank also made another claim seem credible: he maintained that he was merely a "volunteer" in the Ministry of Armaments, serving without pay and on a part-time basis.[20]

At the same time, Hettlage emphasized his contacts with men of the resistance, including Carl Goerdeler, former mayor of Leipzig, and Prussian Finance Minister Johannes Popitz. After his arrest in 1944, Goerdeler testified that he had advised his friend Constantin von Dietze to establish contact with Speer through Hettlage.[21] This testimony may well have triggered Hettlage's own temporary arrest by the Gestapo in the fall of 1944. Although the meeting between Dietze and Speer probably never took place, it is fair to conclude that Goerdeler considered Hettlage a reliable contact in the Speer ministry, even though Hettlage was never an active member of the group of conspirators. Hettlage claimed that he had advised Goerdeler on financial measures to be introduced after the successful coup. Goerdeler did indeed consider Hettlage for a post-Hitler government position, but one should not forget that the conspirators had also planned to include Speer, who was later convicted in Nuremberg as a major war criminal.[22]

In addition, Hettlage provided affidavits from former members of the Center Party such as Heinrich Lübke, later the president of the Federal Republic of Germany, and the former head of the party in the Rhineland, Hugo Mönnig, one of Adenauer's advisers after the war. The denazification panel in Bonn ruled that Hettlage should be considered a confirmed member of the resistance and classified him as "exonerated."[23] Thus, denazification officially turned Hettlage from one of Speer's most influential aides into a member of the resistance.

One year earlier, Hans Globke had also been classified as exonerated by a denazification panel in Aachen.[24] Globke's strategy for self-exculpation had been remarkably similar to Hettlage's. Globke, who also held a Ph.D. in law, emphasized that he had been a member of the Center Party, that he had never joined the Nazi Party, and that he had been an opponent of Nazism with close contacts to the Goerdeler circle. Globke indeed claimed that he was actively involved in the planning of the coup. He provided an impressive array of affidavits: Jakob Kaiser and the bishop of Berlin, Konrad von Preysing, testified that Globke had passed on important information to Catholic officials.[25] Although less blatant in omitting embarrassing truths than Hettlage, Globke failed to disclose that he had unsuccessfully applied for membership in the Nazi Party.[26]

Neither Hettlage nor Globke had been a member of the Nazi Party, but they had joined important affiliated organizations: both had been members of the NS-Rechtswahrerbund and the Akademie für deutsches Recht; Globke had also joined the National Socialist Motorized Corps (NSKK) and the Reichskolonialbund.[27] Moreover, both had served the regime until its demise. Hettlage had even been a member of the SS—which in the process of denazification was considered in his case (probably correctly) to have been merely an honorary rank.[28] Globke, while not a major figure in the Ministry of the Interior, had his name on a viciously antisemitic document that he had produced with his former boss, Wilhelm Stuckart. Even if Globke's interpretation of the Nuremberg Laws was intended to be as favorable as possible to its Jewish targets, as Globke later claimed, his commentary reinforced the policy of pseudolegal racial exclusion of Nazi Germany. In addition, Globke had been involved in drafting the 1939 law requiring German Jews to add David and Sarah as middle names, as well as in other anti-Jewish legislation.[29] The significance of the commentary and other legislation facilitated by Globke is still contested.[30] It is worth emphasizing that Globke had suggested as early as December 1932 that Jews not be allowed to veil their Jewish background through changes of their names.[31]

Globke and Hettlage were two former Center Party members who became perpetrators with ties to resistance circles. After the war, they succeeded in convincing both German and Allied officials that the latter far outweighed the former. In effect, contacts to the resistance annulled more than a decade of service to the National Socialist regime. Lutz Niethammer has referred to the process of denazification as a Mitläuferfabrik: a factory for the production of fellow travelers who could be easily rehabilitated.[32] Both Hettlage and Globke were categorized as less than fellow travelers; both were completely exonerated by their denazification commissions.

Shortly after Hettlage's denazification, Hugo Mönnig attempted to convince Konrad Adenauer that Hettlage be recruited for a position in a postwar government.[33] Adenauer, who apparently thought that Hettlage had been a member of the Nazi Party and the SS, remained lukewarm to the idea. While he believed in the moral integrity of Globke, who had been recommended to him by his confidante Herbert Blankenhorn, Adenauer had reservations about Hettlage. He had known Hettlage in the 1920s, when Hettlage was a young expert on financial law in the municipal administration of Cologne, where Adenauer was then mayor. Adenauer's reservations meant that Hettlage could not immediately assume a government position, but Hettlage still managed to jump-start his career. In 1948 he was appointed chief executive officer (Vorstandsvorsitzender) of the Commerzbank, and in 1951 he became professor of law at the University of Mainz. He was appointed deputy minister of finance of the state of Rheinland-Pfalz in 1956. Two years later, Hettlage joined the federal Ministry of Finance. In 1959 Franz Etzel, the minister of finance, promoted him to state secretary.

While Hettlage's past was well known in government and media circles—even his SS membership was an open secret[34]—his ascent to the position of state secretary in the Ministry of Finance did not trigger any debate. Ironically, Hettlage, who had been far more influential in the Third Reich than Globke, did not have to take the heat of public criticism. Globke, whose name was publicly associated with a staple of antisemitic persecution, the Nuremberg Laws, became the symbol for former Nazis who managed smooth transitions into successful careers in West Germany. Hettlage rose slowly and quietly to a powerful but low-profile position, working for a low-profile minister, Franz Etzel, a member of the Christian Social Union (CSU) who attracted only a fraction of the attention received by his infamous party colleague and successor, Franz Josef Strauss.

INDEMNIFICATION: HETTLAGE, THE BONN REPUBLIC, AND THE VICTIMS OF NAZISM, 1949–1964

One of the first to initiate a process of reconciliation between Jews and Germans was West German President Theodor Heuss, who famously coined the term "collective shame" in 1949 and publicly asked the German people to accept their guilt for Nazi crimes.[35] In his efforts, Heuss was actively supported by top-ranking civil servants in the Chancellery and the Foreign Ministry who had had highly problematic records during the Third Reich. These included Herbert Blankenhorn and Hans Globke, both of whom bent over backward "to be more than accommodating to the Jewish side."[36] Karl Hettlage shared their troubling Nazi-era past and, although he was not involved in the Luxembourg Agreement, he did participate in compensation-related negotiations between West Germany and its European neighbors in the late 1950s. Some people sarcastically commented behind closed doors that if a government of resisters had come to power in West Germany, Bonn would have been far less generous toward the Jews and Israel.[37] The question, then, is whether former perpetrators showed themselves to be especially generous to their former victims and, if so, why? Hettlage, Globke, and Blankenhorn all managed, with a good deal of luck and savvy, to reenter into influential government positions after 1945, and all shared a personal responsibility for atonement. Yet their positions were far from uniform, and the institutional environments in which they operated were also far from uniform.

It should not be forgotten that indemnification for the victims of Nazism—whether it concerned Jewish, non-Jewish, foreign, or German victims—was not popular among ordinary West Germans or among West German politicians.[38] Apart from a handful of deputies in the Bundestag who actively supported indemnification, only the Social Democrats continuously pushed for legislation designed to support the victims. A review of the ratification process of the Luxembourg Agreement, which was concluded with Israel and the Claims Conference in 1952, makes this apparent. All of the Social Democratic Party (Sozialdemokratische Partei Deutschlands, or SPD) deputies voted in favor of the agreement. But of 214 deputies from the Christian Democratic Union (CDU)/CSU, only 106—fewer than half—voted in favor; 5 voted against it; 39 abstained; and the remaining 64 did not participate in the vote. Most deputies of the Free Democratic Party (FDP) abstained as well.[39] Many of the deputies who actively supported indemnification, such as Franz Böhm of the Christian Democratic Union or Jakob Altmeier of the Social Democrats, had suffered personally under Nazi persecution.[40] Ironically, they now found allies in the likes of Globke and Blankenhorn.

Having studied law in Munich and Heidelberg, Herbert Blankenhorn entered the diplomatic service in 1929. Stationed in Athens, Washington, Bern, and ultimately Berlin, Blankenhorn served the Nazi regime while maintaining contacts in the Kreisau circle, particularly to Adam von Trott zu Solz. There is no evidence, however, that Blankenhorn was among the active plotters.[41] Formerly a Center Party supporter, Blankenhorn joined the Nazi Party in 1938 (although a previous application had been rejected in 1934).[42] His overall record during the Nazi era was ambiguous. While he had close contacts to the resistance, some U.S. officials painted a negative picture of him based on assessments of his time in Washington in the late 1930s.[43] Despite his party membership and his continued service in the Foreign Ministry, Blankenhorn was classified as exonerated by a denazification panel in Hamburg in 1947.[44] He became active in the formation of the CDU in the Rhineland, and by 1948 he had become an aide to Konrad Adenauer.

In Adenauer's cabinet, Blankenhorn was the strongest supporter of indemnification for Israel and Jews. He was instrumental in establishing ties with Jewish officials and in pushing the negotiations forward. Praised by Nahum Goldmann, the representative of the Jewish Claims Conference, Blankenhorn understood indemnification for the victims of Nazism as both his personal responsibility and the moral responsibility of the German people as a whole. He saw it as key for "making the German people aware of their horrible past and the necessity of a radical change."[45] Adenauer's State Secretary Otto Lenz claimed that it was Blankenhorn who pushed Adenauer into the Luxembourg Agreement.[46] Blankenhorn, moreover, remained committed to compensation after the Luxembourg Agreement had been concluded.[47]

Blankenhorn paid a price for his support of indemnification. Rumors began to spread that he had been bribed to guarantee that substantial sums of money would be paid to Israel and the Claims Conference.[48] The rumors about bribery, combined with reports about his activities in the Third Reich, were designed to "finally destroy Blankenhorn."[49] There was speculation that the campaign was launched by opponents of the Luxembourg Agreement in the CSU and the FDP,[50] but its origins remain shrouded in mystery. What is clear is that Franz Josef Strauss attacked Blankenhorn for his support of the Luxembourg Agreement, pointing to press articles that Blankenhorn "had been influenced by the Jewish side."[51]

Hans Globke understood perfectly well that he was under close international scrutiny and could ill afford to take a position suggesting that he was hostile toward compensating victims of Nazism. Outspoken support for reconciliation with Israel might soften his image and lend credence to his own claims that he had been an opponent of Nazism. Tom Segev has claimed that Nahum Goldmann used the situation to his advantage. Apparently Goldmann kept a file with material about the Nazi-era records of some members of Adenauer's government. Segev argued that some German officials believed that Goldmann "had the power to ruin them," and that, as a consequence, Goldmann received considerable support from people like Globke.[52] It has been widely acknowledged that Globke did play a positive role in the negotiations toward the Luxembourg Agreement and that he helped foster contacts between West Germany and Israel.[53] In 1960, he arranged the famous meeting between David Ben Gurion and Konrad Adenauer at the Waldorf Astoria hotel in New York.[54] While Globke made arrangements behind the scene, he refrained from publicly supporting compensation to Israel. In fact, his activities remained so discreet that much of the literature on the Luxembourg Agreement does not even consider him worth mentioning.[55]

Globke recognized the political importance of indemnification in the international context. When he was tasked to devise a West German plan for reunification during the Berlin Crisis in 1958–59—a "plan B" in case Bonn had to make concessions[56]—Globke included a provision for compensation of 10 billion DM (deutsche marks) to be paid by a reunited German state. On the one hand, Globke could be fairly certain that the paper would remain a dead letter and the clause could be seen as an easy gimmick. On the other hand, it shows that Globke was aware that on conclusion of a peace treaty with its former enemies, a united Germany would have to face its responsibility for compensation. Moreover, Globke had the courage to put a relatively generous price tag on compensation. In a sense, it was no surprise, then, that in 1964 Kurt Grossmann, while negotiating with West Germany over indemnification payments, said he longed for the times when Globke had been state secretary.[57]

At the time the Luxembourg Agreement was being concluded in 1952, Karl Hettlage was still a professor in Mainz. When he became state secretary in the Ministry of Finance in 1959, West Germany was in the process of negotiating a series of bilateral compensation agreements with its Western European neighbors.[58] In these negotiations, Franz Etzel, the minister of finance, pursued a tactic of conceding as little as possible as late as possible, much as his predecessor, Fritz Schäffer, had done during the negotiations toward the Luxembourg Agreement. Partly due to illness, Etzel left a lot of his day-to-day business to his state secretary, Karl Hettlage. Etzel's stingy approach to compensation was supported by his subordinates in the ministry who were directly involved with compensation matters. Aside from Hettlage, the key figure was Ernst Féaux de la Croix. A lawyer by training, Féaux de la Croix had joined the Nazi Party and the Sturmabteilungen (SA) in 1933 and had served in the Reich Ministry of Justice from 1934 to 1945. He had also been a member of the Akademie für deutsches Recht, for which he had coauthored a racist memorandum in 1938.[59]

Naturally, the Ministry of Finance had to take a cautious approach to what was financially possible for West Germany and to give priority to a balanced budget. However, Constantin Goschler has shown that the ministry was gripped by a "siege mentality,"[60] which led officials to regard themselves as "heroes in the battles against compensation," defending West Germany against excessive, never-ending financial demands from the victims of Nazism. Their perceived enemies were not only the "international lobby" of victims' organizations but also colleagues in the Foreign Ministry.[61] Clashes between the two ministries over the financial sums that should be offered in the negotiations were the inevitable consequence. The Ministry of Finance officials failed to understand that West Germany's international image and moral reputation was at stake. In several instances, Adenauer himself ultimately had to intervene on behalf of the Foreign Ministry in order to prevent a breakdown of the negotiations.

During the negotiations with Greece, for example, Hettlage agreed to the final sum that had been negotiated by the Foreign Ministry (and approved by Adenauer's cabinet) only because of Adenauer's personal intervention in the matter.[62] The Foreign Ministry had emphasized the importance of reaching an agreement with Greece, not only in order to help drive a wedge between Greece and the Communist bloc but also for the sake of "the Federal Republic and its image, in view of recent antisemitic incidents."[63] This argument had been ignored by the Ministry of Finance until forced to give in by Chancellor Adenauer.

However, Karl Hettlage, it should be emphasized, was more ready to compromise than was Féaux de la Croix, whose eagerness to reduce compensation to a minimum had hardly any limits. In the negotiations with France, Norway, and Switzerland, Hettlage ultimately agreed to the sums negotiated by the Foreign Ministry, while in other cases, such as those of Greece or a United Nations fund for stateless victims, he stalled until forced to relent.[64] Hettlage never explicitly stated his position with regard to the principle of indemnification. When he signaled his acceptance of financial compromises, he did so in memoranda of a few innocuous lines. When he expressed opposition to a proposed compensation arrangement, he invoked arguments about costs and legal complications. While probably the one least affected by the "siege syndrome" in his ministry, he clearly did not see financial compensation for the victims of Nazism as his personal responsibility or his chance for personal redemption. In many instances, he passed up the opportunity to show magnanimity to the victims, opting for stubborn haggling instead of an amicable settlement. Ultimately, this was not just a missed personal opportunity. The difficult and drawn-out negotiations damaged West Germany's image in many countries, an effect that negated the political benefits that could have been reaped by showing generosity toward the victims and a genuine desire for atonement.

It would be easy to argue that Hettlage took the least magnanimous position because he was fortunate enough not to be under public scrutiny, as were Globke and Blankenhorn. He also operated in a different environment, the Finance Ministry, in which there was an obsessive concern with saving money. Finance Minister Schäffer's outbursts against compensation were notorious. They were nasty and clearly bore antisemitic overtones.[65] But it is also true that Schäffer was opposed to spending any money for any purpose. The particular "siege mentality" toward compensation in the Finance Ministry stemmed from two factors. First, the costs for compensating Nazi victims were subsumed under the category of Kriegsfolgelasten—expenses resulting from the war—together with items such as the Lastenausgleich or widows' pensions.[66] Consequently, the victims of Nazism (mostly foreigners or émigrés) were placed in direct competition with German widows, orphans, and expellees.[67] Second, the defensive posture related largely to concerns about future demands. "Giving in" to new categories of victims would create new legal precedents and trigger new and larger demands, especially from Eastern Europe. The Cold War had allowed Bonn to ignore demands for compensation from the other side of the iron curtain, a financially advantageous situation that the Ministry of Finance was determined to maintain.

Globke and Blankenhorn, in contrast, operated in a political and diplomatic environment in which compensation was recognized as a precondition for West Germany's reemergence into the international community. Their views were informed primarily by this consideration rather than by financial considerations (or, in the case of Bundestag deputies, by the domestic unpopularity of indemnification). Globke's quiet backing of compensation does not necessarily indicate a more general and thorough reflection on past wrongs and an acceptance of personal and collective responsibility. His support for indemnification, for example, contrasts with his outspoken support for the release of German war criminals from prison.[68] Moreover, as state secretary in the Chancellery he approved government appointments of many individuals with dubious Nazi-era records. Most notoriously, Globke oversaw the recruitment of the intelligence services (Bundesnachrichtendienst), which on his watch became populated with former members of the Security Service (Sicherheitsdienst) of the Reich Security Main Office.[69] Similarly, Blankenhorn, responsible for rebuilding the Foreign Ministry, consistently reappointed Foreign Ministry veterans including former Nazi Party members.[70] In Blankenhorn's case, there may have been an argument for relying on experienced diplomats. But in Globke's case, the recruitment of men who had worked for Heinrich Himmler and Reinhard Heydrich seems hard to justify.

The attacks on Blankenhorn, the stories about a "Jewish conspiracy" underpinning financial compensation for Israel, the "no" votes and abstentions cast for the Luxembourg Agreement, and the general unpopularity of indemnification all reflect the fact that sympathy for the foreign victims of Nazism remained weak in West Germany. Initiatives aimed at addressing the needs and demands of such victims challenged the widespread and self-serving notion that the Germans themselves were victims of Nazism and of World War II. The financial indemnification of foreign victims was regarded as being in competition with financial support for Germany's own victims of those terrible times.[71] Seen in this context, even Karl Hettlage's miserly position with regard to compensation must be characterized as relatively moderate.

CONCLUSIONS

The moral implications of putting individuals such as Karl Hettlage in charge of compensation matters are self-evident. Whether it was ultimately to the benefit of Israel and the Jewish Claims Conference, as some cynical voices claimed, that individuals with tainted pasts were in the government and therefore politically could not afford to reject compensation claims, is questionable as well. This factor may have played a role in international negotiations, where the individuals in the limelight were Globke or Blankenhorn. However, the key expert on compensation in the Ministry of Finance, Ernst Féaux de la Croix, saw himself in a battle against claimants. His memoranda were not under international scrutiny. Despite the recent efflorescence of scholarship on the politics of memory in postwar Germany, we still have no good handle on the question of how many similar officials populated German ministries, compensation offices, and courts. Historians of indemnification have only just begun to investigate this question.

Globke, Hettlage, and to some extent Blankenhorn followed remarkably similar career paths: Globke and Hettlage possessed doctorates in law; both were devout Catholics and before 1933 had been members of the Center Party, with which Blankenhorn also often sympathized; all three had served the Third Reich as reluctant but dutiful bureaucrats with contacts to resistance circles; and all three were exonerated in the process of denazification, enabling them to enjoy successful postwar careers in government. Raul Hilberg has characterized the apolitical, nonideological Schreibtischtäter as the quintessential German bureaucrat who, motivated by loyalty, obedience, and professionalism, contributed to the destruction of the European Jews.[72] Globke, Hettlage, and Blankenhorn might be best understood as reluctant Schreibtischtäter who found themselves hovering between conformity and rejection of the regime. Conformity usually proved to be the stronger impulse. There were strong arguments in favor of conformity: a good, steady income; a young family at home; a deferment from military service; and the sense of being shielded by charismatic, supposedly undogmatic, bosses. Speer and Stuckart in particular were not known to be ideological zealots and were able to protect their employees, particularly after the July 20, 1944, assassination plot. Hettlage admitted that he was personally fascinated by Speer.[73] Another factor was age. They were young (Globke, the oldest, was thirty-five in 1933) and eager to transform their extensive educations into rewarding careers.

Hans Globke hid his unsuccessful application to the Nazi Party. Karl Hettlage purged the GBI from his CV. Rudolf Wolters sanitized the diary that he had kept as Speer's aide at the GBI, deleting all references to the eviction of Jewish Berliners from their homes.[74] Wolters got to the crux of the matter in a poem he composed to honor his friend Karl Hettlage's sixty-fifth birthday in 1967. In the poem, which was exchanged privately, Wolters joked about altering the historical record to cover up misdeeds of the Nazi period. With regard to all the honors that Hettlage had received for his professional accomplishments, Wolters sarcastically observed that the gaps in Hettlage's CV had to be hidden from Nazi-hunter Simon Wiesenthal.[75] In effect, Wolters's poem ridiculed the inadequacies of West Germany's confrontation with the Nazi past. With sanitized CVs, former perpetrators climbed to high positions and received high honors. In the case of Karl Hettlage, a record of dutiful service to Albert Speer did not constitute an obstacle to being awarded the West German Federal Service Cross in 1967, which he received in recognition of his "reliability, dutifulness, and readiness to serve the commonwealth."[76]

NOTES

1. Susanne Willems, *Der entsiedelte Jude. Albert Speers Wohnungsmarktpolitik für den Berliner Hauptstadtbau* (Berlin: Metropol, 2000).
2. Hans Günter Hockerts, Claudia Moisel, and Tobias Winstel, eds., *Grenzen der Wiedergutmachung. Die Entschädigung für NS-Verfolgte in West- und Osteuropa* (Göttingen: Wallstein, 2006).
3. Herbert Hömig, *Das preußische Zentrum in der Weimarer Republik* (Mainz: Grünewald, 1979), 300.
4. Willems, *Der entsiedelte Jude*, 29.
5. Ibid., 29–30.
6. Bundesarchiv Berlin (hereafter BAB), R 4606/370, 94, Hans Heinrich Lammers to Albert Speer, May 4, 1940.
7. Elke Fröhlich, ed., *Die Tagebücher von Joseph Goebbels, Teil 1 Aufzeichnungen 1923–1941*, volume 8 (Munich: K. G. Saur, 1998), September 19, 1940, 333.
8. Ibid., October 6, 1940, 363.
9. Paul Jaskot, *The Architecture of Oppression: The SS, Forced Labor and the Nazi Monumental Building Economy* (London: Routledge, 2000).
10. Hermann Kaienburg, *Die Wirtschaft der SS* (Berlin: Metropol, 2003), 727–45; Jaskot, *The Architecture*, 28–30.
11. Kaienburg, *Die Wirtschaft*, 734–36.
12. Willems, *Der entsiedelte Jude*.
13. Ibid., 180.
14. Ibid., 126–29.
15. Jens Christian Wagner, *Produktion des Todes. Das KZ Mittelbau-Dora* (Göttingen: Wallstein, 2001), 195; Michael Thad Allen, *The Business of Genocide: The SS, Slave Labor, and the Concentration Camps* (Chapel Hill: University of North Carolina Press, 2002), 219–20.
16. Walter Dornberger, *V2—Der Schuss ins Weltall* (Esslingen: Bechtle, 1952), 90.
17. Institut für Zeitgeschichte (hereafter IfZ), Archiv, ZS 920, Prof. Dr. Karl Hettlage, Questionnaire NIQS-II, Office of Chief of Counsel for War Crimes, Nuremberg, December 31, 1946; National Archives (hereafter NA) Kew, Foreign Office (hereafter FO) 1031/141, Report No. 18: examination of Karl Hettlage June 26 and 28, 1945.
18. NA, FO 1031/141, Report No. 18: examination of Karl Hettlage

June 26 and 28, 1945; Landesarchiv Nordrhein-Westphalen (hereafter LA NRW), LK/BO/833/ED 3079, denazification file Prof. Karl Hettlage, CV, undated. Large parts of Hettlage's questionnaire are missing, among them the sections on employment. However, his complete four-page CV does not mention the GBI at all.

19. NA, FO 1031/141, Report No. 18: examination of Karl Hettlage June 26 and 28, 1945; LA NRW, LK/BO/833/ED 3079, denazification file Prof. Karl Hettlage, CV, undated.

20. In fact, Hettlage had received a monthly salary of 1,580 RM (reichsmarks) from the Generalbauinspektion. BAB (formerly in Berlin Document Center), DS/Speer Listen E 92, Blatt 744, payroll 1944/45.

21. Hans Adolf Jacobsen, *Spiegelbild einer Verschwörung* (Stuttgart: Seewald, 1984), 433.

22. Matthias Schmidt, *Albert Speer: das Ende eines Mythos* (Munich: Scherz, 1982), 123.

23. LA NRW, LK/BO/833/ED 3079, denazification, case summary, July 14, 1948.

24. LA NRW, NW 1079/5476, denazification, case summary, September 8, 1947.

25. LA NRW, NW 1079/5476, denazification file Dr. Globke, affidavits by Jakob Kaiser, December 31, 1945, and Konrad von Preysing, January 18, 1946.

26. Erik Lommatzsch, "Hans Globke und der Nationalsozialismus. Eine Skizze," *Historisch Politische Mitteilungen* 10 (2003), 95–128, here 104; and Dan Rogers, "Restoring a German Career: The Ambiguity of Being Hans Globke," *German Studies Review* 31, no. 2 (2008), 303–24, who showed why Globke was able to hide this information.

27. LA NRW, NW 1079/5476, denazification file Dr. Globke, questionnaire; LA NRW, LK/BO/833/ED 3079, denazification file Prof. Hettlage, case summary.

28. Landesarchiv Berlin (hereafter LAB), B Rep. 031-02-01, Nr. 11536, Spruchgericht Bielefeld, Einstellung des Verfahrens, November 18, 1948.

29. Annette Weinke, *Die Verfolgung von NS-Tätern im geteilten Deutschland* (Paderborn: Schöningh, 2002), 153.

30. Lommatzsch, "Hans Globke," 109–113, supported Globke's account. Others have been more cautious: Weinke, *Die Verfolgung*, 410; Henning Köhler, *Adenauer* (Berlin: Propyläen, 1994), 727–28.

31. Raul Hilberg, *Die Vernichtung der europäischen Juden*, volume 1 (Frankfurt: Fischer, 1990), 38.

32. Lutz Niethammer, *Die Mitläuferfabrik* (Berlin: Dietz, 1982), 663.

33. Stiftung Bundeskanzler Adenauer Haus, I 0722, Bl. 240, Hugo Mönnig to Konrad Adenauer, July 30, 1948.

34. "Alles falsch gemacht," *Der Spiegel* 16, no. 4 (January 24, 1962), 20.

35. Yeshayahu Jelinek, *Deutschland und Israel 1945–1965. Ein neurotisches Verhältnis* (Munich: Oldenbourg, 2004), 61.

36. Ibid.

37. Jelinek, *Deutschland und Israel*, 61.

38. For the mood among the population, see Hans Günter Hockerts, "Wiedergutmachung in Deutschland. Eine historische Bilanz 1945–2000," *Vierteljahrshefte für Zeitgeschichte* 49 (2001), 167–214.

39. Jelinek, *Deutschland und Israel*, 247.

40. Constantin Goschler, *Schuld und Schulden. Die Politik der Wiedergutmachung für NS-Verfolgte seit 1945* (Göttingen: Wallstein, 2005), 144. The lawyer Franz Böhm led the German delegation in the negotiations with Israel. He had been dismissed from his university professorship in 1940 after criticizing Nazi racial policy. Jakob Altmeier, who was Jewish, had emigrated during the Third Reich period and returned to Germany after the war. Ibid., 143.

41. Birgit Ramscheid, *Herbert Blankenhorn (1904–1991). Adenauers Aussenpolitischer Berater* (Düsseldorf: Droste, 2006), 65–68.

42. Ibid., 44–45.

43. Ibid., 46, 79–81.

44. Ibid., 94.

45. Ibid., 190.

46. Otto Lenz, *Im Zentrum der Macht. Das Tagebuch von Staatssekretär Lenz 1951–53* (Düsseldorf: Droste, 1989), 571.

47. Krzysztof Ruchniewicz, "Deutschland und das Problem der Nachkriegsentschädigungen für Polen," in Hockerts, Moisel, and Winstel, *Grenzen*, 667–739, here 686–87.

48. Ramscheid, *Herbert Blankenhorn*, 200.

49. Ibid., 201.

50. Ibid., 202.

51. Lenz, *Im Zentrum*, 572.

52. Tom Segev, *Die siebte Million. Der Holocaust und Israels Politik der Erinnerung* (Reinbek: Rowohlt, 1995), 307–8.

53. Köhler, *Adenauer*, 729; Goschler, *Schuld*, 144–45.

54. Franz J. Bach, "Globke und die auswärtige Politik," in *Der Staatssekretär Adenauers*, ed. Klaus Gotto (Stuttgart: Klett Cotta, 1980), 169–70.

55. See, for example, Ronald Zweig, *German Reparations and the Jewish World: A History of the Claims Conference* (London: Frank Cass, 2001); Constantin Goschler, *Wiedergutmachung. Westdeutschland und die Verfolgten des Nationalsozialismus (1945–1954)* (Munich: Oldenbourg, 1992); Ludolf Herbst and Constantin Goschler, eds., *Wiedergutmachung in der Bundesrepublik Deutschland* (Munich: Oldenbourg, 1989).

56. Hans Peter Schwarz, *Adenauer: Der Staatsmann 1952–67* (Stuttgart: Deutsche Verlags Anstalt, 1991), 479. Sometimes the sum of 20 billion DM is mentioned. Hans Günter Hockerts, "Wiedergutmachung. Ein umstrittener Begriff und ein weites Feld," in *Nach der Verfolgung. Wiedergutmachung nationalsozialistischen Unrechts in Deutschland,* eds. Hans Günter Hockerts and Christiane Kuller (Göttingen: Wallstein, 2003), 7–33, here 18.

57. Goschler, *Schuld,* 260; and "Wiedergutmachung: Sehnsucht nach Globke," *Der Spiegel,* 18, no. 25 (1964), June 17, 1964, 35.

58. For details, see Hockerts, Moisel, and Winstel, *Grenzen.*

59. Ernst Klee, *Das Personenlexikon zum Dritten Reich* (Frankfurt: Fischer, 2003), 145.

60. Goschler, *Schuld,* 270, 289.

61. Bundesarchiv Koblenz (hereafter BAK), B126/51593, Ernst Féaux de la Croix to Karl Hettlage, March 8, 1960.

62. Hagen Fleischer and Despina Konstantinakou, "Ad calendas graecas? Griechenland und deutsche Wiedergutmachung," in Hockerts, Moisel, and Winstel, *Grenzen,* 418.

63. Ibid., 416.

64. BAK, B136/1148, Karl Hettlage to Foreign Ministry, September 11, 1959.

65. Goschler, *Schuld,* 140; Jelinek,*Deutschland und Israel,* 211.

66. BAK, B 126/51592, Kriegsfolgelasten (ohne Besatzungskosten) für die Rechnungsjahre 1948–1963, undated; Sowie Kriegsfolgelasten des Bundes für die Rechnungsjahre 1950 bis 1963, Stand January 15, 1958.

67. Goschler, *Schuld,* 130, 137.

68. Lenz, *Im Zentrum,* 374.

69. Wenke, *Die Verfolgung,* 411.

70. Köhler, *Adenauer,* 732.

71. Goschler, *Schuld,* 137.

72. Hilberg, *Die Vernichtung,* Band 3, 1061–68. On Globke, see also Raul Hilberg, *Täter, Opfer, Zuschauer. Die Vernichtung der Juden 1933–45* (Frankfurt: Fischer, 1996), 37.

73. Gitta Sereny, *Albert Speer: His Battle with Truth* (London: Macmillan, 1995), 157.

74. Schmidt, *Speer,* 25–27.

75. BAK, N1340/27, Karl Maria Hettlage zum November 27, 1967.

76. Klaus Vogel, "Karl Maria Hettlage zum 90. Geburtstag," *Archiv des öffentlichen Rechts* 117 (1992), 645.

Suzanne Brown-Fleming

The Vatican and the Nazi Movement, 1922–1939: New Sources and Unexpected Findings on the Vatican's Response to Reichskristallnacht

IN FEBRUARY 2003, IN AN UNPRECEDENTED BREAK WITH VATICAN Secret Archives' policy, the Holy See opened those records pertaining to the Munich and Berlin nunciatures (Vatican diplomatic headquarters) for the period 1922 to 1939.[1] During these years, Eugenio Pacelli, the future Pope Pius XII (1939–58), served as nuncio to Bavaria (1917), nuncio to Germany (1920), and secretary of state to Pope Pius XI (1930–39). The archives of the United States Holocaust Memorial Museum (USHMM) now hold microfilm copies of this subset of critical new primary source material. This collection, acquired by the USHMM in 2006, consists of ninety-five reels of material. The languages necessary for accessing it fully are Latin, Italian, German, and French. Key topics covered in this collection include Nazi attacks on Catholic diplomatic headquarters, associations, schools, priests and other religious, and laymen, and the Church's responses to them; the evolution of the Holy See's position with regard to fascism and National Socialism, including official written protests lodged against the Nazi government by the Holy See; the 1933 Concordat between Pope Pius XI and Adolf Hitler; the dissolution of the Center Party; the conflict between Germany and Poland over the Free City of Danzig; sterilization; the reincorporation of the Saar Territory into the Reich; the assassination of Erich Klausener; the Church's position on the Nazi Labor Service (Arbeitsdienst); the foreign exchange currency (Devisenschmuggel) trials;[2] German rearmament; relations between the German Catholic episcopacy and Reich Minister for Church Affairs Hanns Kerrl;[3] the production and dissemination of the important 1938 encyclical *Mit Brennender Sorge;* Hitler's 1938 visit to Rome; and Reichskristallnacht.

In 2006, Pope Benedict XVI authorized that additional documentation from the Vatican Secret Archives for the 1922–39 period be opened to scholars, who were given access as of September 18, 2006.[4] Thirty thousand new volumes of papers, with pages totaling in the millions, are available for the period, including Pacelli's previously unpublished diaries—his personal notes, written in his own hand after every audience with Pius XI and with the diplomats accredited to the Holy See, from August 1930 through the death of Pius XI on February 10, 1939. These "thousands of hand-written pages, made in Pacelli's normal handwriting" will be published as a series of volumes edited by prefect of the Vatican Secret Archives Father Sergio Pagano. The first volume was to be published in 2007 but did not appear on schedule. Within a few years, the digital edition of Thomas Brechenmacher's work in progress, *Reports of the Apostolic Nuncio Cesare Orsenigo from Germany, 1930–1939 (Berichte des Apostolischen Nuntius Cesare Orsenigo aus Deutschland, 1930–1939),* will also be available to scholars.[5] In the USHMM library are the Vatican Secret Archives' DVD-CD image files of records of the Vatican Information Office for Prisoners of War, covering the years 1939 through 1947 *(Inter Arma Caritas: L'Ufficio Informazioni Vaticano Per I Prigionieri Di Guerra Istituito Da Pio XII, 1939–1947),* first published in 2004. Only a few years ago, Nazi-era decoded cables from the Vatican Secretariat of State to its European nunciatures became available at the National Archives in College Park, Maryland.[6]

These documents suggest a new reality for scholars studying the Catholic Church and the Holocaust. To borrow from the great Holocaust historian Saul Friedländer, the 1930s saw "Catholic appeasement of Hilter's regime."[7] Pinning their hopes on the Concordat signed in 1933, Pope Pius XI and his secretary of state, Eugenio Pacelli, remained "wary" of confrontation with the Nazi regime, Nazi violations of the Concordat excepted. Pius XI's departure from this stance at the end of his life, characterized by the never-published encyclical *Humani Generis Unitas,* never bore fruit because of his death in 1939. With so much new documentation at hand, we may now look at this picture of "Catholic appeasement" anew. This brief essay will test the interpretation of "Catholic appeasement" in light of the documents found in the folio labeled "Reichskristallnacht," which the author has viewed in its entirety.

The Reichskristallnacht folio contains fifteen documents: ten letters from private individuals, some addressed to Secretary of State Pacelli and some to Pope Pius XI and all written in August 1938,[8] and five pieces of official correspondence. Small in number, letters from private individuals illuminate the atmosphere in Europe and the United States in the months before the November pogrom. On August 12, 1938, German American Catholic Dr. Gotthold Steinführer of Chicago, Illinois, wrote a brief and impassioned letter to Pope Pius XI in Rome.

> Permit me to make Your Eminence aware of the words of our Lord Jesus Christ regarding the Jewish question, for example in Matthew 8:11[9] and Revelation 2:9.[10] Your Eminence should not defend the Jews, who [belong to] the Synagogue of Satan. Referring to the above words of Christ, those who defend the Jews defend for Satan. The entire Gospel of John shows the fight of the Jews against Christ. The greatest enemies of all Christendom are the Jews, from Paul until today. Yours Faithfully, Dr. Gotthold Steinführer.[11]

Such ugly sentiments were expressed only in this letter. Catholics whose families were affected by the September 15, 1935, Nuremberg Laws (Law to Protect German Blood and Honor and the Reich Citizenship Law) and other Nazi legal restrictions affecting Jews wrote the remaining letters. Mrs. Georg Marse described herself as "a German Catholic wife to a Jewish German doctor." Their four children, baptized as Catholics and raised in Catholic schools, were now defined by the Nazi state as "half Aryans." Mrs. Marse wrote to Pope Pius XI as a last measure following years of unsuccessful attempts to find financial support for emigration. "I have found no help. The Jewish committees are only responsible for purely Jewish cases! Our family consists of but one Jew and five Catholics! How can my husband expect help from the Jews with his Catholic wife and his [four] Catholic children!? The tragedy of the Jews is shattering, but more shattering [is the tragedy of] the Christian half-Aryans, for the help offered in so many ways for Jews is closed to half-Aryans because they 'are not Jewish,'" she wrote in her impassioned letter.[12] Another letter, addressed to Pope Pius XI and received by the Holy See in August 1938, made the same argument: "I am one of the many thousands of my comrades in fate . . . so-called

'Half-Jews' [Halbjuden]. Our lot is [worse than] that of Jews, in that Jews are caring for their coreligionists and help one another over us, who are Christians; our coreligionists leave us in the lurch—no one cares about us!! One wants to shout to all the world, Christians, where are you?"[13] While too small in number to allow for broader analysis, such letters reflect the general need for further research on discussions and concrete aid efforts within the Holy See regarding those Catholics who were defined as Jews by the Nazi state. Currently, no monograph treats this important subject.

Of greatest interest are three official reports from the Vatican nuncio in Berlin, Cesare Orsenigo, to the secretary of state in Rome, Eugenio Pacelli (the future Pope Pius XII). The first two concern Reichskristallnacht and are dated November 15 and 19, 1938, respectively. The third concerns the ordinance requiring German Jews to wear the yellow star, dated September 13, 1941.

A brief word about Cesare Orsenigo, author of the three reports, is in order. An Italian national who was Pacelli's successor as nuncio to Germany in 1930, fifty-six years of age when he was appointed to Berlin, Archbishop Orsenigo has thus far not fared well in the historiography for the 1933–45 period. His contemporary, George Shuster, described Orsenigo as "frankly, jubilant" about Hitler's appointment to the chancellorship on January 30, 1933.[14] Michael Phayer, in his important book, *The Catholic Church and the Holocaust*, described Orsenigo as "a pro-German, pro-Nazi, anti-Semitic fascist."[15]

Given Orsenigo's disposition, these three reports, with a tone that was decidedly sympathetic to beleaguered Jewry, were an unexpected find. They point to the importance of new documentation that will clarify what is, at present, a very murky picture. Let us begin with Orsenigo's first report about Reichskristallnacht, dated November 15, 1938. His description of the events themselves openly acknowledged the reality of antisemitic vandalism (as he titled the report) and the Nazi and German popular role therein:

> The destructions have been initiated, as if by a single order. . . . The blind popular revenge followed one identical method everywhere: in the night, all display windows were shattered and the synagogues were set on fire; the day after, shops that did not have any defense were looted. Doing this, [the looters] destroyed all the goods, even the most expensive ones. Only towards the afternoon of the 10th, when the masses, having vented their wildest

feelings, and not being restrained by any policeman, did Minister [Joseph] Goebbels give the order to stop, characterizing what happened as venting by "the German people...." All of this easily leaves the impression that the order or permission to act came from a higher authority.... The hour is to follow of ministerial laws and dispositions in order to isolate Jews more and more, prohibiting them every commerce, every [ability to frequent] the public schools, every partaking in places of public diversion (theaters, cinemas, concerts, cultural meetings), with a fine totaling one billion [reichsmarks] to be paid [by Jews themselves].[16]

In the remainder of the report, Orsenigo noted the strong temptation of German Jewry to commit suicide in the wake of these terrible events. He also noted the positive if limited efforts by the embassies of Colombia, the United Kingdom, and the Netherlands to document these events and protect the assets of Jewish nationals, and he openly criticized Poland, writing, "It was . . . Poland that provoked the violent action of Germany" by refusing to extend the expired passports of Polish Jews from Germany, prompting Germany to "suddenly sen[d] back to Poland tens of thousands of Jews, and among these and also the parents [of] the young exasperated boy [Polish Jewish student Herszel Grynszpan], that then assassinated the German ambassador [sic][17] in Paris [Ernst vom Rath]."[18] In the report when read as a whole, Orsenigo appears critical of the events of Kristallnacht, critical of the Nazi state, and critical of the German population.

The second report, dated November 19, 1938, concerned impending legislation declaring "null and void all marriages already conducted" between "Aryans" and Jews, including those marriages in which the Jewish spouse had converted to Catholicism after the marriage.[19] Not surprisingly, Orsenigo objected to the legislation due to its disregard for canon law, but more surprisingly, he added critical commentary about the increasingly radical nature of the Nazi state, noting that "serenity and competence" were "more and more lacking in high places of command" and that there existed a "state of mood that [Orsenigo thought] greased the anti-Semitic events, reveals always more and more turbulence and agitation, and is increasingly less able to be controlled." He lamented, too, that Hitler, whom he referred to as the so-called "Supreme Legislator," was perceived as being above the law.[20]

In his third report, dated September 13, 1941, Orsenigo described with decided sympathy the new legislation prohibiting all Jews still residing in the German Reich or the Protectorate of Bohemia and Moravia from appearing in public without the yellow star. The final paragraph of this memorandum, which again raises the issue of Catholics defined as Jews in Nazi racial law, read:

> Such a law is surely a painful humiliation for the Jews, attesting to the anti-Semitic atmosphere that already encircles them. The baptized non-Aryans [non ariani battezzati] feel especially confused, and are exposed to enormous pain, that will not stop even when they enter church, especially on Feast Days for the customary practices of piety. The echoes of these pains have reached His Eminence Cardinal Innitzer and His Eminence Cardinal Bertram; opportunities were studied to assign to the Jews a reserved place in church, and also, if they were numerous, to offer them special services. The painful situation of non Aryan Catholics [non ariani cattolici] is [a] subject [of jurisdiction] for the Ministry of Ecclesiastical Affairs, but I am of the opinion that it is not possible for the church to function as a mediator, since these laws are accessible to all [and] appear in public. His Eminence Cardinal Bertram examined the proposal which will be turned to the Interior Ministry, but I fear it is useless.[21]

Let us return to Reichskristallnacht for a moment and to Eugenio Pacelli's response. We know that he received both of Orsenigo's reports of November 15 and 19, and, hence, received direct and detailed information about the pogrom described, as we have seen, in surprisingly empathetic prose by Orsenigo. Although no documentation of Pacelli's response to the two Orsenigo reports has yet been discovered, we do have available Pacelli's response to a request from Cardinal Arthur Hinsley, Roman Catholic archbishop of Westminster, that Pope Pius XI make a statement about the pogrom. The story was this: in late November, Cardinal Hinsley sent to Pacelli a request from Lord Viktor Rothschild, whom Hinsley described as "the most famous and highly esteemed amongst Jews in England."[22] On November 26, 1938, Cardinal Hinsley wrote to Pacelli the following:

> On 9 December there will be a public gathering in London in order to ask [for] aid and attendance to all those who suffer from persecution [for reasons of] religion or race. . . . If [in] principle [it] were possible to have an authentic word of the Holy Father being declared that in Christ discrimination of race does not ex-

ist and that the great human family must be joined in peace [by] means of respect of the personality of the individual, such message would [be] sure [to] have in England and America, [and] nevertheless through the entire world, the [effect of] leading to good will towards the [Catholic] Religion and the Holy See."[23]

Pacelli's notes in response to this letter, dated December 3, 1938, are published in *Actes et documents du Saint Siège relatifs à la Seconde Guerre mondial*. They read as follows:

> If the [matter] were of substantially private character, it would be easier. On the other hand, it is necessary to remove the appearance of fearing that which does not need to be feared. Cardinal Hinsley could speak [if] saying he is surely interpreting the thought of the Sovereign Pontiff saying that the [matter] not only finds the Pope in a moment of much worry for his health, but also overwhelmed by the amount of matters before him. It is therefore not possible for [the Holy Father] to [respond] personally. He [Cardinal Hinsley] can say that he is interpreting the thoughts of the Holy Father which view all aid to those who are unhappy and unjustly (unworthily or dishonorably) suffering with a humane and Christian eye.[24]

The preceding response was telegraphed to Cardinal Hinsley on December 3.[25]

On December 9, illustrious figures that included Cardinal Hinsley; William Cosmo Gordon Lang, archbishop of Canterbury; Lord Rothschild; Clement R. Attlee, leader of the opposition in the House of Commons; Sir Alan Anderson, Conservative member of Parliament (MP); and General Evangeline Booth, representative of the Salvation Army, gathered at the invitation of Sir Frank Bowater, Lord Mayor of London, at the Mansion House.[26] A resolution "offering whole-hearted support" for the Lord Baldwin Fund for Refugees was "unanimously adopted."[27] The Baldwin refugee fund for victims of religious and racial persecution, first announced by former prime minister Lord Stanley Baldwin, First Earl of Baldwin, during a radio address on the evening of December 8, 1938, was expressly meant to provide financial aid to Jews and "non-Aryan Christians":

> Tonight, I plead for the victims who turn to England for help, the first time in their long and troubled history that they have asked us in this way for financial aid. . . . Nothing has been more remarkable among the Jews than the way in which the wealthy look after their

poorer neighbors.... The number of these so-called non-Aryan Christians, who, according to German law, are regarded as Jews, certainly exceeds 100,000; in addition there are some half a million professing Jews, and no words can describe the pitiable plight of these 600,000 human souls. What can be done to help?[28]

A brief article in the *New York Times,* entitled, it is interesting to note, "Pope Backs Britons on Aid to Refugees," appeared on December 10. According to the article, "one of Pope Pius [XI]'s rare messages to an interdisciplinary body was read at a meeting representing all faiths and political parties, called by the Lord Mayor of London, at the Mansion House today to support the Earl Baldwin Fund for the victims of religious and racial persecution."[29]

It was Lord Rothschild who read the Vatican telegram to the assembled. Before reading the telegram, Lord Rothschild remarked that Cardinal Hinsley had "written to Rome on his behalf" and that "everyone respected the Pope for his courage and unswerving adherence to the principles which the whole civilized world knew must be maintained if civilization was to persist."[30] The Vatican telegram, as reproduced in the *London Times,* read as follows:

> The Holy Father Pius XI's thoughts and feelings will be correctly interpreted by declaring that he looks with humane and Christian approval on every effort to show charity and to give effective assistance to all those who are innocent victims in these sad times of distress. [Signed] Cardinal Pacelli, Secretary of State to His Holiness.[31]

Cardinal Hinsley's presence at the Mansion House meeting was significant. Significant also was the fact that Pacelli's message was read at a high-level public meeting with the specific purpose of support for Jews—Lord Baldwin's evening radio appeal of December 8 and subsequent reports in the *London Times* were quite clear as to the need for funds for approximately five hundred thousand Jews and one hundred thousand "non-Aryan Christians."[32] Yet here we have a clear example, with clear evidence, that Pacelli, despite being informed about the horrendous details of the pogrom in Germany, was not encouraging of a public statement by the Holy See condemning Nazi Germany, or the November pogrom, or singling out suffering Jews specifically by name—even when asked to do so by a prince of his own church.

He was comfortable only with a statement broad enough to apply to all "innocent victims."

These limited examples suggest that sympathy for Jews existed in important quarters, as demonstrated by Earl Baldwin's December 8 call to active aid, Archbishop Orsenigo's empathetic reports about Reichskristallnacht—though empathy did not mean action for Orsenigo—and Cardinal Hinsley's willingness to intercede for Lord Rothschild and encourage the bishop of Rome to make a public statement about the pogrom. They suggest also that Pacelli's personal response could dictate the Holy See's official institutional response in the months before Pius XI's death on February 10, 1939. In early December 1938, at least, Pacelli was not willing to aggressively and specifically condemn the November 9–10 Nazi pogrom against Jews. Pacelli was willing to authorize (on behalf of the pope) a reminder of the Church's broad commandment and mission to aid the suffering and the persecuted. In those troubled times, such a response was not enough.

NOTES

1. The Vatican Secret Archives (Latin Archivum Secretum Apostolicum Vaticanum; Italian Archivio Segreto Vaticano), located in Vatican City, is the central repository for all of the acts promulgated by the Roman Catholic Church's Holy See. The archives also contain state papers, correspondence, and other documents that the Church has accumulated over the centuries.

2. Only two sources discuss the foreign exchange currency trials specifically: Ernst Hoffmann and Hubert Janssen, *Die Wahrheit über die Ordensdevisenprozesse 1935/36* (Bielefeld: Hausknecht, 1967); and Petra Madeline Rapp, "Die Devisenprozesse gegen katholische Ordensangehörige und Geistliche im Dritten Reich. Eine Untersuchung zum Konflikt deutscher Orden und Klöster in wirtschaftlicher Notlage, totalitärer Machtausübung des nationalsozialistischen Regimes und im Kirchenkampf 1935/36" (Ph.D. diss., Universität Bonn, 1981).

3. Hanns Kerrl received this appointment on July 16, 1935, which made him responsible for all religious communities. After his death on December 15, 1941, no new minister was named.

4. Sandro Magister has noted that the newly available materials pertain to four major categories: (1) archives of the pontifical representatives; (2) archives of the Roman Curia; (3) archive of the secretary of state; and (4) archive

of the Congregation of Extraordinary Ecclesiastical Affairs (Sandro Magister, "The Vatican Secret Archive Has Opened a New Mine for Historians," *Chiesa* [September 30, 2006]. Link: http://www.chiesa.espressonline.it).

5. Thomas Brechenmacher, *Berichte des Apostolischen Nuntius Cesare Orsenigo aus Deutschland, 1930–1939,* is a project of the German Historical Institute–Rome (Deutschen Historischen Instituts–Rom) in cooperation with the Commission for Contemporary History (Kommission für Zeitgeschichte) in Bonn and the Vatican Secret Archives (Archivio Segreto Vaticano).

6. Record Group (hereafter RG) 457 (records of the U.S. National Security Agency [NSA]), Entry 9032, Boxes 517–21, sections 80–90. I thank Dr. Robert Hanyok, Center for Cryptologic History, National Security Agency, for bringing these documents to my attention.

7. Saul Friedländer, *The Years of Extermination: Nazi Germany and the Jews, 1939–1945* (New York: HarperCollins, 2007), 58.

8. Two letters are anonymous and not dated: one originating from Sackingen, Germany, and the other from an anonymous location. The other eight letters that we can identify are from (in alphabetical order) Max Cacheuse of the Rittergut Berkach über Meiningen in Thuringia, Germany (letter dated August 14,1938); Curt Goldberg of Trieste (letter dated August 23, 1938); Magdalena Jankowska of Berlin (no date for letter); Louis Livy of Nancy, France (letter dated November 15, 1938); the wife of Dr. Med. Georg Marx, temporarily in Rome (letter dated August 16, 1938); Dr. Med. Dr. Phil. Erich Simons of Dijon, France (letter dated August 15,1938); Dr. Gotthold Steinführer of Chicago (letter dated August 12, 1938); and Max Weiner of Haifa (letter dated April 11, 1938).

9. Matthew 8:11: "I say to you that many will come from the east and the west, and will take their place at the feast with Abraham, Isaac and Jacob in the kingdom of heaven." Kenneth Barker, gen. ed., *The NIV [New International Version] Study Bible* (Grand Rapids, Mich.: Zondervan Publishing House, 1995), 1450.

10. Revelation 2:9: "I know your afflictions and your poverty—yet you are rich! I know the slander of those who say they are Jews and are not, but are a synagogue of Satan," in ibid., 1927.

11. Letter from Dr. Gotthold Steinführer, Chicago, Illinois, to Eternal Reverend Father, Rome, August 12, 1938. Archive of the Secretariat of State, Section for Extraordinary Affairs, Germany, 1938. In Posizione (hereafter POS.) 742, Fascicolo (hereafter Fasc.) 356, 1938, Reichskristallnacht, RG 76.001M: Selected Records from the Vatican Archives, 1865–1939, United States Holocaust Memorial Museum, Washington, D.C. (hereafter RG 76, USHMM).

12. Letter from Wife of Georg Marse, Dr. Med., Rome, to Pius XI, Vatican, August 16, 1938. Archive of the Secretariat of State, Section for Extraordinary Affairs, Germany, 1938. In POS. 742, Fasc. 356, 1938, Reichskristallnacht, RG 76, USHMM.

13. No author. No date given. Archive of the Secretariat of State, Section for Extraordinary Affairs, Germany, 1938. In POS. 742, Fasc. 356, 1938, Reichskristallnacht, RG 76, USHMM.

14. George N. Shuster, *Like a Mighty Army: Hitler Versus Established Religion* (New York: D. Appleton–Century, 1935), 188, cited in Guenter Lewy, *The Catholic Church and Nazi Germany* (Cambridge, Mass.: De Capo, 2000), 27.

15. Michael Phayer, *The Catholic Church and the Holocaust, 1930–1965* (Bloomington: Indiana University Press, 2000), 27, 44.

16. Letter from Apostolic Delegate to Germany Cesare Orsenigo, Berlin, to Secretary of State Eugenio Cardinal Pacelli, November 15, 1938. Archive of the Secretariat of State, Section for Extraordinary Affairs, Germany, 1938. In POS. 742, Fasc. 356, 1938, Reichskristallnacht, RG 76, USHMM. This letter was first made available to scholars in Pierre Blet, Robert A. Graham, Angelo Martini, and Burkhart Schneider, eds., *Actes et documents du Saint Siège relatifs à La Seconde Guerre mondiale,* volume 6, *Le Saint Siège et les Victimes de la guerre, Mars 1939–Décembre 1940* (Vatican City: Libreria Editrice Vaticana, 1972), Appendix 4, 536–37.

17. Ernst vom Rath was actually third secretary at the German embassy in Paris at the time of his assassination.

18. Letter from Apostolic Delegate to Germany Cesare Orsenigo, Berlin, to Secretary of State Eugenio Cardinal Pacelli, November 15, 1938. Archive of the Secretariat of State, Section for Extraordinary Affairs, Germany, 1938. In POS. 742, Fasc. 356, 1938, Reichskristallnacht, RG 76, USHMM.

19. Letter from Apostolic Delegate to Germany Cesare Orsenigo, Berlin, to Secretary of State Eugenio Cardinal Pacelli, November 19, 1938. Archive of the Secretariat of State, Section for Extraordinary Affairs, Germany, 1938. In POS. 742, Fasc. 356, 1938, Reichskristallnacht, RG 76, USHMM. This letter was first made available to scholars in Blet et al., *Actes et documents,* Appendix 5, 538.

20. Ibid.

21. Letter from Apostolic Delegate to Germany Cesare Orsenigo, Berlin, to Secretary of State Luigi Cardinal Maglione, September 13, 1941. Archive of the Secretariat of State, Section for Extraordinary Affairs, Germany, 1938. In POS. 742, Fasc. 356, 1938, Reichskristallnacht, RG 76, USHMM.

22. Blet et al., *Actes et documents,* 12–13.

23. Ibid., 539, footnote 1.

24. Ibid. The original Italian reads as follows:

Se la cosa fosse di carattere sostanzialmente privato, sarebbe più facile. D'altra parte, occorre togliere l'apparenza di aver paura di ciò che non si deve temere. Si potrebbe incaricare cardinal Hinsley a parlare dicendosi sicuro di interpretare il pensiero del Sommo Pontefice, dicendo che la cosa coglie in Papa in un momento di tanta preoccupazione non soltanto per la Sua salute, ma anche per la quantità di cose. Non ha visto perciò la possibilità di occuparsi personalmente della cose. Egli, cardinale di S.R.C., può dire di interpretare il pensiero che vede con occhio umano e christiano ogni assistenza a quanti infelici e ingiustamente (indegnamente) sofferenti.

I thank Professor Anthony Cardoza of Loyola University of Chicago for his verification of my translation.

25. Ibid., 539, footnote 3.
26. The Mansion House is the official residence of the Lord Mayor of the city of London.
27. See "Help for the Refugees—Ready Response to Appeal—Children's Gifts—Mansion House Meeting," *Times* (London), December 10, 1938, 12.
28. "The Refugees—Appeal by Lord Baldwin—Case for German Cooperation—New Fund Opened," *Times* (London), December 9, 1938, 16. Earl Baldwin's appeal raised approximately £500,000. About half the proceeds were allocated to Jewish organizations and spent on helping child refugees. Louise London, *Whitehall and the Jews, 1933–1938: British Immigration Policy, Jewish Refugees and the Holocaust* (London: Cambridge University Press, 2000), 122. See also A. J. Sherman, *Island Refuge: Britain and Refugees from the Third Reich, 1933–1939* (London: Frank Cass, 1973), 184–85.
29. *New York Times,* December 10, 1938; ProQuest Historical Newspapers, *New York Times* (1851–2003), 6.
30. "Plight of the Refugees—Mansion House Meeting—Lord Rothschild's Appeal," *Times* (London), December 10, 1938, 14.
31. Ibid.
32. "The Refugees—Appeal by Lord Baldwin—Case for German Cooperation—New Fund Opened," *Times* (London), December 9, 1938, 16.

Lissa Skitolsky

Suspending Judgment for the Sake of Knowledge: Agamben's Approach to Auschwitz

THE WORK OF THE CONTEMPORARY ITALIAN PHILOSOPHER GIORGIO Agamben is especially relevant to the theme of the Ninth Biennial Lessons and Legacies conference because he has asked us to reassess two typical assumptions taken by scholars when they explore the meaning of Nazism—first, that the Holocaust testifies to the loss of moral values that we must reaffirm to prevent the recurrence of genocidal intent, especially through our moral judgment of the Nazi regime; and second, that the Nazi regime and the Nazi camp are exceptions to the normal sociopolitical order and so stand opposed to or outside of our moral and political categories.

For Agamben, we cannot judge Nazism to be a singular evil or Nazi Germany to be a site of extremity because it represents the depravity of the sociopolitical world in which we still live. So, Agamben has suggested, the reassessment of these two stances is necessary to change the nature and direction of our social and political life and thus has real implications for the future. In his work *Remnants of Auschwitz: The Witness and the Archive,* Agamben argued for this position through a sustained meditation on the Muselmann—that category of prisoner often referred to as the walking dead—as the foundation rather than the aberration of human nature. And in his work *Homo Sacer: Sovereign Power and Bare Life,* he argued for this position through a systematic historical analysis of the biopolitical foundation of Western politics, which gave rise to the Nazi regime as the radicalization and full realization of a biopolitical state.

I will explain why Agamben's position requires that we suspend two forms of judgment to better explore the philosophical meaning of Nazism. First, we must suspend our moral judgment of victims and perpetrators to heed the real ethical lessons that their experiences offer. Second, we must suspend our historical judgment of the Nazi regime and the concentration camp as "exceptions" to the "normal" order to grasp the true political foundation of Nazism. Though Agamben's position is controversial and unsettling, it has opened up a new direction for philosophical thought on the enduring meaning of Auschwitz for our ethical and political life.

TRACING THE REMNANTS OF AUSCHWITZ IN OUR MORAL WORLDVIEW

For Agamben, as for Theodor W. Adorno, our categories are measured by the phenomena that exceed them. As Adorno famously stated, "If thought is not measured by the extremity that eludes the concept, it is from the outset in the nature of the musical accompaniment with which the SS [Schutzstaffel] liked to drown out the screams of its victims."[1] Yet for Agamben, Nazism does not represent an "extreme" situation or an exception to the normal order, but the hidden foundation of the order itself. In his work *Homo Sacer*, he explained that (Western) politics rests on the distinction between "life" (zoē) and the "good life" (bios), which becomes the basis for the sovereign decision as to what sort of "life" is excluded from the political and moral domains of protection. Sovereign power is based on the right to decide the state of exception, to produce that state of bare or naked life (zoē) that illuminates the value of the good life (bios) or the "normal" order. Thus the opposition between the "normal" and the "extreme" situation is in fact a strategy of political power, one that we must resist through rejecting the logical basis of this very opposition. As Agamben explained in *Remnants of Auschwitz:*

> As long as the state of exception and the normal situation are kept separate in space and time, as is usually the case, both remain opaque, though they secretly institute each other. But as soon as they show their complicity, as happens more and more often today, they illuminate each other, so to speak, from the inside. And yet this implies that the extreme situation can no longer function as a distinguishing criterion.... In this sense, philosophy can be defined as the world seen from an extreme situation that has become the rule.[2]

And yet almost all of the categories with which we describe the condition of the victims and perpetrators of the Third Reich rest on this very opposition between the normal and the exceptional situation, for our ability to judge the perpetrators rests on our ability to distinguish between good and evil, whereas our ability to condemn the camps rests on our ability to distinguish between a human versus an inhuman state of being. However, Agamben has suggested that if our categories rest on this false opposition and so fail to measure the reality of life in concentration camps, they are not simply anachronistic but instead somehow complicit in their creation and continuation. Agamben relied on Primo Levi's speculative observations on the "gray zone" present in camp life that blurred the facile distinction between victims and perpetrators to argue that our categories have obscured the reality of Auschwitz in two ways.

First, since our approach to the ethical lessons of Auschwitz has been expressed almost exclusively through our concern with responsibility, guilt, and judgment, we have consistently confused moral with legal categories and so refused to learn from the ethical evidence presented by the gray zone, evidence that undermines the possibility of judgment and blurs the distinction between guilt and innocence.[3] Agamben explained that "[t]o assume guilt and responsibility—which can, at times, be necessary—is to leave the territory of ethics and enter that of law. Whoever has made this difficult step cannot presume to return through the door he just closed behind him."[4]

Second, since we have failed to heed the evidence of the gray zone and so retained our categories of good and evil as adequate to understand and prevent the recurrence of camp life, we become silent bystanders to those horrors that are still perpetrated in the name of what is good and right.

Agamben referred to a soccer match that took place between the SS and representatives of the Sonderkommando to illustrate these two points:

> This match might strike someone as a brief pause of humanity in the middle of an infinite horror. I, like the witnesses, instead view this match, this moment of normalcy, as the true horror of the camp. For we can perhaps think that the massacres are over— even if here and there they are repeated, not so far away from us. But that match is never over; it continues as if uninterrupted. It is the perfect and eternal cipher of the "gray zone," which knows

no time and is in every place . . . hence our shame, the shame of those who did not know the camps and yet, without knowing how, are spectators of that match, which repeats itself in every match in our stadiums, in every television broadcast, in the normalcy of everyday life.[5]

Agamben was not conflating the atrocities in the camp with the atrocities we might witness in "the normalcy of everyday life," but he did suggest that our concern with guilt, responsibility, and judgment allows us to preserve our moral world and so pretend as if the gray zone did not and still does not exist. Further, in the Nazi regime there was confusion between the ethical and the legal that allowed Nazis to feel responsible, to murder without hate or guilt. Agamben suggested that the same confusion persists in the way we approach and draw "lessons" from the Holocaust, which allows us to keep the events in question at a comfortable distance, to believe that the problem of Auschwitz has been overcome and so feel responsible, to study it without anxiety about its implications for our own moral certainties about the sociopolitical world in which we live.[6] In the previous passage Agamben associated himself with the witness to Auschwitz, who, unlike the judge, viewed this match as the true horror of the camp. For this match evades the judgment of good or evil; it is "simply" a game that goes on in the midst of other "evil" actions. However, the presumption of normalcy in the midst of murder is the condition that allows for our collective participation in state-sponsored massacres; so long as we can still attend our sports games and festivals, we need not worry about the massacres carried out farther away, for the sake of our "safety" and "national security."

Agamben claimed that Levi's "unprecedented discovery" of the gray zone is the new "ethical element" discovered at Auschwitz. It is an area of human experience that is "independent of every establishment of responsibility." Citing Levi, he explained that it is "the zone in which the 'long chain of conjunction between victim and executioner' comes loose, where the oppressed becomes oppressor and the executioner in turn appears as victim. A gray, incessant alchemy in which good and evil and, along with them, all the metals of traditional ethics reach their point of fusion."[7] Agamben did not base his reflections on the ethical implications of the gray zone to affirm with Friedrich Wilhelm

Nietzsche that we are beyond good and evil but, rather, to consider an ethical space that exists *before* them,[8] or before our moral judgment makes martyrs, saints, and sinners out of human beings caught in a zone-of-being that denied the possibility of all three.

Against those scholars who uphold the truth of our moral categories only through judging the behavior of victims or else excluding them from ethics altogether, so that their experience is held to constitute an extreme situation in which ethical categories do not apply, Agamben insisted that our ethical categories are only as relevant as they are to the lives of the victims who perished in the gas chambers. Having rejected the logic of the extreme situation, Agamben would not restore the sense of our moral categories at the cost of excising the victims from our moral universe. This requires two further steps: first, that we "clear away almost all the doctrines that, since Auschwitz, have been advanced in the name of ethics,"[9] and second, that Agamben illustrate how the Muselmann—the "true witness" of Auschwitz—is relevant to an understanding of our ethical life.

FINDING MAN IN THE MUSELMANN: BUILDING AN ETHICS ON THE ONTOLOGY OF THE "WALKING DEAD"

Agamben eschewed moral judgment for the sake of understanding ethical life as that which is informed by the suffering self; he suggested that we should not form an ethics based on what was absent at Auschwitz (respect, recognition of "the other," dignity, spiritual fortitude) but rather on what was present, or on what became of man.[10] His perspective has allowed him to borrow ethical categories from the testimony of Holocaust victims and, in particular, from the testimony of Primo Levi that bears witness to life lived in the gray zone of indistinction between guilt and innocence, victim and perpetrator. In his essay "Shame," Levi stated that the only "true" witness to this form-of-life is the Muselmann, or the one unable to bear witness.[11] This paradox led Agamben to meditate on the significance of the Muselmann—who is defined precisely by the impossible coexistence of life and death, the human and the inhuman—for our ethical life. In his memoir *If This Is a Man* (1959), published in the United States as *Survival in Auschwitz* (1961), Primo Levi provided a well-known description of the Muselmann:

> All the musselmans who finished in the gas chambers have the same story, or more exactly, have no story; they followed the slope down to the bottom, like streams that run down to the sea. On their entry into the camp, through basic incapacity, or by misfortune, or through some banal incident, they are overcome before they can adapt themselves; they are beaten by time, they do not begin to learn German, to disentangle the infernal knot of laws and prohibitions until their body is already in decay, and nothing can save them from selections or from death by exhaustion. Their life is short, but their number is endless; they, the *Muselmänner*, the drowned, form the backbone of the camp, an anonymous mass, continually renewed and always identical, of non-men who march and labour in silence, the divine spark dead within them, already too empty to really suffer. One hesitates to call them living: one hesitates to call their death death, in the face of which they have no fear, as they are too tired to understand.[12]

Other scholars have pointed to the impossibility of fully comprehending that which overwhelms our conceptual categories; Agamben has reflected on the excess that cannot or will not be comprehended. We insist that the Muselmann is not human because we refuse to recognize ourselves in his disfigured state; we do not allow him any significance in the quest for self-knowledge. He remains the extreme situation, one against whom I can derive the distinction between the human and the nonhuman. This approach is the product of a certain tradition of thought that locates ontological truth in what is distinctly *human*, as opposed to what is merely organic or animal, and locates ethical truth in how we must act to realize our humanity.

And yet the Muselmann is a product of this same tradition, as the Nazis held their own conception of a dignified or distinctly human life and were similarly convinced that the Muselmann was less than human. Agamben claimed:

> Simply to deny the *Muselmann*'s humanity would be to accept the verdict of the SS and to repeat their gesture. The *Muselmann* has, instead, moved into a zone of the human where not only help but also dignity and self-respect have become useless. But if there is a zone of the human in which these concepts make no sense, then they are not genuine ethical concepts, for no ethics can claim to exclude a part of humanity, no matter how unpleasant or difficult that humanity is to see.[13]

For Agamben, the Muselmann is "the guard on the threshold of a new ethics,"[14] one that does not operate on the basis of certain ideals and proceed through the act of judgment. Agamben claimed that "in Auschwitz ethics begins precisely at the point where the Muselmann, the 'complete witness,' makes it forever impossible to distinguish between man and non-man."[15] Agamben rejected the validity of moral categories that fail to describe the state of the Muselmann as false and complicit at the same time. When we exclude the Muselmann from our moral considerations, we retain that distinction between the human and the nonhuman that still allows us to remove certain human beings from the moral and legal domains of protection, to subject certain persons to torture and death as part of our political agenda to secure our "freedom" and "safety." Every effort to safeguard our own robust humanity inevitably leads to the judgment and production of persons deemed less-than-human; the only way out of this murderous dialectic is to reject the distinction altogether. The Muselmann represents the radicalization of a form-of-life present in the gray zone that represents the proper object of ethical thought, a form-of-life that is simultaneously subject and object, human and inhuman. This is the only possible position from which to construct an ethics that is not based on false dichotomies that are nevertheless made true in our camps and prisons.

In the Muselmänner of the camps, Agamben recognized a constituent feature of subjectivity—its own potential for desubjectification. He claimed that this potential is felt and expressed through our shame, which both our concepts and our camps have sought to deny and avoid; this denial is felt and expressed through disgust or judgment. When we make a judgment as to what makes Auschwitz atrocious and speculate on how we can avoid such an event in the future, we refuse to associate ourselves with what occurred, to feel shame at what became of man or for the loss of the illusion of self-possession. Shame is felt precisely when the subject bears witness to the loss of the self, when it is moved by its own passivity,[16] consigned to something that cannot be assumed or that cannot be controlled, willed, or known.[17] We feel shame for experiences we did not choose.

Lawrence Langer has described the position of Holocaust victims as one of "choiceless choice," in which every apparent "choice" was so thoroughly compromised as to belie the illusion of true agency. For Agamben, this is the general condition of subjectivity, insofar as it is also always marked by the loss of subjectivity, or desubjectification. We bear witness to this caesura—"the constitutive desubjectification in every subjectification"[18]—through various phenomena such as speech,[19] sadomasochism,[20] and temporality.[21] So, for example, when we utter the word "I" to announce and reveal our subjectivity and instead give voice to an empty signifier with a merely discursive function, we feel discomfort, or shame, at our inability to assume the identity or position to which we are nevertheless consigned.[22] Agamben's point is illustrated in the fact that those who do not speak often exude what we call a "quiet dignity" while those who talk incessantly seem to have lost possession of themselves. This explains the traumatic nature of speech and the utter despair of the poet, who dismembers himself in attempting to explain himself.

The failure of testimony to represent adequately or convey that to which it bears witness is not only a reflection of trauma or proof of the insufficiency of our categories but also the sign, the trace of what is being borne witness to—the "impossibility of conjoining the living being and language,"[23] the impossibility of fully explaining or assuming our suffering. Agamben explained that "*[t]he subject of testimony is the one who bears witness to a desubjectification.* But this . . . can only mean there is no subject of testimony . . . and that every testimony is a field of forces incessantly traversed by currents of subjectification and desubjectification."[24] The paradox of testimony mirrors the paradox of subjectivity itself, insofar as it is simultaneously a possibility and an impossibility of speech that is both present and absent to itself. In the end, it is the witness and not the Muselmann who is the new "ethical subject,"[25] for ethics consists in witnessing for another who cannot bear witness, and so this act of testimony is only realized through the desubjectification of the witness in his failure to adequately testify. *Remnants of Auschwitz* ends with a collection of passages from former victims who testify about their own descent into Muselmänner. From most accounts, it is clear that it was not possible to recover after having once descended, and the term "Muselmann" was coined to refer to the point of no return. So Agamben has indicated that before we can judge the Muselmann as inhuman we must recognize the Muselmann within ourselves, or recognize that we, too, are subject to desubjectification.[26]

How does Agamben's approach work as an alternative to moral judgment in situations of excessive violence? For Agamben, Auschwitz was a radical experiment in biopolitics that was meant to assume total control over the form-of-life but that produced the Muselmann, the radicalization of the very state which the Nazis sought to deny, repress, and destroy. Agamben recognized shame where others see evil. In fact, the "war on terror" is a similar attempt to deny our vulnerability, and it is based on the need to believe that we can preserve ourselves through destroying others, or fully assume our subjectivity through the desubjectification of others, labeled "terrorists," who are nonrational, incapable of negotiation, and immune to therapy.[27] After 9/11, it would have been better to recognize our shame in the face of our powerlessness—or recognize that we are always vulnerable to a meaningless death—rather than attempt to stay alive at all costs through directing our rage at those whom we judge to be guilty, at those with whom we cannot identify, who represent our own alterity and thus provoke our disgust. The more we assume the knowledge of guilt and innocence, the less able we are to grasp the present or learn the real lesson of Auschwitz, and we wind up in an endless cycle of violence as we alternate between disgust and shame.

At the end of *Remnants of Auschwitz,* Agamben stated that the Muselmann represents "the catastrophe of the subject,"[28] the collapse of the inseparable division between our organic and animal, speaking and living being. Agamben's model of ethics requires that the Muselmann be included in our account of human nature so that we do not begin from the position of judgment but from witnessing; we do not aim to realize ideals that allow us to fulfill our humanity (and always require the dehumanization of others, the forced separation between the human and the nonhuman) but instead testify to how certain "ideals" have affected human life, or how human beings are subject to desubjectification in our social practices and political institutions. Agamben has restored the subject as the starting point of philosophy, but not from a humanist or teleological perspective that assumes our historical progression through our gradual realization through time.[29] For Agamben, one does not realize one's humanity through action and decision but instead continually bears witness to the loss of personal humanity, to the inability to master one's self or distinguish between human and inhuman traits. This prevents one from ever taking a position from which one judges others to be inhuman. This is why the witness is the ethical subject but the Muselmann "is the guard on the threshold of a new ethics," for when we exclude him from our considerations we reproduce him through our moral judgments.

THE NAZI CAMP AS THE "NOMOS" OF THE MODERN WORLD

Just as we must recognize that the Muselmann is not an exception to the human condition, so Agamben has insisted that we must recognize that Nazi Germany is not an exception to the Western tradition of politics. In his book *Homo Sacer: Sovereign Power and Bare Life,* he explained:

> If Nazism still appears to us as an enigma . . . this is because we have failed to situate the totalitarian phenomenon in its entirety in the horizon of biopolitics. When life and politics—originally divided, and linked together by means of the no-man's-land of the state of exception that is inhabited by bare life—begin to become one, all life becomes sacred and all politics becomes the exception.[30]

A state's concern with the biological life of its citizens has been characterized as biopolitics, a modern technology of power whose objective is the control and modification of entire populations. Biopolitics refers to the different ways in which biological life enters into the calculations of the state, for example, through government-sponsored sterilization programs, commissions on biomedical ethics, or legislation that regulates the traditionally private concerns of reproduction, sexuality, and death. In Agamben's formulation, a biopolitical state is one in which life itself becomes the supreme political value until the care of life coincides with the fight against the enemy.[31] Though he has traced the political concern with biological life back to the formation and establishment of sovereign power itself, Agamben viewed Nazism as the first radically biopolitical state.[32] In *Homo Sacer,* he faulted Hannah Arendt's penetrating analyses of Nazism for lacking a biopolitical perspective on the nature and significance of totalitarian power.[33] A biopolitical perspective on Nazism assumes that the crimes in question are neither isolated instances of a failure in judgment nor a rupture in social and political life, but rather an expression of fundamental tendencies that have been assuming a greater and greater importance in modern politics.

Agamben recognized the ancient political categories of "life" and "the good life," zoē and bios, as first establishing the biopolitical domain as the real, if hidden, nucleus of sovereign power. Every judgment on life forces its object into reality, which in turn confirms the very validity of the categories involved. Thus, judgments on the good life—which secure the "dignity" of human beings—also require the existence of individuals who embody a state of mere undignified life and so serve as the very exemplars of that against which the sovereign protects us. This is the state that Agamben has referred to as homo sacer, sacred or bare life, which results from the politicization of natural life and signifies a life that can be killed but not murdered, a life that cannot be sacrificed for any higher cause. Agamben discovered the term "homo sacer" as an obscure category of archaic Roman law in which the character of sacredness is tied for the first time to a human life as such: "The sacred man is the one whom the people have judged on account of a crime. It is not permitted to sacrifice this man, yet he who kills him will not be condemned for homicide."[34] The homo sacer represents a life—such as the life of a camp inmate or a detainee—vulnerable to violence sanctioned by sovereign power. Thus, in a biopolitical state, "life" is always included by means of its exclusion, which produces a form-of-life that is neither natural nor political. The paradox of biopolitics is that sovereign power is established by deciding on the state of exception, so that the law is founded through the suspension of law. For Agamben, our political and ethical categories are also ontological categories that function to produce an ever-increasing number of homines sacri.

The Nazi regime sought to transform the sovereign decision on life into the supreme political principle, and the true meaning of Nazi biopolitics can be grasped by the transformation of biological fact—or natural heredity—into a political task.[35] Nazism is the first *radically* biopolitical state because it represents the first politico-juridical structure in which the exception coincides perfectly with the rule, or in which the suspension of the law coincides with the legal order itself. Thus the racial politics of the Nazi regime did not represent a departure but instead the full realization of sovereign power to establish the legal order (the domain of bios) on what is excluded from that order (the domain of zoē). The Nazi camp is a perfect expression of a biopolitical space in which the sovereign decision on life requires the systematic production of bare or naked life. And for Agamben, the Muselmann must be recognized as the very paradigm of homo sacer, or that form-of-life that results from the biopolitical production of "life itself."

Many people have observed that we in the United States are now living in a somewhat permanent state of emergency, as the Patriot Act has suspended many of our fundamental rights and democratic ideals. Further, in the ongoing "war against terror" we have created new "sites of exception" in which certain individuals are judged to be potential "terrorists" and thus inhuman and immoral—and so less-than-human, unworthy of political protection or moral consideration. And yet these disturbing developments are often minimized by the claim that we are fighting a new enemy in a new age, just as we once fought the Nazis and the Communists. We are unable to recognize any commonality between the logic and methods of Nazism and the global war against terrorism because we view the Nazi regime as *an exception* to the Western political tradition.

Critics of Agamben may accuse him of either collapsing the difference between totalitarian regimes and democratic states and/or depriving us of a position from which to condemn the ever-recurring atrocities of genocide and state-sponsored violence. For if Nazism represents the natural outcome of our political tradition, then we cannot simply reaffirm the categories and tools of that tradition to resist the ever-increasing politicization of biological life. Further, Agamben's view of the biopolitical agenda is not as the means to some other insidious end, such as total domination, but as an end in itself; thus it is hard to know how to critique an agenda that has always served to inform the nature of politics as such. This confusion is further compounded by the stance taken in his book *Remnants of Auschwitz,* in which he made a sharp distinction between moral and legal questions and insisted that the categories of guilt, responsibility, and judgment do not properly belong to a moral consideration of the meaning of Auschwitz.

In response to this criticism, I think Agamben might say that our need to judge Auschwitz as evil has not helped to prevent the recurrence of genocidal intent, but instead has served to distance us from the sociopolitical conditions that gave rise to Auschwitz and that continue to inform domestic and foreign policy in the West. These conditions include a preoccupation with self-preservation at all costs and a collective desire to situate the protection and control of biological life as the greatest political priority. They also include a political situation in the United States in which the state of emergency has become the norm and in which the law corresponds with the suspension of law. So, paradoxically, our ability to condemn Auschwitz does not necessarily allow us to understand what is objectionable about it, or those basic social and political principles on which it is based and which must be wholly called into question. In this sense, Agamben's work is devoted to a critique of the present in terms of how we have inherited the past.

In her magnum opus, *The Origins of Totalitarianism,* Hannah Arendt claimed that Nazism represents a historical novum that threatens to act as a new precedent for variations of totalitarian governments. In her various essays on totalitarian power, she suggested that we may resist our own complicity in the theoretical structures that support genocidal intent, through harnessing our powers of judgment against the bureaucratic apparatus and the instrumental logic it employs. On the contrary, Agamben views Nazism as the historical outcome of our politico-juridical structure and has suggested that our capacity for judgment is incapable of recognizing the true moral dilemmas of our time, which are best met by a sober realization of our own impotence and vulnerability. Only in this way can we arrest the ideological commitment to safety and security that always leads to a biopolitical agenda and that seeks to assure the strength and dignity of some only through the desubjectification of others. Once we eschew any claim to dignity, humanity, strength, freedom, or the "good" life, we have no choice but to view ourselves as part of a single community. In this way, we may cease to rationalize the senseless torture and deaths of individuals with a hypocritical reference to our valued "ideals." This is possible only if we suspend judgment for the sake of knowledge or suspend our biopolitical need to distinguish the "best" from the "worst" sort of life to attain knowledge of "life" as that which is inseparable from the "form-of-life" that we all live.

NOTES

1. Theodor W. Adorno, *Negative Dialectics,* trans. E. B. Ashton (New York: Seabury Press, 1973), 365.

2. Giorgio Agamben, *Remnants of Auschwitz: The Witness and the Archive,* trans. Daniel Heller-Roazen (New York: Zone Books, 1999), 49–50.

3. Agamben commented on the noncoincidence of judgment and truth:

> One of the most common mistakes—which is not only made in discussions of the camp—is the tacit confusion of ethical categories and

juridical categories. . . . Almost all the categories that we use in moral and religious judgments are in some way contaminated by law: guilt, responsibility, innocence, judgment, pardon. . . . This makes it difficult to invoke them without particular caution. As jurists well know, law is not directed toward the establishment of justice. Nor is it directed toward the verification of truth. Law is solely directed toward judgment, independent of truth and justice. This is shown beyond doubt by the *force of judgment* that even an unjust sentence carries with it. The ultimate aim of law is the production of a *res judicata*, in which the sentence becomes the substitute for the true and the just, being held as true despite its falsity and injustice. (Ibid., 18.)

4. Ibid., 24.
5. Ibid., 26.
6. Agamben claimed that the trials of Nazi war criminals only compounded this problem:

It is possible that the trials . . . are responsible for the conceptual confusion that, for decades, has made it impossible to think through Auschwitz. Despite the necessity of the trials and despite their evident insufficiency . . . they helped to spread the idea that the problem of Auschwitz had been overcome. The judgments had been passed, the proofs of guilt definitely established. With the exception of occasional moments of lucidity, it has taken almost half a century to understand that law did not exhaust the problem, but rather that the very problem was so enormous as to call into question the law itself, dragging it to its own ruin. (Ibid., 19–20.)

7. Ibid., 21.
8. Ibid.
9. Ibid., 13.
10. The former perspective still assumes the position of looking at Auschwitz and asking "What went wrong?" so that we are able to provide an answer that is at the same time a judgment on how and why the Nazis, long dead, were able to commit such atrocities. As far as I know, Agamben is the first person to develop this approach, and *Remnants of Auschwitz* is still, in my opinion, the only really successful attempt to carve an ethics from the site of genocide. Others have attempted to follow his move only to fall into the trap of assimilating the camp into our moral categories, and so they continue to refuse the Muselmann any role in ethical contemplation.
11. Levi wrote:

[W]e, the survivors, are not the true witnesses. . . . We survivors are not only an exiguous but also an anomalous minority: we are those who by their prevarications or abilities or good luck did not touch bottom. Those who did so, those who saw the Gorgon, have not returned to tell about it or have returned mute, but they are the "Muslims," the submerged, the complete witnesses, the ones whose deposition would have a general significance. They are the rule, we are the exception. (Primo Levi, *The Drowned and the Saved,* trans. Raymond Rosenthal [New York: Vintage Books, 1988], 83–84.)

12. Primo Levi, *Survival in Auschwitz,* trans. Stuart Woolf (New York: Simon and Schuster, 1996), 90.
13. Agamben, *Remnants of Auschwitz,* 63–64.
14. Ibid., 69.
15. Ibid., 47.
16. Ibid., 110.
17. Ibid., 105.
18. Ibid., 123.
19. Ibid., 113.
20. Ibid., 107.
21. Ibid., 128.
22. Ibid., 120–21.
23. Ibid., 130.
24. Ibid., 120–21 (emphasis in the original).
25. Ibid., 151.
26. Agamben's effort to philosophize from the site of Auschwitz has raised several questions that are outside the scope of this essay. These include the following concerns: To what extent can one locate man in the Muselmann without idealizing this state-of-being? And can we forge an ontological similarity between victims then and our position now without exercising a certain fascination that places us in a position of romantic identification with the walking dead? Is it possible to dispense with ideals and instead derive new categories by the light of crematoria? Do we run the risk of indifference to excessive suffering and fall prey to nihilism if there is nothing that we are collectively striving to attain, if there is no way in which I may become more than what I already am?
27. Judith Butler has also argued that the war on terror exposes the need to better accept our vulnerability and dependency on others in her recent work *Precarious Life* (New York: Verso, 2004).
28. Agamben, *Remnants of Auschwitz,* 148.
29. Agamben has claimed that we must reject the teleological urge to realize ideals that supposedly fulfill our humanity, for

> such a conception would once again repeat the dialectic of grounding by which one thing—in our case, bare life—must be separated and effaced for human life to be assigned to subjects as a property. . . . Here the foun-

dation is a function of a telos that is the grounding of the human being, the becoming human of the inhuman. It is this perspective that must be wholly called into question. (Ibid., 158.)

30. Giorgio Agamben, *Homo Sacer: Sovereign Power and Bare Life*, trans. Daniel Heller-Roazen (Stanford, Calif.: Stanford University Press, 1998), 148.

31. Ibid., 147.
32. Ibid., 143.
33. Ibid., 4.
34. Ibid., 71.
35. Ibid., 148.

IV. POST-HOLOCAUST ISSUES

Michael Meng

Did Poles Oppose or Collaborate with the Nazis? Problems with Narrating the Holocaust in Poland

IN 2006, THE POLISH PARLIAMENT PASSED A NEW LAW REGULATING LUStration, the legal process of uncovering those who collaborated with the Communist secret police, which the ruling coalition supported and the president later signed. Buried among its many clauses was a short article that attempted to control debate about the Nazi and Communist periods with surprising consequences for unlawful behavior: "Those who publicly impute to the Polish nation participation, organization, or responsibility for the crimes of communism or Nazism will be sentenced up to three years in prison."[1] Although the Polish president requested that this part of the law be taken out before he signed it, this attempt to restrict discussion about the past is striking in its audacity and breadth. The clause included the term "crimes of communism," but I suspect that the main target was recent research about the participation of Poles in the Holocaust. Brought into the open by Jan Gross's *Neighbors*,[2] a startling book about the massacre of Jews in the village of Jedwabne, the history of Poles as perpetrators challenges precisely the traditional notions of Polish victimization, martyrdom, and resistance that this clause hoped to protect.[3] The measure sought to defend "historical truth" against attacks played out in the "international arena" about "alleged assistance or collaboration in criminal regimes."[4]

This clause uncovered, albeit admittedly in a highly sensational way, one of the basic dilemmas that arise in discussing the Holocaust in Poland. Such defensive posturing has moved not only politicians but also scholars who either implicitly or directly challenge the notion of

Polish collaboration with the Nazis.[5] The dilemma has surfaced over the past decade as Holocaust historiography has shifted from focusing on the decision-making process in Berlin to the implementation of mass murder in Eastern Europe. Since Raul Hilberg's *The Destruction of the European Jews* (first published in 1961),[6] the Holocaust has been narrated mainly from what might be called a German history perspective. This approach focuses on the German perpetrators and more recently on the reaction of German society as a whole and has been adopted by many prominent historians such as Omer Bartov, Wolfgang Benz, Christopher Browning, Ulrich Herbert, Ian Kershaw, Peter Longerich, and Hans Mommsen. Since all of these scholars received their doctoral training in German history, they are inevitably shaped by the broader "German question" that has informed the writing about the German past over the past sixty years: why did Germany, a country that at 1900 stood at the apex of cultural, economic, and political power, only three decades later turn into a dictatorship of racism, war, and genocide?

But after the collapse of communism, several publications started to move away from this "German question" and toward analyzing how the Holocaust unfolded in Eastern Europe, arguing that the periphery shaped the center: solutions to problems arising "on the ground" in the east pushed officials in Berlin to make increasingly radical proposals.[7] As this scholarship came out, historians of Eastern Europe—Jan Gross most famously—pushed the focus even more to the east, eclipsing Berlin altogether and analyzing the direct participation or complicit indifference of the local population to the genocide of the Jews. This new approach poses clear challenges by placing the Holocaust squarely in Polish history. Collaboration clashes with the common hagiographic perception of Poland's past by imputing to the eternal Polish "victims" the crimes of the unequivocal German "perpetrators." Although provoking hyperbolic and disturbing responses in contemporary politics, this shift in focus from the center to the periphery has raised serious scholarly questions about narrating the Holocaust that have not received the attention they deserve. Should the Holocaust be analyzed from a transnational perspective? If historians emphasize the collaboration and indifference of ethnic Poles (or Czechs, Ukrainians, and so on), how do they at the same time clearly articulate the role of Berlin in designing the "Final Solution"? Indeed, as one respected reviewer of *Neighbors* noted, "An insufficiently documented, controversial, and in some respects seemingly unique event does not provide a satisfactory basis for so radically changing our understanding of the Holocaust and for depriving the Nazis of its authorship."[8]

Gross, of course, never intended to change so radically our understanding of the Holocaust, but he has elicited this line of criticism partly because of the double move he has made: pushing out geographically from the German history perspective while remaining analytically embedded in it.[9] The long-standing historiographical focus on the perpetrators and bystanders has shaped the basic analytical framework of Polish research on the Holocaust, which has remained fixated on the behavior, actions, and attitudes of Polish society. Different variations on topics such as collaboration and indifference have become central themes of a growing literature and have appeared in recent issues of journals such as *Zagłada Żydów* (The Holocaust) and *Slavic Review*.[10] In response, other scholars—some with scholarly intentions, others with tendentious aims—have emphasized Polish efforts to save Jews. Without oversimplifying too much, one could say that research on the Holocaust in Poland turns on the central problem of whether Polish society can be characterized as having been complicit in, indifferent to, or resistant against the Nazi campaign against the Jews.

But what are the consequences of this focus on the "bystanders" and "perpetrators"? Is the ensuing division of Polish behavior into conceptual categories of rescue, collaboration, and indifference useful for analyzing and narrating the Holocaust in Poland? This essay grapples with these questions, discussing four books that touch on these broad central themes: *Wokół Jedwabnego, T. 1, Studia* (edited by Paweł Machcewicz and Krzysztof Persak); *U genezy Jedwabnego: Żydzi na Kresach Północno-Wschodnich II Rzeczypospolitej* (Andrzej Żbikowski); *"Ja tego Żyda znam!": Szantażowanie Żydów w Warszawie 1939–1943* (Jan Grabowski); and *Polacy i Żydzi pod okupacją niemiecką 1939–1945* (edited by Andrzej Żbikowski).[11]

Part review essay, part think piece, it hopes to introduce recent research published in Polish to the North American audience, while also thinking through some of the problems associated with narrating the Holocaust in Poland. After having worked through the individual studies, I suggest that such conceptual categories as collaboration, indifference, and resistance do not adequately capture the much more common everyday ways that Polish society became entangled in the persecution, ghettoization, and mass murder of the Jews.

JEDWABNE

The main area of recent research on the Holocaust published in Poland has focused on the kresy, the eastern borderlands where the most widespread violence against Jews by ethnic Poles took place. In 2002, a study by a team of historians associated with the Institute for National Remembrance (Instytut Pamięci Narodowej, or IPN) appeared that considered the issue of anti-Jewish violence in the Łomża and Białystok regions. Established in 1998 to investigate "crimes against the Polish nation," IPN is a government institute that conducts research on both the Communist and Nazi periods. In the wake of the debate about Jedwabne, IPN commissioned a dozen historians to investigate numerous archives in Europe, North America, and the Middle East to study the role of ethnic Poles in murdering their Jewish neighbors. The results of the IPN investigation are impressive. The collection of articles (*Wokół Jedwabnego* [Around Jedwabne], edited by Paweł Machcewicz and Krzysztof Persak), accompanied by a separate volume of documents, provides an important context for understanding the anti-Jewish violence that erupted in the kresy during the summer of 1941. The authors analyze the massacres that took place in the Łomża and Białystok regions and reveal that Jedwabne was not an isolated event. In more than twenty other towns, ethnic Poles, though to varying degrees of direct participation, carried out violence against Jews. As far as the IPN investigation could determine, it was only in the kresy region that Poles participated in anti-Jewish persecution on such a scale.[12]

Thus the volume largely confirms Gross's thesis that ethnic Poles became the perpetrators of the killings. In his introductory essay, Paweł Machcewicz has suggested four main causal factors that do not differ dramatically from Gross's argument: the pervasiveness of antisemitism in the Łomża and Białystok regions; the desire to plunder Jewish property; the role of the Germans as instigators of the massacre; and revenge for the "actual or imagined Jewish cooperation with the Soviets."[13] IPN investigators have, however, revised some of Gross's claims. Machcewicz noted that there were probably a dozen and maybe even twenty Germans present in Jedwabne on the day of the massacre, while Marcin Urynowicz[14] suggested that Jedwabne had approximately 1,000 Jews by the summer of 1941 rather than the 1,600 indicated by Gross. More substantial departures from Gross emerge on the level of emphasis and interpretation. In an essay on Polish-Jewish relations in western Belarus during the Soviet occupation, Marek Wierzbicki[15] has argued that the roots of anti-Jewish hostility lie in both the imagined and actual collaboration of Jews with the Soviets. Wierzbicki noted the significance of the Jewish-communism myth (żydokomuna) and the plight of Jews during the Soviet occupation, but also stressed the support that Jews gave to the Soviets. He pointed out that many Jews welcomed the Soviets and took over leading civil service positions left vacant by ethnic Poles who were forced to leave or who were executed by the Soviets, implying an uneasy and unconvincing causal link between alleged Jewish collaboration and anti-Jewish violence.

The IPN volume also analyzes more carefully than Gross did the possible links between prewar anti-Jewish hatred and wartime violence. Jan J. Milewski[16] indicated that the right-wing, ethnically exclusive National Democracy movement was particularly active in eastern Poland, and that Jews became linked to broad anxieties about capitalism and communism during the economic troubles of the 1930s. In a foreshadowing of his forthcoming book on the Catholic Church, Dariusz Libionka[17] has provided an abundance of information about how local priests reinforced the perception of a growing Jewish threat during the 1930s. These articles together reveal that antisemitism had permeated daily life in eastern Poland, which at first glance appears to be an important point since it was only in the kresy that ethnic Polish hatred against Jews erupted so violently. But on closer scrutiny, it does not seem entirely clear how either the influence of National Democracy or the presence of an antisemitic clergy made Poles more susceptible to Nazi calls for Selbstreinigungsaktionen (self-cleaning actions). As Paweł Machcewicz has noted, Jedwabne was an "oasis of calm" in the region during the interwar period.[18] Indeed, if there is an overarching argument to the IPN volume, it is that the anti-Jewish violence of 1941 stemmed from the brutal experience of the Soviet occupation. Just weeks after the Germans forced the Soviets out of eastern Poland, ethnic Poles avenged the imagined betrayal of Poland by mythic "Jewish communism" through violence and mass murder.[19]

But why did some ethnic Poles react in this way? This question raises the complex problem of perception and reality that Wierzbicki left unresolved: the dynamics between the antisemitic stereotype of żydokomuna and the actual reaction of Jews to the Soviet occupation. In his impressive new monograph *On the Origins of Jedwabne* (*U genezy Jedwabnego*), Andrzej Żbikowski has confronted this issue with unmatched thoroughness.[20] On the basis of a rich collection of sources located in the United States, Britain, Poland, and Israel, Żbikowski has analyzed the position and condition of Jews during the Soviet occupation. On the one hand, some Jews, especially those who were young, became attracted to the equality offered by the Soviets that had long been denied to them by the Polish state (e.g., access to civil service jobs and the official banning of antisemitism). Many Jews also recognized that the Soviets had saved them from the far worse situation of Nazi occupation. As the Zionist Moshe Kleinbaum recalled, "We were sentenced to death, but now it has changed to life imprisonment."[21] On the other hand, the harsh circumstances of occupation severely altered Jewish economic, social, and cultural life. As property owners and small tradespeople, Jews felt the impact of the nationalization of the economy in a particularly harsh way, and Soviet antireligious policies dramatically disrupted everyday life for the majority of shtetl Jews.[22]

Many ethnic Poles did not, however, recognize these adverse changes in Jewish life. A set of stereotypes and prejudices about the role of Jews during the Soviet occupation took hold in Polish society. Numerous reports sent to London by officials of the underground state reported that Jews had welcomed the Soviets en masse and had become beneficiaries of the Soviet occupation at the expense of Poles. In the eyes of many living in the kresy, Jewish Communists had occupied Poland. Żbikowski has clearly showed that this Polish perspective misrepresented reality. Jews did not benefit from the Soviet occupation any more than did their Polish neighbors. A high number of Jews were arrested and deported by the Soviets, and while some Jews did gain from Soviet policies, they were hardly a privileged group; Jews only made up about 10 percent of administrative posts in the Soviet apparatus, roughly equal to their percent per population. At one point, Żbikowski ventured to guess that, overall, probably between 7 and 10 percent of Jews cooperated with the Soviets. It is impossible to know for sure the exact number, but his point is both convincing and important: the alleged Jewish "collaboration" with the Soviets did *not* cause the pogroms in the summer of 1941.[23] Instead, he has rightly emphasized that the violence emerged from the wider context of the Third Reich's evolving policy to exterminate European Jewry. By late

July 1941, ever more extensive shootings of Jews were being conducted by the Einsatzgruppen, Waffen-Schutzstaffel (SS) units in the Kommandostab Reichsführer-SS, and Order Police battalions. Just as the Nazis began to move closer to the "Final Solution," massacres in eastern Poland erupted, taking place mainly between early and mid-July. But while stressing this broader context, Żbikowski has argued that, on the micro level, the role of ethnic Poles in the unfolding of local anti-Jewish incidents was crucial: "After reading [German] sources, I am convinced of the secondary importance of German provocation. Anti-Jewish pogroms were not the outcome of German design, even though the presence of German soldiers and policemen was favorable to their escalation."[24]

Much of what Żbikowski has written in *On the Origins of Jedwabne* is not new, but that does not mean he has not published an important book. If one compares for a moment the Jedwabne debate to a trial, beginning with the passionate opening statement by the dynamic Gross followed by a meticulous airing of the evidence by the more prosaic Żbikowski, then the contribution of *On the Origins of Jedwabne* becomes clear. The book lacks the verve and eloquence of *Neighbors;* it moves slowly and tediously through the archival evidence, but that is precisely its strength. Żbikowski has expertly performed the role of presenting the evidence to a courtroom made up of some who still believe in the stereotype of Jewish collaboration by showing that Jews did not support the Communist regime in any exceptional way. But as the careful cross-examiner, Żbikowski has proved less able to confront the larger question of why. Our understanding of why ethnic Poles decided to participate in the killing of their Jewish neighbors has not advanced nearly as much as has our information about those events. Żbikowski's book fits squarely within a positivist tradition dominant in Poland that stresses a thorough presentation of archival evidence over analysis, but documents standing alone often do not explain. How and why, for a remarkably brief period of time in the summer of 1941, did some Poles living in the kresy become killers? Indeed, the main issues left unresolved in Żbikowski's account are the timing and the place. He does not believe that the Germans coordinated the massacres, arguing that the attacks were part of a broader explosion of Nazi violence initiated by local Poles with German involvement varying from village to village at a moment when the Nazis had not yet settled on the "Final Solution."[25] But immediately on crossing the Polish border in September 1939, the German military proved its capacity to kill thousands of Jews and Poles, and Reinhard Heydrich's orders of 1941 made it clear that "self-cleansing actions" should be encouraged in eastern Poland.[26] Given these direct orders and the brutality of the Nazi occupation in Poland already, why would the German military not coordinate massacres against Jews? Finally, anti-Jewish violence occurred in the kresy precisely because this region did not experience the brutality and terror of German occupation. Some ethnic Poles greeted the Germans as liberators and became willing to collaborate with them in a way that those living in central and western Poland simply never would have.

BEYOND JEDWABNE

One of the most important effects of *Neighbors* has been a surge of research on Polish-Jewish relations during the Holocaust, although "relations" is probably not the right word here. Most studies have explored the general reaction of the Polish population to the Holocaust, partly because the relationship between Poles and Jews was so clearly asymmetrical during the war. Crowded into ghettos and death camps, Jews had little leverage to influence the type of interaction that they had with their Polish neighbors. A recent exploration into this important point is the new book by Jan Grabowski, *"I Know This Jew!" ("Ja tego Żyda znam!")*.[27] Grabowski, a Polish historian working in Canada, has looked at the practice of blackmailing Jews living on the "Aryan" side. On the basis of a rich collection of material from German courts, he has refuted the common perception that only the dregs of society became involved in blackmailing. Only 20 of 260 sample persons involved in the "trade" had a criminal record from the interwar period. The blackmailers (szmalcowniks) came from all parts of society and were made up of Poles, Germans, and even some Jews. They demanded money from Jews spotted outside the ghetto walls in return for not denouncing them. The process often involved negotiation since both sides wanted the matter to be resolved on the street without further referral to the police. Jews felt this way for obvious reasons, but the szmalcowniks would rather avoid interacting with the police given that profiting from Jewish fugitives was illegal and the blackmailer could face either a fine or imprisonment (citizens were supposed to alert the authorities about Jews who had escaped rather than profit from them). Grabowski did not know for certain the number of blackmailers in Warsaw, but he has accepted both Emanuel Ringelblum's guess of szmalcowniks "in the hundreds and maybe even thousands" and Gunnar S. Paulsson's recent estimate of three to four thousand.[28]

But in a sense, the exact number of szmalcowniks is not that important for Grabowski. Even if their number was relatively small, he has emphasized that their impact was wide ranging. Blackmailers effectively became a significant part of the German occupation. They created an environment of fear that reinforced Nazi policies by making hiding an unattractive strategy for survival:

> Although it is difficult to assess the number of Jews handed over to the Germans in this way, the criminal activity of the blackmailers and informers must not be looked at only from the perspective of the anguish and death of their direct victims, but also from the death of all of those who—fearing the threats that awaited them on the other side of the wall—decided to remain in the ghetto and shared in the fate of the majority of Warsaw's Jews.[29]

Grabowski also has argued that the indifference (obojętność) of the underground state and the Warsaw population permitted the practice of blackmailing to flourish. The underground state paid almost no attention to the problem, not even declaring it as a form of collaboration with the Germans until the spring of 1943, which was virtually meaningless since most of Polish Jewry had already perished by that point. The majority of Warsaw's population remained equally indifferent to the szmalcowniks. In 1942, the Delegatura, the representation of the Polish government-in-exile in Poland, published a report about the existence of "three Warsaws": the first, comprising about 25 percent of the population, engaged in "heroic" acts of defiance; the second, making up about 70 percent, attempted just to survive and generally remained indifferent; and the third and smallest, about 5 percent, were involved in blackmail, petty crime, and collaboration. Grabowski has argued that 5 percent might be small, but that szmalcowniks relied on the much broader passive cooperation of Polish society: "Apart from the people actively engaged in the fight against Germany, a wide range of indifferent attitudes sprang up that belonged to 'the Warsaw of

Mr. and Mrs. Kowalski'—to invoke the expression of the Delegatura. And in the shadow of the indifference of the Kowalskis, extortionists and blackmailers built up a booming operation."[30]

Those two sentences end Grabowski's slim book. In a way, *"I Know This Jew!"* is more striking than the other short book that I suspect partly inspired it, *Neighbors*. It lacks, of course, the emotive story that so disturbs: the explosion of hate and violence that surrounded the pushing of Jews into a burning barn. But Jedwabne was rather exceptional; blackmailing and "looking the other way" were not. Many more Poles became beneficiaries of the Nazi persecution of the Jews rather than genocidal killers.

Grabowski powerfully reinforced this point by discussing the seizure of Jewish property by Poles. Although it is not clear how much szmalcowniks were directly involved in the confiscation of property, Grabowski could not be more accurate about its importance. The confiscation of Jewish property in Poland has unfortunately yet to be studied, but if recent research on "Aryanization" in Germany is any indication, the process probably involved extensive participation from authorities and citizens on the local level.[31] And this process occurred in every village, town, and city in Poland.

Some of the broad themes that Grabowski has raised are explored further in an extensively researched collection of essays published by IPN and edited by Andrzej Żbikowski. Under the benign title *Poles and Jews Under the German Occupation (Polacy i Żydzi pod okupacją niemiecką 1939–1945)*, the volume brings together ten essays that deal with Polish-Jewish relations in the geographic areas of Warsaw, Łódź, Kraków, Rzeszowszczna, Białystok, and Katowice and explore such themes as Polish institutional responses to the Holocaust, the rescue of Jews by Poles, the relationship of the rightist-nationalist movement to the genocide, and the general phenomena of blackmail and collaboration.[32] Centered loosely on the fundamental issue of providing assistance to Jews, the volume provides new information, but few of its contributions have made innovative interpretative claims. One might suspect some tendentious aim behind the choice of rescue as a unifying theme given that the volume arose out of the Jedwabne debate and appeared several months before Jan Gross's most recent intervention into the history of antisemitism in postwar Poland.[33] A desire to show the more "positive side" of Polish behavior doubtlessly shaped part of the project, which raises the question of whether government institutions like IPN should be in the business of writing history in the first place. Indeed, this likely political context might partly account for the extremely short introduction written by the editor, Andrzej Żbikowski. How is one to introduce an already difficult and complicated history when conflicting political pressures are added to the mix? Żbikowski went with the safe route of saying little; he avoided drawing out the significance of the thousand pages that follow and steered clear of positioning the volume within broader historiographical debates.[34] But this disappointing introduction is nothing compared to the rather unfortunate article written by Jan Żaryn[35] on five right-wing nationalists who aided Jews. Żaryn has failed to provide the necessary broader context for his discussion of these figures, running the risk of implying that they represented the actions and beliefs of right-wing nationalists as a whole who, to put it mildly, were not sacrificing their lives in droves to save Jews. The inclusion of this odd and clumsy essay takes away from the serious contributions that the other authors have provided.[36]

The rest of the book, in fact, makes a useful contribution in uncovering the various dynamics of Polish-Jewish relations during the Holocaust. Despite Nazi attempts to exclude Jews from the rest of Polish society, interactions between Poles and Jews took place across the ghetto walls to a greater degree than perhaps most historians have realized, as Dorota Siepracka has uncovered particularly well in a vivid essay on Łódź.[37] The nature of these everyday interactions varied significantly. On one end of the spectrum, Marcin Urynowicz has explored organizational and individual factors that both enabled and hindered assistance to Jews. He has showed that Poles helped Jews most often out of humanitarian concerns or because they knew the person they were aiding, and that Poles living in the countryside were much more likely to aid Jews than those living in urban areas. Only about 32 percent of all cases took place in Poland's largest cities, a number that drops to an astonishing 11 percent when the exceptional case of Warsaw is taken out.[38] Since most Jews were confined to cities, these numbers partly explain the overall low level of aid offered to Jews, especially when compared with the frequency of other illegal acts Poles carried out against the Nazis.[39]

Urynowicz also stressed the broader context of the German occupation in shaping Polish actions. The persistent "fear" and "anxiety" of the occupation, combined with traditional perceptions of Jews as strangers, created a "demoralized" environment that was hardly conducive to helping Jews.[40] A central part of this fear, as Urynowicz touched on but Andrzej Żbikowski developed further in his contribution on Polish collaboration,[41] stemmed from those who decided to benefit from and work with the Nazis. In an excellent summary of recent research on this topic, Żbikowski has shown how the presence of denouncers, blackmailers, and the Blue Police reinforced a climate of anxiety, suspicion, and distrust that precluded Poles from helping Jews and dissuaded Jews from looking for assistance across the ghetto walls. He has argued that Poles were motivated by a combination of economic factors such as the desire for Jewish property and by a basic dislike or hatred for Jews.

In the last contribution to the volume, Anna Pyżewska has emphasized the "great polarization of behavior" that shaped Polish-Jewish relations during the Holocaust "from attempts to give aid" to "handing over Jews to the occupation authority" to "pogroms."[42] This IPN work has attempted to capture this polarization by focusing on collaboration and rescue, but it has omitted one central question: if these are the two extreme endpoints of social behavior, how does one characterize the very large middle that has been overlooked here? In confronting this question, some Polish historians have settled on notions of indifference, passive complicity, or neutrality that impute various degrees of complicity or collaboration with the Nazi system. Żbikowski has asked directly: "Can (or should) the indifference in the face of the Jewish tragedy be linked to collaboration?"[43] Urynowicz, in a second contribution on Polish-Jewish relations in Warsaw, put the issue more broadly: "I doubt whether the current stage of research can find the right criteria for contemporary scholars to ascertain how much Polish reaction to the Holocaust was determined by antisemitism or indifference in the face of the Jewish fate, how much by neutrality understood as the inability to give aid, and how much from psychological factors—above all the fear of repression."[44] In short, by focusing on the "great polarization" of Polish behavior, this volume reflects and represents the basic conceptual framework that has shaped recent writing on the Holocaust, searching for answers to the basic question: Was Polish society complicit in, resistant against, or indifferent to the Nazi persecution of the Jews?

As a way to conclude, I would like to suggest, albeit very briefly and broadly by necessity, that this polar approach to studying the Holocaust in Poland has limitations. If on a spectrum of social behavior killing Jews is on one end and saving them is on the other, one can safely say that the overwhelming majority of Poles were neither heroic rescuers nor treasonous collaborators. Instead, most Poles became drawn into, took advantage of, or benefited from the persecution of their Jewish neighbors in a much more ordinary and everyday way. It is not just that Poles and their government officials in exile observed the Holocaust with indifference, no matter if one defines it as passive or complicit. Many other governments and societies certainly reacted in the same way, including those powers that possibly could have done something, such as Britain, the United States, and the Soviet Union. Terms like "indifference" do not capture precisely enough how entangled in the Holocaust ordinary Poles became. In a country where Jews made up 10 percent of the overall population and where in many towns they comprised nearly half of the population, the persecution, ghettoization, deportation, and mass murder of three million people over five years intersected with the lives of so many ordinary Poles to a degree that historians cannot possibly reconstruct with any completeness. The entanglement of the Holocaust with everyday Polish life took on many different forms, from identifying Jews to the Nazis to blackmailing those few Jews living on the "Aryan" side to moving into the homes left behind and considered to be "pożydowski" (a peculiar Polish word invented to denote former Jewish property). To be sure, other Poles reacted with catastrophic fragility or heroic strength by killing or rescuing Jews, but my point is that these were hardly the most common responses of Poles. One could cite many instances to illuminate the more ordinary interactions with the Holocaust that I am thinking about, but the famous writer and literary critic Michał Głowiński has provided one remarkable example in his memoir. He recalled an experience in a café in Warsaw on the "Aryan" side. While his aunt, who looked "Aryan," went to make a phone call, the young Głowiński, sitting by himself, piqued the interest of the women surrounding him who became increasingly anxious about his presence:

> In the beginning, it seemed to me that all was calm. . . . Yet after a while I couldn't escape the realization that the scene was playing out otherwise. . . . The women stared at me as if I were an extraordinary monster, whose very existence called into question the laws of nature, and as if they would have to decide what to do

with me that very moment, for things could not remain as they were.... I heard "A Jew, there's no question, a Jew. She certainly isn't, but him—he's a Jew." ... I heard one of them say, "We have to let the police know." ... Most often they spit out the threatening word "Jew," but also, most terrifying, they kept repeating "We have to let the police know." I was aware that this was the equivalent to a death sentence. If I'd then known something about Mediterranean mythology, I would doubtlessly have thought I'd landed in the possession of the Erinyes, the Furies, desirous of mutilating me. Yet would such an analogy be appropriate? For those women were not possessed by an uncontrollable hatred.... These were normal, ordinary women, in their own way decent and resourceful, hardworking, undoubtedly scrambling to take care of their families in the difficult conditions of the occupation.... They had found themselves in a situation that felt to them trying and threatening, and they wished to confront it directly. They only did not think at what price. Perhaps this transcended their imaginations—although they must have known how it would end if they were to "let them know"—or perhaps such thoughts were simply not within the boundaries of moral reflection accessible to them.[45]

One might be tempted to consider these interactions with the Holocaust as examples of complicity, collaboration, or indifference, but such labels tend toward simplification. Poles who took over Jewish apartments, blackmailed Jews on the tram, or threatened to call the police did not, in their own moral universe, see these actions as forms of collaboration with the German enemy; their moral economy did not necessarily consider these ordinary intersections with the Holocaust as problematic. These types of reactions became integrated and normalized into everyday life to the point that the suffering and humanity of the victim became completely blurred. The climate of fear and anxiety created by Nazi occupation no doubt helped shape this moral economy not least because most ordinary Poles were concerned about their own individual survival, and the persecution of the Jews had virtually no bearing on their everyday existence. But it was also prejudice against Jews, which had taken hold in Polish society over years of increased violence, persecution, bias, and separation since the 1930s, that, crucially, separated the fate of the Jews from that of ordinary Poles. Jews found themselves in the uniquely difficult position of having to worry about both Poles and Germans when they were able to escape to the "Aryan" side. As one Holocaust survivor put it succinctly: "Hiding Jews was a very dangerous activity and no one could expect from people such heroism. Nevertheless there was no need for denunciation of one's neighbor because he was hiding a Jew. I myself lived in constant fear that the Germans would kill me but I was even more afraid of Poles who were able to recognize that I was a Jew."[46] It was the emergence of this moral economy—in which the Jewish fate became utterly separated from the Polish fate—that defined above all Polish-Jewish relations during the Holocaust.

NOTES

1. Article 37, Ustawa z dnia 18 października 2006 r. o ujawnianiu informacji o dokumentach organów bezpieczeństwa państwa z lat 1944–1990 oraz treści tych dokumentów. The law can be downloaded from the Polish parliament's official Web site: http://isip.sejm.gov.pl/prawo/index.html.

2. Jan T. Gross, *Neighbors: The Destruction of the Jewish Community in Jedwabne, Poland* (Princeton, N.J.: Princeton University Press, 2001).

3. Antony Polonsky and Joanna B. Michlic, eds., *The Neighbors Respond: The Controversy of the Jedwabne Massacre in Poland* (Princeton, N.J.: Princeton University Press, 2004).

4. Quotes from Dariusz Stola's critical analysis of the measure: "Historycy za karty," *Gazeta Wyborcza,* September 8, 2006.

5. See, for example, Marek Jan Chodakiewicz, *The Massacre in Jedwabne, July 10, 1941: Before, During, and After* (Boulder, Colo.: East European Monographs, distributed by Columbia University Press, 2005).

6. Raul Hilberg, *The Destruction of the European Jews* (Chicago: Quadrangle Books, 1961).

7. Ulrich Herbert, ed., *National Socialist Extermination Policies: Contemporary German Perspectives and Controversies* (New York: Berghahn, 2000).

8. Dariusz Stola, "Jedwabne: Revisiting the Evidence and Nature of the Crime," *Holocaust and Genocide Studies* 17 (2003), 149.

9. Christopher Browning's *Ordinary Men* (New York: HarperPerennial, 1993) and Daniel Goldhagen's *Hitler's Willing Executioners* (New York: Alfred A. Knopf, 1996) clearly shaped Gross's text.

10. Klaus-Peter Friedrich, "Collaboration in a 'Land Without a Quisling': Patterns of Cooperation with the Nazi German Occupation Regime in Poland During World War II," *Slavic Review* 64, no. 4 (2005), 711–46; John Connelly, "Why the Poles Collaborated So Little—and Why That Is No Reason for Nationalist Hubris," *Slavic Review* 64, no. 4 (2005), 771–

81; Alina Skibińska and Jakub Petelewicz, "Udział Polaków w zbrodniach na Żydach na prowincji regionu świętokrzyskiego," *Zagłada Żydów* 1 (2005), 114–47; and Jan Tomasz Gross, "O kolaboracji," *Zagłada Żydów* 2 (2006), 407–16.

11. The four books I will be reviewing are: Paweł Machcewicz and Krzysztof Persak, eds., *Wokół Jedwabnego, T. 1, Studia* (Warsaw: Instytut Pamięci Narodowej [hereafter IPN], 2002); Andrzej Żbikowski, *U genezy Jedwabnego: Żydzi na Kresach Północno-Wschodnich II Rzeczypospolitej* (Warsaw: Żydowski Institut Historyczny [hereafter ŻIH], 2006); Jan Grabowski, *"Ja tego Żyda znam!": Szantażowanie Żydów w Warszawie 1939–1943* (Warsaw: Wydawnictwo Instytutu Filozofii Socjologii PAN [hereafter IFiS], 2004); Andrzej Żbikowski, ed., *Polacy i Żydzi pod okupacją niemiecką 1939–1945* (Warsaw: IPN, 2006).

12. Andrzej Żbikowski, "Pogromy i mordy ludności żydowskiej w Łomżyńskiem i na Białostocczyźnie latem 1941 roku w świetle relacji ocalałych Żydów i dokumentów sądowych," in Machcewicz and Persak, *Wokół Jedwabnego*, 159–271.

13. Paweł Machcewicz, "Wokół Jedwabnego," in Machcewicz and Persak, *Wokół Jedwabnego*, 40.

14. Marcin Urynowicz, "Ludność żydowska w Jedwabnem. Zmiany demograficzne od końca XIX wieku do 1941 roku na tle regionu łomżyńskiego," in Machcewicz and Persak, *Wokół Jedwabnego*.

15. Marek Wierzbicki, "Stosunki polsko-żydowskie na Zachodniej Białorusi w latach 1939–1941," in Machcewicz and Persak, *Wokół Jedwabnego*, 129–58.

16. Jan J. Milewski, "Polacy i Żydzi w Jedwabnem i okolicy przed 22 czerwca 1941 roku," in Machcewicz and Persak, *Wokół Jedwabnego*, 63–82.

17. Dariusz Libionka, "Duchowieństwo diecezji łomżyńskiej wobec antysemityzmu i zagłady Żydów," in Machcewicz and Persak, *Wokół Jedwabnego*, 105–28.

18. Machcewicz, "Wokół Jedwabnego," in Machcewicz and Persak, *Wokół Jedwabnego*, 69.

19. For a recent discussion of the antisemitic myth of Jewish communism and its discussion among Polish historians, see Joanna Michlic, "The Soviet Occupation of Poland, 1939–41, and the Stereotype of the Anti-Polish and Pro-Soviet Jew," *Jewish Social Studies* 3 (2007), 135–76.

20. Żbikowski, *U genezy Jedwabnego*.

21. Moshe Kleinbaum quoted in Żbikowski, *U genezy Jedwabnego*, 24.

22. Ben-Cion Punchuk, *Shtetl Jews Under Soviet Rule of Eastern Poland on the Eve of the Holocaust* (Oxford.: Blackwell, 1990).

23. Some historians have either implied or argued the opposite: Marek Wierzbicki, *Polacy i Żydzi w zaborze sowieckim. Stosunki polsko-żydowskie na ziemach północno-wschodnich II RP pod okupacją sowiecką* (Warsaw: Fronda, 2001); Bogdan Musiał, *"Kontrrevolutionäre Elemente sind zu erschiessen." Die Brutalisierung des deutsch-sowjetischen Krieges im Sommer 1941* (Munich: Propyläen, 2001).

24. Żbikowski, *U genezy Jedwabnego*, 238.

25. Żbikowski, "Pogromy i mordy."

26. Alexander B. Rossino, *Hitler Strikes Poland: Blitzkrieg, Ideology, and Atrocity* (Lawrence: University Press of Kansas, 2003); Jochen Böhler, *Auftakt zum Vernichtungskrieg. Die Wehrmacht in Polen 1939* (Frankfurt: Fischer, 2006).

27. Grabowski, *"Ja tego Żyda znam!"*

28. Emmanuel Ringelblum, *Polish-Jewish Relations During the Second World War*, eds. Joseph Kermish and Shmuel Krakowski (New York: Howard Fertig, 1976), 124; Gunnar S. Paulsson, *Secret City: The Hidden Jews of Warsaw, 1940–1945* (New Haven, Conn.: Yale University Press, 2003), 149.

29. Grabowski, *"Ja tego Żyda znam!"* 8.

30. Ibid., 131.

31. Frank Bajohr, *"Arisierung" in Hamburg. Die Verdrängung der jüdischen Unternehmer 1933–1945* (Hamburg: Christians, 1997).

32. Żbikowski, *Polacy*.

33. Jan Gross, *Fear: Anti-Semitism in Poland After Auschwitz* (Princeton, N.J.: Princeton University Press, 2006).

34. Żbikowski, *Polacy*.

35. Jan Żaryn, "Elity obozu narodowego wobec zagłady Żydów," in Żbikowski, *Polacy*, 365–428.

36. Since I cannot go into a fuller criticism here, I refer readers to Jan Grabowski's excellent review: Grabowski, "Pomoc organiczona," *Gazeta Wyborcza*, November 10, 2006, 35.

37. Dorota Siepracka, "Stosunki polsko-żydowskie w Łodzi podczas okupacji hitlerowskiej," in Żbikowski, *Polacy*, 691–762.

38. Marcin Urynowicz, "Zorganizowana i indywidualna pomoc Polaków dla ludności żydowskiej eksterminowanej przez okupanta niemieckiego w okresie drugiej wojny światowej," in Żbikowski, *Polacy*, 244–45.

39. Jan T. Gross, "A Tangled Web: Confronting Stereotypes Concerning Relations Between Poles, Germans, Jews, and Communists," in *The Politics of Retribution in Europe: World War II and Its Aftermath*, eds. István Deák, Jan T. Gross, and Tony Judt (Princeton, N.J.: Princeton University Press, 2000), 74–130.

40. Urynowicz, "Zorganizowana," in Żbikowski, *Polacy,* 263–76.

41. Andrzej Żbikowski, "Antysemityzm, szmalcownictwo, współpraca z Niemcami a stosunki polsko-żydowskie pod okupacją niemiecką," in *Polacy.*

42. Anna Pyżewska, "Pomoc dla ludności żydowskiej w Okręgu Białystok w latach okupacji niemieckiej," in Żbikowski, *Polacy,* 952.

43. Żbikowski, "Antysemityzm," in *Polacy,* 430.

44. Marcin Urynowicz, "Stosunki polsko-żydowskie w Warszawie w okresie okupacji hitlerowskiej," in Żbikowski, *Polacy,* 625.

45. Michał Głowiński, *The Black Seasons,* trans. Marci Shore (Evanston, Ill.: Northwestern University Press, 2005), 93–96.

46. Quoted in Joanna B. Michlic, *Poland's Threatening Other: The Image of the Jew from 1880 to the Present* (Lincoln: University of Nebraska Press, 2006), 190.

Paul B. Miller

Just Like the Jews: Contending Victimization in the Former Yugoslavia

FOR ANYONE WHO HAS SPENT TIME IN THE FORMER YUGOSLAVIA recently, the taglines of the Srebrenica genocide are all too familiar: "The largest massacre on European soil since the Holocaust." "The most horrible crime in Europe from the Holocaust to the present." These citations are from Yugoslav sources. They range over different anniversaries of the July 1995 tragedy.[1] What is more, the point that they advertise is at least partly true.

As long as we disregard reprisal massacres against real and alleged fascist collaborators and their families across Europe at the end of World War II; omit the estimated two million ethnic Germans murdered by their Polish, Czech, Hungarian, Serb, and other neighbors as they were forced to flee their ancestral homes in 1945 and the immediate postwar years; and exclude the evil deeds of the Communist regimes, then the cold-blooded murder of some seven to eight thousand Bosnian Muslim males following the fall of Srebrenica to the Bosnian Serb army in summer 1995 surely does constitute the single most despicable thing that has happened in Europe since the Nazi Holocaust. The question I would like to consider here, however, is to what end the correlation? In other words, is calling attention to the Bosnian genocide of the 1990s—or as we shall see, to any of the murderous episodes that plagued Yugoslavs in the twentieth century—by analogy to the Holocaust an effective way to understand that heinous event; or to ensure that its perpetrators are punished; or to bestow meaning on the meaningless? What is achieved and what is lost when the Holocaust becomes the standard trope for a victimized past and when every group has been victimized?

Holocaust analogizing, or what Samantha Power calls "Holocaustizing," is no longer a novelty to those of us who practice what the fiction writer Don DeLillo ironically dubbed "Hitler studies."[2] Titles like *American Holocaust, Late Victorian Holocausts,* and *Eternal Treblinka: Our Treatment of Animals and the Holocaust*—some even important works of scholarship—have proliferated exponentially.[3] Our tolerance for Holocaustizing may fall precipitously when we see references to "the Holocaust of the unborn" or when neoconservatives warn us that the "war on terror" amounts to a choice between "victory or Holocaust."[4] But maybe that is just the price that serious Holocaust scholars have had to pay in the long process of having their work taken, well, seriously.

Moreover, besides its marketing value, the Holocaust analogy is regularly invoked for the altogether positive purpose of pressuring policy-makers to live up to their "never again" rhetoric. This motive was particularly true during the Bosnian conflict that erupted in spring 1992, less than four years after the 1948 United Nations (UN) Genocide Convention finally became law in the United States in November 1988 (in 1986 the U.S. Senate ratified the Genocide Convention and in November 1988 President Reagan signed legislation implementing the Convention). The Cold War having ended, the United States found itself with the global authority and military power to act on the Genocide Convention. What began with televised images of skeletal Muslim men (often aired alongside familiar clips of emaciated Jews in Nazi camps) and an article in the New York paper *Newsday,* headlined "Like Auschwitz," culminated in the 1992 presidential race, when Bill Clinton challenged the incumbent George H. W. Bush's passivity on Bosnia thus: "If the horrors of the Holocaust taught us anything, it is the high cost of remaining silent and paralyzed in the face of genocide."[5] In the end, it would take several more horrors—including Srebrenica—before the U.S.-organized North Atlantic Treaty Organization (NATO) response ended the bloodshed in Bosnia. But that was more than two years after Clinton's inauguration.

By this time, suffering Bosnians themselves had caught the wave of Holocaustization. In an interview with *Newsday* reporter Roy Gutman, Bosnian Muslim student Enver Šišić described the Bosnian Serb capital of Banja Luka as a "big ghetto," adding: "We all felt like Jews in the Third Reich."[6] In what follows, I want to examine several manifestations of the Holocaust analogy among the constituent peoples of the former Yugoslavia. While I clearly regard some as more exaggerated and propagandistic than others, my purpose is not to tear down one group's analogies or to elevate another's. As will become obvious, I think all of them problematic in one way or another and all, at some level, based on factual misrepresentations. Rather, my purpose is to explore one of the seemingly few remaining commonalities in Yugoslav identity—that of the Jewish-like Holocaust victim—and try to figure out why something that is increasingly shared by Orthodox Serbs, Bosnian Muslims, Catholic Croats, and others has also been, and continues to be, their undoing.

SERBIA

Well before there was the fall of Yugoslavia, there was the Fall, with a capital F, of a people—the Jewish people. And ever since those first biblical tumbles in Eden and Egypt, there have been a series of stumblings, both biblical and historical, culminating, as we know, in the Holocaust. Northrop Frye and others have dealt extensively with the ways in which a "covenantal cycle" of Fall and Redemption, epitomized in modern times by the Jews' post-Holocaust return to the land of Israel, often forms a core mythological construct of nationalist ideology.[7] It certainly has for Serbs, who did not take long after Marshal Tito died in 1980 to begin transforming their 1389 defeat at Kosovo by the Ottoman Turks into a teleological morality tale that confirmed Serbian-Jewish affinity—"the thirteenth lost and most ill-fated tribe of Israel," in the words of writer/politician Vuk Drašković. In Drašković's 1985 "Letter to the Writers of Israel," he likened the half millennium of Turkish rule over Serbs to the Babylonian exile, and he consecrated Kosovo the Serbian Jerusalem. But above all, for Drašković, "It was in that last 'genocidal slaughter' [World War II] that centuries of Jewish-Serbian martyrdom were sealed and signed in blood. It is by the hands of the same executioners [the Nazis and their collaborators] that both Serbs and Jews have been exterminated at the same concentration camps ... burned alive in the same ovens."[8]

The genocide against Serbs in World War II at the hands of Croatian fascist Ustasha and, sometimes, at the hands of their Muslim collaborators is, of course, no myth. Likewise, the oft-heard reference to the Ustasha concentration camp Jasenovac as the "Serb Auschwitz" cannot be taken lightly, however inflated the death count.[9] When the Serbian Ministry of Information refers to the Serbian "holocaust," we do not have to guess at what it is trying to prove. But neither can we lightly dismiss the high mortality of Serbs in the Nezavisna Država Hrvatska (NDH, the Independent State of Croatia).[10]

What is problematic is that the mythological construct of a perennial and linked Serb-Jewish victimhood was brought directly to bear on the cause of Greater Serbia. By depicting themselves as the perpetually persecuted, Serb nationalists, including some of the republic's leading intellectuals and politicians, transformed everyone else, particularly Croats and Kosovar Albanians, into serial executioners. "Serbophobia" thus became the undisguised equivalent to antisemitism, with Slobodan Milošević himself playing the analogy to the hilt. In a speech to the Fourth Party Congress on February 17, 2000, he asked delegates to imagine how the Jews would have felt if their persecution by the Nazis had been justified by accusations that they had been committing genocide against the Germans. This, Milošević insisted, was exactly what Serbs faced when westerners accused them of genocide against Albanians.[11] As the writer Dobrica Ćosić put it: "We Serbs feel today as the Jews did in Hitler's day. . . . Serbophobia in Europe is a concept and an attitude with the same ideological motivation and fury as antisemitism had during the Nazi era." Not coincidentally, it was during the Milošević era—when "to be a Serb was . . . to be a victim," wrote Sabrina Ramet—that the home of Theodor Herzl's grandparents in Zemun was converted into a museum meant to affirm Serbia's historic "Jewishness."[12]

The examples of Serb Judeophilism in the 1980s and 1990s are plentiful. The consequences, of course, are well known. But while nearly every study of the breakup of Yugoslavia traces its ideological origins to the 1986 memorandum from the Serbian Academy of Science and Arts alleging "genocide" against Serbs in Kosovo, less has been written on the deliberate efforts to put this Judeo-Serb martyr-in-arms ideology into practice through the Serbian-Jewish Friendship Society. Founded in 1988 by prominent Serbian intellectuals and financed by the government, the society sought to co-opt Serbia's tiny Jewish community into its nationalist program by playing on perceived Western sympathy for Jews and the Jewish state. As member Brana Crnčević put it: "Only friendship with the Jews can save Serbdom."[13]

While most Serbian Jews resisted the political bait, the society did make an impact: it brought a delegation of 440 businesspeople, politicians, and intellectuals to Israel in 1990; established 22 Serbian and Israeli "twin cities"; and took 15 Serb mayors to Israel during the 1991 Gulf War to show solidarity with the beleaguered state (and despite official Yugoslavia's alliance with Iraq). If the society's goal of obtaining Israeli military support for the liberation of Kosovo—the "Serbian Jerusalem"—proved fanciful, it did show just how serious these nationalists were about their contrived victimology.[14]

SLOVENIA/ISTRIA

Although Serbs may have stretched the Holocaust analogy to its ideological and practicable limits, they are not the only Yugoslavs to have pegged their pain and past to that of the Jews. In her study of Slavic and Italian Istrians, Pamela Ballinger showed how both groups mobilized Holocaust narratives to recount their suffering at the hands of Italian fascists or Slavic partisans, respectively. In the case of the Italians, who fled Istria en masse at the end of World War II but also suffered murderous partisan reprisals, Ballinger pointed out that the number of victims has been "grossly exaggerated." Factored into the "thousands" of slain, for example, are Italian deportees, Slavic victims of Nazi-fascist violence, and even German soldiers. Notwithstanding the empirical evidence, Istrian Italians still licking their exilic wounds in the 1990s found in the Yugoslav wars definitive proof of the primitive and genocidal character of their former Slavic neighbors. And again references to the Holocaust abounded.[15]

A similar strategy was adopted by Slovenes in their battle against encroaching Serb hegemony in the late 1980s. When 1,300 Kosovar Albanian miners decided to stay underground until the province's pro-Milošević leaders resigned, their northern countrymen put on a dramatic show of solidarity. On February 27, 1989, during a live broadcast from Ljubljana's Cankarjev dom concert hall, Slovenians donned Albanian skullcaps with a Star of David affixed to them. In one stroke not only had the Slovenians equated Albanians with Jews and thereby the Serbs with Nazis, but by identifying themselves with the Kosovar Albanians in the buildup to their own nation's independence two years later, the Slovenian minority also was linking itself with Jews in their struggle with Serbia.[16]

The Ljubljana concert hall rally might never have provoked a massive counterdemonstration in Belgrade had it not imposed itself on the new Serbian-Jewish foundational mythology. Indeed, the rally had violated one of that mythology's quasi-religious elements: the mystique of the Jadovno pit in the Croatian border region of Krajina. It was into that pit that Croatian and Muslim Ustasha had dumped slaughtered Serbs during World War II. In 1983, the Serbian Orthodox Archimandrite Atanasije Jevtić made a pilgrimage from Kosovo to Jadovno, after which, in his published diary, he consecrated the sites as the consummation of Serbian martyrdom: "The word and reality of Jadovno is the full revelation of the secret of Kosovo and confirmation of the Kosovo choice and Kosovo covenant." By using Jewish symbolism to sanctify a pit in Kosovo that held not murdered Serbs but rather frustrated Albanian miners, the Slovenian action transgressed a hallowed symbol of Serb nationalism. It was left to Matija Bećković, the "Prince of Serbian poetry," to remind Slovenians that while the Albanians eventually came out of the pits "hale and happy," the Jews and Serbs never did.[17]

CROATIA

Considering Croatia's atrocious wartime record as a Nazi puppet state bent on supplementing the Jewish "Final Solution" with one against Serbs—and in view of the blatant antisemitism of Dr. Franjo Tudjman, who led Croatia to independence in the 1990s—it is hard to imagine how Croats might have positioned their Judeophilic plaint of Holocaust-like victimhood in the run-up to the Yugoslav wars.[18] But if four years of the NDH's exceedingly bloody history had ruined Croat nationalists for anything more than a defensive effort to fob their antisemitism off on the Germans and present Croats at large as true allies of their (former) Jewish neighbors, the opposite and more obnoxious strategy of challenging Serbs at their own philosemitic game also came into play. One way to do this was to take on the Serbian myth of not having collaborated with the Nazis in the "Final Solution," a ridiculous claim that grew out of the larger and still prevalent fiction that Serbs are the only people to have lived peacefully with Jews throughout their history.[19] Several figures, including a writer for the official Catholic newsletter *Glas Koncila,* tried to prove the converse: that antisemitism was deeply ingrained in the Serbian national character.[20] Ljubica Štefan's *From Fairy Tale to Holocaust* was typical of this genre. In a work that alleges the Serbs had an independent state during World War II (in fact, they were under German military occupation), Štefan drew attention to Serbian folktales such as "The Yids" (Civuti), a Hansel-and-Gretel-like fable in which the wicked witch was a particularly wicked Jew.[21]

It was during the war itself that Croat nationalists began to construct a victim-centered ideology that depicted Serbs as unrequited genocidal empire builders, impatiently awaiting the opportunity to destroy Croatian national identity and annex Croatian territory. Overlooking the entire history of Croat-Serb cooperation, Croats knew their antisemitic enemy, and it was the Serbs. Accordingly, even the NDH's genocidal crimes could be dismissed as reactionary measures to suppress the Greater Serbian threat. And just as Serbs distorted the nationalism of nineteenth-century Croatian linguist Ante Starčević, Croats depicted his Serbian counterpart Vuk Karadžić's nationalist formulas as "quite similar" to those applied to the Jews in Nazi Germany.[22]

I would be remiss not to mention Bleiburg, the partisan massacre in May 1945 of between twenty and forty thousand Croatian Ustasha, fascist collaborators, partisan opponents of various southern Slavic origins, and, sometimes, family members of all the above. One reason is that this is the one case in which a Jewish-like Holocaust is claimed by Croats, who use terms like "death march" and "exodus" to narrate the plight of surrendering fighters sent by the British back toward partisan lines. Ante Beljo, director of the Croatian Information Center, contended that the partisans slaughtered fifteen thousand Croats a day at Bleiburg, making it "worse than Auschwitz."[23]

But the more crucial reason to highlight the "Croatian Holocaust" at Bleiburg is that it relies on any number of pure fabrications for legitimacy. These include massively inflating the numbers killed, ignoring the ethnic diversity of both victims and killers, and transforming thousands of Ustasha war criminals into innocent Croatians. Moreover, as David Bruce MacDonald pointed out, if the high number of victims claimed by Croat nationalists is to be believed, then this contradicts the myth that few Croats actually supported the NDH. And there is more: assuming, as yet another nationalist myth has it, that Croats comprised the majority of the partisan resistance, then why would they massacre their own or at least not prevent the massacre? In the wake of communism, not only did long-suppressed ethnic identities and histories reemerge, but they also did so in linguistically exclusivist and mathematically improbable ways.[24]

BOSNIA

The Bosnian Muslims, or Bosniaks, certainly do not require comparison with the Jews and the Holocaust to convey their victimization in the recent war—more than 33,000 Bosniak civilians were murdered and more than a million "ethnically cleansed" from 1992 to 1995 as part of the Milošević regime's effort to carve Greater Serbia out of newly independent Bosnia and Herzegovina. In several international court cases involving the Srebrenica massacre, the Serbian campaign has been termed a genocide.[25]

Moreover, the application of the Holocaust analogy during the war by well-intentioned interventionists was bound to leave its mark on Bosnians. For the young conceptual artist Damir Nikšić, this has entailed the wholesale embrace of the European Jewish experience as a metaphor for the Muslims of Bosnia. Nikšić is the passionate purveyor of a victim-based nationalism surprisingly similar to that preached by Serbs in the 1980s and 1990s. Not only has he constructed a pseudomythological history of his people that links anti-Jewish antisemitism to anti-Muslim "antisemitism"; not only does he base that nationalist mythology on the notion of perpetual victimization, dismissing the long-standing (and deadly) animosities among non-Muslim peoples of the Balkans; not only does he dream of a nation-state for his people (again, like the Jews); but Nikšić also literally anthropomorphizes the Bosniak nation as "teenagers" who "have not yet decided what they will be when they grow up." Yet Nikšić has decided that the only conceivable Bosniak future for him is in a state "that is not only and solely Slavic as it has been since 1918."[26]

Nikšić's best-known work to date, "If I Wasn't Muslim," is based on this theory of Bosniak national identity, as he explains on his Web site and in several publications. "If I Wasn't Muslim" is a four-minute music video in which the artist, attired in the baggy trousers and cap of a Bosniak peasant, wallows in the shame and suffering of being a Muslim in Christian Europe, to the tune of "If I Were a Rich Man" from the Broadway musical *Fiddler on the Roof.* As he affectingly bounces and cavorts Cossack-like around the attic of a bombed-out farmhouse,

Nikšić's Tevye sings with profuse self-pity about the litany of humiliations and abuses he must forever suffer simply for being a European Muslim. "If I Wasn't Muslim," the lyrics piteously imagine:

> Life for me would have been fun.
> I could live and prosper.
> My neighbors wouldn't set my home on fire, and surround me with barbed wire.
> Books wouldn't teach you that I was an error in European history.
> I wouldn't have to worry what will happen in a year or two, will I have to leave or stay and die.

The penultimate verse alters the title refrain slightly. "If I were a Christian," Nikšić croons, "I wouldn't have to prove that I am human too. 'Cause when you're Christian you're always civilized, no matter what you wear or do."[27]

As if the associations between the outcast and persecuted shtetl Jew and the long-suffering Bosnian Muslim—Europe's "whipping boy"—are not obvious enough, Nikšić's lyrics pointedly emphasize the commonalities between Muslims and Jews. Twice he refers to the disgrace of being circumcised and never knowing when he will have to "drop my pants to be identified and put aside." Nikšić also expresses shame at "the Semitic language I speak to my God that no one here understands." And the ultimate dream of Jew and Muslim alike? "If I could eat my eggs with ham!"[28]

"If I Wasn't Muslim" is a compelling and funny work. Having lived in Sarajevo, moreover, I am sympathetic with the anguish of Bosnian Muslims, who have to endure the nearly wholesale relativization and often outright denial of their suffering from the very people who tortured, raped, murdered, and ethnically cleansed them in the recent war. It is no wonder that Nikšić has taken to reconfiguring "antisemitism" as Western intolerance of European Muslims.[29]

Not surprising, yes, but such a theory is not unproblematic (or unprecedented, as we've seen), either. For all its humor and pathos, Nikšić's video is no laughing matter. Didn't Bosnian Serbs, too, have much to fear from their neighbors not so long ago? Have Muslims always and alone been the outcast people of Bosnia? Has no one ever understood them or respected their religious and cultural traditions? If this were the case, then how is it that Nikšić can stress a genuine prewar Bosnian identity based on tolerance and what he calls neighbors who are "natural born neighbors"?[30]

It is true that Bosnian Muslim identity has been more precarious in the modern period than that of its Orthodox and Catholic countrymen, whose ethno-religious kin across the Sava and Drina rivers laid claim to large territories of influential populations. Bosniaks, in the meantime, have always shared their ancestral lands with these Christian neighbors. In other words, they have never had anywhere else to go. But more than four hundred years of Ottoman rule in the region favored the Muslims considerably. They constituted more than 80 percent of the landowners in Bosnia-Herzegovina during this time, while the impoverished and often seriously maltreated peasantry was overwhelmingly Serb and Croat.

During the Austro-Hungarian period from 1878 to 1918, when European values and institutions began to impose themselves more directly than ever on the people of Bosnia-Herzegovina, the much-needed land reforms for which the Austro-Hungarian Empire had, in part, been awarded the territory were never forthcoming. Apparently, the new Christian colonizers found it easier to maintain the rural status quo than to risk the chaos that could ensue if Bosniak privileges were stripped away. With this concern for stability, the Austrians also went about cultivating a Bosnian Muslim elite. It is thus wholly ironic that while Nikšić sings despairingly about being a Muslim in Christian Europe, it is his own ethno-religious group in Bosnia that today is doing the most to resurrect the Austro-Hungarian period as one of great cultural and material advancement for the region.

Few would dispute that the tragedy of tragedies in the horrific past century is best represented by the Holocaust. Clearly, like other people worldwide, Bosniaks, Serbs, Croats, and others in the former Yugoslavia have found in the Shoah a kind of new meta-narrative, supplanting the fallen idols of communism and fascism with a universal moral "truth" about where it all ends up. That is why I find an image of a traditionally covered Muslim woman eyeing a poster for the exhibition "Anne Frank and Family" so beautiful and, yet, bothersome. Based on a photograph from Tarik Samarah's collection *Srebrenica,* the woman is, in fact, a mother of Srebrenica. The poster itself, moreover, is based on a photograph: Anne Frank and her sister, on summer holiday, gaze toward the sea and thus also away from the viewer. Taken outside the Anne Frank House in Amsterdam, Samarah's image is a powerful and multilayered means of peering into the past and linking it to the present. We are enjoined to contemplate not only the memories of this Srebrenica mother, but of the countless parents who lost children in the Holocaust. For the picture of Anne and her sister was taken by their father, Otto, the only member of the Frank family—and indeed of all the Jews who hid in the Secret Annex—to survive the war.[31]

Yet this image is not an altogether historically truthful one. For had Anne Frank been in Srebrenica in 1995 rather than just about anywhere in Europe half a century earlier, she would have survived. And while it is certainly not my intent to diminish the hellish experience of genocide, it is this need to equate one's own victimization with that of another group that makes me uncomfortable. Professor Deborah Lipstadt has expressed the problem most eloquently: these sorts of images and interpretations, she has argued, "make the glib suggestion that everything is the same."[32] The Srebrenica genocide—as with Jasenovac, Bleiburg, the ethnic cleansing of Istria, and so on— was unique and tragic enough in its own right. Turning it into the Bosnian Muslim Holocaust in a country that is today 40 percent Muslim (48 percent Bosniak) seems to me to be manufacturing a fixed and morally didactic narrative that leaves little room for exploring the broader context of both the recent war and Yugoslav history generally.[33]

And in that broader context, Bosnian Muslims are not the only ones who have suffered, but they are just one of many groups in the former Yugoslavia who have turned to the European Jewish experience to communicate some aspect of their historical self-understanding. Is that a problem? Should we not at least be thankful to find so much evidence for what I had originally thought of calling this essay: "The Opposite of Denial"? Concluding that Holocaust analogies are problematic because they condense the full complexity of history and identity into one simplified sound bite is not wholly satisfying. Rather, it seems, there are still the Jews themselves to consider—part of the problem, as always, but perhaps part of a solution as well.

CONCLUSION

In a 2007 article in the Sarajevo daily *Oslobođenje,* the journalist Faruk Borić wrote: "Events concerning Jews in Sarajevo during the Second World War have not been fully researched, nor has the historiography been free of ideological influence."[34] Nonetheless, in a city that 11,000 assimilated Jews once called home (a community going back over four centuries and comprising 11 percent of a highly diverse population); in a country that bore the full brunt of Nazi occupation and Jewish persecution; and in a region that has suffered more than its share of what Primo Levi called "useless violence," Holocaust references have been appropriated by a variety of groups to stake claims to their own victimization, all the while ignoring the suffering of their often equally traumatized neighbors or countrymen.[35]

The former Yugoslavia in general, Bosnia-Herzegovina in particular, and Sarajevo above all are very complicated places, and I do not wish to appear insensitive to that fact. In addition to the usual East European medley of Jews and Christians, Orthodox and Catholic, and the whole wondrous blend of ethnicities that once congregated together at marketplaces and trade fairs, the Muslim element has added a dimension that both immensely enriches the region's cultural life and, it seems, has immeasurably bloodied its truly European descent into ethnic homogeneity and uniformity. Moreover, rather than Jews being the central story of World War II, Serbian Četnik violence against Muslims in eastern Bosnia and the Ustasha genocide of Serbs have competed with them for attention. Despite their far higher death rate in World War II (about 80 percent in Yugoslavia), Jews were still a minority among minorities in this ethnically complex country.[36]

And yet in their absence they have become the region's metaphor of choice—one used universally and sometimes disingenuously, then discarded when no longer necessary. As with all other European Communist countries, there was little Holocaust education in Tito's Yugoslavia, which made it easier for Serb and Croat nationalists to hitch their agendas to Jewish suffering without ever having faced up to the role they played in that suffering. And when during the Bosnian war the Holocaust entered people's lives fast and furious as well-meaning foreigners articulated pleas for intervention in the language of the Shoah, Bosniaks naturally followed suit, without giving much thought to what the Holocaust actually was. To offer one example, while Serb and Bosniak communities thankfully still thrive in the region, the Holocaust put an end to European Jewry and its rich panoply of cultural attainments.

Yet more troubling than this forgivable lack of knowledge is that despite the fact that South Slavs are borrowing Jews and Jewish suffering for their own agendas, antisemitism is on the rise in the former Yugoslavia. In Serbia, where political and intellectual elites deliberately nurtured fellowship with the Jewish people in the run-up to the recent wars, the regime wasted little time in undoing this stance during the North Atlantic Treaty Organization (NATO) bombing campaign to expel the Yugoslav army from Kosovo in 1999. Once General Wesley Clark's Jewish ancestry and Secretary of State Madeleine Albright's previously concealed Jewish upbringing (including being a hidden child in Serbia during World War II) became public, they were trumpeted as proof that conniving Jews who did not appreciate all that Serbs had done for them still controlled Serbian destinies.[37] Since then, several antisemitic groups have emerged in Serbia, and the distribution of the *Protocols of the Elders of Zion* has surged, despite there being only some 1,200 Jews in this country of eight million. More hypocritically, "the thirteenth lost tribe of Israel" was the only European nation without official representation at ceremonies marking the sixtieth anniversary of the liberation of Auschwitz.[38] The notion that one's woeful history is "just like the Jews" can, rather quickly, become the more familiar refrain that it is "just like the Jews" to bring all these troubles upon us.[39]

In Croatia, too, the exploitation of the Holocaust has by no means staunched resurgent antisemitism in the post-Communist era, as President Tudjman's own writings and speeches demonstrated. Blatant antisemitism was in fact expressed by all three leaders of the victorious Hrvatska Demokratska Zajednica (HDZ, Croatian Democratic Union) during the 1990 election, in particular to downplay, or deny wholly, the crimes of the Ustasha. In the view of Balkan observer Tihomir Loza, "Croatia's public life has featured pretty virulent antisemitism since the early 1990s."[40]

Much the same could be said of newly minted European Union (EU) member Slovenia. When the Federation of Jewish Communities of Yugoslavia brought charges against the organizer of the Cankarjev dom rally for misusing a Jewish symbol, Joze Školjc (future leader of the Liberal Democratic Party), responded: "Why have the Jews pressed criminal charges? Why, they want money, of course." The charges were dismissed. Shortly thereafter, a journal declared the "closed season" on antisemitism in Slovenia to be over.[41]

Most disturbing of all is the recent and well-documented upsurge of antisemitism in Bosnia-Herzegovina. Barely more than a decade ago, Muslim clerics were referring to their flock as "the new Jews of Europe." Today, due in part to Islamicists from the Middle East who began entering the country during the war, mosques that are fuller than ever sometimes resound with antisemitism more repulsive than has ever been heard before in this proud multicultural land.

In an article entitled "In Need of a Scapegoat: Are the Principal Victims of Genocide in Bosnia Falling Prey to Antisemitism?" the editors of *Transitions Online* concluded that a combination of radical Islamic influences since the war, 9/11, and the second Intifada (and, I would add, the vulnerability of traumatized young people) "may have conspired to create a harder, meaner society that is on the lookout for scapegoats."[42] Indeed, while I was living in Sarajevo from 2004 to 2006, one of the first incidents of antisemitism in public memory occurred when a well-known (though little respected) journalist published an ugly Holocaust denial piece in a Muslim youth magazine. The media and local Helsinki Committee for Human Rights were quick and categorical in condemning it, but this was Bosnia, and this sort of thing did not happen here.[43] In an interview in the Croatian journal *Vjesnik,* Jakob Finci, head of Bosnia's tiny Jewish community, stated ruefully: "Unfortunately, after enough years of being proud that Bosnia-Herzegovina was immune from any form of antisemitism, it appears that the climate is changing."[44]

I do not wish to sound alarmist here, and the purpose of this essay is not to condemn a particular people or to suggest that the ends of Holocaustizing are forever and only self-serving. But the fact is that the climate is always changing, always and everywhere. And since the ferocious wars in the former Yugoslavia, the facts on the ethnically cleansed ground have altered and will continue to alter the way in which ordinary people conceive of themselves and measure their environment. Although they all have tried to use the Holocaust analogy, it has served no single group in the former Yugoslavia because it has achieved little more than calling attention to what they all have in common: an incomplete and unfulfilled sense of their own shared history, responsibility, and identity in this post-Communist, post-Yugoslav, semi-European, semi-Balkan land. Nevertheless, should the Holocaust become less appealing as an analogy in the coming years, let us just hope that it is not because the Jews have, too.

NOTES

1. Tomislav Klauški, "Srbi su ubijali tisuće ljudi i gledali ih u oči," *Slobodna Dalmacija*, July 11, 2005; http://www.bosnjaci.net/print.php?id=184&izvor=teme; http://www.irib.com/worldservice/bosnianRADIO/interviu/ResidHafizovic.htm.
2. Samantha Power, "To *Suffer* by Comparison?" *Daedalus* 128, no. 2 (Spring 1999), 31–66. Don DeLillo, *White Noise* (New York: Penguin, 1999).
3. David E. Stannard, *American Holocaust: The Conquest of the New World* (New York: Oxford University Press, 1993); Mike Davis, *Late Victorian Holocausts: El Niño Famines and the Making of the Third World* (London: Verso, 2001); Charles Patterson, *Eternal Treblinka: Our Treatment of Animals and the Holocaust* (New York: Lantern, 2002).
4. David Frum and Richard Perle, *An End to Evil: How to Win the War on Terror* (New York: Random House, 2004), vii.
5. Alan E. Steinweis, "The Auschwitz Analogy: Holocaust Memory and American Debates over Intervention in Bosnia and Kosovo in the 1990s," *Holocaust and Genocide Studies* 19, no. 2 (Fall 2005), 280.
6. Gutman's interview with Šišić cited in Power, "To *Suffer* by Comparison?" 34.
7. Northrup Frye cited in David Bruce MacDonald, *Balkan Holocausts? Serbian and Croatian Victim-Centred Propaganda and the War in Yugoslavia* (Manchester, U.K.: Manchester University Press, 2002), 15–20.
8. Drašković cited in Marko Zivkovic, "The Wish to Be a Jew: The Power of the Jewish Trope in the Yugoslav Conflict," *Cahiers de l'URMIS [Unité de recherche migrations et société]* 6 (2000), 69, 73.
9. Revisionists claim that seven hundred thousand Serbs died at Jasenovac, a highly improbable number considering the overall population of Serbs in the Nezavisna Država Hrvatska (NDH, the Independent State of Croatia). Ivo Goldstein and Slavko Goldstein put the total number of *all* Jasenovac victims at eighty to ninety thousand (*Holokaust u Zagrebu* [Zagreb: Novi liber and Židovska općina Zagreb, 2001]).
10. MacDonald, *Balkan Holocausts?* 9, 162.
11. Sabrina P. Ramet, "The Denial Syndrome and Its Consequences: Serbian Political Culture Since 2000," *Communist and Post-Communist Studies* 40 (2007), 47–48.
12. Ibid., 43; MacDonald, *Balkan Holocausts?* 74, 83, 87; Rebecca Reich, "A Community Rises Up, and the Young Move Away," *Jewish Daily Forward,* January 24, 2003.
13. Emil Kerenji, "The State of Holocaust Research in Serbia," unpublished conference paper, The State of Holocaust Studies in Southeastern

Europe: Problems, Obstacles, and Perspectives, Sarajevo, October 27–29, 2006.

14. MacDonald, *Balkan Holocausts?* 74–75; Zivkovic, "The Wish to Be a Jew," 74; Philip J. Cohen, "Holocaust History Misappropriated," *Midstream* 38, no. 8 (November 1992), 18–20; Laslo Sekelj, "Antisemitism and Jewish Identity in Serbia After the 1991 Collapse of the Yugoslav State," in *Analysis of Current Trends in Antisemitism* 12 (series) (Jerusalem: The Hebrew University of Jerusalem, Vidal Sassoon International Center for the Study of Antisemitism, 1997).

15. Pamela Ballinger, *History in Exile: Memory and Identity at the Borders of the Balkans* (Princeton, N.J.: Princeton University Press, 2003), 137–40, 146.

16. Zivkovic, "The Wish to Be a Jew," 72; Sekelj, "Antisemitism and Jewish Identity in Serbia."

17. Zivkovic, "The Wish to Be a Jew," 71–73.

18. Sekelj, "Antisemitism and Jewish Identity in Serbia"; MacDonald, *Balkan Holocausts?* 167–68; Ivo Goldstein and Slavko Goldstein, "Revisionism in Croatia: The Case of Franjo Tudjman," *East European Jewish Affairs* 32, no. 1 (Summer 2002), 52–64; Robert D. Kaplan, "Croatianism," *The New Republic* 205, no. 22 (November 25, 1991).

19. Laza Kostić's *The Serbs and the Jews* (1988) has been a key text in spreading the myth of Serbian philosemitism, according to MacDonald (Kostić cited in MacDonald, *Balkan Holocausts?* 147). Jovan Byford, "'Serbs Never Hated the Jews': The Denial of Antisemitism in Serbian Orthodox Christian Culture," *Patterns of Prejudice* 40, no. 2 (May 2006), 159–80.

20. Zivkovic, "The Wish to Be a Jew," 76.

21. Štefan cited in MacDonald, *Balkan Holocausts?* 145–46.

22. Ibid., 108.

23. Ibid., 172–74. At the 2001 Bleiburg commemoration, the parliamentary representative of the Croatian Peasant Party, Ante Simonić, called Bleiburg "the national holocaust" and asserted, improbably, that in the second half of the 1940s "hundreds of thousands of Croats were massacred and killed" (*Novi List,* May 14, 2001).

24. MacDonald, *Balkan Holocausts?* 173–77. Since Tudjman's death in December 1999 and the accession to power of Ivica Račan's Social Democratic Party in 2000 to 2003, Croatian political leaders have shown greater willingness to acknowledge the crimes committed by the genocidal Ustasha regime. Bleiburg, however, persists in being a national symbol of unmitigated Croatian victimhood. Indeed, Ante Simonić was vice premier in the Račan government, and in June 2009 this author noticed that the Web site of Zagreb's main bus terminal was advertising pilgrimage-like tours to the Bleiburg memorial site (http://www.akz.hr/). For an excellent overview of

Croatia's post-Communist efforts to reckon with the past, see Ljiljana Radonic, "Vergangenheitspolitik in Kroatien: Vom Geschichtsrevisionismus zur Aufarbeitung der Vergangenheit?" *Zeitgeschichte* 5, no. 35 (September/October 2008).

25. For statistics on wartime losses in Bosnia and Herzegovina (BiH): http://www.idc.org.ba.

26. Damir Nikšić, "I Jevreji i Bošnjaci su se Našli u Tuđem Ratu," *Dani* 520 (June 1, 2007).

27. The video, "If I Wasn't Muslim," may be viewed on Damir Nikšić's Web site: http://www.damirniksic.com/.

28. Ibid.

29. "Historija je Bazirana na Kampanji Koju je Zapad Vodio Protiv Islama," *Dani* 416 (June 3, 2005).

30. Quote from Damir Nikšić interview with Fareed Zakaria, *Foreign Exchange,* Show 14, July 2005. For a full transcript, see: http://www.damirniksic.com/ifiwasntmuslim.html.

31. Tarik Samarah, *Srebrenica* (Sarajevo: Synopsis, 2005).

32. Conversation between Deborah Lipstadt and the author, Sarajevo, Meeting of the International Association for Genocide Scholars (July 13, 2007).

33. Population figures are drawn from: http://www.state.gov/r/pa/ei/bgn/2868.htm. The prewar Bosnian Muslim population was 44 percent. Sabrina Ramet, *Balkan Babel: The Disintegration of Yugoslavia from the Death of Tito to the Fall of Milošević* (Boulder, Colo.: Westview, 2002), 119.

34. Faruk Borić, "Zavjesa tvrda od svakoga zida," *Oslobođenje,* May 26, 2007, 32–33.

35. Primo Levi, "Useless Violence," *The Drowned and the Saved* (New York: Vintage, 1989).

36. Jozo Tomasevich, *War and Revolution in Yugoslavia, 1941–1945: Occupation and Collaboration* (Palo Alto, Calif.: Stanford University Press, 2001).

37. Jovan Byford and Michael Billig, "The Emergence of Antisemitic Conspiracy Theories in Yugoslavia During the War with NATO," *Patterns of Prejudice* 35, no. 4 (2001), 50–63. Both Albright and Clark were raised as Christians.

38. Kerenji, "The State of Holocaust Research in Serbia," 15.

39. Ramet, "The Denial Syndrome," 49; Tihomir Loza, "Packaged Hatred," *Transitions Online* (November 27, 2006); Sekelj, "Antisemitism and Jewish Identity in Serbia"; "In Need of a Scapegoat: Are the Principal Victims of Genocide in Bosnia Falling Prey to Antisemitism?" *Transitions Online* (January 17, 2005); Byford, "'Serbs Never Hated the Jews,'" 163–64.

40. Loza, "Packaged Hatred."

41. Sekelj, "Antisemitism and Jewish Identity in Serbia."
42. "In Need of a Scapegoat."
43. Dragan Stanimirović, "Recent Incidents Show an Alarming Rise of Anti-Semitic Sentiments in Bosnia," *Transitions Online* (January 17, 2005).
44. Zoran Matkić, "I holocaust i genocid u Srebrenici počeli su riječima," *Vjesnik,* February 24, 2005, 10.

Jerry Fowler

Equivocal Talismans: The UN Genocide Convention and the Responsibility to Protect

ONE LEGACY OF THE HOLOCAUST IS THE CREATION OF THE CONCEPT of genocide and its codification in international law through the adoption in 1948 of the United Nations (UN) Convention on the Prevention and Punishment of the Crime of Genocide (Genocide Convention).[1] Sixty years later, the Genocide Convention is widely celebrated and adopted, yet it is of uncertain, even negligible, practical effect. The Convention has engendered expectations—perhaps summed up in the grandiose but hollow phrase "never again"—that it was not designed to fulfill.

In fact, the Convention represented a small step toward protecting civilians from mass violence: by criminalizing the actions of government officials under certain circumstances, it made explicit for the first time an internationally recognized limit on the treatment that governments could mete out to their own citizens. At the same time, those circumstances were narrowly bounded by the definition of genocide and did not include atrocities that even then were coming to be known as "crimes against humanity." Moreover, although many have assumed that the Genocide Convention provides a mandate for international action, the Convention itself did not articulate what bystander states are permitted to do if another government is committing genocide, much less what they might have some obligation to do. As a consequence, the Convention did not change the political dynamics that have consistently militated in favor of limited or no response to state-sponsored internal mass violence. After sixty years, it is clear that the Genocide Convention is at best an equivocal talisman: with its carefully crafted legalisms, it is generally incapable of transforming political reality and protecting civilian populations at risk.

In the years since 1948, developments in international law have moved beyond the Convention. Most important, internationally accepted limits on state treatment of citizens are significantly broader than genocide, especially with the widespread adoption of various human rights instruments, the general acceptance of a less restrictive definition of crimes against humanity, and the unanimous declaration in September 2005 by the UN General Assembly that states have a "responsibility to protect" those under their control from war crimes, ethnic cleansing, and crimes against humanity, as well as genocide. Yet consensus is still lacking on what international responses are permitted or required in situations of mass violence. Thus, the political dynamics that lead to inaction remain problematic. Ultimately, the "responsibility to protect" doctrine may be as equivocal a talisman as the Genocide Convention that it effectively supersedes.

RAPHAEL LEMKIN AND THE LAW

The word and concept of genocide were first introduced in 1944 by Raphael Lemkin, a Jewish refugee from Poland.[2] As a lawyer and law professor, Lemkin viewed "genocide" as a crime that required a legal response. Moreover, he saw it as inherently an international crime that demanded an international response. In pursuit of such a response, he turned his attention to the newly formed United Nations.

Lemkin's efforts ultimately resulted in the Genocide Convention, which was adopted unanimously by the UN General Assembly on December 9, 1948. The final text was the product of negotiations among sovereign states, and because of that the terms were influenced by various political considerations. But the final product very much reflected Lemkin's legalistic approach to the problem of genocide. Though the Convention's title referred to "prevention" and "punishment," the Convention's details primarily dealt with the latter. And it addressed punishment, understandably, as primarily a legal issue, without recognizing or addressing the fact that prevention (or "suppression") of genocide is first and foremost a political problem.

IN PEACE OR IN WAR

The key principle at the heart of the Genocide Convention is that there are limits to what governments can do to their own citizens.

The cloak of sovereignty is not impermeable; in particular, it does not protect government officials from criminal prosecution for the crime of genocide. This principle is established by several provisions of the Convention. First, Article I specifies that genocide is a crime under international law "whether committed in time of peace or in time of war." Second, Article IV provides for the punishment of perpetrators of genocide "whether they are constitutionally responsible rulers, public officials or private individuals." Finally, although explicit responsibility for trying perpetrators rests with the state on whose territory the genocide was committed (and parties to the Convention promise to pass the laws necessary to make that possible), Article VI also holds open the possibility of trial before an "international penal tribunal." Taken together, these provisions mean that the leaders of a state otherwise at peace with its neighbors can be criminally punished in an international forum for treatment of the state's own citizenry, at least insofar as that treatment constitutes genocide. Moreover, the state itself has a legal obligation to try the perpetrators for their actions.

Piercing the cloak of sovereignty was not quite as novel in 1948 as is sometimes assumed. Noninterference as an attribute of sovereignty, though generally associated with the Peace of Westphalia in 1648, emerged as a widely accepted rule of international law in the latter part of the eighteenth century.[3] But even then it was not without exceptions, leading Stephen Krasner to dub the system of sovereign states one of "organized hypocrisy."[4] During the nineteenth century, in particular, abuses by governments occasionally engendered intervention, including armed intervention, by other governments. After World War I, successor states to the Austro-Hungarian Empire were made to sign treaties that regulated their treatment of minority populations within their borders.[5] These practices led legal scholar Ellery Stowell to claim in 1921 that international law permitted the use of "force for the justifiable purpose of protecting the inhabitants of another state from treatment which is so arbitrary and persistently abusive as to exceed the limits of that authority within which the sovereign is presumed to act with reason and justice."[6]

But these limitations on sovereignty were at best ad hoc and not clearly codified. British efforts to try top officials of the Ottoman Empire after World War I for the massacres of the empire's Armenian citizens were complicated by the view, expressed by Foreign Minister Arthur Balfour, that "strictly speaking, [the officials] had committed no definite legal offences. . . . [Talaat Pasha, minister of the interior in 1915,] had made up his mind to get rid of [the Armenians], and, in consequence, he had massacred them en masse. That was merely a policy, and the offenders could not be tried by court-martial, as they had committed no definite legal offence."[7] Similarly, even as the extent of Nazi atrocities was becoming clear at the end of World War II and the Allies had determined to conduct postwar trials, there was resistance to holding the perpetrators liable for their treatment of German citizens. Robert Jackson insisted on behalf of the United States that "it has been a general principle of foreign policy of our Government from time immemorial that the internal affairs of another government are not ordinarily our business; that is to say, the way Germany treats its inhabitants, or any other country treats its inhabitants is not our affair any more than it is the affair of some other governments to interpose itself in our problems."[8] As a consequence, "crimes against humanity" as defined in the Nuremberg Charter[9] covered attacks on civilians only when committed in conjunction with another crime listed in the charter—that is, crimes against the peace (illegally invading another country) or war crimes (illegal conduct during the international conflict). The treatment of German citizens by the German government before the beginning of the war was not covered.

STATES OF MIND

The Genocide Convention was therefore significant as the multilateral codification of a limit on how governments treat their citizens. This codification was given greater weight in 1951 when the International Court of Justice suggested that the prohibition of genocide was a norm under customary international law and therefore was binding even on states that did not become parties to the Convention.[10] But the substantive limit on governmental conduct was rather narrow.

The essence of that limit is found in Article II, which defines genocide. According to this definition, genocide has two essential components: a specified physical act—such as killing members of a targeted group[11]—and a particular state of mind (technically, a mens rea). This mens rea requirement distinguishes genocide from any other crime: Killing civilians is not genocide—no matter how many perish—unless the perpetrators act with "the intent to destroy, in whole or in part, a national, ethnical, racial or religious group, as such."

Merely intending to commit the killings themselves is not enough. The perpetrators must also have a "specific" or "special" intent to destroy the protected group in whole or in part.[12]

An unfortunate effect of specifying what governments may not do in their exercise of sovereignty is to suggest that other conduct is not prohibited—or at least is not the subject of international concern. States agreeing to the Convention undertook to prevent and punish the murder of, say, six million civilians when done with the intent to destroy a particular political, national, religious, or ethnic group, but not the murder of six million when done without that intent. While there might be a reasonable basis for arguing that there is something uniquely wrong or even evil about acts undertaken with genocidal intent[13] or that genocide is the "crime of crimes,"[14] it hardly exhausts the category of governmental violence that is "so arbitrary and persistently abusive," to use Stowell's phrase, "as to exceed the limits" of sovereign conduct, even from the perspective of 1948. Indeed, the intent to destroy a group was a novel aspect of Lemkin's formulation and had not figured in pre-Holocaust arguments about the type of abusive conduct that fell beyond the limits of sovereign prerogative.

The consequences of the narrow definition are with us today, as evidenced by the extended international debate over whether there is genocide in the Darfur region of Sudan. A UN Commission of Inquiry carefully documented "crimes against humanity," primarily by the government of Sudan and allied militias.[15] It also contended that these crimes are as heinous and deserving of suppression as genocide. But the very need to say so was evidence of some question as to whether it was true. And the attention paid to the difference between U.S. Secretary of State Colin Powell's determination that genocide had been committed in Darfur and the Commission of Inquiry's contrary conclusion on the question of genocide illustrates the persistent notion that the commission of genocide is more consequential than mass destruction without genocidal intent. The irony is that the two contrary conclusions produced essentially the same result—initiation of a process aimed at eventual criminal punishment coupled with generally unavailing diplomatic efforts.[16]

The definition's narrow scope is exacerbated by a second flaw—the inherent difficulty of establishing the existence of the required specific intent. As noted previously, the specific intent standard is demanding and requires more than proof that the relevant acts themselves were done intentionally. The specific intent of the Nazis to destroy European Jewry was clear, both from statements such as Adolf Hitler's January 1939 threat to destroy the Jews in the event of a war and from the circumstances of the unprecedented industrialized murder at Treblinka and the other death camps.

In other situations, however, it can be more difficult to establish intent in real time, especially when perpetrators are well aware that tipping their hands could have adverse consequences. Courts of law may be well equipped to adjudicate intent by weighing evidence and coming to a conclusion.[17] But in the realm of politics, predicating action on a finding of intent is a prescription for paralysis. Even very compelling circumstantial evidence of intent to destroy can be obfuscated with doubts and counterevidence, as well as confusion over how much evidence is necessary.[18] The end result is that for as much as the Convention was a step forward in protecting civilians from their own governments, it was a small step. Another such step was taken in tandem with the Genocide Convention by the adoption of the Universal Declaration of Human Rights.[19] The Declaration was quite sweeping in its terms. But by virtue of being a "declaration," its effect on international law was hortatory rather than obligatory. The Declaration was broad but nonbinding; the Convention was binding but quite narrow.

HALTING IN THE NAME OF THE LAW

Though the Convention clearly provides for the punishment by the territorial state of individuals who commit genocide and holds open the possibility of international prosecution, it is vague regarding other responses. In particular, it has very little to say about what bystander states may or must do to prevent or stop genocide. The preamble observes as a factual matter that "international cooperation is required." Article VIII provides that a party to the Convention "may," but is not required to, "call upon the competent organs of the United Nations to take such action under the Charter of the United Nations as they consider appropriate for the prevention and suppression of acts of genocide." Efforts to require member states to refer cases of genocide to the Security Council were rejected.[20] No other article specifically mentions prevention, except for the ambiguous statement in Article I that parties to the Convention "undertake to prevent" genocide. Parties are permitted by Article IX to submit disputes with other parties to the International Court of Justice (ICJ), "including those relating to the responsibility of a state for genocide."

In sum, bystander nations were not, by the terms of the Convention, required to do anything specific in the event of genocide committed by another state. Nor was it even clear what they were permitted to do, other than refer the matter to the United Nations or seek a ruling from the ICJ. A key pillar of the UN Charter, adopted just three years before the Genocide Convention, enshrined in Article 2(4) the principle of noninterference with the territorial integrity and political independence of sovereign states. The Charter grants to the Security Council the authority to intervene when necessary to maintain or restore international peace and security. But it was almost five decades before the Security Council began to assert that internal events such as massive human rights violations could in and of themselves constitute a threat to international peace and security.[21]

In 2007, the ICJ addressed the issue of what states must or may do in response to genocide elsewhere when it decided a case brought under Article IX of the Genocide Convention by Bosnia and Herzegovina against Serbia. Bosnia alleged that Serbia was directly involved in genocide committed on Bosnian territory in the early 1990s. The ICJ concluded that genocide as defined under the Convention had not been committed, with the exception of the massacres in July 1995 carried out by Bosnian Serb forces near the town of Srebrenica. The court found that Serbia did not have sufficient control or influence over the Bosnian Serbs to be directly responsible for what happened at Srebrenica. Then it took up the separate question of whether Serbia had an obligation under the Genocide Convention as a bystander state to have acted to prevent or stop the genocide.

The court interpreted Article I's vague "undertake to prevent" language to mean that if a party to the Convention "has available to it means likely to have a deterrent effect on those suspected of preparing genocide, or reasonably suspected of harboring specific intent, it is under a duty to make such use of these means as the circumstances permit."[22] Assuming this interpretation of Article I's ambiguous language is valid (even though the court made no effort to ground its opinion in either the legislative history of the Convention or subsequent state practice), there is still less here than meets the eye. When U.S. Secretary of State Colin Powell announced his determination that genocide had been committed in Darfur, he followed that announcement by saying that the determination did not imply new actions by the United States. "We have been doing everything we can," he told the Senate Foreign Relations Committee, "to get the Sudanese Government to act responsibly."[23] Secretary Powell's assertion is echoed in the ICJ's holding that a state must "make such use of the means [available to it] as circumstances permit." Yet the ICJ found Serbia liable with respect to Srebrenica because the Serbs, who had "a position of influence . . . unlike that of any of the other State parties to the Genocide Convention, . . . manifestly refrained" from doing anything.

Short of such an egregious case—manifest failure to act by a party with extraordinary influence—the requirement to use such "means as the circumstances permit" is basically a meaningless standard. The reason why was suggested by ICJ Judge Leonid Skotnikov, who criticized the court's standard as "politically appealing . . . but legally vague, indeed, hardly measurable at all in legal terms."[24] What "circumstances permit" bystander states to do is not measurable in legal terms because it is inherently a political issue, not a legal one. And as a political issue, the determination of what circumstances permit is at the practically unfettered discretion of states. Because states are necessarily the final judge of what political actions circumstances permit them to take, the ICJ interpretation leaves the situation largely unchanged—states are not required to do anything specific in response to genocide in another state. Even what is permitted is left up in the air, for (according to the court) "every State may only act within the limits permitted by international law."[25] The implication of this is that the Genocide Convention does not itself authorize any specific response that might otherwise be prohibited, such as the use of military force.

THE EQUIVOCAL TALISMAN

In light of the definitional issues just cited and the fact that the Convention's vague provisions on prevention and suppression were not designed to overcome the political dynamics of passivity, it should come as no surprise that the Genocide Convention, endowed by many with talismanic qualities, has had at best an equivocal effect. One cannot know whether there were governments that decided not to commit genocide because of its terms. But it is plain that in the decades after its adoption there were several episodes of mass violence that shocked the conscience and arguably fell within even the Convention's narrow parameters, yet the Convention had no apparent impact. The great pioneer of genocide studies, Leo Kuper, complained in 1981 that in fact "the sovereign territorial state claims, as an integral part of its sovereignty, the right to commit genocide . . . and the United Nations, for all practical purposes, defends this right."[26] As for the Genocide Convention, Kuper believed that "there was small comfort to be derived from [it] or from the United Nations. . . . The almost perennial complaint is that the world remains indifferent to the genocide or the genocidal massacres, and that the United Nations turns a deaf ear."[27] In support of this gloomy assessment, he pointed to the lack of response to the "imminent extermination" in the 1970s of the Ache Indians of Paraguay, the mass killing of Hutu in Burundi in 1972, the "murderous regime" of Idi Amin in Uganda from January 1971 to 1979, the radical violence of the Khmer Rouge regime in Cambodia from 1975 to 1979, and the massacres of 1971 in East Pakistan. Concluding his survey with references to Sudan, East Timor, and Equatorial Guinea, Kuper judged that "the United Nations performs a quite negligible role in the direct prevention and punishment of the crime of genocide, and the Genocide Convention is virtually a dead letter."[28]

This desuetude of the Convention up to 1989 might be attributable to the Cold War, which certainly rendered problematic, if not impossible, effective action by the United Nations to stop genocide or other mass violence. But it also stemmed from the fact that the Convention itself, with its definitional limitations and its ambiguous enforcement mechanisms, did not actually embody much of a commitment among its signatories to respond to genocide. And, indeed, the Genocide Convention continued to have limited practical consequence in the years after the Cold War ended. It has contributed little to the prevention or suppression of genocide and in fact may to some degree have hindered efforts by diverting attention into a fruitless debate about whether the term "genocide" describes what is being committed in a given situation. It has played a somewhat greater role in punishment but in a way that illustrates that the Convention has in effect been superseded by the development of the broader category of crimes against humanity and other human rights norms.

AFTER THE THAW

The first major crisis of a genocidal nature to confront the world after the end of the Cold War was the disintegration of the former Yugoslavia. Ethnically based violence occurred first in Croatia in 1991, then began in April 1992 in Bosnia.[29] The Genocide Convention did not provide a basis for a rapid and decisive response to the crisis. To the contrary, the UN Security Council for the most part avoided referring to genocide in its resolutions dealing with the crisis.[30]

As the situation deteriorated and assumed genocidal overtones, the Security Council resorted to the time-tested delaying tactic of appointing a Commission of Experts to assess the situation.[31] Although the commission did not have an explicit mandate to consider the question of genocide, it did anyway. And how the commission considered it is telling. In its first report to the Security Council, it observed that so-called "ethnic cleansing" in Yugoslavia "could . . . fall within the meaning of the Genocide Convention."[32] In its final report, the Commission of Experts concluded with regard to one district in Bosnia, which it considered illustrative of other districts seized by Bosnian Serbs, that "[i]t is unquestionable that the events in Opstina Prijedor since 30 April 1992 qualify as crimes against humanity. Furthermore, it is likely to be confirmed in court under due process of law that these events constitute genocide."[33] The element of doubt in its judgment about genocide and the deferral of any conclusion—in obvious contrast to the certainty of its conclusion regarding crimes against humanity—reflects the legalistic nature of the definition of genocide, the necessarily limited nature of the evidence that could be obtained, and the unavoidable difficulty of determining, under the circumstances, a specific intent to destroy. Equally telling is the Security Council's response to the commission's work. Rather than undertake decisive action to prevent or suppress further acts of "likely" genocide, it instead authorized the creation of a tribunal with a view to ultimately providing punishment.[34] As Aryeh Neier has observed: "Good and bad reasons led to the decision by the Security Council to deal with ex-Yugoslavia in the manner it did. The bad evoke T. S. Eliot's dictum: 'The last temptation is the greatest treason: To do the right deed for the wrong reason.' The wrong reason for the UN Security Council's decision to establish a tribunal was that it was a substitute for effective action to halt Serb depredations in Bosnia-Herzegovina."[35] The terms of the Genocide Convention lent themselves to this substitution. The Convention is after all focused on punishment and includes a reference to possible trial before an international tribunal. Falling back on legal processes was, in 1993 as in 1948, easier than making difficult political decisions to stop the killing.

In establishing the ad hoc International Criminal Tribunal for the Former Yugoslavia (ICTY), the Security Council gave it jurisdiction over not only genocide as defined in the Genocide Convention but also crimes against humanity (without the Nuremberg requirement of a nexus to other illegal conduct) and serious war crimes. By giving the tribunal a broader jurisdiction than genocide, the Security Council was establishing that the conduct that can spark international action (however restrained it might have been) is broader than that undertaken with genocidal intent. This point was reinforced at about the same time when the Security Council undertook a major intervention in Somalia, where there was a grave crisis but where the question of genocide was not remotely in play.[36]

The massive and systematic murder of the Tutsi minority in Rwanda in 1994 presented a clearer case of genocide than Bosnia, yet the Security Council essentially responded in the same fashion: no effective action to stop the violence followed by the creation of an international tribunal to punish those guilty of genocide, crimes against humanity, and war crimes.[37] Samantha Power has documented in great detail the discussions that went on inside the U.S. government during the Rwanda crisis, most of which were aimed at ensuring that the United States was not put in the position of having to commit military force to Rwanda. One theme of those discussions was a concern that acknowledging the killings as genocide would make it more difficult to avoid committing force. The eventual result was a farcical attempt to parse the distinction between "acts of genocide" and "genocide," prompting one reporter to ask the imponderable—"How many acts of genocide does it take to make genocide?"[38] U.S. Secretary of State Warren Christopher ultimately gave up the struggle and said, "If there is any particular magic in calling it genocide, I have no hesitancy in saying that."[39] But there was no magic.

One lesson that many took away from Rwanda was that if government officials can be pushed to recognize a situation as genocide, then they would be compelled to act effectively, in part by the supposed requirements of the Genocide Convention. This lesson misunderstood the actual terms of the Convention. It also overlooked the fact that both the United States and the United Nations recognized the situation in Rwanda as genocide while the killing was still going on (though after many weeks of avoidance)[40] and still found themselves quite capable of making little more than empty gestures—in effect, using such means as they deemed the circumstances permitted.

But as a consequence of this lesson, when the Sudanese government and its militia allies began to use large-scale violence in Darfur, there were calls in many quarters for the U.S. government and other governments to recognize the violence as genocide. The assumption was that calling the violence by "its rightful name" would engender a more effective response. Ultimately, the U.S. government used the word, while disclaiming any responsibility to do more than it was already doing. Nevertheless, whether Darfur was genocide became a point of contention internationally. And the UN Commission of Inquiry's conclusion that the Sudanese government was not pursuing a policy of genocide somehow became a form of vindication, in spite of the commission's copious documentation of Khartoum's crimes against humanity. Some diplomats and government officials will comment privately that many governments did not want to acknowledge Darfur as genocide for fear of what they would be called on to do in response—that is, some of the same considerations that informed discussions within the U.S. government during the Rwanda genocide. Nevertheless, whether a government takes the U.S. position that a determination of genocide carries with it no additional obligations or the apparent sub-rosa position of others that they will not make a determination for fear that it will force some action, Darfur should establish, once and for all, that the Genocide Convention does not magically transform the politics of responding to mass violence and trigger effective action to suppress it.

RESPONSIBILITY TO DO WHAT?

Over the past several years, a new conceptual approach to the problem of mass violence against civilians has emerged in the idea of the "responsibility to protect." The concept originated with the Sudanese scholar Francis Deng, who argued that sovereignty entailed responsibility to the governed.[41] His ideas were amplified by a Canadian-appointed panel of notables, the International Commission on Intervention and State Sovereignty (ICISS). In a December 2001 report, the ICISS asserted the existence of broad international acceptance for the proposition that one responsibility inherent in sovereignty is the responsibility to protect civilians from human rights violations.[42] The foundation for this assertion included the adoption of the Genocide Convention and the Universal Declaration of Human Rights and several subsequent developments. First among those developments is international agreement over the years to a relatively broad and binding latticework of human rights norms, such as the International Covenant on Civil and Political Rights and the Convention Against Torture. Second, the requirement for a nexus between crimes against humanity and other illegal conduct has been abandoned, as confirmed by widespread adoption of the 1998 Statute of the International Criminal Court (ICC Statute). Third, the application of traditional war crimes to internal armed conflicts was broadened through a 1977 revision of the 1949 Geneva Conventions as well as the adoption of the ICC Statute. Fourth, the UN Security Council established that large-scale human rights abuses could constitute a threat to international peace and security even if they occurred inside a single country. This decision gives the Security Council the authority to undertake coercive action up to and including military intervention under Chapter VII of the UN Charter.

Somewhat more controversially, the ICISS went a step further and asserted that when a sovereign state fails to fulfill its responsibility to protect, other states have a residual responsibility to provide the absent protection, including with military intervention under some circumstances. The Commission's formulation conflated two issues that have great practical significance—what bystander states and/or the United Nations are permitted to do in the face of massive human rights abuses and what they are required to do. State practice in the 1990s suggested a broadening but not universal acceptance that coercive action up to and including military action might be permitted; there was little to suggest that states feel obligated to take such action, even when noncoercive steps are manifestly inadequate. By using the language of "responsibility," the Commission was suggesting not just permission but rather some form of obligation.

The first part of the ICISS's formulation—the responsibility of states to their citizens—has received a warmer embrace internationally than its assertions of bystander-state responsibility. In 2005, the

UN General Assembly unanimously declared in Resolution 60/1 that "[e]ach individual State has the responsibility to protect its populations from genocide, war crimes, ethnic cleansing and crimes against humanity."[43] Although not technically binding, the declaration has weight by virtue of its unanimity.

Regarding international responsibilities, the General Assembly was much more circumspect:

> The international community, through the United Nations, also has the responsibility to use appropriate diplomatic, humanitarian and other peaceful means ... to help protect populations from genocide, war crimes, ethnic cleansing and crimes against humanity. In this context, we are prepared to take collective action, in a timely and decisive manner, through the Security Council, in accordance with the Charter, including Chapter VII, on a case-by-case basis and in cooperation with relevant regional organizations as appropriate, should peaceful means be inadequate and national authorities manifestly fail to protect their populations from genocide, war crimes, ethnic cleansing and crimes against humanity.[44]

This language stopped well short of the ICISS's bold assertion of an international responsibility to protect. For example, the responsibility attaches only to the community as a whole "through the United Nations," and not to any individual state. Moreover, the responsibility recognized is to "help" protect, somewhat diluted from the ICISS's assertion of an international responsibility to protect. Most important, the General Assembly only recognized a "responsibility to help protect" using peaceful means. Draft language that would have recognized a "shared responsibility" to use coercive action where peaceful means failed was dropped in favor of the discretionary "case-by-case" approach in the final text. The General Assembly in effect rejected an obligation to use coercive means but accepted that such means would be permitted should the Security Council so decide.

The General Assembly's declaration weakened the doctrine proposed by the ICISS in a subtle but significant way. The ICISS concept recognized that sovereign states had the primary responsibility to protect their citizens from massive abuses. But that was matched by a commensurate international responsibility to act should a state fail to meet its responsibility. Even in this formulation, the doctrine had a significant weak point—the potential for an endless debate about whether a given state had failed to live up to its responsibility and thus forfeited to the international community its primacy over its own territory.[45] But as articulated by the declaration, the responsibilities of the state and the international community are not commensurate. So even if there is agreement that a state is failing to protect its citizens, the international community is responsible only for "helping" to protect civilians, and even then only with limited means and only collectively. With this, the balance of the original ICISS concept has been replaced with a strong tilt toward protecting the prerogatives of the sovereign state and reinforcing bystander passivity.

The declaration's explicit focus on acting through the United Nations left open the question of whether individual states or groups of states have any "responsibility to protect" civilians in another country outside the United Nations. As often as not, the Security Council can be expected to be paralyzed. When this occurred during the Kosovo crisis, the United States and its North Atlantic Treaty Organization (NATO) allies acted on their own initiative and without the explicit authority of the Security Council. The ICISS sought to skirt this issue by putting primary emphasis on Security Council action but recognizing that in some cases where the Security Council fails to act, other options cannot be "entirely discounted."[46] But it conceded—and the declaration essentially confirms—that "it would be impossible to find consensus . . . around any set of proposals for military intervention which acknowledged the validity of any intervention not authorized by the Security Council or General Assembly." It is certainly clear that states have not accepted an obligation to act outside the United Nations; the extent to which such action is permitted remains unresolved.

CONCLUSION

The UN Genocide Convention was a small step toward protecting civilians from their own governments, because it established limits on governmental conduct. But those limits were narrowly drawn. Moreover, the Convention did not include meaningful commitments by bystander nations to enforce those limits. As a consequence, the Convention has had minimal practical effects. More recently, internationally accepted limits on governmental conduct have expanded beyond the narrow prohibition of genocide, as reflected in the 2005

UN General Assembly declaration that states have a "responsibility to protect" their citizens from "war crimes, ethnic cleansing and crimes against humanity" in addition to genocide. But a commitment to enforcement is still lacking, suggesting that as a talisman for protecting civilians from harm, the responsibility to protect may end up being as equivocal as the Genocide Convention.

NOTES

1. Convention on the Prevention and Punishment of the Crime of Genocide, December 9, 1948, 78 U.N.T.S. 277, http://www2.0hchr.org/english/law/genocide.htm (accessed January 16, 2008).

2. Raphael Lemkin, *Axis Rule in Occupied Europe: Laws of Occupation; Analysis of Government; Proposals for Redress* (Washington, D.C.: Carnegie Endowment for International Peace, 1944), 79. Lemkin's story is engagingly recounted in Samantha Power, *"A Problem from Hell": America and the Age of Genocide* (New York: Basic Books, 2002), 17–60; see also William Korey, *An Epitaph for Raphael Lemkin* (New York: American Jewish Committee, 2001).

3. Stephen D. Krasner, *Sovereignty: Organized Hypocrisy* (Princeton, N.J.: Princeton University Press, 1999), 20–25. According to Krasner, "Westphalian sovereignty involve[s] issues of authority and legitimacy," in particular "the exclusion of external actors, whether de facto or de jure, from the territory of the state" (ibid., 4).

4. Ibid.

5. Ibid., 73–104.

6. Ellery C. Stowell, *Intervention in International Law* (Washington, D.C.: John Byrne, 1921), 53. See also Simon Chesterman, "Legality Versus Legitimacy: Humanitarian Intervention, the Security Council, and the Rule of Law," *Security Dialogue* 33, no. 3 (September 2002), 293, 297. According to Chesterman, debate before the middle of the twentieth century "exhibited divisions comparable to that seen now among legal scholars, with some confidently asserting a right of humanitarian intervention and others confidently rejecting it."

7. Gary Jonathan Bass, *Stay the Hand of Vengeance: The Politics of War Crimes Tribunals* (Princeton, N.J.: Princeton University Press, 2000), 131.

8. Quoted in William A. Schabas, *Genocide in International Law: The Crime of Crimes* (New York: Cambridge University Press, 2000), 35.

9. Charter of the International Military Tribunal, Article 6(c), August 8, 1945, available at http://www.yale.edu/lawweb/avalon/imt/proc/imtconst.htm#art6 (accessed January 16, 2008).

10. *Reservations to the Convention on the Prevention and Punishment of the Crime of Genocide (Advisory Opinion)*, May 28, 1951, 21, http://www.icj-cij.org/docket/files/12/4283.pdf (accessed January 15, 2008).

11. The specified acts are: "(a) Killing members of a targeted group; (b) Causing serious bodily or mental harm to members of the group; (c) Deliberately inflicting on the group conditions of life calculated to bring about its physical destruction in whole or in part; (d) Imposing measures intended to prevent births within the group; [and] (e) Forcibly transferring children of the group to another group" (Genocide Convention, Article II).

12. Schabas, *Genocide in International Law*, 217–21.

13. Berel Lang, "The Evil in Genocide," in *Genocide and Human Rights: A Philosophical Guide*, ed. John K. Roth (New York: Palgrave Macmillan, 2005), 5–17.

14. Schabas, *Genocide in International Law*.

15. It is now accepted that crimes against humanity that violate international law do not have to be committed in connection with an international armed conflict. See M. Cherif Bassiouni, *Crimes Against Humanity in International Criminal Law*, 2nd rev. ed. (Boston: Kluwer Law International, 1999), 86.

16. Jerry Fowler, "A New Chapter of Irony: The Legal Implications of the Darfur Genocide Determination," *Genocide Studies and Prevention* 1, no. 1 (July 2006), 29–40.

17. Even then, judicial finality may not be accompanied by general agreement, as evidenced by controversy over the International Court of Justice's finding that there was no genocide in Bosnia other than at Srebrenica. "Genocide Ruling Frustrates Bosnia," BBC News (February 27, 2007), http://news.bbc.co.uk/2/hi/europe/6399319.stm (accessed January 15, 2008); for a generally favorable review of the court's decision, see William A. Schabas, "Whither Genocide? The International Court of Justice Finally Pronounces," *Journal of Genocide Research* 9, no. 2 (June 2007), 183.

18. Fowler, "A New Chapter," 34–35.

19. See Mary Ann Glendon, *A World Made New: Eleanor Roosevelt and the Universal Declaration of Human Rights* (New York: Random House, 2001).

20. Schabas, *Genocide in International Law*, 449.

21. Chesterman, "Legality Versus Legitimacy," 300–301.

22. Montenegro, Judgment of the Court, para. 431, http://www.icj.org/docket/files/91/13635.pdf (accessed August 24, 2009).

23. Colin Powell, "The Crisis in Darfur" (testimony before the Senate Foreign Relations Committee, September 9, 2004), http://www.state.gov/secretary/former/powell/remarks/36042.htm (accessed January 15, 2008).

24. *Application of the Convention on the Prevention and Punishment of*

the Crime of Genocide (Bosnia and Herzegovina v. Serbia and Montenegro), February 26, 2007, Declaration of Judge Leonid Skotnikov, 10, http://www.icj-cij.org/docket/files/91/13705.pdf (accessed January 15, 2008).

25. *Bosnia and Herzegovina v. Serbia and Montenegro,* Judgment of the Court, para. 430, February 26, 2007, http://www.icj-cij.org/docket/files/91/13685.pdf (accessed January 15, 2008).

26. Leo Kuper, *Genocide: Its Political Use in the Twentieth Century* (New Haven, Conn.: Yale University Press, 1981), 161.

27. Ibid., 162.

28. Ibid., 175.

29. Laura Silber and Alan Little, *Yugoslavia: Death of a Nation,* rev. ed. (New York: Penguin, 1997).

30. Schabas, *Genocide in International Law,* 229.

31. United Nations Security Council (1992), Resolution 780, UN Doc. S/RES/780, October 6, 1992, http://daccessdds.un.org/doc/UNDOC/GEN/N92/484/40/IMG/N9248440.pdf?OpenElement (accessed January 16, 2008).

32. *Interim Report of the Commission of Experts Established Pursuant to Security Council Resolution 780 (1992),* UN Doc. S/25274, para. 56, January 26, 1993, http://documents-dds-ny.un.org/doc/UNDOC/GEN/N93/083/51/img/N9308351.pdf?OpenElement (accessed January 16, 2008).

33. *Final Report of the Commission of Experts Established Pursuant to Security Council Resolution 780 (1992),* UN Doc. S/1994/674, para. 182, May 24, 1994, http://documents-dds-ny.un.org/doc/UNDOC/GEN/N94/200/60/pdf/N9420060.pdf?OpenElement (accessed January 16, 2008).

34. United Nations Security Council (1993), Resolution 808, UN Doc. S/RES/808, February 22, 1993, http://daccessdds.un.org/doc/UNDOC/GEN/N93/098/21/IMG/N9309821.pdf?OpenElement (accessed January 16, 2008).

35. Aryeh Neier, *War Crimes: Brutality, Genocide, Terror, and the Struggle for Justice* (New York: Times Books, 1998), 112.

36. Chesterman, "Legality Versus Legitimacy," 301.

37. See Michael Barnett, *Eyewitness to a Genocide: The United Nations and Rwanda* (Ithaca, N.Y.: Cornell University Press, 2002), 97–152.

38. Power, *"A Problem from Hell,"* 363–64.

39. Ibid., 364.

40. One avoidance measure by the Security Council was an April 30, 1994, Presidential Statement that used the terms of the Convention's definition—"killing of members of an ethnic group with the intention of destroying such a group in whole or in part"—without using the actual word "genocide." Statement by the President of the Security Council, UN Doc. S/

PRST/1994/21, April 30, 1994, 1. http://daccessdds.un.org/doc/UNDOC/GEN/N94/199/86/PDF/N9419986.pdf?OpenElement (accessed January 16, 2008).

41. See Francis Deng, ed., *Sovereignty as Responsibility: Conflict Management in Africa* (Washington, D.C.: Brookings Institution Press, 1996).

42. International Commission on Intervention and State Sovereignty (hereafter ICISS) *The Responsibility to Protect* (Ottawa, Canada: International Development Research Centre, 2001).

43. United Nations General Assembly (2005), Resolution 60/1, para. 138, UN Doc. A/Res/60/1, http://daccessdds.un.org/doc/UNDOC/GEN/N05/487/60/PDF/N0548760.pdf?OpenElement (accessed January 16, 2008).

44. Ibid., para. 139.

45. Alex J. Bellamy, "Responsibility to Protect or Trojan Horse? The Crisis in Darfur and Humanitarian Intervention After Iraq," *Ethics and International Affairs* 19, no. 2 (Fall 2005), 31, 52.

46. ICISS, *The Responsibility to Protect*, 53.

V. E·P·I·L·O·G·U·E

*Compiled and introduced
by John K. Roth*

John K. Roth

Ethics During and After the Holocaust

ISSUES ABOUT ETHICS DURING AND AFTER THE HOLOCAUST—THEY involve belief, inquiry, and action regarding what is right, good, and just—make their way between and through the lines of this book. As is often the case, however, historical analysis takes precedence in conferences and books about the Holocaust, and explicit reflection about the ethical implications of that event, including implications for ethics itself, comes last. How is that fact best understood?

When ethics comes last in Holocaust studies, that fact might mean that ethics is an afterthought, something that needs to be mentioned but not highlighted. Or that fact could reveal reticence, a thoughtful caution about speaking too quickly and confidently about "moral lessons" that the Holocaust supposedly teaches. Or it might mean that the Holocaust did so much damage that there is scarcely anything helpful to say about ethics during and after the Holocaust. Many possibilities exist when one considers why study of the Holocaust so often puts ethics last.

As a philosopher who has been tripped up by Holocaust history, I think that we study the Holocaust because it happened, but not only for that reason. We also study it for ethical reasons that are rooted in a deep longing for a more humane world. These ethical reasons have everything to do with careful historical research as well as thoughtfully informed philosophical and religious reflection and literary and artistic expression. Such reflection and expression rightly take plural forms. One-size-fits-all cannot apply to them.

When ethics comes last, that all-too-human fact is perhaps understandable, but I add that "last" must not mean "least." The best scholars of the Holocaust, even when their primary focus is not on ethics, do not disagree with that proposition. They understand that the Holocaust's immense harm affected ethical sensibilities profoundly. The Auschwitz survivor Jean Améry underscored some of those consequences, for when he woke up each morning and saw again the Auschwitz tattoo on his arm, he again lost trust in the world forever.

During the Holocaust, ethics typically ended up last because even humanity's best ethical impulses and traditions were so often overridden, betrayed, subverted, or used in ways that made them ineffectual in preventing genocide or complicit in the atrocities that went on and on. That problem continues to plague human existence and ethics after the Holocaust. Arguably, nothing is more important than figuring out what can and should be done about humanity's moral failure.

For some time, I have been thinking and writing about ethics during and after the Holocaust, often pursuing the question "What happened to ethics during and after the Holocaust?"[1] Fortunately, there are others, participants in Lessons and Legacies prominent among them, who share that concern. What is more, they share that concern because of the diverse approaches that characterize their contributions to Holocaust studies. Therefore, I contacted friends and colleagues in the Lessons and Legacies family, scholars who have significantly informed my Holocaust-related inquiries, and invited them to share their insights on one or more of the following questions: (1) How have ethical considerations affected your research about the Holocaust? (2) What have you discerned about ethics from your Holocaust studies? (3) As you consider your research, what do you think its most important ethical implications may be?

Probing in their distinctive ways important aspects of what happened to ethics during and after the Holocaust, five leading scholars responded to those queries. They did so first in a roundtable discussion at the 2006 Lessons and Legacies Conference. Subsequently, they further focused their presentations for publication here. The contributors are Christopher Browning, author of the classic *Ordinary Men* and the Frank Porter Graham Professor of History at the University of North Carolina, Chapel Hill; Peter Hayes, the author of *From Cooperation to Complicity: Degussa in the Third Reich* and the Theodore Z. Weiss Professor of Holocaust Studies at Northwestern University; Claudia Koonz, professor of history at Duke University and the author of *The Nazi Conscience;* historian Rebecca Wittmann from the University of Toronto, who is the author of *Beyond Justice: The Auschwitz Trial;* and Berel Lang, professor of philosophy and letters at Wesleyan University, whose books include *Post-Holocaust: Interpretation, Misinterpretation, and the Claims of History.*

NOTE

1. See, for example, John K. Roth, *Ethics During and After the Holocaust: In the Shadow of Birkenau* (New York: Palgrave Macmillan, 2005), and John K. Roth, ed., *Genocide and Human Rights: A Philosophical Guide* (New York: Palgrave Macmillan, 2005).

Christopher R. Browning

Encountering Ethical Dilemmas in Writing the History of the Holocaust

FOR MANY, THE HOLOCAUST STANDS AS THE UNDISPUTED SYMBOL OR yardstick of radical evil. I was reminded of how universal this standard had become when I visited China in 1979, in the midst of the China-Vietnam border war. The English-language newspaper at our hotel contained the following cartoon. Ho Chi Minh and Adolf Hitler stand on the shore witnessing the sinking of a boat overloaded with Chinese refugees from Vietnam—the so-called boat people—and Hitler inquires, "Why don't you use gas?" Ho Chi Minh replies, "Because water is cheaper." Thus, unlike many other historical events, the fundamental immorality of the Holocaust is not seriously in question, even in radically different political cultures far distant from the event and among regimes that have their own egregious records in terms of sweeping violations of human rights and mass murder. Even those who in fact approve of the Holocaust must take a public stance not of approval but rather of denial.

The fundamental and undisputed immorality of the event itself does not mean, of course, that there are no ethical challenges or dilemmas in writing about the Holocaust. Two questions in particular have starkly affected my own career. The first concerns writing perpetrator history; the second—with which I have grappled in my recent project on the factory slave labor camps of Starachowice, Poland—concerns writing the history of the victims.

In a review of Robert Lifton's *The Nazi Doctors,* Bruno Bettelheim expressed regret about Lifton's subject and approach that would equally apply to my own work. He noted: "I restricted myself to trying to understand the psychology of the prisoners and I shied away from trying to understand the psychology of the SS [Schutzstaffel]—because of the ever-present danger that understanding fully may come close to forgiving. . . . I believe that there are acts so vile that our task is to reject and prevent them, not to try to understand them empathetically."[1]

Does a historian who attempts to explain and understand the behavior and motivations of the perpetrators, and brings to that task a certain degree of empathy, cross some impermissible boundary that renders his or her own writing of history ethically dubious, as Bettelheim suggests? I would, of course, say no. Some clichés are clichés precisely because they embody basic common sense. But some clichés are simply false, and I reject the notion that to explain is to excuse, that to understand is to forgive.

Another negative reaction to my writing of perpetrator history has important ethical implications as well. This is the tendency to perceive situational explanations, based in part on social-psychological insights about the dynamics of group behavior, as deterministic and hence unacceptable insofar as they are thought to relieve individuals of moral responsibility for their choices and thus to become exculpatory. I think this is a mistaken mixing of categories. As individual human beings, we are all shaped by outside factors, be they cultural, familial, or situational. We are still ethically responsible for the choices we make as individuals, whatever the family into which we are born, the culture in which we are raised, or the situation in which we find ourselves. Close historical study that illuminates the wide spectrum of choices people actually have made in the same situation undermines rather than imposes a deterministic interpretation, even as it also sensitizes us to the vulnerabilities of the human condition.

One constant twofold response to a portrayal of the perpetrators as ordinary human beings that I have encountered, both in the classroom and elsewhere, is first the recognition by others that if they had been there, they too might not have behaved well, and second the assertion that therefore no moral judgment can be made. I think the first aspect of this reaction is important—to have the humility to recognize that we do not know how we might have behaved in similar circumstances. The second aspect, though, is misguided. If we had been there and participated in mass murder, then our behavior would have been immoral and illegal, not beyond judgment. Our potential failings cannot become the very low threshold beyond which moral judgments have no place.

Let us turn to the ethical challenge of writing about victims. Here the normal moral world was totally inverted, in that the basic axiom "do no harm" was often rendered meaningless. Nazi power placed Jews in a less than zero-sum game, in which they had some agency or choice, but all choices caused harm to many and no choice guaranteed saving the life of anyone. As one Starachowice survivor put it succinctly, if you helped one person, it was usually at the expense of another.[2] Lawrence Langer coined the classic phrase "choiceless choice" to capture this impossible situation. One possible reaction to such an impossible situation was to adopt what Primo Levi called "the law of the Lager" —to live by the social Darwinian laws of struggle for survival and survival of the fittest through uninhibited individual self-assertion for self-interest.

In my own study of the complex of factory slave labor camps in the small Polish industrial town of Starachowice, however, I do not find that this was the typical response of the prisoners. Rather than abandoning any notion of moral obligation entirely, the prisoners in effect created a moral system more appropriate to their situation of agency combined with powerlessness. That morality was based on an economy and a hierarchy rather than on universality or annulment of moral obligation. What they expected and accepted of one another was, first of all, loyalty to one's own remaining family members. Second, one had obligations to one's friends and neighbors, third to one's townspeople, and fourth to Jews before other non-Jewish prisoners. I remember my initial shock and discomfort when I was interviewing a Starachowice survivor who told me how his little sister had been taken away in a selection. To this day he would not forgive another survivor, a Jewish camp policeman who had lived on the same street and been his childhood playmate. The camp policeman, he said, could and should have saved his sister because "there was [sic] plenty of people from out of town there that he could have sent."[3] Only gradually did I realize that this unguarded statement reflected precisely the hierarchy of moral obligation within the prisoner community, in which a camp policeman with limited agency was expected to rescue the little sister of a neighborhood playmate, even if at the expense of someone else in a more distant circle of moral obligation.

Survivors from Starachowice do not articulate this version of camp morality openly or even consciously. Indeed, when they tell their stories, they not unnaturally narrate them and frame them from a later perspective of restored conventional morality. Let me give an example. One reason obligation to surviving family was so absolute within the prisoner community in the camps was the legacy of the horrific day when the ghetto was liquidated, families were torn asunder, and nearly 75 percent of the ghettoized Jews were sent to the gas chambers of Treblinka. Everyone in the town knew this fateful day was coming, and people scrambled to purchase factory work cards for themselves and their family members as the single-best protection against deportation and death. Such a survival strategy clearly meant the terrible but nonetheless conscious decision for separation from infants and the elderly who were ineligible for such work cards.

In most survivor accounts this horrific choiceless choice is too unbearable to be narrated as such. There are three typical models of survivor narrative of this event, but what they all have in common is the absence of survivor agency. In the first kind of narrative, the account is both cryptic and told in the passive voice. Workers were simply taken out or separated from the others, and suddenly found themselves on the other side of the marketplace, from which they were marched to the camps instead of to the train. Two brief examples: First, "the men capable of work were immediately separated from the rest."[4] And second: "Some people were summoned and placed with the workers. . . . In that way our family was separated."[5]

The second narrative model is found in the community memory book. "People with work permits refused to part from their dear ones, relinquishing thereby voluntarily the opportunity to be exempt from the expulsion, but the Germans took them by force from their families into the other group."[6] In the words of another survivor: "I did not want to be separated from my wife and my two children, as well as my parents. . . . I was simply sent over to the others with a kick of the foot."[7] In the words of another: "I did not want to separate from my wife. However, I was pulled out of line by [an] SS man who struck me with a club."[8] In this scenario, German force—not Jewish choice—decided who continued to live that day even against their will.

A third narrative allows for Jewish choice. However, it is not that of the survivor but rather of those family members fated to die. In one account, "my sister and I at first wanted to remain with our family. But my father persuaded us to comply with the order. He thought that we might then perhaps remain alive."[9] Another survivor noted that when women with work cards were summoned, "my mother pushed my sister and me out of the line."[10] Some narratives combine familial urging and German force. For instance, one woman was already employed at the factory but did not want to leave her family when holders of work cards were summoned. "I wanted to stay with my mother. But she could not bear that." Thus she "announced that I had a work card, and I was led away by the collar by a Latvian."[11]

In the unusual circumstance in which nearly the entire prisoner community was composed of partial families, almost every prisoner had suffered grievous loss, on the one hand, but still had loved ones alive, on the other. The searing experience did not lead to the total rupture of all bonds but rather to a total commitment to those family members who were still there. Family ties became the key associational and bonding factor of prisoner society in Starachowice and in the end helped to account for the unusually high survival rate. It is no mere coincidence that I know of no fewer than five families in which three sisters survived Starachowice and subsequent camps together. The choiceless choices they had made turned out in this rare instance to be not so choiceless after all, and the camp morality they created helped to alleviate camp mortality and save remaining family members as well.

One ethical challenge in this regard concerns the historian, not the victims. By what right do I—who was not there—sit in judgment of the stories the survivors tell as well as of the behavior and choices they describe? Concerning my treatment of survivor testimonies as evidence subject to the usual rules of critical historical analysis, most survivors have no problem. They recognize and accept the frailty of their own memories, and they want the history of their camp experience to be written and preserved. I remember that at the end of one interview, the survivor turned to me and asked, "How did I do?" He was deferring to me as the expert to judge the quality of his memory of the events. For the survivor who is convinced that he was saved by God in order to tell his story, however, I suspect that my critical approach will be seen not only as presumptuous but also as a kind of blasphemy.[12] But that is the exception, not the rule.

Concerning judgment of prisoner behavior, both I and my readers must recognize, first, that persecution, hyperexploitation, starvation, and murder of family and friends do not turn ordinary people into saints, heroes, and martyrs. No one has the right to expect the survivors to tell or the historian to disseminate feel-good stories of edification and redemption. Second, I will try to tell this story within the moral framework that the prisoners themselves created, including an important exception that at least some of them made. Jews in camp leadership positions, who thereby obtained both greater privilege and greater power, were held responsible for wider moral obligations toward the prisoner community as a whole than those without such privilege and power. In the case of the Starachowice camps, which were notorious for the degree of hierarchy and inequality within the prisoner community, some prisoners took rough justice into their own hands through a revenge killing of the most hated camp leadership. As one survivor who reluctantly told this story concluded, this, too, is history.[13]

NOTES

1. Bruno Bettelheim, "Their Specialty Was Murder," *The New York Review of Books,* October 15, 1986, 62.

2. Author's interview with Howard C., 2001.

3. Author's interview with Henry G., 2000.

4. Zentrale Stelle für Landesjustizverwaltungen zur Aufklärung nationalsozialistischer Verbrechen in Ludwigsburg, 206 AR-Z 39/62, Investigation of Walter Becker (hereafter cited as Becker), 1046 (Moshe Rubenstein, 1968).

5. Becker, 854 (Israel C., 1967).

6. Rachmiel Singer, "Dark Days of Horror and Ruin," *Wierzbnik-Strachowitz Book,* 33.

7. Becker, 973 (Shmuel E.).

8. Ibid., 1190 (Abe F.).

9. Ibid., 1218 (Ben Z.).

10. Ibid., 1059 (Pesia G.).

11. Ibid., 435, 1207 (Toby W., 1966 and 1968).

12. Fortunoff Video Archive for Holocaust Testimonies, Yale University (hereafter FA), T-91 (Israel A.).

13. FA, T-1884 (Regina N.).

Peter Hayes

Ethics and Corporate History in Nazi Germany

AT THE STREET LEVEL, I THINK, MOST PEOPLE UNDERSTAND ETHICS as a system of obligations to persons or principles, obligations that sometimes compete and therefore need to be prioritized in governing behavior. During the Third Reich, the primary obligation felt by most Germans varied among the self, the nation, and an array of intermediate entities (organizations, professions, confessions, employers, and so on). Largely absent from this hierarchy of prime loyalties was the category "fellow human being."

The roots of this tendency to define one's sense of obligation by proximity and similarity were, of course, both anthropological and historical. By the former term, I refer to the widespread, though not universal, human tendency to identify with collective groupings and to strive to be seen as serving them. Such behavior generally brings psychic comfort and sometimes personal advancement as well. By the latter term, I am pointing toward several elements of German life in the 1930s and 1940s that were somewhat different from conditions in our own time and place—notably the prevailing suppositions that most people would reside in the same locale and probably work their entire lives for the same organization, not to mention the ubiquitous propaganda that divided the world between an aggressive and malevolent "them" and an afflicted and virtuous "us." Such circumstances strongly reinforced an ethics of immediacy, an inclination to draw tight limits to the circle of one's obligations and to turn a blind eye to the consequences for those outside that circle.

Over and over in my studies of the corporate world in the Third Reich, I have encountered this phenomenon in the guise of the formulations business leaders used to justify their actions when these aroused moral discomfort. The rationale was almost always in terms of priorities, of responsibility to some calling higher than oneself but not very much so. The need to act "for the good of the firm" is one of the most frequent such escape clauses, the duty to adjust "to the prevailing conditions" a slightly weaker version of the same sentiment. Almost always, the point was that one had to bite the bullet, as we would say today, not for personal advantage and not out of patriotic or ideological feeling, but because one's job created a set of primary obligations (for example, to past, present, and future shareholders and stakeholders in the enterprise) that had to be honored ahead of abstract and general claims of morality.

Should we be surprised to find this pattern in the historical record? I do not think so, especially if one recalls how common the tendency to foreground immediate and/or institutional loyalties is in the history of human behavior. Let me cite two ready examples from our own time and place. The first concerns the Roman Catholic Church's record in multiple nations as well as in most archdioceses in the United States of repeatedly covering up sexual abuse of minors by priests over the past fifty years. In such instances, concern for the potential legal, financial, and reputational damage to the institution, along with feelings of solidarity toward fellow clerics, consistently outweighed a sense of responsibility to vulnerable parishioners in the calculations of the Roman Catholic leadership. Recurrent offenders were moved from place to place, their deeds hushed up, and other children thus were brought, in the words of the Act of Contrition itself, into "the near occasion of sin" by policy-makers who told themselves nonetheless that they were doing the Lord's work.

My second example stems from another walk of life to which people often look for succor, that of law enforcement, and concerns events that occurred a few days after Hurricane Katrina struck and devastated New Orleans in 2005. When groups of mostly African American refugees from that disaster tried to flee New Orleans across the bridge that still connected them with the cozy, predominantly white town of Gretna on the other side of the Mississippi River, the sheriff of that community assembled his small force of deputies at his end of the span of the bridge and ordered them to turn back the crowds of refugees at gunpoint. Whether any of those who had to retreat subsequently died of exposure or some other disaster-related cause as a result of the sheriff's decision is undocumented. If that had happened, neither the sheriff nor his constituents are likely to have been much troubled. In his and their eyes, according to numerous newspaper accounts, he acted to defend their community, its resources already stretched to the limit, against the possible consequences of inundation by hordes of potentially criminal or diseased or drug-addicted urban-dwellers. Like the Catholic bishops and cardinals who reflexively opted to uphold the image of Holy Mother Church first and foremost, the sheriff responded to a choice between alleviating real misery and risking more by looking out for "his own kind."

John Roth asked the contributors to this section to indicate what their specialized research has taught them about ethics. My response to this challenge will seem banal, I am afraid, but it goes as follows: I have been reminded that ethical behavior is hard. In fact, if defined by universalistic principles, it may go against the human grain. Getting people to extend the ambit of solidarity is difficult, all the more so in times of fear or crisis. Corporate leaders in Nazi Germany, when faced with pressures or incentives to commit harmful acts on fellow human beings—from firing Jewish colleagues early in the Third Reich to exploiting unpaid and miserably fed and clothed labor later—disposed of or resolved moral dilemmas in a fashion hardly distinct to their era and nation. They circumscribed their realm of moral obligation to make its demands manageable and less costly to themselves. They engaged, one might say, in a form of ethical triage.

The examples I have cited highlight how easy it was in the Nazi era and remains today to slip into high-minded-sounding justifications of callous conduct (for example, I'm not being cruel or cowardly when I harm others; instead, I'm acting for the greater good of my firm, my church, my town). Indeed, in threatening situations, resorting to these rationalizations is the course of practicality and common sense, and it may well be rewarded by events. The careers of only a few German corporate executives and a handful of Catholic prelates were destroyed by the choices they made in the situations I have described; Gretna's sheriff remained in office, too. Most German corporations, including the ones I have written monographs about, emerged from the cataclysm of Nazi Germany in many respects wealthier than when Hitler came to power.

One of the enduring questions posed by the Holocaust is "Who will defend whom?" Few Germans stood up for Jews, and few German executives defended their Jewish colleagues. Perhaps the most important thing I have learned from the study of corporate history in the Third Reich is that the reasons for these ethical lapses, and the form of the pseudoethical excuses offered by those who committed them, cannot be traced solely to the words "German" and "corporate."

Claudia Koonz

Taking Jean Améry's "Grudge" Seriously

IN 1964, A GERMAN RADIO BROADCASTER INVITED THE AUSCHWITZ survivor Jean Améry to tell listeners about his experiences as a Nazi prisoner and his reactions to post-1945 Germany. His remarks became the basis of a collection of essays that Améry called "a personal confession refracted through meditation" about "the eruption of radical Evil in Germany."[1] Commentaries on the first and second German editions as well as on translations into English, French, and Hebrew have returned again and again to many of the painful questions that Améry raised. With a few notable exceptions, W. E. Sebald among them, discussion of Améry's *Jenseits von Schuld und Sühne* (Beyond Guilt and Atonement) rarely dwells on his anguished descriptions of the masses of Germans who had ostracized Jews, plundered their property, and then deported them to slave labor and death camps.[2] How, Améry wondered, could masses of stalwart believers in a Reich founded on racial principles have so effortlessly become the bulwark of democratic values in a new Europe? Although in the months immediately following German defeat, Améry recalled that he "fancied myself as the conqueror of those who yesterday had tortured me," he quickly realized the futility of such delusions.[3] Far from expressing remorse for their earlier role in catastrophic evil, postwar Germans saw "themselves absolutely as victims" who had courageously endured Stalingrad, bombing raids, occupation, and "the dismemberment of their country."[4] These people, who had been responsible for looting, deporting, and exterminating defenseless victims, were striding into the "industrial paradise of the new Europe and into the majestic halls of the West."[5] Meanwhile, during these years Améry and other survivors experienced anguish, alienation, and displacement. In 1966, Améry insisted that what he called the "moral chasm" between the hangmen and their victims remain open.

As a contribution to that goal, Améry tried to make sense of his own experiences. Having been educated as a philosopher, he thought within the parameters of the classics (including, for example, Immanuel Kant, Franz Kafka, Thomas Mann, and Marcel Proust); and as an exile from his native land after 1945, he added contemporaries such as Frantz Fanon, Georges Battaile, Jean-Paul Sartre, Henri Alleg, James Joyce, and Graham Green. Améry, however, found no reliable guides for thinking about the collective responsibility of citizens who knowingly endorse a regime founded on the persecution of innocent and helpless fellow humans. Had Améry thought about how effortlessly Germans, who were accustomed to the rights guaranteed by the German constitution, gave that endorsement within months of Hitler's takeover, his dilemma would have become even more intractable. But the very language used for both transformations discourages comparisons: Gleichschaltung (coordination) is seen as negative, whereas denazification is positive. If, however, we referred to both transformations as Gleichschaltung or as nazification and denazification, the parallel would become more evident. As Améry well knew, Cold War politics dampened German "war guilt" for mass murder of racial outcasts, prisoners of war, and many other categories of helpless victims.

Although Thomas Aquinas had asked whether the sinner bears a "stain" of his guilt even after he has atoned, philosophers had ignored the questions that Améry asked so urgently about ordinary people who participate in mass crimes. Natural disasters, notably the 1755 Lisbon earthquake, had directed other philosophers' ethical (as well as metaphysical) inquiry. But as Emil Fackenheim noted in the mid-1980s, philosophers avoided thinking about the Holocaust; and, as Zygmunt Bauman commented in 1989, when social theorists did include the Holocaust in their purview, they did not shift conventional analytic paradigms. In the 1960s, when Améry wrote his essays, Europeans may have known about what survivor David Rousset called the "concentration camp universe." (For many Germans, at least during the Third Reich, that "universe" would have existed appropriately for enemies of Nazism.) Only after the trial of Adolf Eichmann (1961) and the Frankfurt Auschwitz Trials (1963–65) did extermination camps and lethal antisemitism enter the public memory of Nazi crimes.

When Primo Levi wrote his observations of life in Auschwitz (*If This Is a Man,* which first appeared in English in 1959), he wrote as an intellectual. But Améry explicitly refused to look for meaning in these terms. For one thing, unlike Levi, his first encounter with Nazi force came in the torture chambers of a Belgian fort. "Whoever was tortured," wrote Améry, "stays tortured. Torture is ineradicably burned into him, even when no clinically objective traces can be detected."[6] Philosophy is useless. "All those problems that one designates according to a linguistic convention as 'metaphysical' became meaningless."[7] Mocking Martin Heidegger, Améry added that one might say that "beings appear to us only in the light of Being, but that man forgot Being by fixing on beings. Well now, Being. But in the camp it was more convincingly apparent than on the outside that beings and the light of Being get you nowhere. You could *be* hungry, *be* tired, *be* sick. To say that one purely and simply *is,* made no sense." Abstract thought "was not only worthless and an impermissible luxury but also mocking and evil. . . . In no other place did the attempt to transcend it [reality] prove so hopeless and so shoddy."[8]

Améry desperately wanted Germans to acknowledge Jewish victims' suffering, and yet his intellect dismissed this desire. After all, Friedrich Nietzsche and Max Scheler dismissed resentment as an emotion typical of servile individuals who succumb to the slave morality of the weak. Améry knew that resentment warps the soul. Where he might have pointed an accusing finger, he deflected his rage with self-parody. How, Améry asked, could he feel resentment against this "peaceful, lovely land, inhabited by hardworking, efficient, and modern people"?[9] With so many Germans professing their desire for reconciliation, how could the ungrateful Améry cling to old grievances? Even to fantasize about retribution no doubt originates from "a barbaric, primitive lust for revenge."[10] Ironically, he passed off his resentment as merely a "grudge."[11]

Commentators on *Jenseits von Schuld und Sühne* mention these sentiments in passing but pursue other topics, particularly (quoting the English subtitle) his "Contemplations by a Survivor on Auschwitz and Its Realities." But torture, not oppression in Nazi camps, constituted the core of his experience. Comparing torture to rape, he wrote, "With the first blow from a policeman's fist, against which there can be no defense and which no helping hand will ward off, a part of our life ends and it can never again be revived. . . . Torture was the essence of National Socialism."[12] The perpetrators, moreover, "tortured with the good conscience of depravity. They martyred their prisoners for definite purposes, which in each instance were exactly specified."[13]

Behind his ironic stance, Améry demanded ethical reckoning and heaped contempt on mainstream Germans who had written paeans to reconciliation. "My personal task is to justify a psychic condition that has been condemned by moralists and psychologists alike . . . I must . . . first accept the sickness as an integrating part of my personality and then legitimize it."[14] Améry wanted revenge. "The piles of corpses that lie between them and me cannot be removed . . ."[15] In titling his book *Jenseits von Schuld und Sühne,* he appropriated Nietzsche's *Jenseits von Gut und Böse"* (Beyond Good and Evil).

Améry experienced firsthand the "guilt of deed, guilt of omission, guilt of utterance, guilt of silence—the total guilt of a people."[16] Against the political correctness of his day, Améry defended his resentment against "guilt-free" Germans, the "indifferent, the malicious and vile, the shrews, the old fat ones and the young pretty ones, those intoxicated by their authority." They had "found that everything was just right, and I am dead certain that they would have voted for Hitler and his accomplices if at that time, 1943, they had stepped up to the ballot box."[17] Améry had experienced the Germans' "atrocities as collective ones. I had been just as afraid of the simple private in his field-gray uniform as of the brown-clad Nazi official with his swastika armband."[18] Surviving as a Jew and a resister had required him to trust no one. "In the midst of the German people, I had to reckon every moment with falling victim to ritual mass murder. . . . I had to accept the notion of statistical collective guilt, and I am burdened with this knowledge in a world and a time that has proclaimed the collective innocence of the Germans."[19] Having given voice to his desire for vengeance, Améry understood the desire's futility. "Our slave morality will not triumph."[20] One day, he predicted bitterly, Auschwitz will simply slide into the landscape of memory and become just another outcropping of horrific inhumanity.

Améry's self-parody allowed him to pose ethical philosophical questions about "collective guilt," a legally meaningless term that ought to be taken seriously as a philosophical concept. In the intervening years, ethics and the Holocaust has become almost a subfield of ethics.

Philosophers ask where ethics went wrong in their moral autopsies; did morality "dupe" perpetrators? What went wrong? Clearly, consequentialism overrode humane considerations in Nazi programs—from involuntary sterilization through euthanasia and the "Final Solution"—and utilitarian considerations contributed to mass murder operations on the Eastern Front. Would stronger moral character or a deeper commitment to human rights make the post-Holocaust world safer? Was moral catastrophe the result of meta-ethical weakness? Of inadequate virtue?

The political philosopher Allen Buchanan doubts that these efforts address the core of "what went wrong" because human rights philosophy allows for moral behavior that violates the rights of particular moral actors in specific situations.[21] Individuals who accept as fact the danger to which their community is subjected may invoke what Buchanan has called "emergency exceptionalism," and they may even understand their crimes against defenseless individuals as preemptive self-defense. Although Buchanan wrote about coercive eugenics, his observations apply both to prewar racist persecution and to wartime extermination. Once we understand the milieu within which perpetrators functioned, we can imagine them thinking cogently about the choices they made as brutal but necessary. When they repressed their memories, we cannot be sure whether they buried the horrifying stench and gore at the mass murder sites or guilt about killing. They may not have perceived moral dissonance between their acts and their culture at the time of their crimes or afterward. Collaborators at every level of persecution and destruction may even have been sustained by the knowledge that they were heirs of a highly regarded culture. Belonging to a humane community beyond the murder sites did not necessarily inhibit their obedience; it may well have facilitated it.

Instead of returning to classical paradigms in relationship to Nazi crimes, we need what Buchanan called a "moral epistemology" that will sharpen our ability to detect ethical weaknesses in the frame within which actors commit crimes. This would mean, in the context of accounting for what Améry called collective responsibility, that rather than dismissing racial beliefs as delusional or crackpot or simply false, we ought to ask whether they would have been credible in the view of the ordinary Germans whose "faces of stone" stared at Améry and other victims locked in boxcars.

With Cold War political constraints behind us and with the Germans' remarkable willingness to come to terms with the Nazi past, we can speculate about ordinary Germans without fearing accusations of normalizing or exculpating Nazi crimes. A wealth of research in newly opened archives has inspired historians to re-create the daily routines not only of guards and supervisory personnel but also of the middle management of genocide. A new consensus suggests that hundreds of thousands, perhaps millions, of Germans and their allies exercised far greater autonomy than previously suspected. Recent studies of Nazi Jewish "experts," racial education, and Joseph Goebbels's dissemination of antisemitism complement research into on-the-ground perpetrators by sketching in the killers' mental world. Far from being either perverted sadists or brainwashed robots, perpetrators were most likely careerists who trusted the experts who demonstrated Jews' supposed lethal influence and the leaders who rallied grassroots support against a foreign foe. Although Améry singled out a few brave Germans, he noted that, for the most part, "we are dealing with society, or with the individual who incorporates himself morally into society and dissolves in its consensus."[22]

One of the first collective pledges of the postwar years, the 1948 United Nations Universal Declaration of Human Rights, proclaimed in Article I: "All human beings are born free and equal in dignity and rights. They are endowed with reason and conscience and should act towards one another in a spirit of brotherhood." During the intervening years, however, it has become apparent that conscience, rather than serving as a steady moral compass, acts like a weathervane. If post-Holocaust historians, literary commentators, and philosophers collaborate well, a better understanding can be forged regarding the ethical frames within which moral individuals contribute to evil projects that they perceive as virtuous.

Meanwhile, Jean Améry felt what he called "the immensity and monstrosity of the natural time-sense," which would seem to call his resentment into question. He even feared that he himself would come to "see the moral desire for reversal as the half-brained chatter that it already is today for the rationally thinking know-it-alls." Post-Holocaust ethical reflection, however, should take seriously Améry's resentments, "their moral value and their historical validity." Resentment may turn out to be, as he put it, the "emotional source of every genuine morality."[23]

NOTES

1. Jean Améry, *At the Mind's Limits: Contemplations by a Survivor on Auschwitz and Its Realities,* trans. Sidney Rosenfeld and Stella P. Rosenfeld (New York: Schocken Books, 1986), viii and xiii.

2. A comparison of the German title and that of the standard English translation identified in the previous note reveals how the cutting edge of Améry's German is softened in the English version of his title.

3. Améry, *At the Mind's Limits,* 65.
4. Ibid., 66.
5. Ibid., 67.
6. Ibid., 34.
7. Ibid., 18.
8. Ibid., 18–19.
9. Ibid., 63.
10. Ibid., 69.
11. Ibid., 67.
12. Ibid., 29–30.
13. Ibid., 31.
14. Ibid., 64.
15. Ibid., 69.
16. Ibid., 73.
17. Ibid., 74.
18. Ibid., 65.
19. Ibid., 75.
20. Ibid., 81.
21. Allen Buchanan, "Institutions, Beliefs, and Ethics: Eugenics as a Case Study," *Philosophy and Public Policy* 15, no. 1 (2007), 22, 40–45.
22. Améry, *At the Mind's Limits,* 71.
23. Ibid., 81.

Rebecca Wittmann

Torture and the Ethical Implications of the Holocaust

WHAT ARE THE MOST IMPORTANT ETHICAL IMPLICATIONS OF MY Holocaust research and teaching?[1] The Holocaust occurred during war. The ongoing war allowed for perpetration, collaboration, passive complicity, and indifference throughout Europe and the world: from the top Nazi ideologues who dreamed up the "Final Solution," able to conquer territory and eradicate the territory's Jewish population; to the guards at concentration camps, driven by antisemitism, opportunism, fear of the front, or careerism; to the civilians in cities throughout Europe, who did not ask where their Jewish neighbor went because they were too concerned with feeding their own families and, in addition, might be able to move into the bigger apartment of the vanished family next door. With war come war crimes. And after war, the reckoning begins. But only a select few will be held accountable—sometimes those at the very top echelons of leadership but usually those who engaged in acts of cruelty, obvious criminality, and torture.

I am less interested here in whether states condone torture and whether it is actively applied policy. We know that states from Algeria to the United States do condone torture, whether they admit it or not. What interests me more is the way that governments—specifically democratic ones—deny their use of torture, after the fact, by staging trials. The official public condemnation of a few "bad apples" is the preferred mode of catharsis that governments offer to their citizens. In general, the public is ready and willing to swallow this mendacious message.

Why do we so quickly distance ourselves from the reality of torture? Why do we allow ourselves to be estranged from the truth? We are all horrified by the images of torture we see splattered across the newspapers, and we demand inquiries. But we then settle for the typical explanation: it was a few sadistic people acting out their dark fantasies. And although we are aghast, we cannot look away. A liberating, breast-beating, collective "that is not us" belies a deeper voyeuristic "of course, that is us," which we quickly, defensively, deny. This is our modern charade: our spurious reaction to the notion of human rights, the Geneva Conventions, the perceived societal duty to seek justice. We pretend to want to get to the bottom of torture; we stage trials that supposedly exact justice. But they do nothing of the sort.

In the wake of World War II and the atrocities committed by the Germans and the Japanese, the newly formed United Nations impressed on democratic nations the need to investigate, prosecute, and punish crimes of excessive cruelty, torture, and atrocity occurring within the framework of war. Prosecutors throughout postwar democratic West Germany undertook a massive program of investigation and legal proceedings against former Nazis suspected of committing heinous crimes. From the outside, this effort appeared to be an earnest attempt to confront the past and properly condemn the unspeakable crimes of the "Final Solution." A closer look, however, shows us that the judiciary deliberately attempted to normalize systemic Nazi crimes by focusing legal attention and public moral outrage on the crimes of a few "excess perpetrators." The public learned to gasp at the crimes of a few sadists, while distancing itself from the system in which so many members of this very same public had been enmeshed. Although Nazism had fallen and West Germany was on its bright new democratic path, the legal system was not so quick to embrace democratic ideals when judging its own past. Postwar judges created a legal system that suited them well and pleased the public, too.

The Trial of the Major War Criminals at Nuremberg conducted jointly by the Allies, and the subsequent Nuremberg trials held by the Americans, set new and bold standards for how war crimes could be prosecuted. The introduction of the four key charges (Crimes Against Peace, War Crimes, Conspiracy to Commit War Crimes, and Crimes Against Humanity) remains the most important development in international criminal law to this day. These charges continue to be used at the International Criminal Court, and they represent the best attempt that we have to address the crimes not only of individuals but also of government systems. Control Council Law No. 10, however, did not sit well with the newly formed West German state, and the Ministry of Justice decided not to adopt it in its criminal code (unlike France or Israel, for example). The national humiliation brought on by the Nuremberg trials smacked of victors' justice, used ex post facto laws that did not exist at the time that the crimes were committed, and forbade the Germans from pointing out Allied atrocities such as the firebombing of German cities and the Soviet massacre of ten thousand Polish officers at Katyn. These factors left the newly formed German justice system—not to mention much of the German population—with a bad taste in its mouth. So trials of Nazis would be conducted according to the regular German penal code after 1949.

The West Germans have brought some 6,500 former Nazis to trial between 1949 and the present for their participation in the "Final Solution of the Jewish Question" as camp guards, members of killing squads, and "desk killers." State attorneys' offices had high hopes for these trials: prosecutors intended to put the whole camp system on trial, to condemn the bureaucrats in charge of the Holocaust, whose pen strokes and signatures sanctioned the murder of millions. And yet, the trials changed course. In the case of the Auschwitz trial, the majority of defendants received mild sentences because they had not shown individual initiative. The investigation of the Reich Security Main Office (RSHA) fell apart after jurists introduced an amendment into the penal code that prevented prosecutors from trying suspects whose base motives—such as racial hatred—could not be proven. The real crime—the methodical murder of innocent men, women, and children in the gas chambers and by the killing commandos—receded into the background, while the full force of the law came down only on the "monsters" on the stand who had created their own instruments of torture, lived out their evil fantasies, and committed crimes so heinous that even the Nazis had investigated them for their excesses. The vast majority of participants in the Nazi racial program came out of the courtroom looking like reluctant, decent people who had gotten confusedly caught up in a madness over which they had no control. The Nazi system ultimately escaped censure when prosecutors had to use as evidence actual Nazi investigations of excessive brutality or corruption to get a conviction of perpetrating murder. And this result has created a most unhealthy and confused relationship to guilt in Germany.

What are the ethical implications of this situation? What relevance does this have for current discussions of torture and war crimes? This is a hugely important discussion and a pivotal moment when we as a society can change how we perceive war crimes. When we talk about the prison guards at Abu Ghraib, we are not dealing with soldiers within a genocidal dictatorship, volunteers working at death camps designed especially for extermination. But the soldiers who engaged in the torturous crimes at that prison have been demonized and held up as monstrous animals that we condemn for their brutality and inhumanity. The U.S. military publicly prosecuted them as examples of exactly what it does not want among its ranks. They have been punished, justice has been served, and the good war can go on. And yet these soldiers did not appear out of nowhere; they are fighters in an ideological battle against "evil." There is a lesson to be learned here about the tendency, in democratic societies, to condemn only the most extreme perpetrators of violence and torture and to turn a blind eye to the system that created them. Perhaps the problem lies with our inability to accept our own responsibility for bringing into office people capable of ordering such barbarities. In that sense, postwar democratic West Germany is not so different from the United States today, except that the West German judiciary was implicated in crimes that had taken place twenty years beforehand, not just twenty weeks beforehand.

We badly want to believe that the laws of our country are being defined, applied, and upheld in a humane and moral way—after all, the laws of a democratic society are supposed to and generally do reflect the will of the people—and we show this through our tacit acceptance of the decisions and pronouncements of our lawmakers. But we need to recognize that when we place such unquestioned trust in the legal system, in the motives of our governments, we allow them to define for us what is normal and what is abnormal, and a vacuum is created in which the public loses its ability to see that justice is not served. Perhaps the scandalous use of torture *does* ultimately delegitimate a bad government; scholarly probing *does* lead to wider public criticism, no matter how much a government and its courts feign abhorrence of this crime. There is an ever-growing suspicion of U.S. governmental policy in its "detention centers" and with its "enhanced interrogation methods." Many Americans now view critically the scandalous treatment of prisoners of war in Abu Ghraib and "enemy combatants" in Afghanistan and Guantanamo. Amazingly, though, the government has attempted to legalize some of the very methods used by the prison guards at Abu Ghraib.

The solution is elusive; it requires *immediate* recognition of guilt, responsibility, and complicity and the commitment to change not only the effects of atrocious policies but also the causes. The decision to support war will always, ultimately, be a decision to support war crimes. It makes no sense to imagine that torture is only the provenance of a few bad apples—it is a fundamental element of war in which "we" attempt to understand, undermine, and eradicate "them." To relegate torture to the margins, to the exceptional, and to the crime of a few sadists is willfully to ignore the nature of war. What a depressing development it is that the Americans, so determined and so successful in putting the masterminds of aggressive war and war crimes on trial at Nuremberg, now refuse to be held to the same legal standards. Robert Jackson, chief prosecutor at the first Nuremberg trial, proudly declared in his opening statement that subjecting the architects of crimes against peace to the rule of law was "one of the most significant tributes that Power ever has paid to Reason." Where is reason now?

NOTE

1. This essay is a revised and shortened version of an article entitled "Torture on Trial: Prosecuting Sadists and the Obfuscation of Systemic Crime," which appeared in *South Central Review*, 24, no. 1 (Spring 2007), 8–17.

Berel Lang

Two Ethical Issues

I WANT TO CALL ATTENTION TO TWO ETHICAL ISSUES RELATED TO both the Holocaust and the post-Holocaust, both of them in my view warranting continued attention. The first concerns the concept and practice of what has come to be known as *group rights*. What I wish to emphasize by introducing this *general* concept into our more specific discussion of the Holocaust can be understood on the model of a straight historical line. The Holocaust, even while it was occurring, led to the conceptualization (and term) of genocide, mainly through the extraordinary efforts of Raphael Lemkin: a development in ethical and legal analysis intended to mark off a distinctive crime (as different, for example, from individual or even mass murder). The conceptualization of *group* murder—a group *wrong*—both assumed and implied (among other things) a right to existence for those groups held to be subject to the crime of genocide; that is, the designation of a *group* right in contrast to those rights that had been more often and traditionally ascribed to individuals as individuals. Three steps, then, historically and conceptually: Holocaust to genocide to group rights.

This schematic, of course, is simplified, as any ostensibly straight historical line must be. Group rights had been intimated and even evoked previously—for example, in Woodrow Wilson's doctrine of the right of national self-determination and in other post–World War I statements on minorities' rights. But in the aftermath of World War II there was an unprecedented emphasis on the detailing and elaboration of group rights—rights that are not just bundles of individual rights but rights in themselves attached to groups. The timing of this development was not, in my view, coincidental. (So, for example, the United Nations [UN] Convention on the Punishment and Prevention of the Crime of Genocide and the UN Universal Declaration of

Human Rights, both in 1948, plus the UN International Covenant on Civil and Political Rights [1966] all tacitly or explicitly cite specific group rights in addition to the individual rights to which they refer.) This development marked a radical shift in ethical and political theory and in jurisprudence.

The history of *natural*—or as they are now usually called, with what appears to be deliberate ambiguity, *human*—rights has focused almost entirely on individual rights, from its origins in medieval political theory and as subsequently epitomized in the American Declaration of Independence (1776) and the French Declaration of the Rights of Man and Citizen (1789). In the post-Holocaust period, however, and to a large extent directly in *response* to the Holocaust and the newly articulated crime of genocide, group rights—not only the group's right to exist but also its right to the means for existence, without which that first right would be vacuous—have come to the fore and have had substantive consequences for the way in which social policy and thinking are formulated. Although not always recognized, the principle of group rights underlies most, if not all, of the programs that have been initiated in the United States on behalf of minority groups, certainly all that come under the rubric of affirmative action. In other countries—notably Canada and Australia—the legislative development of such rights has been even stronger. Above all, in 2002 there was the formation of the International Criminal Court (ICC), which, in my opinion, was a revolutionary achievement. Under the aegis of the United Nations, the ICC is holding hearings focused on the crime of genocide, with trials that have already produced verdicts and punishments. Admittedly, the ICC's powers are limited (partly as a consequence of the refusal by the United States and a small number of other countries to recognize the court). Nevertheless, the ICC's very existence and functioning are significant, amounting to formal and enforceable recognition of group rights as a normal part of the ethical and political landscape. Violations of these rights are open to inspection and judgment across national lines by what is itself an international judicial body.

To be sure, there are serious and recognizable problems related to the concept and practice of group rights. Some of these were evident in early discussion about the UN's Genocide Convention. There were questions, for example, about which groups should be included or excluded in the Convention's provisions and by what criteria; or of what resolution is possible when specific individual and group rights conflict. These issues (and others) are indeed difficulties—as is the more fundamental question of what rights are anyway. Looking both backward and forward in time, I would only say that for every such issue directed at the notion of group rights, either the same or a parallel issue applies to individual rights. And unless one dispenses with the concept of rights altogether (which utilitarian theories often do, but at great cost), such problems have to be faced and at times simply swallowed. Where free lunches are concerned, political theory is not exempt from the judgment that they do not exist.

I do not mean to suggest that the emergent concept of group rights, initiated (on this account) in good measure because of the Holocaust, in any way redeems that event. We know in general, however, that wherever prohibitions appear, they attest to the prior occurrence of the acts that the prohibitions then prohibit. In other words, moral enlightenment as codified reflects prior practice or, more bluntly, transgression. This relationship holds, too, with the Holocaust, genocide, and group rights. Are we, then, entitled to speak of this sequence in any sense as progress? Well, yes and no—or, more precisely, no and yes.

My second ethical issue—uses to which the Holocaust is put—has two parts, both of them commonplace but, in my view, warranting a stronger response than they have received. The first part concerns the use of terms taken from the Holocaust as metaphors or similes that have come to be applied to almost any act or person guilty of almost any wrongdoing: the alleged Adolf Hitlers, or Adolf Eichmanns, or Schutzstaffel (SS) men so labeled since the end of World War II seem as numerous as those who acted within the Holocaust itself; virtually any act of violence or oppression in whatever social or political context turns out now to involve its "Nazis." And if one adds to this development the use of the Holocaust in lectures, sermons, and even academic works that may focus entirely on other subjects but that in the view of the author or speaker—the pundit or clergyman or professor—would benefit from an extra kick of emotive intensity, we arrive at a full house of Holocaust references that have little or nothing to do directly with that event. The effect here is a debasement or devaluation—a form of exploitation often accompanied by straightforward historical and conceptual misrepresentation.

Agreement on this criticism, to be sure, leaves open the question of what can be done about the problem I have identified. Censorship from above is not an option because there is no "above." Refusing to listen or to read is an option—but by the time we decide not to read or listen, we already have. One solution, however, has occurred to me: difficult to enforce but sharp, Dante-esque in its justice. We are familiar with the concept of use taxes levied at parks or on toll roads, when a public utility charges users a specific fee beyond their normal taxes. The analogy here seems fitting: anyone (politician, clergyman, journalist, professor) may employ metaphors or similes or emotive free associations that invoke Nazis or the Holocaust, but for this they pay a use tax (per mention). Such a levy could have both educational and economic value: educational by showing that even metaphors and similes entail historical responsibilities; economic insofar as the funds gathered might then support research and education about the Holocaust—that is, efforts that are not figurative or associative. (An alternate rubric here would be to subsume the proposed payments under the heading of sin taxes such as those levied on tobacco and alcohol.)

The other part of my second ethical issue strikes closer to home for those of us who talk and write specifically about the Holocaust in our professional lives. Much has been said, and much of it tendentious and misleading, about so-called Shoah Business or the Holocaust Industry. One aspect of those charges—less discussed than others—seems to me to have a substantial point. Numerous scholars, writers, and artists have profited financially from their work bearing on the Holocaust. For some of them, the gains have been substantial, even very large; for others, they have at least been actual. I do not refer here to regular employment (as in the ordinary roles of journalist or attorney or teacher), but to profits beyond that, as in public lectures, book royalties, films, conference honoraria, and so on—and the issue there seems to me quite straightforward: is it not a serious ethical question whether anyone who was not himself or herself directly in the Holocaust should profit from its events—from the suffering and loss undergone by others?

Several of the best-known figures who address the Holocaust in their work have acknowledged the force of this question by setting up philanthropic foundations of one kind or another. Few of us, however, come close to having gains on that order, and, of course, there could in any event be no way of compelling compliance on even lesser recommendations. But this need not hinder what seems to me a minimalist response to the *principle,* whereby at least a percentage of such profits—perhaps on the order of tithing, although the specific percentage could be more or less than a tenth—would not be used for one's own personal affairs but voluntarily given up, set aside perhaps to build the fund previously mentioned in support of Holocaust research and education. For surely (I would argue), the gains from these accomplishments ought at least to *recognize* their source. ("Profits with honor" is the name we might give to such "giving back.")

The practical difficulties here seem negligible. The fund could be overseen by one of any number of established institutions concerned with Holocaust research, and the contributions to it would be determined, in percentage or amount, by the contributors themselves. The crucial issue, it seems to me, is the principle on which such contributions would be based—a principle related to but more specific than the general justification for charitable giving. In what is still the immediacy of the Holocaust for those who turn their energies and talents to it—as distinct from many other historical atrocities that are the subjects of other historical and creative narratives—recognition of the source on which they build raises moral considerations beyond those asserted in the compass of "normal" professional principles.

I have two concluding comments. First, in response to the obvious reflexive question: yes, I have myself been doing what I propose—and I would be surprised if several other people were not also already doing this. But a general public fund would obviously have a greater impact than any individual private fund. Second, five years ago, during a year I spent at the United States Holocaust Memorial Museum, I circulated a memorandum recommending a proposal of this sort. It was met with silence—not rejection but glacial silence. Perhaps times have changed.

John K. Roth

Postscript

HAVE TIMES CHANGED? IMPLICITLY IF NOT EXPLICITLY EMBEDDED IN this section on ethics, and indeed in this entire book, that question reminds me that the Serbian novelist Danilo Kiš (1935–1989) was the son of a Montenegrin mother and a Jewish father. Subotica, Kiš's Yugoslavian hometown, stood near the Hungarian border. When the Germans attacked Yugoslavia in April 1941, Subotica came under Hungary's control. Not until March 1944, when the Germans occupied the territory of their faltering Hungarian allies, did the Jews of Hungary face the Holocaust's full onslaught. When it came, that disaster took Kiš's father to an Auschwitz death.

Narrated from the perspective of a boy named Andi Scham, *Garden, Ashes* is Kiš's poignant semiautobiographical novel about the Holocaust. In ways unconventional for that genre, Kiš does not take his readers inside a ghetto, a deportation cattle car, or a death camp. Instead, as the story's title suggests, one is led to consider the Holocaust as an absence, an unredeemed emptiness and unredeemable ruin—ashes—where once there had been life that flowed and flowered like a rich green garden. The absence is personified by Andi's Jewish father, Eduard, who was taken away and presumably killed at Auschwitz, although his son was never quite sure of that and kept hoping and looking for his father's return, which never came.

Eccentric, difficult, but in his own ways loving and lovable, Eduard Scham was a writer whose masterpiece remained unfinished. The lack of closure, however, was not due entirely to the murder of its author. Scham's project was to be the third edition of his previously published *Bus, Ship, Rail, and Air Travel Guide*. In its revised and enlarged form, this book became a mystical, metaphysical exploration that included not only "all cities, all land areas and all the seas, all the skies, all climates, all meridians" but also spiraling roads and forking paths that carried him "afield both in breadth and depth" so that "abbreviations became subchapters, subchapters became chapters" with no end to their multiplying enigmas.[1]

Like Eduard Scham's travel guide, which led in so many directions without arriving at a certain destination, *Garden, Ashes* lacks closure, too. One of the reasons involves the Singer sewing machine that belonged to Andi's mother. The novel's early pages describe it and include a sketch of the machine, adding to the specificity that Kiš conveys. Andi's mother created beauty with that machine, and thus the sewing machine itself was beautiful, for it signified home and a world in which one could be at home. It is even possible that the destination sought by Eduard Scham's travel guide might have been the place where that sewing machine belonged and where it could be found. The sewing machine, however, was not to be found. Apparently it belonged nowhere, for, Kiš wrote, it "vanished in the confusion of war."[2] The garden it had helped to create was turned to ashes by the Holocaust.

Garden, Ashes ends on somber notes.[3] "We are witnesses to a great breakdown in values," said Kiš, and Andi Scham observes that his vanished world has left him in a house with a kitchen stove that cannot "generate a real flame: we lacked a real blaze, there was no glow." The novel's last words belong to Andi's mother, who has no husband and no Singer sewing machine: "Lord," she says, "how quickly it gets dark here."

Have times changed? Especially when we think about the themes in this book's title—*Memory, History, and Responsibility: Reassessments of the Holocaust, Implications for the Future*—the argument that ethics should come first grows not only stronger but also more urgent. Shouldn't ethics come first? Holding us accountable, that question stands out, lingers, and haunts all the more by coming last.

NOTES

1. Danilo Kiš, *Garden, Ashes,* trans. William J. Hannaher (Champaign, Ill.: Dalkey Archive Press, 2003), 34, 37, 39. The discussion of *Garden, Ashes*

POSTSCRIPT

draws on my contributions to David Patterson and John K. Roth, eds., *Fire in the Ashes: God, Evil, and the Holocaust* (Seattle: University of Washington Press, 2005).

2. Kiš, *Garden, Ashes,* 169.

3. For the quotations that follow, see ibid., 168–70.

Abbreviations and Acronyms

ASG	Ankieta Sadów Grodzkich
AŻIH	Archiwum Żydowski Instytut Historyczny (Jewish Historical Institute, Warsaw)
BAB	Bundesarchiv Berlin
BAK	Bundesarchiv Koblenz
BAL	Bundesarchiv Ludwigsburg
BFL	Budapest Főváros Levéltára (Budapest City Archives)
BuF	Bevölkerungswesen und Fürsorge (Population and Welfare)
CDJC	Center for Contemporary Jewish Documentation
CDU	Christian Democratic Union
CSU	Christian Social Union
CV	curriculum vitae
DaChO	Derzhavnyi arkhiv Cherkas'koi oblasti
DAKO	Derzhavnyi arkhiv Kyivs'koi oblasti
DM	deutsche marks
Dok. Bd.	Dokumenten Band
DöW	Dokumentationsarchiv des österreichischen Widerstandes
DP	displaced person
DVA	Deutsche Verlags Anstalt
EU	European Union
FA	Fortunoff Archive
FDP	Free Democratic Party
FO	Foreign Office
GBI	Generalbauinspektion
GBK	Generalbezirk Kiew

GDL	Gouverneur des Distrikts Lublin
HDZ	Hrvatska Demokratska Zajednica (Croatian Democratic Union)
HSSPF	Higher SS and Police Leader
HVA-SVHF	Holocaust Video Archives—Shoah Visual History Foundation
ICC	International Criminal Court
ICISS	International Commission on Intervention and State Sovereignty
ICJ	International Court of Justice
IFiS	Wydawnictwo Instytutu Filozofii Socjologii PAN
IPN	Instytut Pamięci Narodowej
JNSV	*Justiz und N-S Verbrechen*
JSS	Jüdische Soziale Selbsthilfe (Jewish Social Self-Help Organization)
KMF	Kolektsiia materialiv i fotodokumentiv
KTB	Kriegstagebuch (War Diary)
LAB	Landesarchiv Berlin
LA NRW	Landesarchiv Nordrhein-Westphalen
LCVA	Lithuanian Central State Archive, Vilnius
Lfd. Nr.	Laufende Nummer (running number)
LG	Landgericht Kassel
LYA	Lithuanian Special Archive
MGB	Ministry of State Security
NA	National Archives, United Kingdom
NARA	National Archives and Records Administration
NATO	North Atlantic Treaty Organization
NDH	Nezavisna Država Hrvatska (Independent State of Croatia)
NOKW	Nuremberg Oberkommando der Wehrmacht
NSA	National Security Agency (U.S.)
NSKK	National Socialist Motorized Corps
OL	Országos Levéltár (Hungarian National Archives)
POW	prisoner of war
RFSS	Reichsführer-Schutzstaffel
RG	Record Group
RKU	Reichskommissariat Ukraine
RM	reichsmarks
RSHA	Reich Security Main Office

ABBREVIATIONS AND ACRONYMS

RZ	Rada Żydowska w Lublinie
SA	Sturmabteilungen
SBU	Sluzhba Bezpeky Ukrainy
SD	Sicherheitsdienst
SPD	Sozialdemokratische Partei Deutschlands (Social Democratic Party)
SS	Schutzstaffel
TsDAHOU	Tsentral'nyi derzhavnyi arkhiv hromads'kykh orhanizatsii Ukrainy
TsDAVO	Tsentral'nyi derzhavnyi arkhiv vyshchykh orhaniv vlady i upravlinnia Ukrainy
UdSSR	Union der Sozialistischen Sowjet-Republiken (former Soviet Union)
UN	United Nations
USHMM	United States Holocaust Memorial Museum
WAPL	Województwo Archiwum Państwowe w Lublinie
YVA	Yad Vashem Archive
ZBL	Zentralbauleitung
ŻIH	Żydowski Institut Historyczny

Notes on Contributors

MICHAEL ALLEN is the author of *The Business of Genocide: The SS, Slave Labor, and the Concentration Camps,* which won the German Studies Association DAAD Book Prize in 2002–3.

SUZANNE BROWN-FLEMING is the senior program officer in the University Programs Division of the United States Holocaust Memorial Museum's Center for Advanced Holocaust Studies in Washington, D.C. Her publications include *The Holocaust and Catholic Conscience: Cardinal Aloisius Muench and the Guilt Question in Germany.*

CHRISTOPHER R. BROWNING is the Frank Porter Graham Professor of History at the University of North Carolina at Chapel Hill. He is the author of *Ordinary Men: Reserve Police Battalion 101 and the Final Solution in Poland; The Path to Genocide: Essays on Launching the Final Solution;* and *The Origins of the Final Solution: The Evolution of Nazi Jewish Policy, September 1939–March 1942.*

TIM COLE is a senior lecturer in European social history at the University of Bristol. He is the author of *Selling the Holocaust* and *Holocaust City: The Making of a Jewish Ghetto.* He is currently completing a social history of the Holocaust in Hungary.

MARTIN DEAN is an applied research scholar at the United States Holocaust Memorial Museum's Center for Advanced Holocaust Studies. He is the author of *Collaboration in the Holocaust: Crimes of the Local Police in Belorussia and Ukraine, 1941–44* and coeditor of *Robbery and Restitution: The Conflict over Jewish Property in Europe.*

• 329

JERRY FOWLER is president of the Save Darfur Coalition. Prior to that, he served as director of the Committee on Conscience at the United States Holocaust Memorial Museum. His publications include "Out of That Darkness: Preventing Genocide in the 21st Century" in *Century of Genocide: Eyewitness Accounts and Critical Views*. He also directed the short film *A Good Man in Hell: General Romeo Dallaire and the Rwanda Genocide*.

SAUL FRIEDLÄNDER is a professor of history at the University of California–Los Angeles, where he holds the 1939 Club Chair in Holocaust Studies. His publications include *The Years of Persecution: Nazi Germany and the Jews, 1933–1939* and *The Years of Extermination: Nazi Germany and the Jews, 1939–1945*. In 2007 he received the Peace Prize of the German Book Trade.

SIMONE GIGLIOTTI is an assistant professor of history at Victoria University, Wellington, New Zealand. She is coeditor of *The Holocaust: A Reader*.

CHRISTIAN GOESCHEL is a postdoctoral research fellow at Birkbeck College, University of London. He served as the Charles H. Revson Foundation Fellow at the Center for Advanced Holocaust Studies, United States Holocaust Memorial Museum during 2005–6 and has just completed a major monograph on suicide in Nazi Germany.

PETER HAYES is the Theodore Z. Weiss Professor of Holocaust Studies at Northwestern University. His publications include *Industry and Ideology: I. G. Farben in the Nazi Era* and *From Cooperation to Complicity: Degussa in the Third Reich*.

RACHEL ISKOV is a doctoral candidate in Holocaust history at the Strassler Family Center for Holocaust and Genocide Studies at Clark University in Worcester, Massachusetts.

CLAUDIA KOONZ is a professor of history at Duke University. She is the author of *Mothers in the Fatherland: Women, the Family, and Nazi Politics* and *The Nazi Conscience*.

NOTES ON CONTRIBUTORS

BEREL LANG is a professor of philosophy and letters at Wesleyan University. His publications include *Post-Holocaust: Interpretation, Misinterpretation, and the Claims of History* and *The Future of the Holocaust: Between History and Memory.*

MICHAEL MENG recently completed his Ph.D. in modern European history at the University of North Carolina at Chapel Hill and is currently teaching at Davidson College. He has published articles in *Central European History* and *Contemporary European History,* and in the volume *Beyond Berlin,* edited by Gavriel Rosenfeld and Paul Jaskot. He is working on his first book, *Shattered Spaces: Encountering Jewish Ruins in Germany and Poland After 1945.*

PAUL B. MILLER is an associate professor of history at McDaniel College and the International University of Sarajevo. In 2004–5, he was a Fulbright scholar in Bosnia-Herzegovina.

JONATHAN PETROPOULOS is the John V. Croul Professor of European History at Claremont McKenna College. He is the author of *Art as Politics in the Third Reich* and *The Faustian Bargain: The Art World in Nazi Germany.* His most recent book is *Royals and the Reich: The Princes von Hessen in Nazi Germany.*

ALEXANDER V. PRUSIN is the author of *Nationalizing a Borderland: War, Ethnicity, and Anti-Jewish Violence in East Galicia, 1914–1920.* He is an associate professor of history at New Mexico Institute of Mining and Technology.

LYNN RAPAPORT is the Henry Snyder Professor of Sociology at Pomona College. She is the author of *Jews in Germany After the Holocaust: Memory, Identity, and Jewish-German Relations,* which won the 1998 Most Distinguished Publication Award in the Sociology of Religion from the American Sociological Association. She is currently working on a project about how the Holocaust has been portrayed in popular culture from the 1940s to the present day.

JOHN K. ROTH is the Edward J. Sexton Professor Emeritus of Philosophy and the founding director of the Center for the Study of the Holocaust, Genocide, and Human Rights (now the Center for Human

Rights Leadership) at Claremont McKenna College, where he taught from 1966 through 2006. His numerous Holocaust-related books include *Ethics During and After the Holocaust* and *Holocaust Politics*. He is the coeditor (with Peter Hayes) of *The Oxford Handbook of Holocaust Studies*.

SUSANNA SCHRAFSTETTER is an associate professor of history at the University of Vermont. She is the author of *Avoiding Armageddon: The United States, Western Europe and the Struggle for Nuclear Non-Proliferation, 1945–1970* (coauthored with Stephen Twigge).

DAVID SILBERKLANG is a senior historian at Yad Vashem in Jerusalem, where he is editor in chief of publications and of *Yad Vashem Studies*. He is also adjunct professor at the Hebrew University in Jerusalem and was the Rosenthal Visiting Fellow at Case Western Reserve University from January to May 2007.

LISSA SKITOLSKY is an assistant professor of philosophy at Susquehanna University. Her article "Applied Ethics: Bush's Totalitarian Logic" appeared in *Free Inquiry*.

REBECCA WITTMANN is an associate professor of history at the University of Toronto. She is the author of *Beyond Justice: The Auschwitz Trial*.